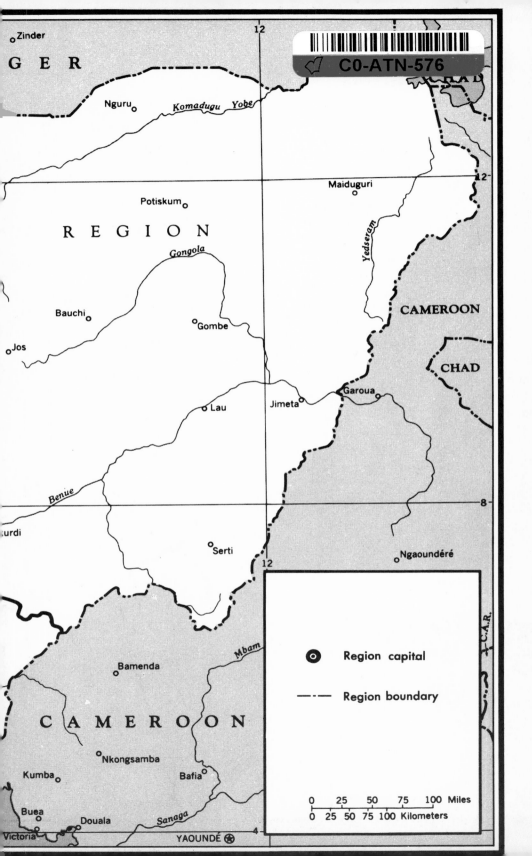

NIGERIA

The Tribes, the Nation, or the Race—
The Politics of Independence

NIGERIA

The Tribes, the Nation, or the Race —
The Politics of Independence

Frederick A. O. Schwarz, Jr.

The M. I. T. Press

Massachusetts Institute of Technology
Cambridge, Massachusetts, and London, England

To M. L. S.

Preface

This is a book about Nigeria, Africa's most populous nation. Because so many issues are viewed by Nigeria's citizens in an African rather than a national context and because the country's own policies can often best be evaluated by comparison with those of other African countries, it is also in a sense about all of Africa. Because of racial prejudice against the black man, the crisis of confidence engendered by that prejudice, and the consequent sense of racial solidarity in Africa, it is also a book about race.

The focus of the book is political. It is political in the broad sense of what the people desire and why their leaders act as well as in the narrower sense of who is in power and how the government operates.

The first political question for every African nation is whether it is a nation. Each country could be ripped apart by tribal jealousies, and all are weakened by them. Nigeria brings together more people and more ethnic groups than any other African nation. Much of the book is about ethnic jealousies and the manner in which they have molded and distorted her development. The book will also suggest that she will hold together because of economic reality, her federal system, the prestige of being big, and hope of becoming part of a still larger political community.

Nigeria remains a democracy with several parties in part because she is deeply divided ethnically. Similarly, the bill of rights in her Constitution is there largely because of the fears of minority tribes and minority religions. But those divisions and fears are also the greatest threat to Nigerian democracy.

The book is also in large measure about democracy in Nigeria and the forces that support and undercut democratic practices and ideals.

The successful practice of democracy in Africa has been thought to prove the equality of Africa with the West. That notion will increasingly become a less significant prop for democracy in Africa as Africans increasingly turn inward for approval. But a common distaste for racial prejudice and an association of the vestiges of colonialism with racial prejudice remain central to Africa's future. That distaste explains some anomalous thoughts in this book such as the prediction that Nigeria and Ghana will retain English as their national language because they are so anxious to be rid of the vestiges of colonialism. It is central to the Pan-African movement, an aspect of which is the aim of political union of all of Africa or all of black Africa.

Nigeria's cautious, methodical approach to African unity reflects her own political history. It is probably realistic to say, as do Nigeria's leaders, that you cannot have internationalism before you have nationalism. But frequently Nigeria's leaders have appeared to have underestimated the power of emotion and the need to restore their people's pride, both of which Africa's leading Pan-Africanists have better appreciated. As the book develops, however, the reader will note the beginnings of a change in Nigeria as evidenced by the Government's increasing awareness of the need to cut some of its ties—particularly symbolic signs of continued dependence—with Great Britain, Nigeria's former master.

Nigeria and all African countries will increasingly turn away from the West to idealize the African way and the "African personality." That tendency is, the book suggests, in the West's long-term interests. From the point of view of the immediate struggle between the West and the Communist world, Communism will find it harder to use Africa's pressing emotional need for disengagement from the West, because Africa can aspire to a third way, the African way. Ultimately, the West, if it can overcome its tendencies toward racial prejudice, has a better chance than the Communists to be close to Africa because it is better able to accommodate a pluralistic world.

The struggle to acquire pride, self-respect, and the respect of others is the crucial struggle in Africa. This is a subject which Americans should understand as well as any other group in the world. Colonialism plus racial discrimination has had the same destructive effect upon the African as slavery plus racial discrimination has had upon the American Negro. One of the remedies will be the same. As the Negro people with their new militancy are winning that pride that comes from struggle and the confidence of true independence, so the Africans must struggle in order to recover their pride and confidence.

I did not go to Africa to write. I went to work for the Northern Nigerian Government, in the Attorney-General's office, primarily as the Assistant Commissioner for Law Revision, for a year in 1961 and 1962. I thank that Government for giving me the opportunity to work in Africa.

My job was lined up by the Fellows in Africa Program of the School of Industrial Management of the Massachusetts Institute of Technology, with Ford Foundation backing. To the School, the Institute, and the Foundation, I am indebted for support in Africa and during the fall term 1962, when I was able to write the first draft of most of the chapters while a research associate on the faculty of the School. For the creative and practical inquisitiveness and the thoughtful energy of Professor Carroll Wilson, who conceived of and guides the Program, I have the greatest admiration and respect.

I am conscious that it is presumptuous for a foreigner to tell some of a nation's political history, speculate about its future, and try to describe the spirit underlying that history and shaping that future. Only one of the people written about can fully capture the aspirations and frustrations that are vital to understanding. To my Nigerian friends who helped me learn something of their country, I am deeply grateful.

FREDERICK A. O. SCHWARZ, JR.

New York City
June, 1965

Contents

The Roots of a Nation

Nigeria's history has just begun. The history of her tribes goes back as far as man remembers. Her greatest need is that the different tribes become but strands woven into the web of her national history; her greatest danger is that tribal jealousies will explode and cut the ties that hold the nation together.

The problem of building a nation from a collection of tribes is one which all new nations of Africa face today. By her very size, Nigeria has a greater problem than most. With a population of over 50 million, Nigeria is almost twice as populous as any other country on the continent of Africa. Approximately one-quarter of the Africans south of the Sahara are Nigerians. Estimates of the number of distinct languages ranging from 150 to 248 give some idea of the country's ethnic diversity.[1]

Nigeria, which became independent on October 1, 1960, after being under British colonial rule for periods ranging from approximately 50 to approximately 100 years, is a federation. When it became independent it was divided into three large regions (Eastern, Western, and Northern Nigeria), and in July 1963 a fourth region, the Midwest, was carved out of Western Nigeria. The regions' relationship to Nigeria's Federal Government is analogous to that of the American states to the American Federal Government. Nigeria's federation is unique, however, in that one of its federal subdivisions, the Northern Region, has much more land and a few more people than the rest of the country combined.

Each region is dominated by an ethnic group, the vast majority of whose members live within it. In the Eastern Region the Ibo dominate, in the Western Region the Yoruba, in the Northern Region the Fulani and Hausa, and the Midwestern Region is dominated by the Edo-speaking people. Each of the dominant groups has its own history, tradition, and language* and each has a contemptuous expression with which to describe the others, or all strangers. Each of the dominant groups (other than the Edo-speaking people of the Midwest) has a population of approximately 10 million — more than any of the four countries that border upon Nigeria. Each would be quite capable, had history developed differently, of being a medium-sized African nation itself. Their jealousies have dominated Nigeria's politics.

Within each region there are a number, and in the North a multitude, of other ethnic groups. Each of them has its own language and traditions. Some had no historical relationship with the dominant group in its region, others were enslaved, still others were once secure in their proud kingdoms, and some recall an earlier day when they were the country's leading merchants and their city-states far outshone the villages of their dominant neighbors of today. As power passed from British to Nigerian hands, and the dominant position of the Ibo, the Yoruba, and the Fulani and Hausa within the three original regions became clear, separatist movements sprang up among many of the minority groups. Often the ethnic minority of one region allied itself with the ethnic majority of another, and thus regional politics have had the same ethnic cast as national politics.

Added to the ethnic differences between Nigeria's peoples are religious differences and differences in the impact of Western civilization. Those factors have resulted in a sharp distinction between the Northern Region, or its northern two-thirds, and the Eastern and Western regions which together, along now with the Midwest, are often referred to as the South. The North is strongly influenced by traditional Islam and has been changed far less than the South by Western civilization. The South has many Christians and has been influenced profoundly by its contact with the Western world, particularly by Western education.

*The Fulani and Hausa have an intermixed tradition, and many Fulani speak Hausa.

The Long Road to Unity

Some observers, both Nigerian and foreign, have considered all the differences among Nigeria's peoples and have derided the very concept of a Nigerian nation. Thus, Obafemi Awolowo, leader of the opposition at the time of independence, stated early in his career:

Nigeria is not a nation. It is a mere geographical expression. . . . The word "Nigerian" is merely a distinctive appellation to distinguish those who live within Nigeria from those who do not.[2]

Similarly, a British governor characterized the Nigerians as a

. . . collection of self-contained and mutually independent Native States, separated from one another . . . by vast distances, by differences of history and traditions, and by ethnological, racial, tribal, political, social and religious barriers. . . .[3]

Other countries once dismissed as mere geographical expressions have proved their right to be known as nations. Italy is an example. But, unlike Italy, Nigeria has neither a common faith, nor a common language (except to the extent that English serves as one for the elite) nor a historical tradition with the unifying force that the Roman Empire had for the modern Italian nation. Until independence in 1960, there was never a Nigerian, or a group of Nigerians, who governed the entire country, or even one of its regions, though in the last few years of colonial rule the British had turned over more and more responsibility for government to the Nigerians.

Further difficulties that face Nigeria in its effort to build a nation out of a host of ethnic groups can be illustrated by comparing it with the United States. By and large, Nigeria's peoples still live in their ethnic homelands. Those who came to America had all left theirs. America's peoples may have brought their languages and customs with them, and most came in groups. But they had, by cutting themselves away from the ethnic homeland, or by being torn away from it, taken a long first step toward the development of a new loyalty.

Nigerian ethnic groups not only still live in their respective homelands, they also are not geographically intermixed. Though there are exceptions, it is generally true that the members of an ethnic group still reside in the ancestral territory and few members of other ethnic groups live within that territory. (Map 1 helps illustrate the cohesiveness of Nigeria's ethnic groups.) The possibility of reducing differences through continual

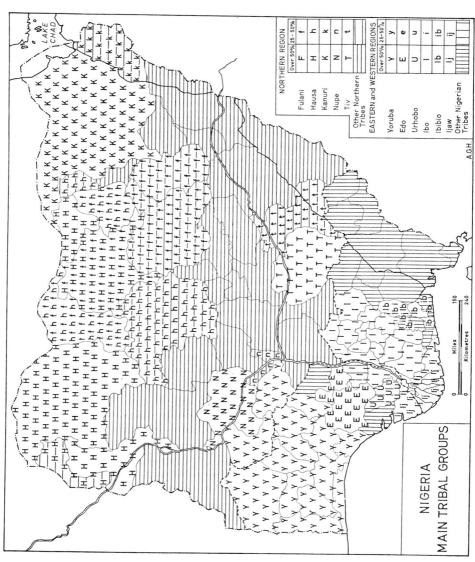

MAP 1. *Principal Ethnic Groups of Nigeria (courtesy of H. M. Stationery Office and R. M. Prothero). The map shows the Southern Cameroons as part of Nigeria, though in 1959 it became a part of the Cameroon Republic.*

NIGERIA
MAIN TRIBAL GROUPS

NORTHERN REGION		
	Over 50%	25 - 50%
Fulani	F	f
Hausa	H	h
Kanuri	K	k
Nupe	N	n
Tiv	T	t
Other Northern Tribes		

EASTERN and WESTERN REGIONS		
	Over 50%	25-50%
Yoruba	Y	y
Edo	E	e
Urhobo	U	u
Ibo	I	i
Ibibio	Ib	ib
Ijaw	Ij	ij
Other Nigerian Tribes		

A.G.H.

LAKE CHAD

Miles 0   150   240
Kilometres

contact of various ethnic groups is thus less than it was in America where, despite various ethnic pockets, there was more mixing.

Nigeria, moreover, lacks the American asset of an open frontier beyond which there is empty land into which adventuresome spirits from all ethnic groups can pour. Some land in Nigeria is quite empty; parts of Niger Province in the southwestern part of the Northern Region, for example, have good soil, but fewer than five persons per square mile because of nineteenth-century internal slave raiding. Despite some relatively empty land, however, there is none or very little which is available to all comers. It all lies within a traditional tribal domain, and throughout the British era the traditional rights to land were respected. Reinforcing the customary hold of peoples to their ancestral land are regional jealousies. A Southerner may not use or even occupy land in the Northern Region without the consent of the Northern Nigerian Government, and that consent is seldom granted. The constitutional prohibition against discrimination based on "community, tribe, place of origin, religion or political opinion" does not, moreover, apply to "restrictions with respect to the acquisition or use by any person of land or other property.[4]

The geographical cohesiveness and exclusiveness of Nigeria's ethnic groups has both advantages and disadvantages. It reduces the chances of abrasive communal friction such as has occurred on the Indian subcontinent where Muslim and Hindu were mixed together. But it also slows the development of mutual understanding. It is the basis of Nigeria's federal system.

A federal system requires that each group desiring autonomy or protection be identified with a particular piece of territory which can be made a federal subdivision that it can control; federalism is not a device with which to protect minorities scattered throughout a country and intermingled with other groups. Nigeria's federal system provides that matters which are of greatest concern to the dominant regional ethnic groups — land tenure, local government, customary law, education — are in the hands of the regions which they, rather the Federal Government, dominate. Thus it assures the major ethnic groups that their customs will not be interfered with. The other side of the coin, of course, is that it tends to perpetuate differences. Furthermore, it gives rise to demands by ethnic minorities within each region for their own regions.

Tradition and Change

The difficulty Nigeria faces in building a nation out of her many tribes cannot be appreciated by merely stating that there are a number of tribes, many of whose traditions are different and most of the members of which are geographically separated. It is also important to realize that most Nigerians are members of traditional societies, where the majority of people look upon themselves as part of the ethnic group rather than as individuals who happen to be members of an ethnic group.

Members of a traditional society are like the spokes of a wheel that turns as it has always, no one of them being able to escape the wheel. The force of immemorial custom upon the life of the Nigerian peasant-farmer — and most Nigerians are peasant-farmers — is strong; his days are spent tilling the soil of his ancestors; of the outer world he knows little. Usually belonging to a relatively classless society, he does not feel a bond with members of his class in other ethnic groups. He is not a mobile individual whose loyalty is split among many groups, each encompassing different individuals from different ethnic groups.

The extent to which most Nigerians remain a part of their traditional societies is suggested by the comment of the Federal Government newspaper that

> . . . the truth is that most of our people still have more faith in the natural ruler [chief] than even in the Parliament which makes the rules by which the natural ruler governs.[5]

Many Nigerians have of course moved away from their traditional societies (and many of those who have done so are loyal to the nation more than to the tribe). It is those who have moved away from the traditional society who are the center of attention in Nigeria, and certainly outside of Nigeria, because it is they who express themselves in writing, and speak on the problems of today — colonialism, racism, democracy, socialism, and nationalism. Groups of them come together or fall apart on issues that are devoid of ethnic implications: ideological agreement or controversy, economic self-interest, fascination with one academic subject or another.* But even as to them Nigeria's ethnic

---

*Similarly, within any ethnic group there are, obviously, groups who share interests different than other members of the ethnic group. The Yoruba women traders, whose highly competitive search for buyers and colorful light and dark blue shawls dominate markets in the Western Region and Lagos, have been a strong pressure group for their own particular interests though remaining by and large within a Yoruba society.

variety is of enormous importance. Accusations of ethnic favoritism or bias frequently erupt within the governments, among university faculties and even among students overseas. Furthermore, in Nigeria, as in any country composed of several ethnic groups, there is conflict between the desire to overcome ethnic hostility and separatism and the desire to retain the culture of various ethnic groups and avoid stamping out individuality in the name of national unity.

Three forces from outside have disrupted Nigeria's traditional societies. The first is Islam and the second Christianity. The third is secular Western civilization, brought by Europeans beginning with the Portuguese in the fifteenth century and by British colonial administrators beginning in the nineteenth century.

Converts to Islam and Christianity have a bond with their coreligionists that cuts across ethnic lines. Both universal religions, moreover, brought with them tools and skills necessary to widen man's horizons beyond his tribe. They are, for example, responsible for writing in Nigeria. With Islam came the Arabic script to the North; Christian missionaries in the South first put the Southern languages into writing and taught English as well. With the Western influences came a more sophisticated cash economy and a belief in individual liberty, both of which reduced the hold of the traditional society.

But while those forces have reduced ethnic differences in some ways, they have reinforced them in others. Their differential impact has also created a wide divergence between North and South which, while it cuts across ethnic lines, is nonetheless a debilitating drain upon the vitality of the Nigerian nation.

Islam has great influence upon most Northern groups, a lesser, though substantial, influence in the West, little in the Midwest, and next to no influence in the East. Christianity, conversely, has had great success in the South, but has met with almost no success in the northern two-thirds of the Northern Region, where Islam was firmly established before the Christian missionaries arrived. (Map 2 helps illustrate the varying strengths of Islam, Christianity, and animism in different parts of Nigeria.)

Similarly, Western secular civilization has affected Nigeria's ethnic groups in very different ways. Because modern power depends largely upon acquisition of the skills of the West, new tensions have been thereby created. The Yoruba often regard themselves as superior to other Nigerian groups because the effects of Western education have spread

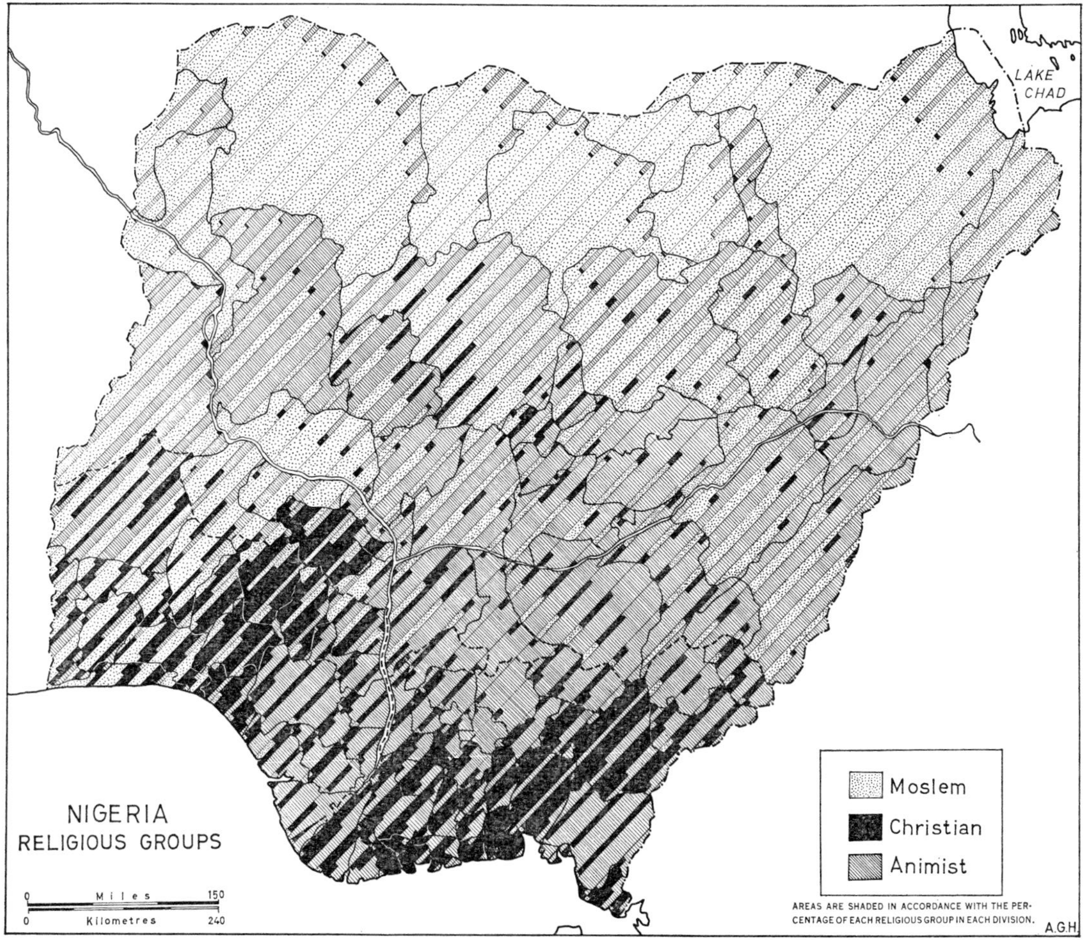

MAP 2. *Principal Religious Groups of Nigeria (courtesy of H. M. Stationery Office and R. M. Prothero). The map is based on the 1952–1953 census.*

NIGERIA
RELIGIOUS GROUPS

Miles 0 ... 150
Kilometres 0 ... 240

Moslem
Christian
Animist

AREAS ARE SHADED IN ACCORDANCE WITH THE PER-
CENTAGE OF EACH RELIGIOUS GROUP IN EACH DIVISION.   A.G.H.

LAKE CHAD

widest and deepest among them. The Ibo, starting later, have almost caught up, but their aggressive efforts to do so have made the Yoruba jealous and angry. The Islamic peoples in the North have only very recently perceived their need for Western education which, with British encouragement, they had rejected earlier. They are still far less willing than the Southerners to adopt Western ways, though, anomalously perhaps, the Northern elite is less self-consciously African than the Southern elite.

Geographical differences between the North and the South help explain the varying impacts of Islam, Christianity, and Western technology upon them.

The northern portion of the Northern Region belongs to an area geographically and historically known as the Western Sudan. Bordering upon the southern section of the Sahara and typically consisting of open savannah, it was tied to North Africa and through it to the Middle East for centuries before the European "discoveries" of West Africa. Waves of migrating peoples had come to West Africa from North Africa and perhaps the Middle East. Northerners today will often still show Hamitic or Semitic Arab features just as their names — Muhammed, Ali, or Abubakar, and Ibrahim, Musa, or Isa — recall the heroes of Muslim Arab history and Arab transliterations of Biblical names.

After the migrations, trade began. From the Western Sudan across the desert to North Africa went camel caravans loaded with gold, salt, slaves, and the red goatskins which became "Moroccan" leather. With the Arab and Berber traders and raiders from North Africa came the faith, the law, and the learning of Islam.

The legends of origin of some of the Southern Nigerian peoples like the Yoruba also tell of migrations from North Africa or the Middle East, and some of them felt the influence of Islam and Arab culture through the Northern peoples. But those influences were not nearly as strong in the South as in the North. The Northern part of Nigeria is, obviously, closer to North Africa. Even had the northern peoples or the Berbers and Arabs wished to penetrate further south, the terrain was a barrier. Their horses, or camels, could neither penetrate the thick southern forest nor survive the bite of the tsetse fly infesting it.

Christianity and Western technology were brought to Nigeria by Europeans who sailed across the sea. They first affected the coastal peoples, not the Northerners who had first felt Islam's impact. From their first "discoveries" in the fifteenth century until the nineteenth century,

9

moreover, the Europeans usually waited on the coast in their ships for African middlemen to bring them the goods they sought, including slaves. On their occasional forays inland they usually went up the rivers or creeks and waited on their ships for trade. Their contact with the Northerners, distant inland, was much less than with the Southerners.

Because it was close to the coast, moreover, the British imposed their control over Southern Nigeria approximately fifty years before doing so in the North. Finally, when they did extend their control, the North was more resistant to Western innovation, and that in large measure was due to the fact that the North had a strong conflicting civilization based on Islam.

Lest the impression be felt that all the tensions in Nigeria are ethnic, communal, geographic, and religious, it is worth noting at the outset one of the several quite different sorts of tension — that between the established and the new elite. In part this is a conflict between the outs and the ins. That conflict is accentuated by the fact that the established generation moved easily into civil service and political jobs which opened up as the British left. It gives no sign of relinquishing its privileges, which are all the more significant since industry and other sectors of the economy have not expanded fast enough to offer equivalent jobs. In part it is also a conflict of ideas, with the rising generation being more outspokenly nationalistic, anticolonial, and fearful of economic exploitation by the Western world. Frustration at being shut off from jobs, nationalism, and anticolonialism all contribute to the rising generation's frequently voiced criticism of the established generation for cutting itself off from the masses through selfish insistence on continuation, even expansion, of the privileges in pay and other perquisites that were offered to colonial administrators in order to persuade them to work in tropical Africa.

Precolonial History

A common history can help hold a nation together, but the most significant general comment that can be made about precolonial history in Nigeria is that it is not Nigerian history but rather the history of different tribes, or, occasionally, groupings of tribes. Of course it is true, as Thomas Hodgkin points out in his anthology of the history of Nigerian peoples, that a "variety of links existed between the various states and peoples which were the predecessors of modern Nigeria."[6] But those links were of some groups with their neighbors and not of all Nigerian groups together. One part of the country, the North, had its most important historical relationships with groups outside the country. Others were completely isolated. Some of the links that did exist between Nigerian groups, moreover, consisted of war between groups or enslavement of one group by another.

Nigeria's peoples did not have a sufficiently common history so that a sage writing as few as seventy years ago could have foreseen the emergence of a nation which unites the peoples brought together in Nigeria today. The country's boundaries have no basis whatsoever in history; nor, except for the Atlantic ocean, which forms the southern boundary, are they meaningful geographically. The western frontier, between Nigeria and Dahomey, splits the Yoruba tribe, and many Hausa live across the northern frontier in Niger. Instead of the frontiers being reflective of Nigerian history, they were fixed by bargaining between the British and their rival colonialists, the French and the Germans.*

But though it is true that Nigeria's precolonial history does not provide the basis for a Nigerian nation, it is also true that there is little in her precolonial history that adds to the difficulty of preserving and building the Nigerian nation. There are relatively few unsettled scores, historic grievances, or thwarted drives for expansion that could have been expected to erupt after the British departure. Generally speaking, each group controls the land that it remembers as its own. The Fulani conquests of the early nineteenth century stand as something of an exception. Since the effect of the Fulani triumph is still felt in independent Nigeria in a number of ways, it is worth describing in some detail.

The Fulani, along with the Hausa whose language most of them speak, are today the dominant group in Nigeria's Northern Region. The Hausa lived in the area before the Fulani migrated into Hausaland in the thirteenth century "bringing with them books on Divinity and

---

*"We have been engaged," said Lord Salisbury after the British and French agreed upon the rough limits of the British sphere of influence in the North, "in drawing lines upon maps where no white man's foot has ever trod; we have been giving away mountains and rivers and lakes to each other, only hindered by the small impediment that we never knew exactly where the mountains and rivers and lakes were."

Of the frontier between British and German territory in the east, Sir Claude Macdonald reminisced: "in those days we just took a blue pencil and a rule and we put it down at Old Calabar and drew that line up to Yola."[7]

Etymology."[8] For many years the Hausa were politically dominant. Their city-states, Kano and Katsina particularly, were great commercial entrepôts for the camel-caravan trade with Morocco and other kingdoms across the Sahara Desert. Kano, whose chronicle describes the reigns of forty-eight kings from 999, was said by the wandering Leo Africanus* in the early sixteenth century to be a town of "rich merchants and most civil people."[9]

Both the Hausa and the Fulani had been converted to Islam. The Hausa, however, were not always constant in their Islamic faith. In the early nineteenth century, their tendency to revert to ancestral paganism was one of the things which inspired Usuman dan Fodio, a Fulani, to lead a reform movement to restore the true faith and to spread it further.

Usuman dan Fodio was a strict Muslim of the Maliki school who taught and preached in Gobir, a Hausa kingdom in what is now the Republic of Niger to the north of Nigeria. There he sought to instill religious zeal in the people and denounced reversion to ancestral paganism. For that Usuman earned the enmity of the king of Gobir, and upon the accession to the throne of the king's son, Usuman's former pupil, Usuman was forced to flee in February 1804. With him came supporters in such numbers that he was able to defeat Gobir the following June. He and his supporters then declared a Jihad, a holy war, and Usuman was given the title of Sarkin Musulmi — Commander, or Chief of the faithful.

The Jihad met with great success. Fulani rulers, Usuman's followers, were established throughout Hausaland and beyond in previously pagan territory. By 1809, when Usuman retired, the conquest was nearly complete. By 1831, an area of 180,000 square miles, larger than California or Italy, had been brought under Fulani rule.

Accompanying the Jihad, and indeed inspiring it, was "an important intellectual movement, involving in the minds of the leaders a conception of the ideal society."[10] A total of 258 books and pamphlets have been provisionally attributed to Usuman dan Fodio, his son, Muhammed Bello, and brother, Abdullahi, who together succeeded him upon his retirement, a retirement which he sought in order to give himself more time to read and write.

---

*Leo Africanus was a North African, born in Granada, Spain, who traveled in his youth through much of West Africa which bordered upon the Sahara. After being captured by a Sicilian corsair, he was converted to Christianity, given the Pope's name, and wrote descriptions of the lands through which he had traveled.

The Fulani empire was governed upon principles related to European feudalism. Owing allegiance to the rulers at its two capitals and paying tribute to them were local rulers known as emirs. The emirs in turn headed a pyramid with district and village heads beneath them. The local rulers of most of Northern Nigeria today are the descendants of Usuman's followers, and the emirate system of government, described more fully in the next chapter, still is of great significance.

The Jihad, and the emirate system created by its leaders, brought a measure of unity to a huge area. By strengthening the Muslim faith of those who came within the Empire, it provided a bond which helped to override ethnic differences. It is one of the reasons why the Islamic portion of Northern Nigeria is today relatively cohesive politically.

The Fulani triumph lives on in more subtle ways as well. The Fulani-Hausa have political influence in Nigeria out of all proportion to their numerical strength, particularly since they, with the rest of the Islamic North, were the least exposed to modern influences during the British era and therefore fell behind in modern skills. They form the core of the Northern Peoples Congress (NPC) which, led by the Sardauna of Sokoto,* a great-great-grandson of Usuman dan Fodio, governs the Northern Region and is the senior partner in Nigeria's coalition Federal Government. Of course that power is largely the result of a pyramiding of advantages: the Fulani-Hausa are the largest group in the Northern Region, which in turn is the largest region in the Federation. But it also stems from the pride and confidence of the Fulani and the Hausa, and particularly of their leaders. Those qualities have had much to do with their success, and those qualities come, in large though incalculable measure, from their pride in their historical glory, the Jihad that increased it, the learning and governmental system that sustained it, and the religion that inspired it.

There is another side as well. There is in some Northerners a certain narrowness, a disinterest in national events outside the North, not to speak of international events, and a contempt for those outside their tradition. This too stems in part from pride in the past. Both disinterest and pride help explain why the NPC is not open to Southerners and why the party has made only halfhearted efforts, meeting with negligible success, to enter directly into the politics of the rest of the country.

*Sardauna is a title restricted to members of the ruling house of Sokoto, one of the two Fulani capitals, a new town established by Usuman's son. It means, roughly, Captain of the Bodyguard.

All this helps explain the fervor with which the NPC opposes proposals to split the Northern Region so as to create a new region out of its southern portion. The words of the Sardauna of Sokoto, speaking in the Northern House of Assembly against such a proposal, help show that side of the Northern spirit. "If I may further say," he concluded, "whoever thinks he has words with which to attack me, I can assure him that I learnt more than he knows before he was born . . . our empire is going to last forever because it was inspired by the Creator of the universe and his criticisms do not come within our fold."[11]

In the southwest section of what is today the Northern Region, the Fulani warriors met the Yoruba. Yoruba legends say that the tribe had once been united under the political leadership of Oyo and the religious supremacy of Ife with power resting in the hands of the descendants of the legendary tribal ancestor, Oduduwa. By the late eighteenth century, however, the Yoruba had split into four states and the process of disintegration, caused in part by slave wars, continued further thereafter. Thus as the Fulani and their allies, inspired and united by the Jihad, began to push down upon the Yoruba, the Yoruba were falling apart.

In 1817, one Afonja of the Ilorin subtribe of the Yoruba was in revolt against his overlord, the Alafin (King) of Oyo. He sought help from the troops of Alimi, a Sokoto Fulani, and, receiving help, won independence. Independence was short-lived, however, for Alimi's son killed Afonja, ascended the throne as an emir, and brought Ilorin within the Fulani empire.

Ilorin and the Ilorin Yoruba are today part of the Northern Region, which includes all of the old Fulani empire that lies within Nigeria. Efforts by the Action Group, a political party based primarily upon Yoruba support, to redraw the regional boundary to include the Ilorin Yoruba with the rest of the Yoruba in the Western Region have embittered Nigerian politics more than any other issue that stems from Nigeria's precolonial history.

The Fulani were prevented from penetrating further into Yoruba territory by the Ibadan subtribe of the Yoruba along what is now approximately the border between Northern and Western Nigeria. When the British began to extend their power to that area at the end of the nineteenth century, the Fulani with their Ilorin allies and the Ibadan Yoruba still faced each other in armed camps. Once the British did extend their power to the area, the armed camps were dissolved, but occasionally a Northerner will suggest that his people will move again.

Abubakar Tafawa Balewa, who later became the Federal Prime Minister and is a Northerner, though not a Fulani, spoke in 1947 against the British departure from the country at that time, warning that if they departed "the Northern people would continue their interrupted conquest to the sea."[12]

There are other areas in what is today the Northern Region where the Fulani met with successful resistance or at least failed to penetrate. One was the heavily forested area near the Benue River, where the Tiv were the dominant group.

The Tiv and some other groups in the Middle Belt (roughly the southern third of the Northern Region) have resisted being included in the Northern Region. In the hope of delaying independence until given their own region, the Tiv staged a minor revolt just prior to independence, and in 1964 they began another insurrection. In large measure their resistance stems from the fact that they did not come within the Fulani-Hausa sphere of influence at the time of the Jihad, and their separate traditions therefore retained their vitality. Some groups in the portion of the Middle Belt area conquered by the Fulani also have resisted inclusion in the Northern Region, stating, as a member of one such group did in the Nigerian Parliament a few months before Independence, that the Sardauna of Sokoto, who is Premier of Northern Nigeria as well as leader of the NPC, regards them "as the inherited wealth of his great-grandfather."[13]

Another area that the Fulani failed to conquer in what is today the Northern Region was Bornu, the home of the Kanuri tribe in the Region's northeast corner bordering on the shores of Lake Chad. The Kanuri-speaking people had been converted to Islam at the end of the eleventh century, before the Hausa. Their ties as part of the Kanem-Bornu Empire were with Egypt and the northeast coast of Africa rather than, as the Hausa, with the Kingdoms of the Western Sudan and Morocco. The Kanem-Bornu Empire reached a height in the sixteenth century under Mai (King) Idris Alooma, who used to good advantage horses and Turkish muskets which had been obtained in trade primarily for slaves. For a time the Bornu Empire had a loose control over some of the Hausa city-states, but by the time of Usuman dan Fodio's Jihad, Bornu had declined in strength.

The ruling mai was driven into exile and his capital occupied by the Fulani. The Kanuri then turned to Muhammed al-Kanami, who liberated most of the Empire.

15

Before doing so, he wrote in Arabic to Muhammed Bello, Usuman dan Fodio's son and successor, saying that attacks upon Bornu were unjustified, for

> we are innocent of paganism and it is far from our compound . . . . No age and no country is free from its share of heresy and sin. If, thereby, they become pagan, then surely their books are useless.[14]

Bornu's separate historical traditions have been reflected recently by the Bornu Youth Movement, one of whose aims was the separation of Bornu from the rest of the Northern Region in order to create a new state. At the moment, owing to the skillful use of patronage and harassment, the secessionist movement seems dead. Still the Kanuri continue to have an independent spirit.

In the South as well, there are some separatist tendencies which stem from Nigeria's precolonial history. In the Eastern Region, the Efik and Ijaw separatist movements in part reflect their great commercial power in the seventeenth, eighteenth, and nineteenth centuries as compared with the Ibo, their now dominant neighbors. While the Ibo mostly lived in dark little villages and were frequent victims of slavers, they ruled city-states busy with the slave trade and later with the palm-oil trade. In the Western Region, the separatist tradition, which led to the creation of a separate Midwest Region in July 1963, centered upon the old Kingdom of Benin and was based in large measure upon memories of its considerable historical glory. Benin reached its height in the fifteenth and sixteenth centuries, and its bronze castings of that period and earlier have received world acclaim. A measure of its power is gathered from the fact that at the end of the fifteenth century, when Columbus was voyaging to America, Benin exchanged ambassadors with Portugal.

Slavery played a major role in Nigeria's precolonial history. The coastal regions which now are part of Nigeria were known as the slave coast, just as present-day Ghana was known as the Gold Coast and the present-day Ivory Coast was known by that name. What is now Nigeria provided a high percentage of the Africans who were cruelly torn from their families and homes, crowded into the stinking dark holds of ships, and, if they survived the voyage, put to work in the New World as beasts of burden. Captain John Adams, an Englishman who sailed frequently to West Africa in the eighteenth century, estimated that during a twenty-year period 370,000 people from the Ibo tribe alone were sold into slavery.

The constant insecurity caused by slave raiding had an extremely harmful effect upon progress in Nigeria. Slave wars, slave raiding, and hiding from slave raiders all kept Nigerian groups fragmented.

There has been no greater crime committed by the Western world than the role it played in the transatlantic slave trade. To complete the record it should be noted, however, that some Africans as well played a tawdry role. The European slave traders usually waited in their boats for African middlemen to bring the human chattels to them. Certain groups, notably the Aro clan of the Ibo tribe and the Efik and Ijaw tribes on the coast of what is today the Eastern Region, became rich and powerful from their part in the transatlantic slave trade and resisted the eventual efforts of the British to put an end to it.

In addition to the role played by Africans in the foreign slave trade, slavery of Africans by Africans was traditional. It remained common until the British extended their rule over the whole country, defeating as late as 1903, for example, the Emir of Kontagora, who was reputed to have said, "Can you stop a cat from mousing? When I die I shall be found with a slave in my mouth."[15] It is said, with some truth perhaps, that such slavery was not as cruel as the slavery of Africans by white men in the Americas.* And, particularly in Bornu and the city-states of the Eastern Region, it was not uncommon for able slaves to rise to leadership positions.† But the now empty spaces in Niger Province which were once ravaged by the Emir of Kontagora, and the lips of the women of the Zaranda tribe, still expanded to the size of small plates as a legacy of the days when that was done to make them undesirable as slaves, suggest that it had its cruel side as well.

The years of slave raiding and slave wars have left many legacies for modern Nigeria. But there is obviously no desire to return to the old slave-raiding days. And the memories of slave wars between various ethnic groups divide Nigerians less than might be expected because descendants of both slavers and slaves, raiders and fugitives, share resentment of the brutality, the exploitation, and the indignity of the transatlantic slave trade.

*In one way at least some Nigerian slaves were fortunate. When the British first established their authority in an area, they would sometimes tell the local chief to supply a certain number of boys for school. Often he would include his slaves' sons among those sent, sometimes instead of his own sons.

†Jaja of Opobo, for example, was purchased as a slave in 1860 and within ten years had become the head of the large trading house in the Niger delta area that had purchased him.

17

Race, History, and Unity

With all their differences, what are the forces that tend to keep Nigerians together? There are two dominant ones. First, even though the British created some new differences, Nigerians were brought together and differentiated from their neighbors by the period of British colonial rule, to be discussed in the next chapter. The second major unifying force is a strong feeling of racial solidarity, a bond that stems from long years of prejudice and derision. Nnamdi Azikiwe, Nigeria's President (then her Governor-General), recently said that "the problem of Nigerian unity would have been extremely difficult but for our racial homogeneity." He then went on to say

> In other words, whilst we must admit that we have hundreds of nationalities in Nigeria, by which I mean Nigerian societies whose inhabitants speak different languages and whose cultures are influenced by their environment and by the constant impact of other cultures on their own, yet we must also concede that our racial homogeneity and the sociological problems created by peoples of different racial stock and cultural complexes coming into contact with us have facilitated the crystallization of a sense of oneness among Nigerians. . . .

The feeling of racial solidarity and two questions arising from it — does it continue to be relevant after the British surrendered political power, and can it be transformed to produce national unity or does it rather suggest the union of all of black Africa — are of focal importance throughout the whole book. Here they are merely introduced.

Though all of Nigeria's ethnic groups do not share a common precolonial history, they do tend to be united by a certain point of view concerning Africa's precolonial history. They have a common distaste for the idea that black Africa either had no history before the Europeans came or had a history of unparalleled savagery and superstition, the bloody tale of a dark continent.

The assumption that black Africa's history begins with the coming of European explorers, traders, and missionaries has been widely held. "Africa," said an early edition of the *Encyclopaedia Britannica,* "with the exception of the lower Nile Valley and what is known of Roman Africa is, so far as its native inhabitants are concerned, a continent without history. . . . The negro is essentially a child of the moment, and his memory, both tribal and individual, is very short."[16] Sometimes when discoveries such as the ruined cities of Zimbabwe in central Africa have been made, it has been asserted that the Negro could not have been responsible because of the "well accepted fact that the negroid brain never could be capable of taking the initiative in work of such intricate nature."[17]

As the foregoing quotations show, generalizations about the emptiness of black Africa's history have often been coupled with generalizations about the emptiness of the Negro's brain. Capacity as well as past performance has been discounted. But there are other students of Africa who, believing fully in the capacity of the African, have nevertheless argued that his history was barren before the Europeans came. Thus Margery Perham stated, in arguing for a different policy toward Africa than toward Asia:

> The dealings between tropical Africa and the West must be different. Here in place of the large unities of Asia was the multicellular tissue of tribalism: instead of an ancient civilization, the largest area of primitive poverty enduring into the modern age. Until the very recent penetration by Europe the greater part of the Continent was without the wheel, the plough or the transport-animal; almost without stone houses or clothes, except for skins; without writing and so without history.[18]

The natural tendency among all Africans, Nigerians included, is to seek to correct the record. Great artistic or political accomplishments, like the Benin and Ife bronzes or the Muslim reform movement of Usuman dan Fodio, are extolled and romanticized. The theory is put forward that African kingdoms during the European Middle Ages were as advanced as the European kingdoms but that their growth was stunted. In 1962, Nnamdi Azikiwe told a score of African heads of state:

> Those nations compared most favourably with their contemporaries in Europe and Asia. Then came the revival of learning and the invention of gunpowder as a weapon of warfare and as an instrument of political control. Those African empires and kingdoms disintegrated partly as a result of disunity created by fratricidal struggles for power and partly because of the slave trade.[19]*

Sometimes, admitted historical deficiencies in technological or secular skills are countered with an asserted superiority of the African way of life, with emphasis upon the closeness of the relationship between members of the community and upon a capacity for zestful enjoyment of

---

*Azikiwe's reference to gunpowder recalls the lines of Hilaire Belloc explaining the power of the Europeans by saying:
> Whatever happens we have got
> The maxim gun and they have not.[20]

life. Finally, as in the lines of a Ghanaian poet, Michael Francis Dei-Anang, the significant past history is said to be man's beginnings in Africa. Thus he wrote

> My race was great
> And ever so will be
> For man's primeval dawn
> Began its course
> Upon my land.[21]

Because attacks have been made upon the history and often the capacity of the Negro race as a whole, Africans tend to respond as members of that race and not as members of a particular nation in Africa. The Nigerian Governor-General pointed to all the kingdoms of Africa. Nigerian historians take equal pride in the political accomplishments of Mansa Musa, Emperor of Mali, who in the fourteenth century made the pilgrimage to Mecca, crossing the Sahara Desert with thousands of men, and in the artistic or engineering accomplishments of Zimbabwe, as in accomplishments within Nigeria itself.[22]*

There is, therefore, an emotional force to precolonial history — even though it may consist of the history of many tribes — which serves to unite Africans. They are united in a way similar to other groups such as the Jews which have felt the slights of prejudice. But the emotional force serves to unite them not as members of a particular nation but as mem-

---

*Nigeria's Government was urged by many to change the country's name after independence to one like Songhai that would recall the glories of some former African kingdom. (Songhai was a kingdom of the Western Sudan to the north and west of Nigeria that had slight influence over Hausa states. Presumably a name of a non-Nigerian kingdom was suggested because to suggest one of the former kingdoms of Nigerian groups might exacerbate ethnic jealousy as other groups put forward a great name from their past.) The Government decided not to change the country's name, unlike the former Gold Coast that adopted the name of Ghana, a kingdom of the Western Sudan which was located many miles from the Ghana of today, the territory to which some of old Ghana's peoples are said to have migrated. Mali is another modern African nation that adopted the name of an old African kingdom. Nyasaland changed to Malawi and Northern Rhodesia to Zambia. Southern Rhodesia (now Rhodesia) will probably eventually be known as Zimbabwe.

The name Nigeria was probably first suggested by Flora Shaw, a commentator on colonial affairs for the London *Times* who later became the wife of Lord Lugard, Nigeria's first Governor-General. In the *Times* of January 8, 1897, writing about what is now Northern Nigeria, she suggested "Nigeria" as a "title for the agglomeration of pagan and Mohammedan states which have been brought . . . within the confines of a British protectorate, and thus need for the first time in their history to be described as an entity by some general name."[23]

bers of the Negro race joined in spirit with other members of the race in Africa and outside it. Thus, so far as precolonial history is concerned, the natural political community would be, if not the tribe, then the race or the continent.

It is wrong to think that black Africa accomplished nothing before the white man came to carry some of its inhabitants into slavery and to bring other attributes of his civilization to the rest. Many of its accomplishments, a few of which are mentioned or briefly outlined in the preceding paragraphs, were admirable. Nevertheless, it undoubtedly is fair to say that when the European came the black African was in many ways backward. More than anything else, perhaps, it is a sign of his weakness that there was no writing until outsiders, first Muslim Arabs and then Christian Europeans, introduced and taught it.

Assuming that the African was backward, does it follow that he and his nations are necessarily destined to remain so forever? History does not support such an inference. Two thousand years ago, the tribes whose descendants became citizens of today's dominant states of Northern Europe and North America were to the Romans barbarians. As those who were backward have risen to lead, so those who once led, the Egyptians, for example, have fallen behind. The crucial question is capacity, and past performance is only one of many guides to it.

History suggests, moreover, that capacity in many instances has been realized only after the stimulus of contact with an established civilization. Greece owed much to Egypt, Rome much to Greece, and Northern Europe much to Rome.

Black Africa until recently has been isolated from the rest of the world. On three sides it was surrounded by ocean, and even if its distant coasts could be reached by probing strangers, they were, certainly in West Africa, choked with growth. The Sahara, to the north, formed the fourth side. It could be crossed, and along its southern borders outposts of Islamic civilization grew up. But it too was a formidable barrier to communication.

Professor Arnold J. Toynbee in his *Study of History* develops the theory that civilizations arise as a response to challenge. But the challenge must be neither too hard, for then the people cannot respond, nor too easy, for then the people need not respond. Life in Africa was at once too hard and too easy. It was too hard because of the jungle, which never surrenders, and because subtle and unseen carriers of disease were favored by the climate. If they did not kill the African, tropical diseases such as bilharzia and malaria would slowly sap his strength. On the other hand, if one survived disease, life was relatively easy in the tropical sun. (Can an environment less conducive to diligence be imagined than one where, as is true in much of Nigeria, a tree — a species of palm — can be tapped and an alcoholic wine obtained within minutes?)

Africa's historic backwardness has a parallel in the historic backwardness of other peoples who later became powerful, and it can be explained as arising from Africa's isolation and its cruel but kind natural environment. But having been behind does not make the task of Africa's nations any easier, particularly in this age when growing publicity about differences can breed discouragement as well as ambition. The climate, too, still remains, though man has more control over it now.

In Nigeria's case, the chief stimulus from outside, the chief transmitter of the world's developed light and learning, and the chief challenge has been the British colonialist.

The British: Catalysts
for Nationalism

The British cut Nigeria out of Africa. Much of themselves they left behind. Colonial rule left a new country with a measure of both political and economic unity, but the British did more to unify the country economically than politically. And the political unity that did develop stemmed much more from Nigerians' assimilation of alien ideas and their common desire to oust alien rulers than from any design of the colonialists. Even economically, much that was done by Britain was in her interest and not in the interest of the colony. Racial prejudice and class snobbery mar the record.

The British kept the peace in a land that had been beset by war. They brought new and more just means of administration. They built roads. For the Romans, those accomplishments assure their mark in history. Today colonialists are held to tougher tests.

Criticism of the British must be tempered with understanding that the standard to which colonialists are now held is new in emphasis if not in basic conception. The thought that the relationship between rich countries and poor colonies consists primarily of the duty of the rich to develop the poor evolved recently. After all, the idea that governments have a responsibility to develop even their own peoples and to remove the barriers between their own rich and poor is also new in emphasis.

More should be said to temper criticism of the British. The differences between Nigeria's peoples were great before the British came; new differences were created by the varying times at which areas first felt the disruptive impact of the Western world. The people were very backward technologically before the British came. The British were not in the country long. Lagos, the first territory annexed, was not annexed until 1861, much of the North was not conquered until 1903, and parts of Nigeria remained under only the most theoretical control for many years thereafter. In the early years, much of the available energy had to be devoted simply to keeping the peace. During the slightly more than fifty years that the entire country was under British control, moreover, the mother country fought two world wars and lived through an enervating depression. The time during which she could devote the necessary resources to Nigeria was short indeed. But, until the rush toward independence after World War II, it was believed that the time available before Britain would be judged by what she left behind was long indeed. Also, many people had assumed that Britain would be judged not by whether she left behind a Nigerian nation but by whether she left behind a collection of well-administered tribal states. Considering all these factors, much was accomplished.

It will be recalled that many of the differences among Nigeria's peoples could be explained by geography. Northerners accepted Islam because they were closer to its source. Their trade ran north where there were richer markets, more enticing goods, and more open terrain than to the south. The forest dwellers in the South, particularly the Ibo of the Southeast, were cut off from contact with other peoples and even from each other by the choking growth. Finally, the Southerners, because their land touched the coast, came into contact with the revolutionary ideas and techniques of Europeans long before the Northerners.

The British opened up the country. Old geographical barriers no longer keep Nigerians apart; today, because of the economic development undertaken during the period of British rule, Nigeria's geographical diversity has become a strong unifying force.

The natural trade routes of the northern peoples now run south toward the ocean and through the rest of Nigeria rather than out of Nigeria across the Sahara Desert. The railroad running south and ships waiting at the shore have replaced the camel gliding north. As a result, one of the strongest forces holding the Northerners in the Nigerian Federation is their realization that secession would leave them poor, landlocked, and at the mercy of the coastal peoples across whose land their goods must pass.

Reversing the natural flow of the Northerners' trade so that it ran through the rest of Nigeria was the most significant consequence of the British policy of opening up the country. That policy made a difference everywhere and to all Nigerians. The Ibo of the Eastern Region, for example, is no longer isolated in his thick forest. The forest grows on, but it is parted by roads. Using those roads, and benefiting from the peaceful conditions in the country and new opportunities for employment in the cities, he more than any other Nigerian has moved out of the ancestral homeland. The Ibos' need for outlets for their surplus population and their continuing interest in those who have already departed from the homeland are, incidentally, important forces which hold them in the Nigerian Federation.*

With the country at peace and opened up by rail and road, its geographic diversity helps hold it together and thus reinforces the British influence. As one leaves Nigeria's Atlantic Coast and heads into the interior, the vegetation becomes less thick, the soil sandier, and the rainfall less. At the coast is a belt of swamps and thick mangrove growth; inland is a belt of tropical forest with numerous varieties of trees and bushes, the most noticeable of which are the palms and the most productive of which are the oil palm and the cocoa. Still further inland, beginning north of the Eastern Region's northern border and south of the Western Region's northern border, the country opens into bush savannah, which gradually becomes drier, only occasionally dotted by wispy thorn trees or bulbus baobabs. That is the general pattern, though there are departures from it, such as the well-watered Jos plateau rising in the Northern Region.

Because of variations in soil and rainfall, the economies of Nigeria's northern and southern portions are complementary. Different crops are grown both for export and for domestic use. For export, the North,

---

*The Eastern Region is by far the most densely populated of Nigeria's three regions and Iboland is the most densely populated portion of it. Though it has fewer large cities than either the North or the West, it had under the 1952-1953 census 245 persons per square mile, compared with 134 in the West and 60 in the North. Of the ten most densely populated provinces in Nigeria, eight including the first four were in the Eastern Region, and six of those eight were inhabited primarily by Ibos. Owerri Province was the most crowded, with 654 persons per square mile, 873 in its most crowded division.[1] The 1963 census showed further growth in the population of the Eastern Region.

drier and with sandier soil, grows groundnuts (peanuts) and cotton; in the South, with more rainfall and forests, the Western Region produces cocoa, timber, rubber, and palm products, and the Eastern Region produces palm products in greater quantity than the West. Domestically, the North grows grain crops while root crops like yams and cassava grow in the South. Cattle are bred only in the North; kola, a bitter nut used for ceremony and chewed for pleasure, staining the mouth brown, grows only in the South. The variety in export crops means that Nigeria, 85 per cent of whose foreign exchange comes from agricultural exports, can withstand fluctuations in the price of a crop which would ruin a one-crop country. The variety of domestic crops strengthens the ties of trade.

In raw materials for industry, the regional resources are not so clearly complementary but are still different enough so that the benefits of unity are obvious. In the East there is coal, lignite, limestone, iron, and oil (in amounts that now appear to be very substantial); in the West, there is limestone, and in the Midwest lignite and a lesser amount of oil; in the North there is tin, limestone, coal, iron, and, once the dams proposed in the 1962–1968 development plan are built, the North will have the country's major source of electric power. Unity makes easier the exchange necessary to start a steel mill, for example; it means that there is an internal market large enough to make industrial schemes feasible that would be impossible in smaller nations.

In addition to roads and railways, the British left Nigeria with other underpinnings of a unified economy. There is a common currency, the Nigerian pound on a par with sterling, and there are nationwide post, telephone, and telegraph systems. There are no internal customs barriers or other such impediments to trade.

Even though the basis for a unified economy exists, it does not mean that Nigeria has nearly developed her economic potential. Her people are very poor. Their average income is less than $100 per year.*

Nigeria was developed economically in the interest of the mother country rather than the colony. In many ways those interests coincided

---

*The estimate for 1956–1958 in the *Economic Survey of Nigeria, 1959* (Federal Government Printer, Lagos, 1959), pp. 15–18, was under £30 or $84. Even assuming that the annual increase per capita has increased from the 2½ per cent estimated to have been the rate from 1950–1951 to 1956–1957, the average income is not likely to be over $100 since the abortive 1962 census and the 1963 census revealed that Nigeria's population had been undercounted when the per capita estimates were first made.

and, to be practical, if the economy had not been developed in Britain's self-interest it might be even less advanced than in fact it is. But Nigeria inherited an economy which it must change for many reasons, not the least of which is the need further to cement the economic foundations of unity.

The roads and the railroads were designed primarily to serve the export-import trade and not to encourage internal trade or communication. The major lines run from north to south, to and from the ocean, while east-west lines are few. There is no railway running between Eastern and Western Nigeria and a decent road was begun only after Nigerians came to power. Similarly, though the Niger and Benue Rivers are bridged by north-south lines, there is as yet only a ferry running from west to east across the Niger after it, joined by the Benue, turns south to run toward the ocean, though a bridge is planned under the 1962–1968 development plan.[2] As for communications with Nigeria's neighbors — the ex-French territories to the east, west, and north — both the British and the French were jealous of their preserves so that there are no railway links and very few roads.*

The British created a greenhouse economy in Nigeria. And, as with a greenhouse, the important thing from the master's point of view was to ensure that more and more fragrant flowers arrived at his table. Nigeria relies heavily upon agricultural production and exports for its income† and imports almost all its manufactured goods. Even goods manufactured from Nigeria's own raw materials are imported. Soap using Nigerian palm oil is imported, as is peanut butter from Nigerian peanuts; until the reins of power had been almost completely transferred to Nigerian hands, there was no cotton cloth made in Nigeria from Nigerian cotton.

*In 1958, .18 per cent of Nigeria's imports were from other West African countries, and 1.01 per cent of her exports went to other West African countries. In 1962, the import percentage was down to .12 per cent and the export percentage was up, but only to 2.88 per cent (Central Bank of Nigeria, *Economic and Financial Review*, Vol. 1, No. 2 [Dec. 1963], p. 39). Given the agricultural base of the economies of Nigeria and her neighbors and the overlaps in crops, it is not surprising that the figures are low. However, trade between Nigeria and her neighbors is undoubtedly hampered by the fact that during the colonial days little attention was paid to developing such trade or to creating the infrastructure for it.

†In addition to yielding 85 per cent of the country's foreign exchange, more than 75 per cent of Nigeria's work force is in agriculture or related fields, from which comes about two-thirds of her national income. Secondary trades dependent upon agriculture produce a large portion of the rest of her income.

27

That Nigeria should import her manufactured goods and concentrate on the export of tropical agricultural produce was of course in Britain's interest as a shipping and manufacturing nation. For the short term, at least, it was in Nigeria's interest as well, for in the past the quickest way to generate money with which further to develop the country was, as is still true, to increase agricultural production. Nevertheless, the country encompasses a big enough market and has sufficient raw materials to develop a substantial supplementary industrial sector.

To make the economic balance sheet more complete, it should be noted that much of Nigeria's economic development — including remotely related expenditures like the payment of civil servants' salaries — was paid for by the Nigerians themselves, though until recently it was primarily inspired by British initiative and guided by British hands. Until 1918, the imperial treasury subsidized the colonial budget, particularly the Protectorate of Northern Nigeria before 1914 when it was amalgamated with the richer Protectorate of Southern Nigeria and the Colony of Lagos. After World War II, grants began to be made under the Colonial Development and Welfare Act of 1940. Agricultural produce has benefited from a small preference on the British market. But those contributions were small compared to the contributions made by the Nigerians themselves. They paid for development through direct taxes and, more importantly, duties on imported goods and on the export of agricultural produce and through profits made by the government-owned marketing boards on the sale of produce grown by Nigerians.

Some of the political changes wrought by the economic development of Nigeria during the colonial period have already been described. Thus the need for the Northerners to remain in the union is strong, because the British redirected their trade toward the south, and the Ibos are tied to the nation in part because the British built roads out of Iboland to urban centers in the West and North where there were new jobs stimulated by the new economy. The emergence of a cash economy undercut tribal power, which rested upon an age-old sharing of tasks within a subsistence economy.

The British left their imprint upon all of Nigeria's citizens. The appearance of the police and the wigs of the lawyers, the cars driving on the left-hand side of the road, the positioning in Parliament of government and opposition benches directly opposite each other, "leaves" taken in London, the curriculum of the schools, the English language —

small things and large — all show the British mark and the British style. They add greatly to the elements that Nigerians hold in common. Furthermore, they push Nigerians toward each other by cutting them off from their neighbors, who have been as profoundly influenced by France.

Those who have led the new Nigeria, moreover, are those who (often after education in Great Britain or America, and usually living in changing urban centers) acquired strong weapons from their rulers — a strengthened belief in individual freedom and national self-determination. It was they who were chilled and then angered by the cold hand of racial prejudice as white men less worthy than they got better jobs and more pay in their own country. The new leaders were those Nigerians from all groups who had entered the modern world, who had participated in the cash economy, who had partaken of Western education. Once they had done so, their resentment of alien tutorial rule was inevitable. And it was an inevitable consequence of the British presence that these Nigerians would acquire those strong ideological weapons and enter the modern world.*

Certain British policies, however, slowed the growth of a politically cohesive nation. Indirect rule perpetuated ethnic differences and favored the traditional aristocracy as opposed to a new class free of tribal shackles. Isolating the North from disruptive influences that were transforming the South left the North backward, fearful, and resentful, and the South scornful of the North. The resulting tension has distorted and bedeviled Nigerian politics and made national integration infinitely harder.

Under indirect rule the imperial power uses the existing institutions

---

*That was realized, and to an extent welcomed, by the wiser Englishmen like Sir Frederick (later Lord) Lugard, who wrote, "If there is unrest and a desire for independence . . . it is because we have taught the people the value of liberty and freedom . . . . Their very discontent is a measure of their progress."[3]
The only thing wrong about Lugard's statement is that people are not taught the value of liberty or freedom: they feel it. The British did help educate the Nigerians so that they could better articulate their feelings. While they were there, more Nigerians were released from that poverty that drugs the feeling than ever had been released before. The British also were something more obvious than ever before from which to be free. To be sure, nationalists early demanded the rights of Englishmen and British justice. The relatively high standards of liberty in England did make an impression on her colonial subjects. But a desire for independence, a release of the latent desire for freedom, would have come irrespective of British traditions. Britain's traditions have much to do with the way in which she lost an Empire; they have little to do with the desire of her subjects to become free.

of the indigenous communities as its instrument of government. It rules through the chiefs rather than directly operating upon their subjects. It gently guides the chiefs and reforms indigenous institutions, retaining much it finds strange and even repugnant. It is a policy based upon respect for other societies and doubt that the institutions of the home country are necessarily suited for all peoples. Indirect rule is a practical way to administer large areas with few men and creates the least risk of resistance from the existing rulers. By retaining the structure of the conquered society, indirect rule increases the likelihood that the conquered society will remain stable. Indirect rule is cheap.

The contrasting method is direct rule. Confident in their virtue and careless of the cost, the colonialists transport wholesale their own institutions, trying to remold the natives entirely in their own image or, as in the white colonies, disregarding the natives and ruling through their own countrymen as settlers.

The principle of indirect rule was first systematically applied in Nigeria by Frederick Lugard, Governor of the Protectorate of Northern Nigeria, which was proclaimed at the beginning of the present century. Incredible as it seems, at the end of his first year he was operating with a total staff of 304 men (104 civil and 200 military), of whom one-third were away on leave at any one time. With a budget of £ 135,000 he governed a territory the size of Texas, although his control over much of this vast area was only nominal at the beginning. In 1903 he conquered Kano and Sokoto and brought most of the Protectorate under his control. At the end of that year, his staff and budget had grown, but to only 417 men, 278 estimated to be in Africa, and £500,000.

Faced with an imperial treasury that guarded every farthing and a British public tired from the Boer War and in no mood for colonial wars, Lugard had little choice but to operate through the emirs. The emirate system operated by the descendants of Usuman dan Fodio and his followers was the ideal tool for an imperial system of indirect rule: it was relatively well organized, efficient, and easily understood.

The emirs possessed almost absolute power. Rule was hereditary, though the emir's successor was not necessarily his eldest son but could be chosen in a variety of ways from a single royal dynasty, or even from a number of royal dynasties in succession. Beneath the emir were selected officials of aristocratic birth, some with specific functions at the emirate center and others with general supervision of an outlying district or village.

Appointed by the emir as well were the alkali (Hausa transliteration of the Arabic words for "the judge"), who presided in courts applying Muslim law of the Maliki school. There was also a fully developed system of taxation that was accepted by the people. The emirs collected taxes upon cattle and other stock, upon arable land, upon irrigated crops, and upon those who acceded to office; they imposed tolls upon the movement of merchandise and license fees upon handicrafts and trades; and they were the beneficiaries of the Koranic right to a tithe.

The British eliminated some of the crueler practices of the emirates such as the cutting off of the hands of thieves and the dungeons in which the "legs of those sentenced to death were thrust up to the thigh [where] they were left to be trodden on by the mass of other prisoners till they died of thirst and starvation."[4] They changed the tax collection system somewhat to cut down oppression and corruption. They changed the style of administration to some extent by requiring the district or village heads to live among the people in their outlying fiefdoms rather than lounging at the emir's court. But basically they ruled through the traditional emirate system, retaining in authority the existing emirs or their relatives.

After an absence from Nigeria to serve as Governor of Hong Kong, Lugard returned, charged with the task of amalgamating the Protectorate of Northern Nigeria, the Protectorate of Southern Nigeria, and the Colony of Lagos, a task which he accomplished in 1914. After amalgamation, he attempted to apply the principle of indirect rule in the southern provinces. There he was less successful. In the West, the British were unable to understand the system of chiefly rule. In the East they were unable to find the chiefs.

The Yoruba chiefs appeared to have the same sort of autocratic power as did the Fulani emirs or the Tudor monarchs; in fact, theirs was a constitutional monarchy built upon overlapping family, lineage, and clan units. At the center of a Yoruba state there was an oba, or king, but substantial power was also held by the heads of families and clans and subchiefs who did not owe their office to the oba. They were chosen by a process of selection from below, beginning with the small family unit and continuing upward. Instead of the feudal pyramid from emir to village among the Fulani, there were interwoven or overlapping lines of authority resulting in part from the Yoruba retention of clan and lineage loyalties after they had migrated to the many urban centers in Yorubaland. Moreover, though the oba was regarded as semidivine when ruling, others, applying an unwritten constitution, determined who would become an oba and could remove an oba who offended the people. Traditional electors or councilors chose him from among the eligible males of the royal families; if the councilors decided that his rule should end, he would be politely sent a parrot's egg as an indication that he should depart. When that happened he would commit suicide.

Obafemi Awolowo, analyzing in 1947 the effects of indirect rule upon his people, the Yoruba, wrote

> There is no doubt that in its original treatment of Paramount Chiefs the British Government mistook a part for the whole. It invested the part with powers, the exercise of which properly belonged to the whole. . . . The dictatorial powers which some Yoruba chiefs are wielding today are the making of the British Government, who at the beginning misconceived the true nature of Yoruba monarchy.[5]

The Yoruba system was not easy to understand, and the British administrator, without training as an anthropologist or having the benefit of anthropologists' studies, had to act quickly on the basis of what he saw. Moreover, even when the true nature of the chiefly system began to be understood, the need of the British administrative officer for a quick and efficient response led to continued exaltation of the chiefs and unnatural isolation of them from their councilors and their people.[6]

In the East, the problem was to find the traditional authorities through whom to rule. On the coast Lugard, reversing the policy of his predecessors, decided not to use the "Houses" (commercial and governmental institutions which flourished in response to the European traders' reliance upon African middlemen) because their power was founded upon slavery. They gradually withered away. Inland in Iboland, the effort to find rulers who could be used by the British was ceaseless and frustrating. Contrary to the large-scale monarchial political institutions traditional in Yorubaland, the Islamic North, Benin, and some other places, the Ibo (perhaps because of the thick forest which made it difficult for him to communicate with his fellows and cut him off from outside pressure) traditionally were organized on village, clan, and even family lines. Along with smallness in scale went an essentially democratic, or consultative, method of political decision making. A recent report on the position, status, and influence of chiefs in the Eastern Region described the traditional political process (which had not significantly changed) in the following manner:

> The usual pattern here is for public matters to be discussed at a general meeting at which every able-bodied male who is a full-bodied member

of the community has a right to attend and to speak if he so wishes. After a general discussion, the elders retire to consult and when they return a spokesman announces their decision to the meeting who either accept it by general acclamation or refuse it. The community, particularly in the Ibo area, is not prepared to surrender its legislative authority to any chiefs, elders or other traditional office holders . . . .[7]

Indirect rule was a necessary expedient at first. It became a fetish. Its natural political evolution was toward a host of separate tribal states. It depended upon the continued vitality of tribal authority and that in turn depended in part upon keeping tribes apart, upholding traditional restrictions on land, and maintaining existing differences among tribal customs. As it developed, indirect rule supported the most conservative elements, who were least likely to have a horizon wider than the tribe. Its legacy for independent Nigeria has been to delay and make more difficult the process of national integration.*

The British also made national integration more difficult by sheltering the North from the foreign influences that were transforming the South and by keeping Northerners and Southerners isolated from each other. The most important aspect of this British policy was the obstacles placed in the path of Christian missions that wished to establish schools in the North. The mission schools until very recently have been by far the most important and numerous in Nigeria.

The reasons for discouraging mission schools in the Islamic North have much in common with those that led to the use of indirect rule there. To permit the schools would have risked violent and costly opposition from the Muslim emirs.† When Lugard captured Kano, he promised that the "government will in no way interfere with the Mohammedan religion."[9] That promise was taken, particularly by Lugard's successors, to mean not only that missions and mission schools should not be forced down the throats of the emirs but also that the emirs should be urged to reject them.

Secular education as well as mission education was neglected in the Islamic North — with the exception of a few belated efforts like Katsina

*It also delayed the introduction of democracy at the grass roots, where it is most easily understood by the people, with the anomalous result that Nigeria was holding national elections on a universal suffrage basis, except for women in the North, at the same time as many of its local government units were controlled by chiefs or other traditional officeholders.

†The strength of their feeling is suggested by the report that the Emir of Zaria killed an official who had given a missionary shelter by having him repeatedly thrown up against the palace ceiling.[8]

Training College, largely for the heirs or wards of the aristocracy. Here again indirect rule played a part, for it was feared (correctly) that modern education would undermine the structure of indirect rule, resting as it did on the continued power of traditional authority.

Added to fear of the effect of modern education upon the structure of indirect rule was the distaste of most Englishmen for the educated African with whom they had come in contact elsewhere in Nigeria. Joyce Cary, several of whose novels were based on his youthful experiences as a district officer in Northern Nigeria, expressed the typical contempt for "black parsons and lawyers" in a letter saying that Northern Nigeria was a paradise because it was without "the hybrids we see in the coast towns."[10] Reinforcing the British dislike of the educated African was the British fondness for the traditional aristocracy, particularly in the North. The British have always been fascinated by Muslims, and Muslims on horseback in glorious dress, surrounded by elaborate ceremony like the Fulani emirs, were too much to resist. Some Northern aristocrats even learned to play an excellent game of polo, thereby making communication infinitely easier.

For whatever reason the British disliked the educated African — whether because they feared their eventual replacements, resented "airs," were racially prejudiced, or, themselves usually upperclass Englishmen, were saddened by the passing of the old dignity — that dislike clearly had some influence upon British policy.

In part because of the British lack of enthusiasm for education in the North, its peoples fell far behind their Southern countrymen in the acquisition of modern skills. In 1952, the time of the last census before independence, only 2 per cent of persons more than six years old in the Northern Region were literate in Roman script (5.4 per cent were literate in Arabic). The almost entirely Muslim provinces of Sokoto, Kano, and Bornu in the far North had 1 per cent or less literate in the Roman script, compared with 16 per cent literacy in the Roman script in the Eastern Region and 18 per cent in the Western Region, including Lagos. As late as 1951, there was only one university graduate among the Northerners, whereas there were hundreds of Yorubas, Ibos, and other Southerners with graduate and postgraduate degrees. In 1961, there were still many fewer Northerners in school than Southerners. The North, with a larger population than the rest of the country, had 6,487 students in secondary schools; the West (which then included the Midwest) had 127,751, and the East 25,908. There were 316,264 Northerners in primary schools as compared with 1,136,409 Westerners and 1,274,383 Easterners.[11] Those figures, coldly counting the future leaders of Nigeria, show how hard it will be for the North to catch up and how long it will take. Northern backwardness has been and will be one of the country's most basic causes of tension.

A side effect of the educational backwardness of the Islamic Northerners is that their neighbors in the Middle Belt, the southern third of the Region, are more important to the Region than one would expect from their numbers and from the fact that most are outside the dominant Fulani and Hausa culture and historical tradition. Though they had fewer schools than the Southerners, they had more than the Islamic Northerners. Accordingly, they are very important for matters like staffing the Regional Civil (Public) Service.

In addition to discouraging education in the North as compared with the South, the British discouraged associations among the people of the two areas. Southerners came into the North as government employees down to the lowest levels because there were too few educated Northerners. In the North, it suited the British and the local authorities to isolate these Southerners in separate areas, *sabon garis,* or new towns. Northerners were discouraged from going to the more radical South. None, for example, sat in the Legislative Council established under the Constitution of 1922, a weak body, but the only common political institution in the country for many years.

Though North and South were amalgamated in 1914, in practice they had quite separate administrative traditions. The loyalty of Englishmen to their particular area became so intense that it was said that if all Nigerians were removed from Nigeria the British administrators of North and South would go to war against each other. Their attitude and British policy reflected and encouraged similar attitudes among Nigerians.

Nigeria is virtually without European white settlers. It moved toward independence, therefore, without all the added tension caused by the efforts of a white minority to perpetuate its power and privilege that marked the pre-independence years of Kenya and Algeria, for example.

Climate and geography help explain why Nigeria has no settler class. Once known as the "white man's grave," West Africa was extremely unhealthy for Europeans. Of 48 Europeans who steamed up the Niger River in three ships in 1832–1834 to explore, trade, and convert, 38 died of fever. Even though shortly thereafter quinine's prophylactic utility against malaria was discovered, tropical disease remained a dangerous killer. Of the 150 Europeans in Lagos in 1896, most of whom were young, 28 died within a few months. Realizing that their political

35

path has been smoothed by the absence of white settlers, Nigerians sometimes say that the mosquito should be recognized as a national hero.

The lack of such settlers was caused by more than the fact that Nigeria was unhealthy and that there was no land in Nigeria as suitable for settlement as the white highlands of Kenya. Shipping and manufacturing interests in Great Britain urged white settlement upon the colonial government in the belief that white plantation ownership would increase agricultural production. Their proposals were rejected by the early proconsuls and their successors in part because white settlement would inevitably have cut away the roots of indirect rule, and perhaps in part because of foreknowledge of the trouble it would cause.

Compared with East Africa, Nigeria (and West Africa as a whole) is not only without a white settler class but also has many fewer Asians or Levantines. There are a few Syrians and Lebanese, but compared with the omnipresent Asians in East Africa, they are insignificant in number and in influence. The vast majority of the Asians in East Africa are descendants of men from British-ruled India who were brought in for minor supervisory and even laborers' jobs on the building of the railway from the Kenya coast to the headwaters of the Nile in Uganda. In West Africa, Africans filled analogous jobs. Whether that was because they were more sophisticated and accustomed to the concept of employment, or because West Africa is further from an alternate source of labor, is arguable.

As a physical block of territory, Nigeria may be less developed economically than it would have been with European settlers and Asian shopkeepers and laborers. But as a result its people have acquired many more modern skills. They had to fulfill the functions which non-Africans fulfilled in East Africa.

Nigeria's job of national integration has been made easier by not having to face the added complexity caused by white settlers or an Asian lower middle class.* Still, the job of building a nation out of a multitude of tribes, each with different languages and traditions, brought together in a loose way by an alien power for only an instant, with some tribal differences reinforced by religious and educational differences, is tough enough.

---

*That is not to say that a country with a racial mixture is unfortunate. The two-way challenge of making race irrelevant will increasingly become the world's as it shrinks. If an end of life is to love others and know oneself, then one cannot rest surrounded only by the familiar. But those are rather metaphysical, spiritual considerations. From the point of view of short-run political development, an African country is better off without white settlers.

Language and Religion

A common language and a common faith may both be a basis for the development of national unity. Nigeria has neither a common language (though her elite speaks English) nor a common faith.

Where lands that were linked have broken apart, they have broken, more often than not, along linguistic or religious lines. Men will fight for their songs and their God.*

*India serves as a recent example of the divisive effect of differing religions and languages. First came the partition of British India along religious lines into the countries of Pakistan, largely Muslim, and India, largely Hindu. "Partition" is a euphemism for religious massacres and the fearful movement of peoples from land that had been their fathers' for centuries. The countries are still enemies.

After the partition, the divisive effect of differing languages has been felt in both countries, but particularly in India. As in Nigeria, English was a second language for the elite, and India also had a host of indigenous tongues. The Constituent Assembly which promulgated India's Constitution decided that the new nation should replace English as its official language and substitute instead one of its many indigenous languages — "Hindi in the Devanagasi script." However, it was also provided that English should be used for official purposes for fifteen years (though Hindi could be used as well) and that Parliament could extend the time limit for the replacement of English after the fifteen-year period.

The results have not been those envisaged. There has been increasing resistance to Hindi by those who use another tongue. Instead of increasing linguistic uniformity, successful demands for new states based upon language have been made. As for the replacement of English, the late Prime Minister Nehru stated that even after the fifteen-year period English would continue as "an associate additional secondary language in the central sphere."[1] And in 1965 when steps

However much a boon a common language and a common faith may be to an inchoate nation, the record does not prove that either is essential.* Among established nations, Switzerland, Belgium, and Canada are all multilingual. The United States has a mixture of Catholics, Protestants, and Jews; Germany, where nationalism has been carried to perhaps its greatest excess, was once a religious battleground, and the Germans remain divided between Protestant and Catholic. Nigeria, of course, must live (as must some other nations) with both linguistic and religious differences. The religious differences which exist — between Muslim, Christian, and pagan — are, moreover, greater than the differences in the established nations between sects of the Christian faith or between Christians and Jews.

This chapter examines the effect that Nigeria's linguistic and religious diversity may have upon her prospects as a nation and recounts her governments' hitherto skillful treatment of the problems created by those diversities.

Language

Nigeria's future treatment of the linguistic issue depends so much upon emotion that it is hazardous to predict what will happen. There is the further danger that this writer has an emotional bias in favor of English, particularly because he remembers friendships with Nigerians made possible by the use of English. Nevertheless, trying to discount such a bias and risking a prediction, it seems likely that Nigeria will retain English as its national language. Most of Africa, like Nigeria, will retain the colonial languages, whereas Asia is more likely eventually to replace them. This is, anomalously, in part because the African states are more ambitious in their aim to rid themselves of the vestiges of colonialism.

Why is it a drawback that Hausa, Yoruba, and Ibo; Kanuri, Tiv, Efik, and Edo; and the others of Nigeria's hundreds of languages are mutually unintelligible? The answer is expressed by the saying, "Let me

---

toward recognition of Hindi were taken there were serious and sustained riots in southern India, and Prime Minister Shastri was compelled to promise legislation that would in effect give non-Hindi–speaking Indians control over change.

*Joseph Stalin, who first received acclaim as an ideologist for his work on minorities and nationalities, argued to the contrary so far as language was concerned. He stated that "a national community is inconceivable without a common language. . . . There is no nation which at one and the same time speaks several languages."[2]

write the songs of a people and I care not who writes its laws."* As a social animal, man remains suspicious of those with whom he cannot communicate. Without a common language, friendship, love, marriage, are all unlikely. Linguistic differences are the seed from which secession can grow.

English now serves as a common language for Nigeria's elite. It is learned as a second language which is spoken well and easily by those who have pursued it through their schooling into secondary school and beyond, and poorly by those who came into brief contact with it at school or have learned a few words for their jobs. English is, by virtue of the Constitution, the official language in the Federal Parliament and all the regional legislatures (in the North being so jointly with Hausa). It is the language used by the civil service, the superior courts, and the major newspapers. It is the medium of instruction in all the secondary schools and in the last years of all the primary schools. Where a school draws students from a number of linguistic groups or where the indigenous language is not one of the major ones, it is customary for the beginners to go "straight for English," hard as that may be.

Yet, despite the obvious advantage of English as a means of communication between Nigeria's elite from different linguistic groups, it is hardly satisfactory for the elite to speak a language which the masses do not. Because Nigeria is committed to operating as a democracy, its people must be given access to the thoughts and words of all who govern, not merely those who speak their native tongue.

So there are two problems. The differences between indigenous languages keep the people apart, perpetuate ethnic hostilities, weaken national loyalties, and increase the danger of separatist sentiment. English, which unites the elite of various ethnic groups, divides the elite from the masses.

To overcome those divisions, there are a number of policies which Nigerian governments could pursue. They could pick one of the indigenous languages as the national language. They could teach all Nigerians to speak the other major indigenous languages without making any one the official national language. Finally, they could continue with English as the national language and the major unifying language, but

*Or, as newspaper columnist Tai Solarin said, "Nigeria will never really become a nation until the Yoruba can joke in Ibo or Hausa, or the Hausa young man can make the Ibadan damsel blush as she listens to a courting monologue rounded off in a beautiful epigram in her own tongue."[3]

reduce the gap between the elite and the masses by further widening education in English. None of the solutions is easy; all present great problems. The governments seem to be pursuing the second and third, with primary emphasis on the third.

There are a number of dry, rational arguments why it would be foolish to replace English as the national language and the chief language of instruction in the schools. First, the translation which would be required would be staggering and would call for major expenditures of the asset Nigeria has least of — trained manpower. Textbooks, parliamentary debates, judicial reports, and legislation* would all have to be translated into the chosen indigenous tongue and reprinted in it. The number of man-hours would be enormous: for most of the work, highly skilled people with a sound knowledge of the subject matter being translated would be needed. In addition, the language chosen would itself have to be somewhat further developed through the addition of technical terms not part of its vocabulary.[4]

The existing high-level manpower force in Nigeria, the group from which the translators would have to come, was recently estimated at 30,000 persons, of whom 15,000 are "Senior" ("top administrators and managers of sizable establishments [public and private] and professionally-trained persons of all kinds") and 15,000 are "Intermediate" ("technical and supervisory personnel . . . [who have] some technical training, but not of professional standard and often are in executive or supervisory, but not policy-making, positions.")[5] That is less than one-tenth of 1 per cent of the population, and is substantially lower than in other underdeveloped countries such as Ghana (over three-tenths of 1 per cent), or India and Egypt (over one-half of 1 per cent).[6] Moreover, it is estimated that about 10,000, or one-third, of the group in Nigeria are foreigners, of whom a negligible proportion speak a Nigerian language fluently; of course many of the Nigerians in the group would also not speak the indigenous language that was chosen as the national language. Finally, the economic development planned for the coming years is going to strain Nigeria's trained manpower supply to the utmost, and finding the translators is not, therefore, likely to become any easier in the foreseeable future.

The conclusion from the foregoing statements is clear: if a new national language is to be adopted, many Nigerians will have to be trans-

*Criminal legislation is already translated into the major languages within a region.

ferred from the jobs they were doing and expensive expatriates hired to take their places. It is illustrative to note that Israel, which recently has succeeded in modernizing Hebrew and in making it the common language of a people many of whom had not spoken it naturally before, is blessed with an abundance of Nigeria's scarcest resource, skilled manpower.

Another argument against the replacement of English is that no matter how thorough and continuous the translation, the loss of English would cut the Nigerian off from much of the world's learning, though English could still be learned by the elite as a second language. A more significant argument derives from the lesson that can be learned from the history of other multilingual nations that have attempted to elevate one language above the others. Bitterness, bloodshed, and the reawakening, rather than the elimination, of narrow linguistic loyalties have often been the result. The riots in Ceylon in 1956 caused by the effort to give Sinhalese priority over Tamil, and the riots between the Walloons and the Flemings in Belgium in 1962 are recent examples of the feeling. Canada's constitution guarantees linguistic autonomy to her French-speaking province, and it is doubtful whether even that stable nation could survive an effort to force the French Canadians to speak English.*

In Nigeria, some of the tension that would follow adoption of a traditional African tongue as the national language is shown by a debate on the subject in the Nigerian parliament shortly after independence. A member put forward a motion which urged the Federal Government "in consultation with the Regional Governments, to introduce the teaching of Hausa, Yoruba, Ibo and other languages into institutions of learning throughout the country with a view to adopting one of them as an official language in the near future." An amendment was proposed which urged the regions to adopt Hausa as a *lingua franca*.

That produced an outburst from Anthony Enahoro. Enahoro, whose native tongue is Edo, the language of Benin and the surrounding area, said

> As one who comes from a minority tribe, I deplore the continuing evidence in this country that people wish to impose their customs, their languages, and even more their way of life upon the smaller tribes. My people have a language, and that language was handed down through a thousand years of tradition and custom. When the Benin Empire exchanged ambassadors with Portugal, many of the new Nigerian languages

---

*Of course the other side of the coin is the survival of Quebec nationalism within the Canadian nation.

of today did not exist. How can they now, because the British [have] brought us together, wish to impose their language on us.[7]*

That Enahoro was the man who spoke these words and that he also called for the retention of English is significant. For, though he is now one of the members of the opposition party convicted of conspiring against the Government, he has always been a passionate and radical Nigerian nationalist, having gone to prison three times, for example, for his biting attacks on the British.

An attempt to make one of the Nigerian languages the national language would, most likely, meet with more than verbal opposition.

In one respect Enahoro was being unfair in his remarks. What support there is for the adoption of Hausa as the national language is not limited to the Hausa; indeed, its most ardent supporters have been other than Hausa.† The motion advocating Hausa to which Enahoro responded was proposed by a man from Benin and seconded by a Kanuri. An Ibo,

---

*The Federal Government rejected the amendment which advocated Hausa, but, speaking through the Minister of Education, supported the original motion as "the natural consequence of our independence," though warning against the "hasty replacement of English."[8] Since then the Federal Government has given no indication that it wishes to raise the political temperature by doing anything to adopt a new national language, and the regions, who under the Constitution are responsible for primary and secondary education except in the Federal Capital of Lagos, have continued to base their instruction upon English. A comparison between the Independence Constitution, under which Nigeria was governed for its first three years of independence, and the Republican Constitution, which became effective on October 1, 1963, demonstrates the extent to which Nigeria appears to be committed to the retention of English as its national language. The principal aim of the constitutional changes was to drop those aspects of the Independence Constitution which served as symbolic reminders of Britain's colonial control or which constituted remnants of British colonial power. Thus, the Queen of England was replaced as head of state by a President chosen by the Nigerian Parliament, and her Majesty's Privy Council was no longer empowered to hear appeals from the Nigerian Federal Supreme Court or to play a role in the removal of judges. At the same time, the Republican Constitution continued without change the provision of the Independence Constitution that English should be the language of Parliament.

†There are four main reasons why Hausa has been advocated as a replacement for English more than any other indigenous language. It is simpler than its chief competitors, Ibo and Yoruba, being less tonal. It is spoken as a native tongue by more Nigerians than any other. (Many Fulani, as well as the Hausa, speak it from birth.) It is spoken as a second language by more people than any other, and it is most often spoken outside Nigeria. In one way, however, Hausa would be particularly difficult to introduce as the national language. Educated manpower is scarcest in the Hausa-speaking North, and thus teachers of Hausa could even less easily be spared than teachers of Ibo or Yoruba.

Mbonu Ojike, first raised the issue when at the General Conference on Review of the Constitution in 1950 he moved that Hausa be made a compulsory language in elementary and secondary schools. (The Conference resolved instead that "consideration be given to the establishment of a common language for Nigeria," its caution reflecting the tension that would have resulted from an attempt to agree upon one of Nigeria's indigenous languages.) [9] Through his weekly newspaper column, Tai Solarin, a Yoruba, has become the leading advocate of the adoption of Hausa.

Those men, and others like them, have become Nigerians first and members of their tribes only incidentally. They are exceptions. And many Nigerians, like Enahoro, who are also strong nationalists, would rebel if they were forced to learn the language of another tribe to speak in Parliament or the courts or if their children were forced to learn their lessons in that language.

There are many arguments against replacement of English by an indigenous tongue. It would divert the energy of much of the country's talent; it would limit the flow of information from the outside world; it would risk increasing ethnic tension.

But, the reader may ask, have we not missed the crucial point — the power of national pride? Is it not too great an indignity to ask those freed from colonialism to speak forever the language of their conquerors, and will not emotion overcome all dry, rational arguments to the contrary? And if English is "foreign" can Nigerians ever think in it as well as in a "native" tongue? And finally, do not the Nigerians need an African language to develop or recover the pride in their past, respect for their countrymen, and confidence in themselves that colonialism took from them? And is that not one of their greatest needs? For analogous, emotionally powerful, reasons, most of the new Asian nations have turned, albeit with qualifications and setbacks, toward one of their indigenous languages to replace the colonial language.

Those are powerful arguments, but there are answers to them, and it seems unlikely that Nigeria's leaders will replace English. In many ways, the most relevant Nigerian past is that in which the participants played their roles in English. The speeches and writings of Nnamdi Azikiwe calling for freedom, or the early words of Alhaji Abubakar Tafawa Balewa on chieftaincy reform, or Chief Rotimi Williams' analyses of the Constitution were spoken or written in English. It is that history, the history of the struggle for freedom, that most unites the

Nigerians, regardless of how much they may have quarrelled among themselves during the struggle. As one goes back to a more remote past where the language of thought and action was Ibo, Yoruba, Hausa, or Arabic, history does less to unite Nigeria's peoples and sometimes divides them. The Nigerian languages, moreover, have not been written until recent times. Yoruba and Ibo were first written when the missionaries came; though there was writing in the North long before that, the language used was Arabic, and it is nowhere suggested that Arabic should become the national language. Thus, if English is retained as the national language, the loss may be less than in some Asian countries where literature and history have been written in the indigenous tongues for a long time.*

In addition, efforts to replace English would conflict with a desire close to the hearts of many Nigerians. The hope that they will move closer to other African peoples, know them, and eventually join with them is very strong. Though the Government has rejected the concept of immediate political union with other African nations, its stated objective is union through more gradual means. Nigeria's most militant anti-colonialists, the men who might be expected to lead the movement for the replacement of English by an indigenous tongue, moreover, accuse the Government of moving too slowly toward African unity.

To discard English for an indigenous language would lop off one of the existing springboards to increased African unity. The elite in many other African countries speak English.† Their indigenous languages, however, are different from those of Nigeria. With English as a common language, Nigeria and the other English-speaking countries have taken a long first step toward understanding, one that makes eventual union

---

*A decision to retain English as the national language and a means of communication between the various ethnic groups does not mean that their languages will be lost. They will remain as part of the people's culture. Though the danger of linguistic separation will remain, it is inconceivable that any government would try to wipe out the existing languages. To the contrary, it is extremely likely that there will be increasing pressure from nationally minded and nationalistic Nigerians to teach at least the three main indigenous languages in all schools, beginning at least at the secondary school level. And it is quite likely that that will be done.

†French is the other widespread common language in Africa. At the Monrovia Conference, a conference of leaders of the majority of independent African nations held in 1961, the ex-English colonies resolved to make a "special effort" to teach French, and the ex-French colonies pledged themselves to do the same for English.[10]

possible, though certainly not inevitable.* Thus the strong emotional power that there is in the desire for greater African unity counterbalances the strong emotional power that one might expect to support the replacement of the colonial language with an indigenous language.

Even Ghana, hardly a moderate in the effort to develop national spirit and hardly casual about the African cultural heritage, provides that English shall be the language of its civil service, constitutional courts, and National Assembly and that no one may be elected to its National Assembly unless he can speak and read English sufficiently well to be able to "take an active part in the proceedings of the Assembly."[11] Ghana, like Nigeria, provides that English shall be the medium of instruction in the schools.

In the African setting, therefore, it seems likely that the language of the ex-colonial powers will remain as a means of fostering unity within the country and strengthening links with the outside world, particularly with other countries in Africa.

If English survives the first few years of Nigeria's independence, what pressure there is for its replacement should decrease. A language belongs to its users. There are now fine Nigerian novelists, poets, and playwrights writing in English: Achebe, Soyinka, and Clark, for example. Their best work reflects an African heritage (just as American English reflects the distinctive American heritage), and in the future should do so even more as national pride increasingly wipes out the colonial mentality which has caused some Nigerians to find little good in things Nigerian and to follow too closely the model of the English.† With their success, as measured both by world acclaim and, more importantly, by their ability to describe Nigerians' emotions and experiences in English, will come growing pride in Nigerian English.

Religion

Nigeria is one of the places where Islam and Christianity meet. The followers of the Prophet Muhammed came down across the desert from

---

*It should be noted, however, that political associations of African states explicitly based upon a shared colonial language, such as the much-maligned Brazzaville group of former French colonies, are suspect in the eyes of many committed Pan-Africanists.

†Where Nigerian writing in English is poor, it is often because it follows an English manner of speaking that is inapplicable to Nigeria. In one Nigerian novel, for example, the hair of an African girl is likened to black "silk" and she is called "damsel."[12]

the north and the followers of Christ came up from the sea to the south. Map 2 (p. 8) shows how the adherents of the two religions (and Nigeria's pagans or animists) are geographically dispersed. It shows that though there are a substantial number of Muslims in the Yoruba West, even down to Lagos on the coast, most Muslims are in the North and most Christians are in the South.

Thus far, the country has been blessed by the absence of serious religious antagonism. Her Christians have not set forth to pillage the land of Islam as did the Crusaders. Her Muslims have not sought to convert the Christian infidel by the sword or overrun Christendom as did the Moors and Ottoman Turks.

Though one of the spurs to the zeal of the early Christian missionaries in Nigeria, as throughout Africa, was to stop Islam's march south, proselytization of the pagans rather than conversion of the Muslims — containment — was their principal aim. As we have seen in the previous chapter, moreover, the British discouraged what efforts the missionaries did make to go among the Muslims in the north of Nigeria.

The relative lack of interference by Christian missionaries with the faith of Nigeria's Muslims is one factor which minimizes hostility of Muslim toward Christian in Nigeria today. Another is the appreciation of many of the Muslim leaders for mission hospitals and schools. The social value of the missions continues to be meaningful to Muslim leaders. Thus, Alhaji Abubakar Tafawa Balewa, the Federal Prime Minister and a Muslim who has made the pilgrimage to Mecca, sent a son to a Catholic school.*

As for the attitude of the Nigerian Christian toward his Muslim countrymen, the historical background of the two religions in Nigeria also contributes to tolerance. Islam is regarded as indigenous to Africa. It was and is spread by African traders or teachers wandering into pagan communities and living with the people. Christianity, on the other hand, was brought to Nigeria by Europeans. It was largely spread by European missionaries, who often were culturally isolated from their flock. The Church has sometimes been slow to substitute African for European leadership. Some of its customs, such as the ban upon polygamy, a common practice in Africa which is permitted by Islam, are regarded by many as unsuited to Africa. For all those reasons, the Christian

---

*A measure of the Prime Minister's character can be gained from the fact that he did not seek to wield his power or demand special favor when his son was expelled for misbehavior.

church in Nigeria, as in much of Africa, must be somewhat on the defensive. As a matter of tactics, it could not risk antagonizing Islam, whose roots are imbedded deeper in Africa soil.

The individual Nigerian who accepts the teachings of Christ as universal truth equally meant for all races (and there are many Nigerians who do so) has necessarily a different attitude toward his Muslim countrymen than, say, a European crusader toward a Turk or an Arab, or a Spaniard toward a Moor.[13] The Muslim is, to begin with, his countryman. The Muslim is, moreover, of a tradition that is clearly not European. And such traditions are what racially conscious, anti-European, Nigerians want desperately to retain or develop. Interestingly, in the Nigeria of today there are more Christians who are racially conscious and anti-European than there are Muslims.

Christianity had an enormous indirect impact upon the development of nationalism in Nigeria. With the missionaries came education; with education came unrest and a desire for freedom. Christian teaching itself strengthened the demand for equality. The speeches of Nigerian nationalists were often filled with Biblical illusions. Thus, Nnamdi Azikiwe, Nigeria's first great nationalist leader and now her President, after being convicted of sedition by a colonial court said

> . . . when a son of the New Africa is faced with the travails and tribulations of Gethsemane, and Golgotha and Calvary, there is no need for the spirit to weaken. At this stage of my life, I cannot be mere flesh. . . . I am the living spirit of an idea — the idea of a New Africa. I am the living spirit of an ideal — the ideal of man's humanity to man. . . .
>
> Happily for the gospel according to the New Africa, there exist today on this continent Renascent Africans: literate and illiterate, poor and wealthy, high and low; and they have expressed to me, by their words and deeds, during the last few days of the crucial moments of the existence of my flesh on this earth, that the New Africa is born to me.[14]

Nationalist agitation and political parties came to the South before the North in large measure because the unsettling effects of Christianity and its handmaiden, mission education, were not felt in the Muslim North.

However, for all that it did to start the wind of change blowing through Nigeria, Christianity itself has not dominated any political movement and is not likely to do so in the future. Islam is a political force. It is closely associated with Nigeria's largest political party, the Northern Peoples Congress (NPC).

Perhaps one reason why Islam is more directly associated than Christianity with politics in Nigeria is that the religion is more pervasive. Islam is a total religion without the Christian concept of separation of secular and religious concerns. There is no Koranic verse corresponding to the biblical "Render therefore unto Caesar the things which are Caesar's, and to God the things which are God's."

That is a difference between Christianity and Islam which would apply equally in all times and in all lands. It is reinforced in Nigeria by the difference between the local histories of the two religions. When the British conquered Nigeria, Islam was an existing political force, particularly in the Fulani empire. It was easy, therefore, for Nigerians to tie a political movement to Islam as an alternative to British rule. Christianity, on the other hand, was closely associated with the colonialists themselves. It had inspired no Nigerian empire. Islam, whose adherents held back more impatient Nigerian nationalists during the move toward independence, and which did far less than Christianity to bring Nigeria into the modern world, is in some ways regarded as a more fitting faith for a Nigerian nationalist than Christianity because of its longer association with the people.

There is more that can and should be said about Muslim than about Christian tolerance. That is not to suggest that Christians are inherently any more tolerant than Muslims. Rather, tolerance on the part of Muslims is more significant to Nigeria's welfare because Islam is more closely associated with a political movement than Christianity (and that seems likely to continue as a difference). It is also more significant because there are more Muslims than Christians and because they feel a certain shared resentment of being left behind during the British era.

The NPC is not an explicitly Muslim party. It is a Northern party, and Muslims from the southern regions are excluded. Christians and animists from the Northern Region, as "people of Northern descent," are eligible for membership. The NPC has met with great success in the non-Muslim part of the Region. Its slogan, "one North, one people, irrespective of religion, race or tribe," includes a pledge of religious tolerance.[15]

Nevertheless, the NPC has a very strong Muslim cast, as would be expected for a Northern party, since approximately two-thirds of the regional population is Muslim. Its leadership is almost entirely Muslim, with the party President, the Sardauna of Sokoto, being a direct descendant of the Muslim reformer and empire builder Usuman dan Fodio. As will be seen, a common NPC device during political campaigns is to call upon the faithful to resist the southern parties lest they desecrate the holy Koran. Women are not permitted to vote in the North, not even in its non-Muslim parts, though they may vote elsewhere in the Federation. When the Federal Senate delayed in 1961 an amendment to the Constitution of Northern Nigeria that would have permitted a judge trained in Muslim, but not English, law to sit with the Northern Nigerian High Court on certain appeals, the Sardauna of Sokoto thundered that the nation's unity was at stake.[16]

The Muslim-dominated NPC has taken one very important step which fulfilled its pledge of religious tolerance. That step, a reform of the criminal law, was a most hopeful sign of Nigeria's ability to grow as a religiously pluralistic society.

Under the British system of indirect rule existing native courts continued to function. They applied traditional "native law and custom" unless, as with the practice of cutting off the hands of thieves, it was found to be contrary to "natural justice, equity and good conscience."

In the Northern Region, approximately 95 per cent of the cases were, and are, heard in native courts. Those with the greatest power, including in some cases even the power to sentence to death, were the numerous Muslim courts of emirs or alkali (Muslim judges). Those courts applied Muslim law of the Maliki School.

Under the Maliki, as under other schools of Muslim law, the law applied is derived from the Koran, from the Sunna — traditions concerning the life and views of the Prophet — and from the consensus of great early Muslim jurists. The law is divinely ordained and unchangeable, though perhaps its interpretation can change.[17] For criminal law, only six or seven crimes are defined. As for the rest, the divine text provides merely that all wrongdoing shall be suitably punished. The courts are thus left with almost unfettered discretion to define and punish offenses, including political ones.

Under Muslim criminal law, there are a number of distinctions drawn between Muslims, Christians, and pagans. In the case of murder (where the most extreme provocation is irrelevant), the penalty awarded depends upon whether the relatives of the victim demand the killer's life, require blood money, or choose to let him go. But the relative of a pagan can never demand the life of a Muslim killer and can demand only one-fifteenth of the blood money that would be due had a Muslim been killed. The status of Christians is halfway between pagans and Muslims. Further, though the testimony of uninterested male Muslim witnesses or fifty oaths of Muslim heirs of the blood is almost conclusive, non-Muslims are not even eligible as witnesses in cases where Muslims are involved. Women's testimony is also inadmissible.[18]

One of the fears expressed by some minority elements, mostly Christians and animists, in the southern portion of the Northern Region, as they agitated for separation from the Islamic North shortly prior to independence, was that Muslim law was unfair to those of them it covered and might be extended further after the British departure.[19] After the issue came to a head, the NPC-controlled Northern Nigerian Government sent delegations to the Sudan, Libya, and Pakistan to investigate their legal systems, and in the summer of 1958 appointed a panel of jurists to suggest judicial reforms in light of "the legal and judicial systems obtaining in other parts of the world where Muslim and non-Muslim live side by side."[20]

The panel, which was chaired by the Chief Justice of the Sudan and had as associate members three Northern Nigerians (two Muslims and a Christian), a retired judge from Pakistan, and a British professor (an ex-missionary, who became an expert on Islamic law) made sweeping recommendations. Most were accepted. Most important was its recommendation that a penal code should be written which defined all offenses and ended the alkalis' discretion under Muslim law to define and punish offenses as they saw fit. A Penal Code was passed in 1959 pursuant to that recommendation. Under it, distinctions between the punishment of Muslims and non-Muslims for having done identical acts were no longer sanctioned. Moreover, provocation became relevant, to reduce the penalty for homicide, and the victim's relatives were no longer permitted to determine the punishment of the accused. Under a new Procedure Code passed in 1960, courts were no longer permitted to exclude the testimony of non-Muslims or women.

A few special concessions were made to Muslim orthodoxy in the new codes. It is still a crime for Muslims to drink alcohol. The decision to base the code upon the Sudan's (which itself was based upon an earlier Indian Penal Code designed by Lord Macauley) was taken because Muslim opinion in the North was hostile to the existing Nigerian Criminal Code, which applies in all courts in the South.

Despite those concessions, the Code is one that non-Muslim communities can live with without feeling menaced because of their religious beliefs. The decision to enact it was a courageous step for the predominantly Muslim NPC Government to take in the face of traditional opinion. As Professor J. N. D. Anderson, the British member of the Panel, said in an article discussing the changes:

> Such, however, was the dead weight, in the North, of rigidly traditional opinion, that we were repeatedly warned that to . . . [recommend substitution of a Penal Code for the alkali's discretion] would be the equivalent of crying for the moon; and it is to the eternal credit of the Northern Nigerian government that they not only saw the need for such a revolutionary change but also had the courage to carry it into effect, in the teeth of considerable opposition.[21]

The changes were a major advance, and it is doubtful whether any Government or party other than one headed by a man like the Sardauna of Sokoto, whose Muslim credentials are impeccable, could have accomplished them without extremely serious opposition from traditionalists. Even as it is, the implementation of the reforms remains a source of friction between the Government and some of the more conservative emirs.

In the South there have been religious issues, but none of the importance of the North's. In the Western Region, Christians play a more important role in the leadership of the Action Group party than would be 'expected from the nearly even division between Christians and Muslims among the Yoruba, who provide the party with most of its support. That is because the Action Group represents in large measure the rising new class, a high proportion of whom are Christians who early benefited from mission education. The Action Group, however, is clearly not a religious party, as is shown by the fact that when, during the spring of 1962, it sought to replace its erstwhile deputy leader, a Christian, as Premier of the Western Region, it put forward a Muslim as his successor.

In 1957, the National Muslim League was formed as a politico-religious party, chiefly to demand more Muslim schools from the Western Region Government. It was greeted with strong opposition by the Action Group leader, Obafemi Awolowo, who said, "we of the Action Group, Muslims, Christians and others, must leave no stone unturned to combat what is really a diabolical threat to the peace and tranquillity of this country, and a calculated assault on the freedom of religion."[22] The party soon opened its membership to non-Muslims, changed its name to the National Emancipation League, and was soundly trounced in the next election, the 1959 federal election, in which it won no seats.

In the Eastern Region, there are very few Muslims. Religion has been of some political importance because Catholics have claimed their schools were getting less support from the regional government than Protestant schools.

Though Islam and Christianity each cut across tribal lines and thus sometimes reduce the significance of tribal distinctions, the religious differences among the Nigerians are clearly not going to make the process of national integration any easier. But thus far toleration has been the rule, and differences have been handled calmly without extremists of any group getting the upper hand.

For the future, there are at least three crucial questions. The first is whether the Northern Muslims, after they have caught up educationally to the point where they no longer need help to run the government, will continue their relatively tolerant policy toward non-Muslim Northerners. The second, similar, question is, what will happen to the attitude of Christians toward Muslims if Nigerian Christianity loses its slightly European taint?

The third can serve as an introduction to one of the several themes running through Nigeria's political history. The North has been Nigeria's most conservative section, and the Islamic Northerners have been Nigeria's conservative leaders. Southerners have by and large been far more radical, excitable, and impatient. The North has also been the least nationalistic of Nigeria's regions; the Northern Party, the NPC, has confined its own activities to the North. Southerners, though they have their regional and tribal biases as well, have been by and large far more nationalistic.

There is a relationship between the North's general conservatism and regionalism and its Islamic heritage. Because much of the North had a strong civilization based on Islam when the British arrived, the British were unwilling to risk resistance to mission and secular Western education. Because they therefore fell far behind in the acquisition of modern skills, the Northerners feared too quick a march to independence, which they thought would leave them at the mercy of their more advanced countrymen. Because they feared their countrymen, the Northerners banded together politically. In Northern nationalism there is also a strain which readily lends itself to conservatism, a strain less often found in Southern nationalism. The Southerner, for all the genuine attention that may be paid to African culture and history, looks forward to and presses for more and more change. The nationalism of many Northerners places much more emphasis upon a return to lost greatness — greatness which was based on Islam.

Islam thus helps explain Northern conservatism and regionalism. But it is an explanation that depends upon the recent history of Islam in Nigeria; conservatism is not a necessary consequence of the religion itself. Though the all-embracing nature of Islam combined with the age of its rules lends itself to conservatism, some Muslim countries, Egypt and Algeria, for example, are radical today. In Northern Nigeria there is a radical party, the Northern (now-Nigerian) Elements Progressive Union, which has, as does the NPC, a strong Muslim character.

But if conservatism continues to be the dominant note in the North, and if its chief party continues for many years to be regional in nature, it is quite possible that the impatient Southerners will turn against conservative Islam. For the most obvious difference between North and South is the strong Islamic influence in the Northern Region. Northern leaders have said things that, perhaps quoted out of context or ignoring other parts of the record, could be used to show that Islam itself is the conservative force. The Sardauna of Sokoto, for example, made a most fatalistic remark in his autobiography, one that conflicts with the vociferous activism of Southerners. Recalling a fiery, patriotic, anti-imperialist speech of a Southern politician who had attacked the Northerners for their refusal in 1953 to support a demand for independence in 1956, he wondered whether anything had been gained by the speech, and said

The hand of God was moving as always, using us men as its pieces on the wide field of the world events. Nothing which we could have said or done would have moved the date of Independence forward, or put it back a single hour from the moment in which it was ordained from the dawn of time itself.[23]

Tribalism, Regionalism, and National Politics

Constitutional controversy and a pure struggle for power have been the recurring themes in Nigeria's political history. The main question has been whether Nigeria does indeed constitute a desirable, workable, political community. Not only the rules of the game but also the size of the playing field itself has been at stake. Even on the assumption that Nigeria should remain a political community, much of the controversy has been over what kind of government it should have rather than what its government should do. Thus far the main issues have been constitutional rather than legislative.

The threshold question was whether the British would leave. If they would, what should follow? Indirect rule suggested to some people that the country should revert to tribal kingdoms, each led by its traditional ruler. Others, at another extreme, saw a Republic of Africa or of black Africa as the only desirable successor of the colonialism they hated and the tribalism they wished to put behind them forever. But what happened was that the political community remained the block of West Africa known as Nigeria* with Nigerians substituted for Britishers at the helm.

Within that framework many choices remained. First, should the new

*Plus, eventually, a portion of the British-administered Cameroons Trust Territory.

elite, generally young and Western educated, or the traditional elite, older and less well-equipped with alien skills, take command? Second, how should the new nation be organized? Here the choice was between, at one extreme, a strong center without regard to separate tribal traditions and, at the other, a weak center, a federal system, and a separate state for each linguistic or ethnic group. In this chapter the story is carried through the first definite steps toward independence, through the decision to organize Nigeria as a federation with three large regions (each with a dominant ethnic or religious group), and through the emergence of three major political parties, each based primarily upon one of the dominant groups.

The Beginnings of National Politics

World War II was a great turning point in Nigerian politics. During the war, nationalism's force began to be felt beyond the coastal cities, and the first national political party was organized. The series of constitutional reforms, which bore fruit in independence within fifteen years, began at the end of the war. A few months after the war, the Nigerian people first showed the strength they could muster by acting together.

Earlier, almost all political activity had taken place in Lagos. Lagos, an old Yoruba coastal city in contact with European traders and missionaries long before the British annexed it in 1861, was the first place in Nigeria to come under British control, the only place to be administered as a colony (which, as opposed to a protectorate, gave her citizens the rights of British subjects), and was the focal point of Nigeria's intellectual and political life.* It was the capital. It had a newspaper from 1880 on, and by the beginning of World War I it had five. The vast majority of Western-educated Nigerians in the early days were Yorubas who lived in Lagos and a few other nearby Yoruba cities. Some of them came from families who had been exposed to Western education for many years. Thus, Miss Kofoworola Moore (now Lady Ademola, wife of the Federal Chief Justice), who was born in 1913, had a great-grand-

---

*Until 1951, Lagos, along with Calabar, a coastal city in the Eastern Region, was the only place in Nigeria to elect representatives. In 1920, its wealthier citizens were given the right to elect a town council and in 1923 to elect three members to the Legislative Council. The country's first significant political party, the Nigerian National Democratic Party under the leadership of Herbert Macaulay, was formed in 1923 to contest the first Legislative Council election; during its fifteen-year reign it confined its activity to Lagos.

father who was a minister of the Church of England, and a grandfather who was educated at an English public school before being ordained; her father was trained as a lawyer at the Middle Temple, London. She has recalled:

> I was brought up against the background of essentially western ideas, and from my earliest childhood my mind was formed in relation to western culture and not to the background of untouched tribal life.[1]

Lagos also was a center for "native foreigners," the term applied to Africans, often freed slaves, who had come to Nigeria from, among other places, Sierra Leone, Liberia, Brazil, and the United States. Many had ancestors who had been carried off from Nigeria by slavers and who had had most of the roots into their tribal culture bent, if not broken.

While early political activity in Nigeria was concentrated in Lagos, the politically conscious often thought in terms of a community wider even than Nigeria. Thus, as a Nigerian historian put it, "at the end of the nineteenth century, the driving force of nationalism in Nigeria was not loyalty to Nigeria as such, but racial consciousness as Africans."[2] The existence of African nationalism as opposed to Nigerian nationalism reflected both the newness and the artificiality of Nigeria. It also stemmed from the background of those who were then involved in politics — "native foreigners" and westernized Yorubas — who had far more in common with the coastal, Western-educated elites in other colonies than with the masses in Nigeria's own interior. Racial consciousness was also a reaction to the racist undertones of colonialism.*

The racial nature of political thinking was also influenced by American and West Indian Negroes such as W. E. B. Du Bois, a pioneer of Pan-Africanism, and Marcus Garvey, leader of the Back to Africa Movement and popularizer of the slogan "Africa for the Africans." Such men had no ties with a particular tribe or country, though they did feel a community of interest as members of a race.†

Contrasting with racial nationalism was tribal nationalism, expressed in efforts to recapture the glories of particular tribes. If the educated

---

*To this day the British usually refer to the indigenous residents of Nigeria as "Africans," where they do not refer to a man or group by tribal origin. Of course it was not that innocent, if somewhat dated, lumping together of Africans that contributed to *African* nationalism, but rather the tendency of many colonialists to lump Africans together as inherently inferior fools.

†That such men often thought in racial terms does not, of course, mean that they always thought alike. Du Bois and Garvey, for example, were strongly opposed to each other.

Nigerian did not turn his attention to all of Africa he tended to turn to his own tribe, not to Nigeria itself. Samuel Johnson's *History of the Yorubas* was one of the earliest of many books written by Nigerians on their tribal customs or histories.[3] Many of those books implied that the tribe was the natural political community for the future as it had been in the past. Thus, Akiga, a Tiv, told "his Tiv brothers of the new generation that can read . . . [to read his book] and tell others, who cannot, of the things of our ancestors. And," he continued, "do you, however great your knowledge may be, remember that you are a Tiv, remain a Tiv, and know the things of Tiv; for therein lies your pride."[4]

The events during and after World War II did not end belief that the desirable and natural political community was the Negro race, or black Africa (Pan-Africanism), and certainly did not put an end to tribalism. But Nigeria as a nation-state became a realizable alternative to an African continental state and to a tribal state, and Pan-Africanism and tribalism can be seen after the war as conflicting themes running through the score of *Nigerian* politics.

The war itself had something to do with the intensification of nationalism. The Japanese victories over the English and their allies dealt a blow to colonialism's crutch — white supremacy. During the war, Nigeria became a stopping place for over 100,000 white troops on their way to the Middle East and India; some of them spread radical political ideas, others aggravated racial tensions and showed that the average white man was less exceptional than the select colonial administrators. The Italian invasion of Ethiopia brought forth a sense of African nationalism and anti-European feeling among some Nigerians.

The wartime idealization of freedom and democracy by Britain and her allies and specific pledges like that of the Atlantic Charter supporting "the right of all peoples to choose the form of government under which they will live" were taken by Nigerians as applicable to themselves as well as to Europeans under the yoke of Hitler. In that view they were encouraged by Americans of the stature of President Roosevelt and Wendell Wilkie,* though not by Winston Churchill, who flatly rejected the suggestion that "all peoples" included colonial peoples.

More than 100,000 Nigerian troops served in the war, 30,000 of them outside the country in India, Burma, East Africa, and the Middle

*American support for African self-determination eventually bore fruit in America itself, as African independence was one factor increasing the frustration and militancy of the American Negro in the late 1950's and early 1960's.

East. They vastly increased the ranks of those who formed the core of the nationalist movement — educated or partially educated, wage-earning Nigerians who had left their tribal homeland. Still others were added to that class as the war stimulated the country's economy; at the same time, wartime economic controls added grievances.

Other events which stimulated national consciousness or had an effect upon the British attitude toward Nigeria's future occurred somewhat fortuitously during the war. Unrest in the Caribbean colonies just prior to the war led to a royal investigative commission. Out of its recommendations grew the Development and Welfare Acts of 1940 and 1945, which put new emphasis upon the economic and social development of the colonies by the Imperial Government. Because the Labour Party was part of the wartime coalition, the influence of the Colonel Blimps among the Conservatives was lessened, and Labour was able to influence policy toward "constructive trusteeship."[5] The Indian struggle for independence continued unabated through the war and, shortly after, was successful, inspiring many Nigerians.

Irrespective of the wartime events, an upsurge of nationalism in Nigeria would have come soon. Antipathy toward British rule grew as more Nigerians were changed by it; nationalism was a function of the number of generations under colonialism. As Obafemi Awolowo expressed it in 1947:

> Our grandfathers, with unbounded gratitude adored the British who emancipated them from slavery and saved them from the "horrors" of tribal wars. Our immediate fathers simply toed the line. We of today are critical, unappreciative, and do not feel we owe any debt of gratitude to the British. The younger elements in our group are extremely cynical and cannot understand why Britain is in Nigeria.[6]

The nationalist leaders, at least in the South, were Nigerians who had gone abroad for study and returned as lawyers, teachers, journalists, doctors, sometimes businessmen, and often agitators. The majority went to Great Britain; a minority (mostly Ibos), which turned out to include many of the most militant, went to America. They returned, having seen the white man "warts and all" in his homeland, having been influenced by liberal thought, and convinced that the backwardness of their people, the supposed justification for colonialism, was removable.

Chief among them was Nnamdi Azikiwe.* By heritage, Azikiwe was

*Azikiwe had been christened Benjamin Nnamdi Azikiwe, and while studying and teaching in the United States wrote articles signed Benjamin. On his way back

an Onitsha Ibo, but he was born in 1904 in Zungeru, Northern Nigeria, where his father was a clerk in the Army. (His father later resigned after being insulted by a young British officer.) His early life was typical of many Nigerians who entered the modern elite — education at mission schools (in Onitsha, Calabar, and Lagos), followed by service as a government clerk in Lagos.

In 1925, at twenty-one, he broke from the pattern and took a boat to the United States. There he remained for nine years. He attended Storer College (a preparatory school), Howard University, and Lincoln University (Pa.),* where he received his undergraduate degree and a graduate degree in political science, and where he taught; he also obtained graduate degrees from the Columbia School of Journalism and the University of Pennsylvania. His life was much more difficult than that of most foreign students of today. Without multiple sources of financial aid, he worked as a dishwasher, a coal miner, and on a road gang; he also fought as a boxer. While in America he also encountered racial impatience for justice, and since in those days Americans behaved no less badly to foreign black men than to American black men, he was faced with racial prejudice unrelieved by the special consideration today given, sometimes, to the feelings of the native-born African.

In 1934, Azikiwe (or "Zik," pronounced "Zeek," which was his American nickname and which became the cry of his Nigerian supporters) returned to Africa. Despite his education, and possibly because it had been American, his application to teach was turned down in Nigeria and in three other British West African Territories. Frustrated as a teacher, he became the most exciting, sensational, and militant newspaper editor that West Africa had ever seen. He began in Ghana (then the Gold Coast) where, along with I. T. Wallace-Johnson, he edited the Accra *African Morning Post* from 1934 until he was convicted of sedition in 1937 (his conviction was eventually reversed). Then, in 1937, he returned home to Nigeria to found the *West African Pilot,* whose motto was, "Show the light and the people will find the way."

The *West African Pilot* was published in Lagos, but was distributed

---

to Africa in 1934, he tried to represent Nigeria in the Empire Games at London. After protests from South Africans, however, he was barred by the London Amateur Athletic Association. He then decided to drop his English name.

*Lincoln was also the alma mater of Ghana's Kwame Nkrumah, who was influenced by Azikiwe and followed him to America. Azikiwe's son also came to America for his higher education. He came, in 1961, to Harvard.

nationally and featured the common man and provinces as well as Lagos and its elite. The Zik chain of newspapers, a profitable operation, incidentally, was soon joined by provincial dailies in Ibadan, Onitsha, Port Harcourt, and Kano, and was a crucial factor in the spread of nationalism and race consciousness to the interior. Pride was the dominant note of the papers. Every graduation, every new lawyer or doctor, was a triumph. With pride, grievance was joined. Why was it that those new lawyers or doctors were second-class citizens in their own country?

As indicated by the titles of newspapers and his early books — *Liberia in World Politics* (1934), *Renascent Africa* (1937) — Azikiwe at first used his eloquent tongue and pen primarily to foster race consciousness, and considered Africa or West Africa, rather than Nigeria, to be the coming political community. In doing so, he was true to his own early mobility and consistent with the traditional broad view already remarked upon. Increasingly, however, he became caught up in Nigerian affairs as Nigeria began to emerge as a nation; indeed, one of the crucial events in the political development of Nigeria after World War II was the charge that he had become not a Nigerian nationalist but an Ibo tribalist.

Azikiwe was a little older than the radical educated youths who emerged toward the end of World War II as a powerful political force. Nigeria's first national political party grew out of student dissatisfaction upon which Azikiwe and others built. In the spring of 1944, students at Kings College, Lagos, struck in protest against the use of their dormitories by soldiers; seventy-five were expelled, and eight were drafted into the army. Thereupon, the Nigerian Union of Students, frustrated by the lack of a central organization which could coordinate the political activity of existing groups, called a meeting at Glover Hall in Lagos. At the meeting, on August 26, 1944, the Nigerian National Council, which soon changed its name to the National Council of Nigeria and the Cameroons (NCNC),* was formed. Herbert Macaulay was elected President and Nnamdi Azikiwe General Secretary of the Council, which, "believing our country is rightfully entitled to liberty and prosperous life," resolved to "work in unity for realization of our ultimate goal of self-government within the British Empire."[7]

Membership in the NCNC at its formation was organizational rather

*In 1962, after the Southern Cameroons had decided to join the Cameroon Republic and the Northern Cameroons had been incorporated into Northern Nigeria, the NCNC changed its name, but not its initials, to the National Council of Nigerian Citizens.

than individual. Existing political parties, literary societies, social clubs, professional associations, labor unions, and over one hundred tribal, village, or clan unions, including the Ibo union, became members. Among the organizations that declined membership, the most important numerically was the Nigerian Union of Teachers, the nation's largest trade union, and the most important politically was the Nigerian Youth Movement (NYM).

The NYM had been formed in 1936, and in 1938 it had challenged and ended the fifteen-year Lagos rule of Herbert Macaulay's Nigerian National Democratic Party. Though its activities were centered in Lagos, it aimed at the unification of Nigeria's tribes, had branches in the provinces, and criticized the older Democratic Party for being dominated by "native foreigners." Azikiwe became a member of the NYM's executive committee but resigned this position, though not his membership, for "business" reasons in 1939. (Some people said it was because the NYM had begun to subsidize the *Daily Service* newspaper under the editorship of Ernest Ikoli in competition with Azikiwe's *West African Pilot.*)

In 1941, the NYM was permanently split, and tribalism came to the fore of Nigerian politics. The occasion was a contest within the NYM for a vacant seat on the Legislative Council. The contestants were Ernest Ikoli, who was an Ijaw, and Samuel Akinsanya, an Ijebu Yoruba. Ikoli was chosen. Azikiwe and most Ibos and Akinsanya with some Ijebus left the NYM on the ground that the majority had rejected Akinsanya because he was an Ijebu.* The NYM was left with an almost entirely Yoruba membership, and thus began the political tension between Ibo and Yoruba that has plagued Nigerian politics ever since.

After the organization of the NCNC, however, the underlying tribal tension was overshadowed for a while by a surge of nationalistic feeling against the British which was highlighted by a general strike in the summer of 1945. The chief grievance of Nigerian workers was that their

---

*The Ijebu subtribe of the Yoruba have been noted for their acquisitiveness, and are no more popular with their neighbors than other groups with that reputation. They had, moreover, remained outside the mainstream of Yoruba history. Other Yorubas have had some prejudice against them, a prejudice which appeared during the crisis that split the Action Group, the political party backed by most Yorubas, in 1962. Prejudice may well explain the rejection of Akinsanya, but two facts point the other way. First, his opponent, Ikoli, did not belong to the Yoruba majority; second, Obafemi Awolowo, himself an Ijebu Yoruba, spoke in favor of Ikoli.

wages had not increased with the great wartime increases in the cost of living. European civil servants, on the other hand, had been given some cost-of-living allowances. Seventeen unions with 30,000 workers who controlled such vital industries and services as the railways and the postal system joined the strike. They succeeded, in a sense. An impartial fact-finding commission was appointed, and secured increased allowances for them.[8] Their success showed both Nigerians and Britons that organized Nigerians had power. But the pattern of victory was one that recurred time and again in Nigeria's move toward independence. The Colonial Government made a timely concession before the Nigerians could build from their grievances a truly national and united force.

During the strike, Azikiwe sought national power. He came close to winning it, closer than anyone before or since; he spread nationalist feeling wider than ever before; he set Nigeria on the path to freedom. But in a sense he also failed.

The Government shut down his two Lagos newspapers for allegedly misrepresenting the facts about the strike. He then announced in his "last testament" that he was willing to give "my most prized possession — my life — for the redemption of Africa," accused the Government of plotting his assassination, and went into hiding in Onitsha.[9] The assassination story, seen against the background of Azikiwe's earlier opposition to the Government, was believed by many.* It made him a hero and dramatized the nationalist cause. But unquestionably Azikiwe could have become more of a hero, could have dramatized the cause still more, and could have molded a more united Nigeria if he had stood his ground instead of fleeing, if he had defied the ban on his papers, and most particularly if he could have driven the British to jail him. He never was jailed, and that is one reason why the Nigerian people did not unite behind him quite as much as the Ghanaian people united behind his one-time disciple, Kwame Nkrumah.

Shortly before the general strike, Nigeria's new Governor, Sir Arthur Richards, suddenly presented a new constitution to the country. The Richards Constitution was in some ways an advance and a response to the changes in Nigerian and British opinion that had taken place during

---

*In his sketch of Azikiwe, Anthony Enahoro stated: "But let there be no two opinions about this — the common people believed and were completely satisfied that the white man had planned to assassinate him." Enahoro went on to say that, "We interpret Nnamdi Azikiwe's prompt retirement to Onitsha as a huge joke, a cowardly act or a wise and judicious step, according to our several opinions of the man."[10]

the War. Northerners were to be members of the Legislative Council for the first time. For the first time persons (known as "unofficials") other than colonial administrators were to be in a majority in the only national legislative body, the Legislative Council. The same was true in the newly created regional houses of assembly. But the Richards Constitution was greeted with almost universal disapproval by Nigerian nationalists.

The Constitution represented no real advance toward Nigerian control of the government. The Legislative Council and the regional houses were merely forums for discussion, and Nigerians were not added to the executive branch, where real power lay. The Constitution was tainted, moreover, by being suddenly announced from on high. Despite his predecessor's promise, Governor Richards did not give Nigerians an opportunity to participate in the planning of their country's future.

Governor Richards' Constitution also seemed to be based upon assumptions about Nigeria's future that were a challenge to the new nationalists. Native authorities, the traditional tribal instruments of indirect rule, were given the crucial role. They selected the members of the regional houses, who in turn selected from their ranks the members of the Legislative Council. The elective principle was not extended at all; indeed, the existing franchise for Lagos and Calabar was retained only upon the insistence of the British Cabinet member responsible for the colonies. In the same vein, emirs and other chiefs were included within the "unofficial" majorities.*

Most politically aware Nigerians, who then were almost all Southerners, resented the Richards Constitution. Some, like Obafemi Awolowo, favored giving it a test. Azikiwe and the NCNC, on the other hand, decided to take their protest to the country.

An NCNC team led by Herbert Macaulay and Azikiwe set off on a national tour in the spring of 1946 to protest the Constitution and even more the four so-called "obnoxious ordinances." One, the Minerals Ordinance, vested in "the Crown" control of all Nigeria's minerals and rivers. Two others designated as "Crown lands" all land acquired for public purposes. The fault, of course, was in the use of the expression

*There were two objections to their inclusion. First, it was further proof that the British sought to hand over power to the traditional rather than the new class. Second, along with the inclusion of representatives of European commerce among the unofficials, it made a mockery of the claim that the "unofficial majorities" represented a break-through for nationalism, since the emirs and chiefs had become more and more dependent upon Government support.

"Crown." Responsibility lay with the rather inflexible legal draftsmen of the Colonial Government. The "Crown" in fact meant the Nigerian Government, which the Nigerians were said by the British to be destined to control. But it appeared to mean a distant monarch exploiting Nigeria's land and natural resources.*

During the NCNC tour, Herbert Macaulay died. Azikiwe gave the funeral oration, speaking, as he had in his own "last testament," of dying for *Africa,* not for Nigeria. "Come and mourn with me, heroes and heroines of the New Africa," he said, "He had one life; yet this had been sacrificed for the redemption of Africa."[11]

Azikiwe succeeded Macaulay as President of the NCNC and the tour went on. Along with the provincial newspapers of the Zik chain, the tour, as much as anything else, stimulated the political consciousness of the interior. It was also a financial success. The money collected was used to send a protest delegation to London which met with no tangible success and which upon its return fell to squabbling over its failure to account for the use of the funds. While it may not have met with obvious success, that delegation represented a high point in Nigerian nationalism. It included representatives of a wide spectrum of Nigeria's peoples, including a Northerner, Bukar Dipcharima, a Kanuri, and upon its return was reportedly greeted by a Lagos crowd of 100,000 shouting, "NCNC: FREEDOM OR DEATH."[12]

Militant Nationalism

Protests and petitions were not the way of those militant young Nigerians known as the Zikists. "We have passed the age of petition," Zikist President Mallam H. R. Adballah told a rally. "This is the age of action — plain blunt and positive action."[13] Another Zikist argued: "If we tell the Governor to come down, he will not; we must drag him down and take over."[14]

The Zikist Movement was born in 1946 as a response by Azikiwe's

---

*The fourth obnoxious ordinance, the Appointment and Deposition of Chiefs Ordinance, was merely a consolidation of the government's existing powers to control chiefs. Those were great, yet were wider on paper than generally in practice. But the nationalists, while on the one hand believing that they rather than the traditional chiefs should inherit power, have always known that most common people still revere their chiefs, and hence have often defended them. Furthermore, many of the early nationalists were themselves from chiefly families, who, if they wished, had had easier access to education than most.

militant supporters to ridicule by the NYM's newspaper of his charges that the British plotted his assassination. The Zikists vowed "nevermore [to] allow this evangelist to cry his voice hoarse when millions of youths of Nigeria can . . . echo it all over the world."[15] The movement became in effect an activist youth branch of the NCNC.

At the end of 1948, growing impatient with the NCNC, the Zikists stepped up the call for revolution. Included among their plans was an effort, apparently unknown to Azikiwe, to get the Government to jail him in the belief that that would set off a revolution. But the Government instead arrested ten of the most militant Zikists on charges of sedition; most were convicted and sentenced to prison.

Zikist activity, though hampered, did not end. In November 1949, twenty-one Nigerian coal miners were shot and killed by policemen under the orders of a jittery European police officer. The shooting led to a revival of Zikist militancy.* In four Eastern towns, Zikist leaders stirred the people to riot and the people assaulted Europeans, looted European-owned stores, and damaged Government property. In each town the police were called upon to disperse the mobs, and they fired upon the leaders.[16] Then, in February 1950, a Zikist tried to assassinate Hugh Foot, a high Government official who later won reknown as a tough Governor of Cyprus, and still later became the Labour Party Ambassador to the United Nations after leaving British Government service in protest against its reluctance to give power to African nationalists in the Rhodesias. Again there was a governmental crackdown culminating in an order declaring the Zikist Movement illegal.

Though the movement reorganized under another name, it and militant nationalism as a whole became less significant. For that there are three reasons, the least important of which was the vigilance of the Colonial Government. More important, Azikiwe, the natural catalyst of any revolutionary movement, never gave his full support. He wavered

---

*It also led to a temporary truce between the NCNC and the NYM. Together they formed the National Emergency Committee, but it fell apart within a year. It was no more long-lived than an earlier coalition, the United Front Committee, which was formed in 1947 to protest racial discrimination — the specific incident being the refusal by the Bristol Hotel in Lagos to let a Colonial Office official of African descent occupy a room. In both cases, the coalition stemmed from an incident with explicit or implicit racial overtones. The victories of both coalitions were limited to forcing the Government to take steps against racial discrimination. The United Front Committee forced the Government to issue a circular condemning discrimination in public facilities, and the NEC saw that formal discrimination on the teaching staff of University College, Ibadan, was abandoned.

between creating the Order of African Freedom to be awarded to all imprisoned for sedition and warning against "high sounding slogans and plans that fizzle out into a nine day's wonder."[17] Because of his substantial business interests, Azikiwe would have risked much in a violent revolution. Moreover, he came to believe that the British were going to set Nigeria free peaceably and saw the advantage both to himself and to his country of cooperating "now that we have been offered freedom on a platter of gold."[18] Skillful British concessions also weakened the militant nationalists and changed the emphasis in Nigerian politics from whether the British would go, or even when they would go, to who would succeed them.[19] Most Nigerians agreed that the British *should* go — though they were divided as to when; the Nigerians split when the question became who would inherit British power.

Tribal Tension in the South

Concessions made by the British in 1948 took some of the rancor away from Nigerian-British relations. Many nationalists were, moreover, immobilized from politics by being appointed to the Senior Civil Service. Further, constitutional discussions which culminated in the General Conference of 1950 led to increasing attention being paid to the role that the various Nigerian groups would play in the nation that was being formed.

The chief protagonists at first were the Yoruba and the Ibo. The Yoruba, dominant in the Western Region, were the established leaders. They had been exposed to Western education at a much earlier date than any other group in Nigeria; they were the wealthiest Nigerians, with a substantial middle class based on cocoa farming, and their cities, Lagos, Abeokuta, and Ibadan, were Nigeria's intellectual and political centers. The Ibo, dominant in the Eastern Region, were the energetic, land-hungry newcomers.

When Yoruba young men were obtaining their education in England, the Ibo on the whole were still living their isolated life in their small village communities.* The Ibo were poor and land hungry. By great energy and the sacrifices of village improvement unions to provide

---

*It is possible that the absence of large-scale political communities among the Ibo in the precolonial days made it easier for the Ibo to become a cohesive political community as the Nigerian nation emerged than was true for the Yoruba, who still are affected by the divisions between various Yoruba states during precolonial days. The Tiv can be analogized to the Ibo.

scholarships, however, the Ibos reduced the gap so much that by the late 1930's there were more Ibos than Yorubas at most of the important Nigerian schools.

The Ibo came into conflict with the Yoruba in two ways. Because of the crowded conditions in their homeland and their willingness to leave home to advance themselves, Ibos had spread all over Nigeria, including the Yoruba cities. Lagos, for example, had 264 Ibos in 1911, but 26,000 in 1951. Ibos also tended to be more militant nationalists than Yorubas — though there were exceptions in both directions — and as such challenged the economic and political interests of the established Yorubas.

During the 1930's, various Ibo villages and clans formed "progress" and "improvement" unions, one of whose primary functions was raising money for education. In 1936, after Francis Ibiam (now Governor of Eastern Nigeria) returned from England as the first Ibo doctor, many of those unions were federated under the Ibo Union (Lagos) and in 1944 the Ibo Federal Union was inaugurated. The function of that pan-Ibo body was not primarily political, but was to build schools in Iboland. The Ibo Union (Lagos), however, was one of the chief supporters of the NCNC, and provincial branches of the Ibo Federal Union frequently played host to the NCNC leaders on their national tour.

In 1948, a pan-Yoruba organization, the aims of which are described at the conclusion of this section, was formed. Known as the Egbe Omo Oduduwa (Society of the Sons of Oduduwa, the legendary Yoruba tribal ancestor), its members made remarks which were taken by Ibos as tribalistic attacks. Azikiwe was referred to as an "Arch Devil,"[20] and the Egbe's President promised that the "Big Tomorrow" for the Yoruba was coming when they "will hold their own among the other tribes of Nigeria."[21]

During the summer of 1948, tension between Yorubas and Ibos in Lagos nearly led to violence, for which both groups prepared by purchasing all available machetes. The tension resulted in the conversion of the pan-Ibo movement into an explicitly political body. All personal attacks upon Azikiwe were resolved by the Ibos of Lagos to be attacks upon the Ibo nation, because "if a hen were killed, the chickens would be exposed to danger."[22] At the end of 1948, the Ibo Federal Union was converted into the Ibo State Union and Azikiwe, by this time President of the NCNC, was elected its President.

At the first meeting of the Ibo State Union, Azikiwe made a speech in which he linked the destinies of Africa and his tribe in a way that his opponents said proved that he was a tribalist. He said

> The God of Africa has specially created the Ibo nation to lead the children of Africa from the bondage of the ages. . . . The martial prowess of the Ibo nation at all stages of human history has enabled them not only to conquer others but also to adapt themselves to the role of preserver. . . . The Ibo nation cannot shirk its responsibility.[23]

Azikiwe's first great rival for national political power, Obafemi Awolowo, emerged out of the Ibo-Yoruba tension as the champion of Yoruba nationalism. Awolowo was an Ijebu Yoruba born in 1909 of a moderately well-to-do family with some aristocratic antecedents. His father, a convert to Christianity, pushed him to school and encouraged him to improve his skill at home through exercises such as writing in chalk all over the walls.* When Awolowo was eleven his father died. Because of a Yoruba custom whereby a dead man's property went to his younger brothers and sisters and to the children of his older brothers and sisters before going to his own children, Awolowo's future became less rosy.†

The next few years saw a series of broken promises by relatives who said they would pay for his schooling but who found it more profitable to put the boy to work. He moved countless times in efforts to obtain schooling on his own. However, with the money earned from odd jobs such as writing letters for a blind letter writer and selling water to housewives — a profession at which he claims to have excelled because of his ability to push his way to the only standpipe — Awolowo managed to get enough schooling (at Anglican, Catholic, Baptist, Wesleyan, and Salvation Army schools) so as to be able to pass the exam for Wesley College. Wesley College was the equivalent of a high school, training teachers for elementary schools.

Frustrated by the restrictions at Wesley College, Awolowo left after

---

*His father's life story is a saga of the coming of Christianity to Nigeria. His marriage to Awolowo's mother was delayed, first because the father and other village Christians had to flee their pagan neighbors because they had eaten some sacred fish, and then because the pagans, including Awolowo's mother, fled the British-led troops who occupied the village. The father was an "unfailing church-goer" who "abhorred paganism"; he did, however, marry a second wife when Awolowo was ten. The father died of smallpox contracted after he had led a group of Christians to destroy a pagan shrine dedicated to a smallpox cult.[24]

†Awolowo was given only a robe from his father's estate. That he sold nine years later to help pay for correspondence courses.

one year, when he was eighteen, and taught for the two following years. He then became in succession a shorthand typist with a German commercial firm, a clerk at Wesley College, a reporter and free-lance journalist, and a trader-contractor whose corporation went bankrupt. As he matured, he became increasingly interested in politics and became a minor official in the NYM and the Nigerian Motor Transport Union. Finally, in 1944, after profiting from a contract to supply yams to army units, he realized a lifelong ambition and sailed to England to study law at the Inner Temple. He was called to the bar in two years and proudly recalls in his autobiography that he did better on the bar finals than the man who is now Nigeria's Attorney-General.*

While studying in England, Awolowo wrote *Path to Nigerian Freedom*. In it he summarized his proposals for Nigeria's future. His premise at that time was that Nigeria was not a nation but "a mere geographical expression."[26] More than that, each separate ethnic group was divided; as he put it:

> On top of all this, the country is made up of a large number of small, unintegrated tribal and clannish units, who live in political isolation from one another. The Yoruba, for instance, belong to the same racial stock. But they are divided into a number of tribes and clans, each of which claims and strives to be independent of the others.[27]

His solution was a federation of all of Nigeria's ethnic groups. Each ethnic group should rule itself so that "the barriers of tribalism and clannishness within each ethnical unit . . . [will] be totally destroyed"; no member of one ethnic unit should "poke his nose into the domestic issues of the other."[28] There were two aims; first, to end the internal divisions within various ethnic groups; second, to enable the various ethnic groups to move toward nationhood together. At the beginning, at least, the first was probably more important to Awolowo.

---

*Awolowo's autobiography, *Awo*, contains an intimate and revealing portrait of his early years. The outstanding note is determination, mixed with an optimistic ambition. A motto "formulated on my thirtieth birthday anniversary" and "recorded . . . in my private journal" expresses much of the spirit of that self portrait. It reads

> After rain comes sunshine; after darkness comes the glorious dawn. There is no sorrow without its alloy of joy; there is no joy without its admixture of sorrow. Behind the ugly terrible mask of Misfortune lies the beautiful soothing countenance of Prosperity. So, tear the mask.[25]

Those words are particularly interesting in the light of Awolowo's conviction in 1963 of plotting to overthrow the Federal Government, a plot born, said the convicting judge, of Awolowo's frustration at not becoming Prime Minister in the 1959 election.

The Egbe Omo Oduduwa, founded by Awolowo in London in 1945 and formally organized in Nigeria after his return, was an application of Awolowo's theories to his people, the Yoruba. Its constitution laid primary stress upon the needs of Yorubaland and secondary stress upon the needs of Nigeria. Awolowo's thinking was most clearly reflected in its resolve to "unite the various clans and tribes in Yorubaland and generally create and actively foster the idea of a single nationalism throughout Yorubaland" and to "accelerate the emergence of a virile, modernized and efficient Yoruba state with its own individuality in the Federal State of Nigeria." To help foster Yoruba nationalism and individuality, the Egbe also resolved to promote study of the Yoruba language, culture, and history. Somewhat more broadly, the Egbe resolved to encourage similar groups among other ethnic groups and to cooperate with them "so as thereby to attain unity in federation."[29]

The split between Yoruba and Ibo, between Western and Eastern Regions, was further institutionalized in 1951 when Obafemi Awolowo inspired and molded a new political party with the aim of challenging the NCNC and of winning power in the Yoruba-dominated Western Region. The existence of the new party, the Action Group, was made public after a year of secret meetings, most of which were held in Ibadan in Awolowo's house and the Egbe Secretariat. Awolowo was chosen as leader, other Yorubas were prominent in its leadership, and the Egbe and the leading Yoruba Obas soon pledged their support. Though its base was primarily Yoruba, the Action Group had some support among other Western Region groups such as the Beni or Edo and the Itsekeri, representatives of which like Chief Anthony Enahoro and Chief Arthur Prest were officers.*

The Action Group was different from the NCNC in a number of ways. Membership was individual, and discipline was tight. From its inception it issued policy papers on all aspects of its program, whose "Prussian-like thoroughness and efficiency" were, according to one unfriendly observer, characteristic of the party.[31] Those papers reflected the fact that the Action Group attracted a large proportion of the country's intellectuals. The most significant difference from the NCNC,

---

*There was apparently at first some doubt as to whether non-Yorubas should be admitted. At the seventh secret meeting, Awolowo is reported to have said: "He felt that the Yorubas should first weld themselves together so that it might be difficult for other tribes to break through them. . . . We should ensure that the Yorubas were first strongly organized and that . . . non-Yorubas could be drawn in later."[30]

however, was that the Action Group was, when organized, a regional party seeking only to capture power in the rich Western Region.

At its inception the NCNC, on the other hand, had national aspirations. As we have seen, however, the connection between Ibo groups and the NCNC was close. The connection was highlighted by the fact that Azikiwe was President of both the NCNC and the Ibo State Union. In 1952, moreover, the NCNC became more closely associated with the Ibo-dominated Eastern Region as Azikiwe left the national assembly to become the East's Premier. Azikiwe's political base in Nigeria had always been Lagos, from which he had been elected to various national assemblies. But in 1951 a constitutional change gave the Western Region legislature power to pick representatives from Lagos to the national assembly from several men nominated by the Lagosians. The Western legislature, dominated by the Action Group, passed over Azikiwe. Closed out of the center, he went to the East. With that change, neither of the two leading Southern political leaders, Azikiwe and Awolowo, had a national office.

The North Against the South

Until the constitutional conferences called for by Governor John Macpherson, who had succeeded the unpopular Governor Richards in 1948, political activity had been centered in the South. Southerners had tended to take Northerners for granted, as backward children who would follow their lead once the British were gone. To the Northerners, the Southerners appeared to be a menace, a greater threat than the British. Southerners had moved into the North in great numbers, taking most of the jobs in the modern economy. As late as 1953 Southerners held 82 per cent of the clerical service jobs in the North. Seeing that and the Northerners' educational backwardness, the editor of *Gaskiya Ta Fi Kwabo* (a Hausa newspaper whose title means "Truth is worth more than a penny") said

> Southerners will take the place of Europeans in the North. What is there to stop them? . . . There are Europeans but, undoubtedly, it is the Southerner who has the power in the North.[32]

The Northerners became a new conservative force in Nigerian politics. They did not want the British to depart immediately; they sometimes also doubted whether Nigeria should stay together when the British did depart. They did not want the British to depart because they feared

Southern domination; they doubted whether Nigeria should stay together as a nation because they resented and feared and yet felt superior to the Southerners. Thus, Abubakar Tafawa Balewa, who became Nigeria's Prime Minister, replied in the Legislative Council to a motion by Azikiwe which called for a united Nigerian outlook by saying that many Nigerians

> . . . deceive themselves by thinking that Nigeria is one. This is wrong. I am sorry to say that this presence of unity is artificial and it ends outside this Chamber. . . . The southern tribes who are now pouring into the North in ever increasing numbers . . . do not mix with the northern people in social matters, and we in the North look upon them as invaders.[33]

Controversy between North and South dominated the General Conference for review of the Constitution held at Ibadan in 1950. The General Conference met to consider the constitutional recommendations of a drafting committee that had been guided by the recommendations of successive village, provincial, and regional conferences. The committee's aim was "to maintain the unity of Nigeria," and it therefore recommended a strong central government in which all regions would be represented. But its chief premise and most significant recommendation was that

> In a country of the size of Nigeria with its diversities of history, race, tradition and religion, real unity will not . . . be achieved by attempting to concentrate all power at the centre, but rather by further decentralization of authority to the regions.[34]

Accordingly, it suggested that Nigeria adopt a "federal" system with three regions, the North, the East, and the West.

There was some dissent from Eastern delegates, but the General Conference agreed without great controversy to a federal system with three large regions. The struggle was over the relative power of the three regions and, more particularly, over the power to be given the Northern Region as opposed to the East and West. The Northern delegates (eighteen of the fifty-three) turned the Southerners' democratic speeches against them, and insisted that their region, which had more than half of the country's population, should be given one-half of the members of the proposed Central House of Representatives. If their demand was not granted, said the Emirs of Zaria and Katsina, the North "would ask for separation from the rest of Nigeria on the arrangements existing before [Lugard amalgamated the Northern and Southern Protectorates in] 1914."[35]

The Conference (in which there were thirty-two Southern as opposed to the eighteen Northern delegates), however, adopted a resolution proposing that the North be given forty-five members compared to thirty-three each for the Western and Eastern Regions. The Northerners then unanimously recorded their determination to disassociate themselves from all the other recommendations of the Conference unless they were granted half the seats in the Central House of Representatives.

On two other issues, the North stood adamant against the South. The North contended that tax revenue should be divided on a per capita basis, thereby giving it more than half, rather than according to its derivation, which would give it substantially less than half. The Conference did not resolve the issue but instead left it to a commission of fiscal experts. The commission eventually compromised, but did much to meet the wishes of the North by making a substantial portion of the annual grants depend upon the number of adult male taxpayers within each region and by recommending a grant of two million pounds to the North to make up for past deficiencies.

The other issue which divided North and South was also left for outside decision, and again the North was ultimately victorious. The Yoruba-dominated Western Region Conference had resolved that the boundary between the Northern and Western Regions should be redrawn to include the Northern Yorubas in the Western Region. At the General Conference, the Northerners opposed even an investigation of regional boundaries, stating that people could move but the land could not. Over their opposition, the Conference agreed to leave the boundary question to the Governor; he eventually decided against revision.

Though the West has stood against the North on the questions of representation in the Central House of Representatives, revenue allocation, and revision of boundaries, those were issues where the narrow interests of the West were obviously contrary to those of the North. The general premise from which the North argued — that each region should develop in its own way — was one which most Western delegates accepted, however. It was consistent with Awolowo's and the Egbe's premise that Nigeria should be governed as a federation of ethnic groups (though each of the three regions included several ethnic groups) and that the various ethnic groups should avoid interest in the affairs of other groups. The Easterners were not as prepared to accept this premise.

Their disagreement was expressed over a resolution supported by Northerners and Westerners stating that for five years only Northern

Nigerian adult males should be qualified for election to the Northern House of Assembly. Because of the definition of "Northern Nigerian," the resolution barred anyone of Southern descent from a seat in the Northern House, no matter how long he or his parents had lived in the North. The Minority Report in opposition to that resolution was signed by all Eastern delegates and by no one else.[36]

On the question of the future role of chiefs and emirs — the symbols of continued ethnic separation as well as of the traditional order — Easterners again took the most radical position and Northerners the most conservative.* Two Easterners, Eyo Ita and Mbonu Ojike, both members of the NCNC and both educated in America, said respectively

> Today we are out to abolish feudalism, not to reform it. We must leave the archaic in the limbo where they belong.

and

> The people who carry umbrellas for their majesties are people. Enfranchise them.

The Sardauna of Sokoto replied for the North, saying

> The gentleman thinks that a new era for them [commoners] has opened, yes, but since when? . . . If my friend can live for centuries he might still see the natural rulers in the North.[37]

After the General Conference ended with the North still adamant in its demand for half of the seats in the Central House of Representatives, the British referred the issue to the Legislative Council. The Council decided to give in to the Northern demands. Azikiwe, who then still represented Lagos in the Legislative Council, submitted a minority report in which he argued that if the North were to have power equal to the East and West combined, there should also be an upper house, like the United States Senate, in which the regions would be equally represented. He also attacked the very concept of three large regions, ad-

---

*Delegates to the General Conference were selected in a way that produced a higher number of conservative members than was representative of nationalist sentiment. Half were delegates by virtue of being members of the Legislative Council. It was relatively conservative because of the role played by the native authorities in selecting the regional houses of assembly, which in turn selected the regional members of the Legislative Council. Most of the remainder were selected by regional conferences, which reflected the same conservative bias, since they were composed largely of members of the regional houses of assembly. The fact that the General Conference was not a constituent assembly of nationalist leaders is probably why Azikiwe boycotted it.

vocating instead the division of the country into more, and weaker, states organized to be more homogeneous ethnically and linguistically.

Elections under the new constitution were held in 1951. For those elections, two new political parties were organized. One was the Action Group, the other the Northern Peoples Congress (NPC).

Class Struggle in the North

The NPC became a political party in response to a dual threat: the threat of Southern domination and the threat of Northern radicalism.

Early stirrings of nationalism among indigenous Northerners (as opposed to Southerners in the North) came in Bauchi in 1943. Mallams Sa'ad Zungur and Amino Kano founded the Bauchi General Improvement Union, one of whose members was Mallam Abubakar Tafawa Balewa. The union was soon disbanded because it displeased the Emir of Bauchi. But the spark was not quenched. Abubakar Tafawa Balewa and Amino Kano were among the Northern teachers sent by the colonial government to Britain to study at the end of the war. Upon his return, Kano organized the Northern Teachers' Association.

In the meantime, Dr. R. A. B. Dikko, a Fulani converted to Christianity, the first Northerner to get a University degree and the only Northerner to go abroad for higher education before 1945, organized the Northern Peoples Congress in December 1949. The Congress was not designed as a political party. It was to be a Northern cultural association. In this work Dr. Dikko was aided by Amino Kano, Abubakar Tafawa Balewa, Yahaya Gusau, Aliyu Mai Bornu, and a few others from the educated group.

In the North as in the South young men educated abroad for at least a short time were in the vanguard of political activity. The greater strength of traditionalism and of the older men in the North was apparent from the outset, however.

At its inaugural conference, NPC leaders were careful to say that they would not usurp the authority of "our Natural rulers"; instead, their "ardent desire" was to enhance those rulers' authority and to "help [them] in the proper discharge of their duties" and "in enlightening" the peasants.[38] Deference to tradition combined with hints of reform were the dominant notes at first.*

*Abubakar Tafawa Balewa's speech in the Northern House of Assembly in 1950 typified the mixture of respect for tradition and desire for change:

In August 1950, the more radical members of the NPC under the leadership of Amino Kano formed the first Northern political party, the Northern Elements Progressive Union (NEPU). In the five-stage elections held in 1951, the NEPU began with great success. Its success frightened the conservative leaders into converting the NPC into a political party to fight the later stages of the elections. Success was complete; at the final stage not a single NEPU candidate was elected to the House of Assembly. That was due in large measure to the substantial advantage given to the conservative elements by the electoral rules. Each native authority, then often an emir acting alone, was permitted to appoint 10 per cent of the membership of the final electoral college in its area. The effectiveness of this device was shown in Kano Emirate, where not one of the twenty men eventually chosen had been chosen at the first stage where all adult males were eligible to vote; ten had been defeated and ten had not run.

The NPC and the NEPU were both Northern parties, though the NEPU allied itself with the predominantly Southern NCNC. Membership in the NPC was open to "people of Northern descent" and its aim was "regional autonomy." Both the parties were predominantly Muslim despite the NPC's slogan of "one North, one people, irrespective of religion, rank or tribe."[40] The differences lay in their attitude toward traditional authority.

The NEPU *Declaration of Principles* promulgated in 1952 decried the "shocking state of social order" caused by the "autocratic" rule of the native authorities and their "unscrupulous and vicious system of Administration." It saw a class struggle, supported the depressed peasant class, the talakawa, and therefore stated it was "diametrically opposed to the interest of all sections of the master class" and "hostile to the party of the oppressors."[41] The NPC's *Aims and Objects*, also promulgated in 1952, limited its program for local government to "local government reform within a progressive Emirate system based on tradition and custom," the last five words having been added in 1952 to the NPC's original program.[42]

The difference between the parties was further reflected in the background of their leadership. The NPC's position as the party of tradition

---

Our Natural Rulers should realize that Western education and world conditions are fast creating a new class of people in the North. That this new class must exist is certain, and the Natural Rulers, whom the North must retain at all costs, should, instead of suspecting it try to find it proper accommodation.[39]

is shown most graphically by its selection of the Sardauna of Sokoto, great-great-grandson of Usuman dan Fodio, as its leader. The traditional rulers, the Fulani, had power in the NPC that was out of proportion to their share of the regional population. In 1958, about 32.4 per cent of the party's National Executive were Fulanis, though Fulanis make up only some 18 per cent of the regional population. At the same time, 69 per cent of the National Executive had been native authority function-aries, and in the 1959 election 135 of the NPC's 161 candidates were associated with the native authority system.[43] The NPC leaders and candidates, therefore, were largely aristocrats, their scions, or their loyal retainers. On the other hand, petty traders, shopkeepers, inde-pendent artisans, and craftsmen were heavily represented among the NEPU leaders and candidates.

It was in the North that political parties were most closely correlated with class.* A society based upon class had existed there at least since the emirate system had been created by Usuman dan Fodio's Jihad at the beginning of the nineteenth century. The traditional social system of the North had weathered the British era well because of indirect rule and the North's educational isolation. In the South, traditional society (to the extent that it had ever been based upon class) had been substan-tially weakened during the British era, and a new society based upon class is only now beginning to appear as wealth and power are concen-trated in the hands of those fortunate enough to have acquired a Western education, particularly those who have connections with the government.

The North Against the South: Round II

Resolved "that this House accepts as a primary political objective the attainment of self-government for Nigeria in 1956." That resolution, moved in the House of Representatives by Chief Anthony Enahoro of the Action Group on March 31, 1953, plunged Nigeria into crisis, nearly led to the secession of the North, was followed by bloody tribal rioting, and made certain that Nigeria would be a federation rather than a cen-tralized unitary state.

*Class considerations were not irrelevant elsewhere. For example, in Ibadan, the Mabolaje (the name meaning "do not diminish the splendor") represented the interests of the indigenous, largely Muslim population of Ibadan against the largely Christian, newcomer elements of the Action Group, whose adherents, generally speaking, had benefited educationally and financially more than the Mabolaje's supporters from the forces of the modern world.

77

After Enahoro made his motion, the Sardauna of Sokoto, speaking for the North and the NPC, moved to substitute the words "as soon as practicable" for "in 1956." The North, he said, "does not intend to accept the invitation to commit suicide." With the North unwilling to commit itself to setting a date for freedom, and with the two main Southern parties vieing to appear as nationalistic as possible, the debate was stormy and bitter.[44] It ended with the Action Group and the NCNC joining together to walk out of the House as their two leaders, Azikiwe and Awolowo, embraced on the steps outside, in one of their few gestures of reconciliation.

On the following day, after the Northern members, distinctive in their flowing white rigas, had been booed and abused by Lagos crowds, the House met again for an even more tempestuous session. Two Action Group members, who resigned as ministers of the government, reported to the House that the Northern ministers had been frustrating Nigeria's true nationalists by continually voting with the British official ministers. "We refuse to associate ourselves," said Bode Thomas, "with Africans who have not got the guts to speak their minds." Contrasting himself with the Northerners, S. L. Akintola said, "I am not appointed an Imperialist Minister to do the will of the Imperialist agents in Nigeria." Seething with anger, the Sardauna of Sokoto then announced, "The mistake of 1914 has come to light and I should like to go no further."[45] The Northerners departed for home. Their desire to secede — and thereby end the amalgamation of North and South accomplished by Lugard in 1914 — was strengthened as they were abused by crowds of Southerners at each stop of the train carrying them home and by Southern railway employees all the way.

During the acrimonious debate, the Northerners gave two reasons for being unwilling to agree to the 1956 date. They said they could not commit themselves on such an important matter without consulting the people. That argument was interesting because it showed the Northerners, for all their conservative and even autocratic tendencies, using arguments based upon a democratic premise as they had at the 1950 General Conference when they insisted upon equality of representation. The response of Obafemi Awolowo was also interesting in view of his party's later insistence that it was the party of the common man. He ridiculed the Northerners' desire to consult the masses, saying:

> Who are these masses? The generality of the people are not interested in self-government or in government generally. What they are interested in

is their food, shelter, clothing, to get married, bear children, and drink plenty of palm wine, and, if they have the money, to drink some gin as well.[46]

The chief reason for the Northern reluctance to agree to advocating a date for self-government was the fear of Southern domination that had always shaped their political thinking. They were convinced that the vastly greater numbers of educated Southerners would control the country, leaving the North, as the Sardauna reflected in his autobiography, with "quite simply, just nothing, beyond a little window dressing."[47]

After the Northern politicians left Lagos, the Action Group and the NCNC followed upon their heels to campaign in the North for self-government in 1956. Upon the visit of S. L. Akintola of the Action Group to Kano in May, rioting broke out.* In four days of rioting, at least 36 were killed and 241 wounded.[48]

The Northern leaders thought hard about secession, finding the idea, according to the Sardauna of Sokoto, "very tempting."[49] Eventually they rejected it, primarily because they realized that they needed an outlet to the sea. Instead they proposed an eight-point program under which there would be no central legislature or executive, but only an agency for the assessment of customs duties which would immediately be passed on to the regions.[50]

On May 21, 1953, at the end of the Kano riots and just before the Northern House of Assembly passed the eight-point program, the Secretary of State for the Colonies "regretfully" announced in the British House of Commons that the Nigerian Constitution would have to be redrawn to provide for greater regional autonomy.[51] Conferences then were held between representatives of the Nigerian political parties in London in 1953 and in Lagos in 1954 which set the constitutional pattern for the Nigeria of today. The trend toward decentralization and regionalization was accentuated. Nigeria was to become a federation with three strong regions invested with the residual powers. In addition, the transfer of power from British to Nigerian hands was to be speeded, though it was recognized that each region could go at its own pace. Any region

---

*Though Akintola and most of his companions were Yorubas, the fighting in Kano was primarily between Ibos and Hausas. That is one reason why many Nigerians, commenting on the lack of violence when Yoruba leader Awolowo was arrested in 1962, told the author, depending upon their persuasion, that the Yoruba were a peace-loving or a cowardly tribe.

could if it so desired have full internal self-government, within the still-dependent federation, in 1956. The political as well as the constitutional pattern was to move toward regionalization. The NCNC and the NPC emerged as the overwhelmingly dominant powers in the East and North respectively, and the Action Group increasingly solidified its hold on the West.

As far as it has been traced, through 1954, Nigerian political development seems a tale of unhappy disintegration and increasing parochialism. World War II saw the birth of the NCNC, a national party. After the war, for the first time, politically conscious Nigeria became something more than Lagos, and national spirit began to spread through the country. Within a few years, however, new parties had been born with tribal or regional-religious bases and the NCNC itself had become increasingly an Eastern Region and Ibo party.

The trend toward tribal and regional-religious political parties is surely not something that Nigerians could be happy about. Yet, given the power of tradition and pride of tribe among most of the Nigerian populace, it was the inevitable consequence of another, desirable, trend — the trend toward greater participation by the people in the country's affairs. As long as the intellectual elite of Lagos dominated politics, tribal loyalties were relatively unimportant. But as long as Lagos remained the political center, the British would refuse to surrender power on the ground that the politicians were in no way representative of the people. The development of political parties enlisting the support of the common people throughout the country — notwithstanding the fact that their chief appeal may have been to tribal, regional, or religious loyalties — gave political leaders the mass support necessary to make realistic their demands for independence. Millions of people immersed in tradition first felt the music of change when they were drawn into the political struggle, even though the dominant note in that struggle was the familiar one of *only my tribe, only my faith, only my culture.*

Nor were the narrow loyalties of the early days of Nigeria's political development wholly destructive. Ibo pride meant sacrifices for Ibo education. Northern pride and the memory of the glory of the Islamic kingdoms in the North inspired the Northerners to seek to match the Southerners in modern skills. The Egbe Omo Oduduwa and the Action Group united the clans of the Yoruba as they had not been united since the slave wars, if ever before.

The development of political parties that were relatively parochial in the sense that they drew most of their support from a constituency limited by tribe or region, therefore, was not something which should be looked upon as entirely detrimental. Nevertheless, it was obvious that it was extremely dangerous. As it reflected, so it accentuated Nigeria's major political problem — the absence of a firm consensus among Nigerians that their several destinies would be best served by working together.

Minority Group Politics

After it had been agreed that Nigeria would be governed as a federation with three strong regions, minorities within each of the regions began to agitate for their own regions or states in which they would be safe from domination by the majority ethnic groups. As independence approached, the most significant question in Nigerian politics became whether new regions should be created for minority groups. Controversy between the major parties on that issue was a principal cause of the political crisis that shocked Nigeria two years after her independence.

The new-region controversy is the prime example of how basic and unsettling the central issues in Nigerian politics have been. The structure of the political system has been at stake rather than the specific actions which should be taken by governments operating within a generally accepted framework. The proponents of new regions directly challenge the legitimacy of the existing governments. Both proponents and opponents have sometimes felt the issue to be so vital that victory became essential, compromise impossible, and observance of the rules of the game unnecessary.

Before the minority movement became a potent political force, increasing the number of regions had been advocated by the Action Group and the NCNC and their respective leaders, Awolowo and Azikiwe. That discussion, however, was focused primarily upon whether Nigeria should have a strong central government or strong regions. It was not until that issue was resolved in favor of having three strong regions that the demands of the minorities themselves became the central issue.

Awolowo's arguments for a decentralized federal system were based on the premise that each ethnic group was entitled to manage its own affairs without interference. Accordingly, in *Path to Nigerian Freedom* he argued that the ultimate goal should be a "truly" federal constitution under which "each group, however small, is entitled to the same treatment as any other group, however large." "Each must have its own Regional House of Assembly," he said, and "even as many as thirty to forty Regional Houses of Assembly would not be too many in the future United States of Nigeria."[1]

Azikiwe also had written in favor of redrawing Nigeria's internal boundaries so as to create additional states. In 1943, in *Political Blueprint of Nigeria,* he suggested that Nigeria should be organized as a federation made up of eight "protectorates" organized along ethnic lines.[2] The NCNC "Freedom Charter" of 1948 further developed that line by proposing the creation of states on a linguistic basis.[3] At the Ibadan General Conference in 1950, the only delegates to object to three powerful regions within a federal system were officers of the NCNC — Eyo Ita and Mbonu Ojike. Their dissent was echoed by Azikiwe's vigorous contention in the Legislative Council three months later that the existing system was an "artificial creation" which would "inevitably tend towards the existence of chronic minority problems." All three suggested that the country, instead of being divided into three large polyglot and practically self-sufficient regions, should be divided along ethnic and linguistic lines.[4]

Though Awolowo and Azikiwe both advocated the creation of more regions, their reasons for doing so in those early days were significantly different. Azikiwe and his followers were the strongest proponents of a united and cohesive Nigeria. Ita and Ojike opposed having three powerful regions "because it divides the country" and advocated organization along ethnic lines in order to "remove the problems of Boundaries, minority and Pakistanistic dangers now threatening the unity of Nigeria."[5] That the NCNC's main reason for supporting new states was to ensure that Nigeria hold together is further suggested by its abandonment of support for new states at its 1951 Kano Conference. There it came full circle, and resolved instead to strive for a unitary government as being better for Nigeria "in view of recent divisionist tendencies."[6] Either more, and weaker, states within a federal system, or a unitary system would satisfy the NCNC's desire in the early 1950's for a strong central government.

As the first militant and the first national political party in Nigeria, the NCNC had naturally attracted a large proportion of those Nigerians who thought in national terms. Moreover, the area in which it was the strongest, the East, and the people from whom it received its main support, the Ibo, both had good reasons to support a strong central government. The East (then before the discovery of oil) was the poorest of the three regions, the least able to stand alone; the Ibo had the greatest need for national unity because they, more than any other group, had left their homeland to spread over the rest of the country.

The NCNC's support for a unitary system, its opposition to Nigeria's brand of federalism, reflected not only the NCNC's concern for national unity but also the fact that in 1951 it was the NCNC which was being hurt by the existing three-region system. The NPC in the North and the Action Group in the West were at that time merely regional parties that benefited from the solidarity of the ethnic groups which provided their support. They also benefited from a system in which those ethnic groups formed the majority of a region *and* the regions stood on their own as powerful units of government. The NCNC, on the other hand, was being closed out of areas, particularly in the West, that a strong national party would hope to hold. Thus, in the 1951 elections for the Western Regional House of Assembly the Action Group won a solid majority in the Yoruba areas; the election in the region as a whole, however, was very close. But enough NCNC members soon declared for the Action Group to give it a clear majority. After the Action Group had organized the House, others from the NCNC crossed the carpet to give the Action Group 75 per cent of the membership of the House.

In the early 1950's, the Action Group and Awolowo appeared to be much less concerned with national unity than did the NCNC and Azikiwe. Awolowo in the early days was primarily a Yoruba leader who saw a decentralized federal system organized along ethnic or linguistic lines as the means to protect the Yoruba from interference. For him, at that time, additional states were primarily devices to preserve differences. For the NCNC, additional states were primarily devices to render differences unimportant.

One might have expected that a party which emphasized Yoruba interests would find three powerful regions within a federal system, which left the Yoruba in a large majority in the West, to its liking. Instead, the Action Group became the strongest advocate of new states for minorities. The reason can best be understood after discussing the emergence of the minority movements in each of Nigeria's three original regions.

The minority movements arose because of the ethnic composition of the three regions. Each region, as we have seen before, had a large ethnic majority — the Yoruba in the West, the Ibo in the East and the Islamic peoples, particularly the Fulani and the Hausa, in the North. In each region some minorities became fearful of domination by the ethnic majority. Map 3 shows the territory sought by the various new state movements.

Until the nationalist movement had colonialism on the run, the minorities were not fearful, because under indirect rule each ethnic group was given a large measure of autonomy and the British rulers were in principle neutral between ethnic groups. But the shield of indirect rule was bound to crumble, and the minorities were not so sure about the neutrality of their fellow Nigerians. Also, the role of government would increase with the end of colonialism. A Nigerian government would undoubtedly do more to develop the country than had the colonial government, and increased development made the question of whether the minorities were to get their share more important. Moreover, as Nigerians began to acquire power over the purse and the prestige and monetary rewards of ministerial appointments, it seemed to the minorities that they could best share in those benefits in a state where they ruled supreme.

Against that background, political and constitutional developments accentuated the minorities' fears. Each of the major political parties was solidly supported by one of the ethnic majorities — the Action Group by the Yoruba, the NPC by the Hausa-Fulani, and the NCNC by the Ibo. That fact was particularly frightening to the ethnic minorities within each region during the 1950's when heavy emphasis was placed upon regional power. Until 1954, representatives to the central legislature were elected by the regional houses of assembly, thereby allowing a regional majority to pyramid its advantages. Thereafter, until 1959, the leaders of each of the three major parties served as premiers of the regions in which their respective parties were solidly entrenched rather than seeking to enter the Federal Government. Until independence in 1960, moreover, the federal powers over defense and foreign affairs were still exercised by the Colonial Government, while Nigerian control of regional matters such as education and local government had come much sooner.

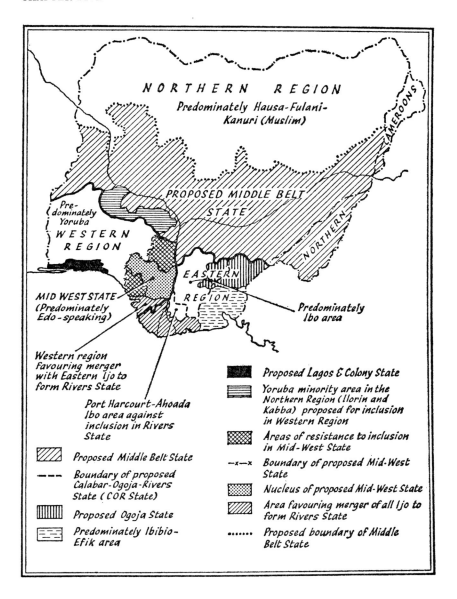

MAP 3. *Territory for Proposed New Regions* (*adapted from* The Story of Nigeria *by Michael Crowder, and reprinted by permission of Faber and Faber, Ltd., London*). *The map was drawn prior to the creation of the Midwest Region. The areas shown as resisting inclusion within that region in fact voted for its creation. The area shown as Northern Cameroons is now part of the Northern Region.*

86

The relationship between regionalization and the emergence of minority movements is shown most clearly in the Eastern Region. Minority movements demanding a separate state did not develop there until (1) Azikiwe had returned to the Region from Lagos to become its Premier after a ministerial crisis forced the ouster of Eyo Ita, himself a leader of the Efik minority, and (2) the NCNC had abandoned the stand taken at its Kano Conference in 1951 favoring a unitary government and instead had agreed to accept three powerful regions, though at the same time promising to work for more regions.

Agitation by the minorities was, moreover, accentuated by rivalries between the major political parties themselves. Because the dominant political party in each region was solidly supported by the region's ethnic majority, the other political parties were forced to concentrate on soliciting minority votes.

Although the same considerations affected the minority movements throughout the country, the relationship between minority and majority in the two southern regions was somewhat different from the relationship in the North. In the South, the important minorities could look back to an earlier time when their power and culture were as great or greater than the majority's. Thus, in the Western Region, Benin Kingdom had been as glorious as any Yoruba kingdom; in the Eastern Region, the city-states of the Efik and Ijaw peoples had outshone the villages of the Ibo. Now, however, the majority ethnic groups had taken a lead. In the West intensive missionary influence and with it modern education had reached Yorubaland before the Benin area. In the East the Ibo had taken to education with an avidity unsurpassed elsewhere in Nigeria, and as a result had gone ahead of all the minority groups except the Efik of Calabar. Moreover, much of the Eastern and all of the Western Region minority areas were remote and thus poorly served with roads, water, electricity, and other social amenities.

In the North the situation was reversed. It was the majority which had the glorious past, but the minority which had benefited most from modern education and which had been supplied with the most social amenities. The main minority area, the Middle Belt, was the most accessible part of the region because it was closest to the sea and was served by navigable stretches of the Niger and Benue rivers.

The strongest and most cohesive minority movement grew up in the West. It was centered around the Edo-speaking peoples of the old kingdom of Benin. But its aim was the creation of a larger state covering all of Benin and Delta Provinces, an area which came to be known as the Midwest. (In July 1963 its aim was realized.) In 1950, at the Western Region Conference held prior to the Ibadan General Conference, representatives of those two provinces put forward their claims. Because the claims were rejected, the Oba of Benin boycotted the General Conference. In 1953 a new party, the Benin-Delta Peoples' Party, aiming at the creation of a Benin-Delta state, was born with the Oba as its leader. The party entered an alliance with the NCNC.

The Action Group, though largely Yoruba, did have among its leaders some Midwesterners such as Chief Anthony Enahoro and Chief Arthur Prest. But it had little success in its attempt to widen its popular base into the Benin-Delta area. The NCNC and its ally, the Benin-Delta Peoples' Party, won most of the seats in the Midwest in the 1951 regional and 1954 federal elections, campaigning in the latter election on the promise that the Midwest would be made a new region.

Following the 1954 election, the Action Group made a move which it was not allowed to forget. On June 14, 1955, a private member in the Western Region House of Assembly sponsored a motion urging the creation of a Midwest Region. The Action Group supported the motion and it carried unanimously.[7] Later in the same month the Oba of Benin joined the Action Group Government of the Western Region as a Minister without portfolio, presumably feeling that cooperation was now in the interest of his people because the Action Group had committed itself to the establishment of the new region. The Benin-Delta Peoples' Party then changed its name to the Midwest State Movement, an avowedly nonpolitical movement, under the leadership of Chief Dennis Osadebay, a member of the Ibo minority in the Western Region and leader of the NCNC opposition in the Western House of Assembly.

Support of the motion was in accord with Chief Awolowo's ideas about the right of ethnic groups to be free from interference from other ethnic groups. In addition, there were sound political reasons for the Action Group's support of the creation of a Midwest Region, or at least for its saying that the party supported it. The recent elections seemed to show that the Action Group could not win in a Benin-Delta area which was attached to the Western Region and fearful of Yoruba domination. Perhaps if the desire for a separate state were met, the party would have greater success. Even if it did not, it might be worth discarding an area which was voting heavily against the party and thereby giving the opposition a chance to capture all of the region if it could win close to a majority in the Yoruba West.* Finally, the Action Group commitment to support the creation of a new state out of the region in which it was strongest would be useful in attracting the support of minority movements in the other regions.

The Action Group did succeed in aligning itself with minority groups in the East and North. In the East, it was inevitable that the minorities would turn to the Action Group, because the minorities were opposing the NCNC and the other major party, the NPC, was not interested in Southern politics.

The minority movements in the Eastern Region were, as stated previously, related to the ministerial crisis in 1952 and 1953 that was climaxed by the return of Azikiwe to the Eastern Region.† After Eyo Ita was expelled from the Premiership, he and other ousted NCNC Ministers formed the National Independence Party which found its chief strength in the Efik-Ibibio area. A constitutional conference held in London in 1953 rejected its proposals for a strong central government, and thereafter the party concentrated upon the creation of a new state or states. As the United National Independence Party (following merger with another small party in the East), it formed an alliance with the Action Group to accomplish that end.

The United National Independence Party (UNIP) had as its aim the creation of a Calabar-Ogoja-Rivers (COR) Region that would include the varied peoples from those three provinces — the Efik-Ibibio from Calabar, the many small tribes in the non-Ibo portion of Ogoja and the Ijaw from Rivers, and in addition a substantial number of Ibos in Rivers Province. There were also separate movements for a Rivers State, for a Cross River State (including Calabar and Ogoja Provinces), and for an Ogoja State.

When minority agitation first arose in the East, the NCNC, like the

---

*In the 1954 federal election, the NCNC won a majority of the Western Region seats through combining a few Yoruba seats with most of the Midwest seats. The Action Group-controlled Regional Government was, of course, not affected by that federal election.

†At the time of the ministerial crisis, the peoples living in the southern portion of the Cameroons Trust Territory — an ex-German territory administered by the British since World War I — increased their pressure for a separate state, saying that their interests were being sacrificed during Eastern Region squabbling. After the Kamerun National Congress, campaigning on the issue of separation, had won all the Southern Cameroons seats to the Eastern Region House of Assembly, the Lagos Constitutional Conference of 1954 endorsed the Colonial Secretary's proposal to separate the Southern Cameroons from the Eastern Region.

Action Group in the West, found it necessary to support the demands for separation. As late as the 1957 election of the Eastern Region House of Assembly, the party's manifesto stated that the country should be carved into fourteen regions; in his election eve broadcast, Dr. Azikiwe sought the minorities' support by saying, "we have reaffirmed our faith in the right of any community to self-determination," and, more specifically, that the rights of Calabar, Ogoja, and Rivers are "conceded."[8] Such statements may have helped the NCNC hold down the Action Group-UNIP vote in the minority areas. The alliance won, but it won only eighteen seats opposed to seventeen for the NCNC. The victory was more impressive, however, if the five seats won by the NCNC in the Ibo area of Rivers Province are excluded.

After the election, the NCNC abandoned its verbal support for new states in the East. Azikiwe announced "the situation in the East is exceptionable," and "the East can no longer stand dismemberment as a sacrifice either for administrative convenience or for national unity."[9] The combination of the election results and Dr. Azikiwe's statement cemented the marriage of the minorities and the Action Group. For the minorities, the Action Group was the only major party supporting their claims. For the Action Group, the returns had confirmed their belief that it was only by concentrating on the minorities that they could make any headway whatsoever in the East — of fifty-two Ibo seats, the NCNC had won fifty, independents two, and the Action Group none.

In the North, minority separatist movements arose in three areas. Each met with the implacable opposition of the NPC, adhering firmly to its slogan of "One North, One People."

In the non-Muslim southern third of the region, a number of minority movements came into being. In view of their people's relative advantage in education, which helped them win governmental posts, some of them believed that their interests would best be served not by separation but by cooperation with the NPC. By 1957, however, one party, the United Middle Belt Congress (UMBC) led by J. S. Tarka, a Tiv, was steadfastly supporting separation.*

*Its origins demonstrate a zigzag course between the tactics of cooperation with the NPC and separation. In 1950, the Non-Muslim League (later the Middle Zone League) was founded by Pastor David Lot and allied itself with the NPC. Three years later, the Middle Belt People's Party was formed with the backing of the NCNC and the NEPU. It sought a separate state, and opposed the NPC for its unwillingness to demand self-government in 1956. The Middle Belt People's Party and the Middle Zone League joined together in 1955 to form

The UMBC at first included the Northern Region's largely Yoruba Provinces, Ilorin and Kabba, within its proposed Middle Belt State. But after the Constitutional Conference of 1957 the Action Group and the UMBC agreed that the Action Group would support the UMBC but that the UMBC would abandon its claim to those two Provinces. The Action Group sought to join them with the rest of the Yoruba territory in the Western Region.

In the early nineteenth century the Yoruba of Ilorin had obtained Fulani help in their revolt against the Yoruba empire at Oyo; the helpers had then taken over Ilorin and added it to the Fulani emirate system. Later, with its armies still facing south against the Ibadan Yoruba, Ilorin emirate was included within the Niger Company's sphere of influence, which became the Protectorate of Northern Nigeria, now all in the Northern Region. The Constitutional Conference of 1950 had referred to Governor Macpherson the question of whether the boundary between Western and Northern Nigeria should be redrawn so as to include the Yoruba from Ilorin and Kabba within the West. He had decided that it should not be.

The Action Group did not accept his decision as final, and continued to demand the boundary revision. In 1956, it formed with the Ilorin Talaka Parapo (Commoner's Party) and a number of smaller Yoruba parties in Ilorin Province a fruitful alliance, winning all four Ilorin seats in the 1956 Northern Regional election. Thereafter, the allies won elections to the Ilorin Town Council, the Ilorin Native Authority Council, and a majority of the district councils throughout the province. Those local bodies then passed resolutions favoring transfer to the Western Region, with the elected members from the alliance outvoting the elected NPC members and the traditional members nominated by the Emir. As was the case with the UMBC, however, the Ilorin Talaka Parapo was not unanimous in its support for separation from the North; a minority resigned because it was opposed.

---

the UMBC. It first allied with the NPC and promised not to ally itself with parties that sought the dismemberment of the North; for the 1956 regional election, it issued a manifesto stating (1) that though a new region would be "desirable," it was "for the present, impracticable" and (2) that party representatives in the regional government would adequately protect the area's interests.[10] During the election, however, the NPC was accused of breaking its promise not to challenge UMBC candidates, the alliance was broken, and thereafter the UMBC under Tarka pressed for a new state. Some members, however, led by Pastor Lot, continued to cooperate with the NPC.

The third separatist movement in the North grew up in Bornu, which, though sharing the Islamic faith with the Fulani and Hausa, had a separate historical tradition. Bornu had, for example, successfully repulsed the Fulani Jihad at the beginning of the nineteenth century. In 1954, Bornu's separatist tradition was politically expressed by the Bornu Youth Movement, led by Ibrahim Imam, a onetime General Secretary of the NPC. The party differed from the NPC in the same way as did the NEPU — it was impatient of delay in democratizing the feudal system of the region and in ousting the British. It also sought creation of a Bornu State. In the 1956 regional election it won both seats for the urban Maiduguri-Yerma area, unseating in the process Shettima Kashim, then the powerful Waziri of Bornu and now the Governor of Northern Nigeria. At that time the party was allied with the NCNC and the NEPU, but in 1958 it joined most of the nation's other separatist movements in an alliance with the Action Group.

The Minorities Commission

At the Constitutional Conference held in London in 1957 the agitation for new regions came to a head. Claims for no fewer than fifteen were put forward. After lengthy discussion the delegates decided to turn the matter over to a Minorities Commission instructed to ascertain the fears of minorities and propose means of allaying them.[11]

At the conference, and consistently thereafter, the United Kingdom made clear that it was very reluctant to agree to the creation of new regions. It was concerned lest the Federation break up, worried about the economic and administrative viability of new regions, and anxious to disengage itself from Nigeria without beginning all over again the process of constitution-making.* At the conference the United Kingdom stated that while the creation of even one new state in any region "would create an administrative problem of the first order, the creation of more than one such state in any region could not at present be contemplated."[12] The Minorities Commission's terms of reference, drawn up by the Colonial Secretary, further reflected the British government's antipathy toward the creation of new regions. The Commission was charged first to consider other means of allaying minority fears and "if, but only

---

*It may also be that it believed that the existing system with three large regions dominated by the North helped the conservative forces which it probably hoped would rule Nigeria.

if, no other solution seems to the Commission to meet the case, then as a last resort to make detailed recommendations" for the creation of more regions.[13]

The Commission consisted of four Englishmen. It visited Nigeria in late 1957 and early 1958, hearing from the various governments, from the minority groups (whose cases, said one member of the Commission after its report was issued, were "badly presented"[15]), and from organizations like the Citizens Committee for Independence, an articulate group of Nigerians from different ethnic groups whose pamphlets called for more regions as a way to ensure the nation's unity.[16]

In its appearances before the Minorities Commission, the NPC took its usual position, heatedly opposing proposals for the creation of a Middle Belt Region and not being concerned with the issue in the rest of the country. The NCNC's position was less straightforward. It presented the traditional NCNC view that Nigeria needed a strong Federal Government attainable by dividing the country into several small states with less power than the existing regions. Despite Dr. Azikiwe's earlier statement that the "East can no longer stand dismemberment," the NCNC said that it would agree to the division of the Eastern Region into smaller states if the same were done to other regions. However, the NCNC adamantly opposed creation of a COR Region for which the most vociferous case was being made. Such a region would not satisfy one of the conditions the party had said a new region must meet — that it should be ethnically homogeneous. This it was not, because it contained the Ijaw from Rivers, the Ibibio-Efik from Calabar, the polyglot collection from Ogoja, and several other groups who were united, said the NCNC, only by "a negative dislike for the Ibo tribe" and that, said the NCNC, was no basis upon which to build a region.[17]

The other proposed states, Rivers, Cross River, and Ogoja, met all their requirements, and the NCNC said it saw no objection to their creation. The Commission's report casts some doubt upon their sincerity in that regard. The Commission was not very likely to suggest the creation of all three states, since its terms of reference implied it could at most suggest one new state in a region. A clearer indication was the following:

*The Chairman, Sir Henry Willink, had been a minister in the wartime British cabinet and then became the head of Magdalene College at Cambridge University; Philip Mason, who wrote most of the report, was Director of the Race Relations Institute; one of the remaining two members had been in the Indian Civil Service and the other, the only one with West African experience, Deputy Governor in the former Gold Coast.[14]

the chief advocate for the Cross River State was a NCNC supporter; he stated that he had the personal approval of Dr. Azikiwe and displayed a telegram from him stating, "Memorandum Cross River excellent go ahead"; the covering letter describing the memorandum, however, stated that the motive for its submission was "to break that atmosphere in the unanimity of the COR demand on the one hand and to save our faces with our people on the other."[18]

The Action Group was accused by the Midwest State Movement of similarly working against the Midwest while at the same time claiming to support it. Following its consistent course since the 1955 resolution of the Western House of Assembly, the party advocated the creation of a Midwest Region. However, applying its principle of ethnic self-determination, the area which the party contended should be included within the state was less than the whole of Benin and Delta Provinces, the area sought by the Midwest State Movement. The Action Group argued that the Itsekeri of Warri Division, and the people of Akoko-Edo Division who had increasingly adopted Yoruba customs and whose language is related to Yoruba, should remain attached to the Yoruba West upon which they bordered. The Ijaw in the Niger Delta should be united with their fellow Ijaw of Rivers Province in the East in a separate state, and the Ibo living on the Western Region side of the Niger river should be united with the rest of the Ibo in the Eastern Region. Though they could accept the loss of the others, without the western Ibo, said the Midwest State Movement, they would not have a state worth having; even to suggest such a state was "a subtle attempt to discredit the whole idea."[19] Perhaps the Movement was correct in its analysis of Action Group motives. But later events saw the Action Group support a Midwest Region, including within it the Western Ibo so long as it believed there was a chance that the other regions would also be divided.

After public sittings in eighteen Nigerian cities and additional private sessions, the Commission issued its report recommending against the creation of any new regions. The Commission said that most proposed new regions would themselves create new minority problems. Within their borders there were groups afraid of their minority status in the proposed regions. Thus, in the Midwest, "in Warri and the Western Ijaw Division dismay would be much more prevalent than pleasure"; in COR "many of the other tribes expressed at least as much fear of Efiks and Ibibios as of Ibos"; and, though the Tiv and some others strongly favored a Middle Belt Region, "there was some anxiety at the thought of a state in which the Tivs would be the dominating element; one witness expressed the view succinctly in the statement that he preferred the Fulani because they were further away."[20]

In locations where a boundary could be drawn which would not itself create a new minority problem, the Commission found that the new state would be too small, or too poor or, as in Ogoja, that there was no strong sentiment for it. They found strong support for unity among the Ijaw in the Niger Delta but, noting the economic backwardness of the area and the difficulty of combating the creeks, barriers which produced backwardness, they reasoned that "to sever themselves from the wealthier parts of the Region is surely not the way to get the schools and floating dispensaries they want."[21]

For the North, the Commission was impressed by the NPC's argument that the Region would be seriously harmed by the loss of the Middle Belt, particularly in the Civil Service, where the departure of Middle Belters would leave "the rump of the North without experienced officials."[22]

The Minorities Commission also dealt with the dispute as to whether the Yoruba of Ilorin and Kabba should be transferred to the Western Region. That troubled it more than anything else. It found that natural ties between the Yoruba groups had grown stronger, and would probably grow stronger still, while the historical enmity of the Ilorin Yoruba for the Ibadan and other Yoruba was growing weaker. But, said the Commission, there was great advantage to the educated young men of Ilorin in staying with the North; taxation would probably be higher in the West, and many people would suffer by the "revolutionary speeding up" of the area's democratization that would follow transfer to the West.[23] The Commission, which based its chief conclusions upon its faith in democracy, appeared to fear too much democracy too fast. There had, to be sure, been votes by a number of local government bodies in favor of joining the West, but the Commission said it was not sure the people had understood the issue when they chose their representatives.

Finally, after much anguish, the Commission recommended that a plebiscite be held in the Ilorin-Kabba area if, and only if, all parties agreed to the details of its supervision and agreed to abide by the result. If, in such a plebiscite, 60 per cent voted for transfer, the transfer should be made. The NPC, as must have been expected, succeeded in successfully resisting the holding of any such plebiscite and the area remains part of the North.

95

The Commission expressed fear that the creation of new regions would perpetuate tribal differences and set back efforts to build a nation. Until recently, it said, tribal differences had been diminishing through education and greater contact in urban centers. Then the anticipation of independence and the transfer of power to Nigerian hands brought about "a sharp recrudescence of tribal feeling." That, said the Commission, should gradually die down again and therefore:

> It would be a pity if, at the moment when Nigerians achieved independence, separate states had been designed which enshrined tribal separation in a political form designed to be permanent.[24]

It is worth commenting at this point on the counterargument that the Action Group, which continued to support the creation of new states, later made. The party manifesto published shortly before independence began by taking a position with which few disagreed:

> Nigeria must be rid of the trappings of tribalism. The individual must be taught to regard the nation as an organic whole demanding from him a loyalty superior to that which he owes to his small ethnic unit.

Then it went on to argue that it was "to achieve this end" that

> The Action Group advocated the division of the country into states based on linguistic or ethnic lines. Any system of political grouping which allows of the domination of one ethnic unit by another strikes a blow at the unity of the country. So long as one unit is constitutionally made to occupy a position of inferiority to another, so long will the inferior unit exaggerate and emphasize its own ethnic identity — a situation which bids fair to imperil the national solidarity.[25]

The Action Group was stating a truism — ethnic jealousy and hostility will obviously be greater when one ethnic group is "made to occupy a position of inferiority" than when it feels secure. The Minorities Commission undoubtedly accepted that proposition but, beginning with the premise that it was affirmatively undesirable to have more states, asked whether security for the minorities could be attained through ways other than the creation of new states, and concluded that it could.

Considering the Commission's premise, its judgment will appear right or wrong depending upon whether in the light of hindsight the devices that it concluded could allay the fears of minorities without new states in fact succeed in doing so. The enormous majority in favor of a Midwest Region (570 thousand as opposed to 7 thousand) suggests that it underestimated the strength of minority secessionist sentiment, as does the continuing unrest in the Tiv area. But it is too early yet to tell whether the Commission's judgment — given its major premise — was correct.

The Commission and the British Government that framed its terms of reference are perhaps at fault, however, for so uncritically accepting the premise that new regions were affirmatively undesirable. The validity of the point that new regions would tend to enshrine tribal separatism was somewhat undercut by the fact that the new regions proposed would, as the Commission itself pointed out, have been multitribal. The observation that new regions would add to the cost of government was correct, though some compensating savings would derive from transportation and administrative efficiencies. Some new regions would have been hard pressed to find administrative talent, though reduction in the size of the existing regions would have released talent from them. All those matters are quibbles. But more significant was the failure of the Commission to consider (or at least to comment upon) whether it was dangerous for the federation to enter upon independence with one region larger in population and area than the rest of the regions combined.

In any event the Commission concluded that the minorities could be made to feel secure without new regions. It recommended some formal constitutional safeguards to allay fears. Ultimate control of the police should rest in federal hands, though there should be consultation with regional officials concerning the use of the police. The theory was that the risk to minorities came from regional governments, whereas the Federal Government was more likely to be multitribal and therefore neutral. The Commission also recommended that the Constitution guarantee certain fundamental human rights — freedom of religion, freedom of speech, freedom from discrimination, and the right to a fair trial, for example. With some modifications, those recommendations were incorporated into the Constitution and are discussed in later chapters.

But the Commission placed most faith in democracy. It argued that upon independence the Federal Government would become more significant as the powers over foreign affairs, defense, and the ultimate responsibility for law and order in the country was passed to Nigerian hands. The major parties would then focus their energies upon winning control of the Federal Government, and to do so they would have to seek the votes of minorities. Furthermore, the monolithic solidarity of the majority ethnic groups should gradually break down. That had already begun to happen among the Yoruba, the most highly educated group in Nigeria. If more than one party had a chance to win the support of the majority ethnic group, each would have to appeal to the minorities.* If, as planned, Nigeria follows the road of liberal democracy and parliamentary government, said the Commission, "votes will count and in the last resort it is the votes that will win fair treatment for the minorities."[26] That conclusion points up a paradox. Though democracy is a safeguard for Nigeria's minorities, perhaps the greatest threat to democracy is the ethnic parochialism of which the minorities' issue is one aspect. For an elite may come which finds itself national in spirit and which becomes impatient of democracy which rests upon a people more divided than it is.

Independence or New States

The Commission's report was reviewed by the Resumed Constitutional Conference held in London in the fall of 1958. There the Colonial Secretary, commenting that the Conference could not "lightly disregard" the Commission's unequivocal conclusions, presented those pressing for new states with a cruel choice. If Nigeria wanted to be independent in 1960, no new states could be created. Nigeria must either abandon its demand for independence in 1960 and agree to put the question of whether there were to be new states to an election or series of plebiscites (following which, even if the results were favorable, there would have to be another constitutional conference at which those opposed would be consulted), or it could continue to press its claim for early independence. No political party which hoped to be a major force in an independent Nigeria could afford further to delay independence. Hence, faced with the Colonial Secretary's choice, all the major delegations reaffirmed their desire for early independence.[27]

Instead of creating any new regions before independence, the Conference agreed upon a procedure by which they could be created after independence. The effect of the formula adopted was that a new region could not be established unless two-thirds of both houses of the Federal

---

*In three areas the Commission recommended special bodies that would periodically publicize the treatment of minorities and thereby hopefully bring the democratic processes to bear to right any wrongs. For the Edo-speaking peoples in the West, Calabar Province in the East, and the Ijaws of West and East, the Commission proposed that a council or board be selected which would respectively lay before the Western and Eastern legislature and Federal Parliament annual reports on the development of the area and the welfare of its peoples. Those recommendations, with minor modifications, were adopted in the Constitution.

Parliament, two of the three existing regions, and 60 per cent of the registered voters in the proposed region agreed that it should be.[28] But that formula did not come into effect until independence.

At the Resumed Constitutional Conference, both the minorities and the Action Group argued that the creation of new states was not incompatible with the early grant of independence. Some minority spokesmen had already said they would prefer to delay independence if they were not to get the security of their own state.[29] Such remarks had provoked heated replies from, for example, the pro-NCNC *West African Pilot,* which said, "If the tree of unity must be watered by the blood of insurgents against the order of society and constitutional authority, let us not hesitate to do it."[30]

The Action Group would not ask the British to delay independence, but it decided to fight the 1959 election on a platform calling for creation of more states before independence in 1960. That was a decision for which it was to be made to suffer.

Before the election all three regional governments took steps which they hoped would quiet the fears of the minorities in their region. The most concrete was taken in the North and that was the enactment of the Penal Code, which replaced the system of Muslim and customary law that had hitherto been applicable in the native courts. (Muslim law discriminated against non-Muslims and it and customary law gave the judges wide discretion to define and punish offenses.)

In each region the minorities' fears had stemmed from their beliefs, first, that the majority ethnic group would always vote as a unit and hence control the regional government, and, second, that the regional government was overwhelmingly powerful and thus able to damage their interests. Limited steps were taken in each region to counter the second belief by increasing local autonomy.[31] In the Eastern Region, legislation was enacted to provide for a provincial assembly in each province. Comprised of representatives of local councils and chiefs, it was to serve as a consultative body and an outlet for provincial opinion. In addition, a House of Chiefs was created as a second chamber of the Eastern Region Legislature. Since the chiefly tradition was strongest in the non-Ibo areas of the East, that in itself was a gesture to the minorities and the House was, moreover, organized to give weight to provincial interests.* The

---

*The House of Chiefs, however, like the previously existing House of Chiefs in the West, had only limited delaying powers. The Northern House of Chiefs had greater power.

provincial lines were redrawn and new provinces created in order to decrease the fears of minorities who had been combined with Ibos in various provinces. The non-Ibo areas of Ogoja, for example, were separated from the Ibo areas.

In the West, the Government had already established an Advisory Council for the Midwest Area chaired by Chief Anthony Enahoro, Minister for Midwest affairs. Pursuant to the recommendation of the Minorities Commission, it agreed to declare the Midwest, minus Warri Division and Akoko-Edo District, as a minority area, with a minority council the majority of whose membership would be composed of the legislators elected to the Federal House of Representatives and Western House of Assembly rather than nominated by the Government.* As with the provincial bodies in the Eastern Region, the minority council was an outlet for public opinion and a means to publicize the treatment of the area rather than a body independent from the Regional Government or possessing any direct power of its own.

In the North, there were no provincial assemblies created, and the Minorities Commission had not recommended that any minority council be established. The Government did, however, establish provincial courts of appeals and promised to nominate one of its twelve Federal Senators from each of the twelve provinces in the Region. The West made a similar commitment, and the Eastern Government agreed to consult with the opposition on the nomination of Senators.[32]

One reason for making those changes and promises was to retain or attract minority support in the election for the Federal House of Representatives in 1959. That election was held to determine who would govern independent Nigeria and is a subject to which we now turn.

---

*The Eastern Region was committed to create an analogous Minority Council for Calabar.

The 1959 Election

Much was at stake in the 1959 election for the Federal House of Representatives. The United Kingdom had promised that if the newly elected government passed a resolution asking for independence on October 1, 1960, independence would be granted. To the victor would come the glory of forming the first government of a free Nigeria. For the first time Nigerians were to control their own foreign relations. At home it was still to be decided whether the existing regions were to be divided and new ones created. All the power, prestige, and patronage of the largest government in Africa was at stake.

In the outgoing House of Representatives, Alhaji Abubakar Tafawa Balewa, second in command of the NPC, presided as Prime Minister over a "National Government" that included NCNC and Action Group ministers in addition to those from the NPC. After constitutional reforms in 1957, he had been appointed as the country's first Prime Minister, and had formed a coalition government with both of the other major parties in order to present a united front until independence was won. Now the struggle for independence was all but over, and each political party sought to garner the fruits of the struggle for itself.

Both Chief Awolowo and Dr. Azikiwe, as leaders of the Action Group and NCNC, stood for election to the Federal House, announcing that they would give up their positions as regional premiers. The Sardauna of Sokoto, the leader of the NPC, on the other hand, decided to stay on as Premier of the North and to let Alhaji Tafawa Balewa continue to lead the NPC in the Federal Government.

The NPC, like the Sardauna, avoided the South. The party entered only two candidates in the South, and formed a few alliances with very small parties. The NPC presumably had nothing against votes from the South but realized undoubtedly that a party that did not permit Southerners to join could expect to win few votes from them. The party's ability to concentrate on the Northern Region alone was enhanced by the fact that the North contained more than half of the seats at stake, 174 of 312.*

The effect of the size of the North upon the NPC's national political strategy has been one of the crucial political facts in Nigeria. Whether or not it has been responsible for NPC and Northern insularity is debatable, but it is clear that it has made it easier for the NPC to continue to emphasize regional interests. As long as one region has more than half of the seats in the House of Representatives, the forces of democracy — upon which the Minorities Commission placed such trust in recommending against new regions — cannot operate with their full force to break down regional insularity or to minimize ethnic and religious differences that coincide with regional differences.

The same mathematical logic which enabled the NPC to concentrate on the North alone put pressure upon the NCNC and the Action Group, who were national by inclination, to seek to win a majority of seats by contesting the election in every region, including the North.† The tactics of the NCNC and the Action Group were very different, however. The NCNC did not push for new regions and, while critical of remnants of feudalism and political repression in the North, was also understanding; the Action Group put its trust in the minorities and the strength of their desire for new regions, and minced no words in criticizing the NPC.

In addition to the major parties, there were several minor parties con-

*A side effect of the great power given to the NPC by the North's size was that it attracted the support of some minority movements. The Niger Delta Congress allied itself with the NPC at the time of the 1959 election, stating that it aimed to make the Niger Delta a federal territory.[1]

†The substantial size of the Eastern and Western Regions, however, does increase the likelihood that a political party could afford to limit its efforts to a single region. Therefore, as with the size of the North, though to a lesser degree, the large size of those regions could limit the pressure a democratic system places upon political parties to appeal to all elements of a nation. In fact, as described in the next chapter, the Action Group split in 1962 in part over the question whether it should confine its efforts to the Western Region.

testing the election. In each region there was a party whose efforts were limited to obtaining the support of the dominant majority in the region. In the North that party, of course, was the NEPU. In the East it was the Democratic Party of Nigeria and the Cameroons, composed of former NCNC members, led by K. O. Mbadiwe, who had quarrelled with Azikiwe and been expelled from the party. In the West it was the Mabolaje, whose efforts were limited to Ibadan where it represented the interests of the predominantly Muslim, long-time inhabitants against the predominantly Christian and Western-educated newcomers supporting the Action Group. In the North and East, and to a lesser extent the West, there were also minor parties representing the interests of minority groups. Many of these allied themselves with the Action Group and sought secession. But the Niger Delta Congress allied itself with the NPC and sought federal status, and others, such as parties representing the Idoma and Igala tribes in the North, did not seek secession.

There was a different tone to the campaigns of the three major parties. The Action Group mounted the most intensive, best organized, and expensive campaign that had ever been seen in Nigeria. During the campaign, the Western Region Government, which it controlled, launched the first television service in Africa; the party's most noticeable campaign device — the use of helicopters to fly party leaders to rallies — was also expected to impress upon the country that the Action Group was best equipped to deal with the modern, scientific, technological world that Nigeria was about to enter on its own. The helicopters would descend upon dumfounded pagan villages or into quiet Muslim towns and out would step the neatly dressed, articulate Action Group spokesman. It is possible that such tactics backfired. The NPC vigorously and repeatedly asserted that the helicopters, and indeed all the Action Group's aggressive campaigning, were offensive to the Northern people; the helicopters came to represent to the NPC all they hated about the Action Group. Thus, Alhaji Aliyu, Makaman Bida, Northern Minister of Finance, told a rally that the helicopters had violated tradition by enabling their occupants to hover over compounds and see women in purdah, "a crime for which they will never be forgiven."[2] The NCNC as well charged the Action Group with violating sacred traditions with its helicopters. While the party was holding a ceremony at the Lagos grave of Herbert Macaulay, an Action Group helicopter had irreverently dropped leaflets on their heads, complained Dr. Azikiwe.[3]

Contrasted to the flashy, hustling, modern style of the Action Group, the NPC was sober, dignified, and conservative. Its ability to solicit the public's vote "in the most decent way" was reason enough to vote for it, said the Northern Minister of Education to a rally at Zaria.[4] The party manifesto promised that its government would be founded upon "respect for traditional institutions," belief in "orderly progress," and "above all, its Government will be based on fear of God."[5]

The dominant note in the NCNC campaign was emphasis upon its great contributions to the independence movement. Nigeria was said to owe a debt of gratitude to the NCNC for its work and sacrifice as the first national political party.[6] Reminders that Dr. Azikiwe had been the first of the party leaders to enter the nationalistic struggle were made again and again. Interestingly enough, when the NCNC reviewed the record of the other parties it was not the NPC, which had sought to delay independence to catch up with the rest of the country, but the Action Group, which had become at least as aggressive as the NCNC in demanding independence, that the party condemned, asking in its manifesto:

> Where was the Action Group, which now poses as the champion of Nigerian Independence, during the early and bitter periods of this national struggle? Surely it was in the womb of its tribalistic mother and today it is making a devilish bid to reap where it did not sow.[7]

No such reference was made to the NPC.

All parties promised to bring more schools, roads, hospitals, water pipes, and other welfare services to the people. The Action Group relied heavily on its record in supplying welfare services to the people of Western Nigeria, a record made easier by the fact that the West had been the richest of the three regions. "What this party has done for one Region, and more than that, the party and its allies will do for the whole country if they win the Federal elections," said the Action Group.[8] Even the NPC, despite its strong regionalism, advocated Federal Government schools in all regions open to students of all tribes. During the campaign the NCNC abolished fees for a fourth year of primary school. In emphasis on welfare, there was little to choose between the parties.

There were slight differences on foreign affairs among the parties. Both the Action Group, particularly Chief Awolowo, and the NPC came out strongly in favor of continued close association with Great Britain and the other Western democracies. Neutralism, said leaders of both parties, was immoral. Awolowo, when speaking of the Western and Communist worlds, argued

To pretend that neither of two diametrically opposed ideological camps is right or wrong, especially if we occupy an influential position in the assembly of nations, is to encourage evil-doing, and to damp the ardour for well-doing.

To woo both East and West for aid is a tactic "both disreputable and dangerous," he said, "acts of double-dealing — whether diplomatic or otherwise — never pay in the end."[9]*

The NPC manifesto stated that its foreign policy would be based upon principles as well as national interest and that therefore neutralism must be ruled out. "It is to those countries whose policies are animated by the same beliefs as her own that Nigeria must look for real friendship and support," said the NPC. "For this reason over and above her membership in the Commonwealth Nigeria must maintain the closest relationship with the United Kingdom."[11]

Chief Awolowo's similar argument, though long, is worth quoting in full in view of his later shift of position.

There are two distinct ideological camps in the world today: the Western democracies and the communist bloc. For reasons which I will presently give, my preference is unhesitatingly and unequivocally for the Western democracies. No nation in the world is absolutely good or absolutely evil. There is still a colour-bar in the Western democracies. Negroes in America are still being discriminated against, and can still be lynched with impunity. For her part, Britain is still guilty, as before, though in a decreasing order of magnitude, of injustice toward the black peoples in East and Central Africa. But such evils as are committed in the countries of the Western democracies toward the weaker peoples of the world are not only diminishing, but are being constantly subjected to strong and sharp criticism in those countries by their nationals, without any risk to their lives or personal freedom. If you did likewise behind the iron curtain you would not live to fight another day.[12]

The NCNC, and its NEPU ally, professed a desire to remain in the British Commonwealth, and for a "very intimate and cordial relationship" with the United States and promised to "spike neutrality because it is defeatist and lacks moral conviction." More than the other two parties, however, they saw an advantage in increasing contact with the Communist bloc, though they were "strongly opposed to Communism as a way of life." Their program was described not as neutrality

---

*Awolowo found support for his attitude toward neutralism in the Bible: "I know thy works, that thou art neither cold nor hot: I would thou wert cold or hot. So then because thou are lukewarm and neither cold nor hot, I will spue thee out of my mouth."[10]

but as "an independent non-alignment policy making sure that Nigeria does not follow any nation or group of nations blindly."[13] As the campaign developed, the NCNC increasingly attacked the Action Group for favoring alignment with the West, a policy which Dr. Azikiwe said in an election eve appeal "can violate the integrity of the nation."[14]

The second foreign policy issue in the campaign was the attitude taken by the parties toward the movement for political Pan-Africanism, the union of African States, of which Ghana's Kwame Nkrumah was the best known apostle. All the major parties agreed that it was at present premature, though the NCNC — and even more the NEPU — were extremely enthusiastic in endorsement of political union as a long-term objective.[15] Nkrumah became a secondary issue because of the Action Group's attacks on him for repression of the Ghanaian opposition and undermining of liberal democracy. Such attacks upon "Ghana's internationally respected nationalistic Prime Minister" showed, said the NCNC, that the Action Group planned to "carry its deeply imbued tribalistic and jingoistic internal policy into the international sphere."[16]

On one issue the NCNC-NEPU alliance and the Action Group united against the NPC. Political liberty was being suppressed in the North and their supporters were being victimized, they protested. Permits for rallies kept being denied to NCNC, NEPU, or Action Group campaigners.[17] The NPC controlled virtually every native authority (local government unit) in the northern two-thirds of the region, and the native authorities had the police power to control political demonstrations. They were not hesitant to use that power. The alkali, responsible for justice in the native courts, were almost invariably NPC supporters whose jobs depended upon the good will of their respective emirs, who backed the NPC.

While one should be wary of accusing any alkali of unfairness, there being no clear proof, it seems likely that many remembered their strong belief in the NPC's conservative ideals when it came time to deliver judgment in cases involving supporters of other parties. And again, though protests against repression in the North have been extremely poorly documented, one gets the strong impression that a disproportionate number of cases have involved opposition members. Upon appeal many of those convictions have been reversed. Ibrahim Iman, leader of the Bornu Youth Movement, was convicted of accepting a bribe when he had been Minister of Works in the Bornu Native Authority, but upon appeal there was found to be no evidence.[18]

Occasionally opposition leaders have been convicted by the native courts for acts which clearly were not criminal. Sule Maito and seven other leaders of the Ilorin Talaka Parapo were convicted of holding an unlawful assembly on the basis of a peaceful meeting at one of their houses to discuss the construction of bridges and roads in Ilorin District.[19]* Certainly no one who has lived in Northern Nigeria could believe that opposition to the NPC in Northern Nigeria is looked upon with favor or that it is not risky.

The difficulties faced by opposition campaigners in many parts of the North were a function of public hostility and conservatism as well as official discouragement. The Action Group and the NCNC-NEPU alliance at times attacked traditional rulers as well as seeking to reform them. In the villages of Northern Nigeria, the people are often not yet prepared to tolerate criticism of the chiefs, let alone oppose them.

Violence is close to the surface in all political campaigns in Nigeria, South as well as North. The following is a sample of stories that appeared during the 1959 campaign in the *Lagos Daily Times,* an independent British-owned but Nigerian-edited newspaper:

Four NCNC-NEPU supporters accompanying Dr. Azikiwe on his tour of the North attacked at Bida; 7 NEPU men hospitalized following fight after the tour stops at Nguru; 11 Democratic Party of Nigeria and the Cameroons and NCNC men charged with breach of the peace at DPNC meeting in Enugu, Eastern Region, following fighting and damage to Action Group helicopter; NPC member of Northern House of Assembly sentenced to two years imprisonment for assault on Action Group organizing secretary;[21] Governor-General Robertson makes broadcast calling for an end to violence; all public processions banned in the Western Region from November 26 to December 8; Governor-General Robertson makes a second radio broadcast decrying violence; troops moved to Bauchi, Bida, Funtua, Jos and Kano in the Northern Region to guard against violence; NEPU supporter killed in Bida Emirate after NPC meeting; 11 Action Group supporters in Calabar charged with being violent with intent to provoke a breach of the peace in that they "did sing and use abusive words" about the NCNC and throw stones and shoot arrows at NCNC cars.[22]

A further indication of the volatile nature of political competition in Nigeria, particularly in the North, can be found in the Report of the

---

*The Action Group Party Manager charged that when Sule Maito was in prison before his appeal succeeded he was made to collect "latrine refuse" from the Emir of Ilorin's palace.[20]

Nigerian Police for the year 1959. Of twenty-seven "Disturbances and Major Incidents" during the year, fourteen stemmed from conflicts between political parties, and of those, twelve were in the North.[23]

Despite the existence of political violence in the South as well as the North, the NCNC and the Action Group agreed that they were being victimized in the North. Both put pressure upon the Governor-General to bring into force the constitutional guarantees of fundamental rights that had been agreed upon at the 1958 Constitutional Conference so that they could rely upon them to protect their supporters campaigning in the North. In the midst of the campaign the Governor-General did make the guarantees operative.

The different ways in which the parties approached the question of new regions for minorities turned out to be more important than differences concerning foreign affairs, internal social services, or civil liberties. As always, the NPC was against the creation of a Middle Belt Region and any other reduction in the size of the North. The Action Group championed the cause of the minorities, promising if elected to create before independence a COR Region out of the East, a Midwest Region out of the West, and a Middle Belt Region out of the North.[24] The Action Group's aim was to capture enough seats in the Yoruba West, the minority areas, and (with less confidence) in the heartland of the North and East to win a majority of the seats.

The NCNC played a much more cautious game, aiming as much toward paving the way for a coalition with the NPC as toward winning a majority itself. That helps explain why the NCNC attacked the Action Group for failing to support the independence movement while not mentioning the NPC. Its tactics were most clearly revealed by its program with respect to new regions. Faithful homage was paid to the NCNC's traditional ideal of a strong central government with more, and weaker, regions. But that was for the vague future; for the present the only changes which the NCNC promised to support were those that ate into the Region controlled by the Action Group. It promised to create a Midwest Region and to extend the borders of the Federal Capital Territory (Lagos) to include more of the Yoruba West.[25] As for the North, the NCNC made its ability to collaborate with the NPC in the running of a national government one of its chief claims. By comparison, it said, the Action Group was unable to collaborate because of its "rigid intolerance." The NCNC added that it could "show sufficient understanding of the Northern Region to march with its people along the path of social democracy."[26] The party fully realized that to "collaborate" with the NPC after independence and to show "understanding" of the NPC version of Northern Nigeria it would have to avoid any support for a Middle Belt Region. So it did.

Dennis Osadebay, leader of the Midwest State Movement, advised others that a Midwest Region could only be created by voting for the NCNC. Although his advice undoubtedly was colored by the fact that he himself was a NCNC leader, he foresaw the future well. He said

> Owing to the constitutional position no one major party in this country can create new Regions without the concurrence of at least one other major party.* Owing to its habit of antagonizing all and sundry, the Action Group will not be able to count on the NPC or NCNC to aid it. So those who want the Midwest Region created must support the NCNC and its good friend the NPC who are the only parties capable of creating the Midwest Region.[27]

During the campaign there were indications that the NPC and the NCNC had reached an understanding that, though they might fight hard and bitterly for seats in the Northern Region, the Action Group was their common enemy and the major threat. In the North, Dr. Azikiwe would attack NPC victimization and oppression, warning that its continuation would lead eventually to a Communist-inspired revolt. Speakers for the NPC in the North told their audiences to vote against the NEPU, "because if the NEPU comes to power it will appoint an Ibo man [Dr. Azikiwe] as the first Prime Minister of Nigeria."[28] In the South, however, the NPC even gave some campaign help to conservative NCNC candidates against their Action Group opponents. S. A. Ajayi of Kabba Province, then Parliamentary Secretary to the Sardauna of Sokoto, was sent with a team to campaign for Chief Festus Okotie-Eboh in Warri, where he said there was a "common understanding" between the NPC and the NCNC and that it would be a "national calamity" if the Action Group won.[29]

Even in the North, the NPC was more hostile to the Action Group than it was to the NCNC or the NEPU. It was the Action Group that the Sardauna said would ban Islam, and it was Chief Awolowo who, he said, had shown contempt for Islam. That ugly charge could not be made with much success against the NCNC since it was represented in the North primarily by the NEPU, an essentially Muslim party whose

---

*That of course was true only so long as the existing party line-up, with each party strongly entrenched in one of the three regions, continued.

leader was a devout Muslim. The NPC had an altogether different attitude toward the NEPU opposition than toward the Action Group. The NEPU was a brother who had strayed, or, as the Sardauna put it in a later election, a "misguided youth."[30] The Action Group was the alien enemy, the brash intruder, and in 1959 the greater threat.

Voting for the 312 seats of the Federal House of Representatives finally took place[31] at the end of the second week of December 1959. Over 7 million persons voted for an extremely creditable turnout of just under 80 per cent of the registered voters. In the North almost 90 per cent of the registered voters cast a ballot. Abubakar Tafawa Balewa, Dr. Azikiwe, and Chief Awolowo all won in their own constituencies. The NPC was the party victor, emerging with 148 seats, only 9 shy of an absolute majority. It won 134 seats in the North; to that were added 14 allies or independents who declared for the NPC after the election.* The regional nature of the NPC was underscored by the fact that of the 134 seats and 2,027,194 votes it won itself, all the seats and all but 33,159 of the votes came from the North.

The NCNC-NEPU alliance received the greatest number of votes† but won the second largest number of seats — 89. Fifty-eight came from the East, where the NCNC won all 51 of the predominantly Ibo seats; 21 came from the West; 2 from Lagos; and 8 from the North. The alliance's total in the North was disappointingly low. The NEPU had shown greater strength in previous elections in the North even though various indirect methods of voting had reduced its eventual totals. It was expected that the first direct and designedly secret elections in the North would result in a much larger vote for the party of reform and protest. But as it turned out the NEPU only won 6 of the approximately 100 seats in the Islamic North. It is likely that its alliance with a tainted Southern party hurt it with the voters. It also may have been hurt by the great power of government, which has meant that parties in control of governments have good opportunity to enhance their control. Finally, many who sympathized with its objectives undoubtedly

---

*Seven of those added seats came from independents and the allied Igbirra Tribal Union in the North. Six persons elected in Ibadan by one wing of the feuding Mabolaje Grand Alliance declared for the NPC, and one seat was won in the East by the allied Niger Delta Congress.

†The NCNC-NEPU alliance received approximately 2.5 million votes while both the NPC and the Action Group received just under 2 million votes. Had women voted in the North, and voted in the same proportions as the Northern men, however, the NPC would have received the most votes.

reasoned that the best way to achieve their own career goals or to accomplish the reforming aims of NEPU was to work from within the NPC.

The Action Group's attempt to attract the votes of minorities through its promise to create new regions was a qualified success. In the North it and its allies won only 25 of the approximately 74 seats in the Middle Belt area. Its ally in the Islamic North, the Bornu Youth Movement, was swamped at the polls. Where the demand for a new region was the most intense, however, it had pockets of great strength, as in the Tiv area where its ally the UMBC won all 7 seats and 84 per cent of the vote. In the East, the result was the same. There was great strength in the Ibibio and Efik areas where the desire for secession was the strongest. The 14 seats the Action Group won, however, were less than half the seats in the COR area, though nearly two-thirds of the 22 non-Ibo seats. In the Midwest, non-Yoruba, area the party record was most disappointing; it won only 3 out of 18 seats (and after the election was joined by two victorious independents).

In all, the Action Group and its allies obtained 75 seats: 35 from the West (33 won by the party plus two independents who declared for it) 1 from Lagos, 25 from the North, and 14 from the East. Although the Action Group had not done as well with the minorities as it had hoped, it was the only one of the three major parties to win a majority of its seats outside the region of its traditional strength, and that was because of minority support.

The voting pattern demonstrates conclusively that the dominant factor in the 1959 election was ethnic, or regional-religious, cohesiveness. In the East the NCNC won all 51 of the Ibo seats, obtaining over 80 per cent of the vote in 25 of those constituencies. In the North, the NPC won over 80 per cent of the vote in 42 constituencies in Kano and Sokoto Provinces and Bornu Division. The NPC lost only a few seats in the North outside the Middle Belt, some of which, such as Kano East, were notable because of the number of Southerners registered in the constituency. In the West, the Action Group won 30 of the 35 Yoruba seats. All the NPC seats and almost two-thirds of the NCNC seats came from the regions which those parties respectively controlled. Though the Action Group won slightly more than half its seats outside the West, it won support in the North and East from minority ethnic groups expressing resentment or fear of the dominant majority in their region. From the election one could derive no clear picture of the direc-

111

tion in which the Nigerian voters would like their government to proceed, either in domestic policy or in foreign policy.*

A Coalition Government

Since no party had a majority of seats, it was necessary that a coalition government be formed. Governor-General Robertson gave Alhaji Abubakar Tafawa Balewa the first chance to form a government, and he succeeded in putting together an NPC-NCNC/NEPU coalition.†

The coalition was a strange one; it brought together the most conservative and the then most radical parties, and it put the NEPU into a coalition with the NPC at the federal level while it was its traditional rival in the Northern Region. But it was a natural consequence of the animosity that both the NPC and the NCNC felt toward the Action Group because of its efforts to create new states and stir up minority fears in their home regions. For the NCNC, moreover, the election results seemed to prove the need to cooperate with the NPC and concentrate the party's fire upon the Action Group. Their NEPU ally had done very badly against the NPC in the North, but they had done quite well against the Action Group in the West; that clearly was the place to strive in the future.

The coalition could not be said to be founded primarily upon a program for the development of national unity, but by design or not, it did avoid a very serious threat to the unity of the country that would have

---

*That is not to say that it is a purely academic exercise to consider the party programs and manifestos. To be sure there may not have been many votes that were changed by the manifestos. But sections of the manifestos were expressive of popular desires sometimes held in common — such as the emphasis upon welfare services — and sometimes held by particular groups — such as promises to create new regions. Furthermore, the presumed lack of attention by the vast majority of voters to matters such as foreign policy covered by the manifestos does not make views on those subjects any less significant. Indeed, the fact that only an elite takes an interest in a particular subject makes the views of the elite particularly significant.

†The NEPU received no ministries, and as between the NPC and the NCNC, the NCNC was definitely the junior partner in the cabinet. Nevertheless, among its ministries were some extremely significant ones: Finance, Information, Labour, and eventually Foreign Affairs. Dr. Azikiwe was not in the cabinet, but in January he became President of the Nigerian Senate, and in November 1960, six weeks after Independence, became the first Nigerian to hold the distinguished, but largely ceremonial, nonpolitical position of Governor-General.

arisen if the NCNC and the Action Group had arrayed themselves in a coalition against the NPC. The most basic tension within the country was between North and South. Perhaps the tension was less than it had been in 1953, when the North had come close to seceding because it felt the Southerners were pushing too hard for an independence in which the North would be unable to take care of itself. But the underlying causes of the tension had by no means disappeared. A government which excluded Northerners — other than the NEPU (which for all its vision was very much a minority party) and the secessionists allied with the Action Group — would certainly have kept alive and increased the tension.

The Role of the Sardauna

During the coalition negotiations, the Sardauna of Sokoto announced that he would retire from politics as soon as the negotiations were finished and, like his ancestor Usuman dan Fodio, hand over power to his lieutenants. Ten days later, he said that pressure from the party, public telegrams, etc., had changed his mind. The effect was a reminder that the Sardauna was still the leader of the country's most powerful party even though his lieutenant had been selected as Federal Prime Minister and he himself had not been a candidate.

The Sardauna has made it quite clear that his heart is in the North. Speaking shortly after independence, he said, "Consolidation of the North is what is uppermost in my mind and which I have achieved with God's help. And to show our thanks to God we shall continue to rule justly as we have hitherto done in the past. . . ."[32]

To consolidate the North, regional matters such as local government and education were more important than federal concerns like foreign affairs. Indicative of the priority given by the Sardauna to Northern Nigeria over Nigeria itself is the fact that his autobiography, written in 1961 and published in 1962, does not even refer to national independence in 1960. He finishes by saying it is fitting to stop the story with the granting of "our long-sought self-government."[33] The event he refers to is regional, not national, self-government.

Emotion as well as a reasoned judgment as to how best to help the North played a part in keeping the Sardauna in the North. The Sardauna's roots are deeply embedded in the Northern tradition to which his ancestors contributed so greatly. When speculation first arose that he was interested in becoming Nigeria's president if she became a republic, he stated with an aristocrat's air:

> My hereditary title is what I treasure and not the imported one. I am sure I have able lieutenants and not only able but also capable. I have implicit confidence in them and I have dedicated my life to their service. And with God's help, victory will always continue to be on my side. . . . I now leave it to other parties to have their squabbles but not within my party.[34]

The taste the Sardauna had had of political "squabbles" in the Federal Capital was not likely to have made him anxious to return for more. The insults and abuse from the "Southern elements" (as the Sardauna is wont to call his Southern countrymen)[35] during the 1953 crisis over the timing of self-government have always rankled. The Northern tradition stands against public criticism, not to speak of abuse, of those in authority. The Sardauna, just as was true for many of the British who were products of another aristocratic tradition, was not happy among the more exuberant, vociferous, volatile, and to him ill-mannered, Southerners.

The Sardauna is an extremely controversial man in Nigeria and is often bitterly attacked for giving a higher priority to the North than to the nation, for being too cautious about modernizing the North, and for being arrogant. It is obviously not healthy to have the nation's most powerful man emphasizing a region over the nation. Nevertheless, one of the most unhealthy characteristics of Nigeria, one of the greatest obstacles to national unity, is the backwardness of the North. Though the Sardauna does not particularly assert the national interest in emphasizing the needs of the North, and indeed sometimes aggravates North-South tension by appearing to be blind to the needs and aspirations of the South, the tendency of his program, if not his public relations, is to serve the long-term interests of the nation by concentrating upon overcoming that backwardness.

It is correct that the Sardauna is at times cautious about social change in the North. To endanger the prestige of the emirs, "or even to remove any of their traditional trappings, would be to set the country back for years,"[36] he has said. Any other attitude would be surprising coming from a man who is so much a product of the North's tradition. But the Sardauna has also taken steps to reduce the independent power of the emirs, both by increasing the checks of the regional government against them and by encouraging increased power of the councilors around them.

It may well be that the social structure of the North should be changed more rapidly. But once again, in defense of the Sardauna's historic role, it should be said that his impeccable qualifications within the Northern traditional order have made it a great deal easier to accomplish the changes that have occurred.

On to Independence

In January 1960 the Federal House of Representatives convened and unanimously passed a motion calling upon the United Kingdom to fulfill its promise and grant Nigeria its independence. The final constitutional arrangements were then completed, an enabling act passed by the British Parliament without dissent, and arrangements begun for October 1, 1960, when the new green and white flag of Nigeria would replace the Union Jack. That was a happy time in Nigeria. Yet there was much about the country's political scene that was worrisome.

Its strongest political party, the NPC, was not a national party. It did not even permit Southerners to join, and the regional government it controlled admittedly discriminated against Southerners. It was not possible to become a Northerner by settling in the North. One had to be born into a Northern tribe. No matter how long a non-Northerner had lived in the North, he was to be treated in certain respects as an outcast, since his tribe was not indigenous to the North. There were restrictions placed upon his use of land that were not placed upon a Northerner. Southerners were being systematically eliminated from the regional civil service, and even Englishmen and other foreigners were preferred to them.[37]

The regional nature of the NPC and the discriminatory policy of the Northern Government against Southerners were both terrible threats to the unity of the country. Of course the NPC policy was understandable: the North was still very much behind the South, and special privileges for her people were necessary if it was not to remain a permanently backward area. Despite the great political power of the NPC, Northern backwardness still weakened the Region greatly. Thus despite NPC control of many ministries at the top, at the time of independence only 1 per cent of the Federal civil service was from the North, and of those most were in the lower grades.[38] But understandable or not, the NPC policy of discrimination was very cruel to those Southerners living in the North who were affected by it, and was resented by all politically aware non-Northerners. That the nation's largest and strongest political party was regional and not national would keep alive regional, ethnic, and (because of its close association with Islam) religious jealousies.

To a lesser extent the other two major parties were also regional and ethnic. Of course they were national in aim, admitted people from any region or ethnic group as members, and in the past election had won seats in all three regions. But the election had shown that both still found their most solid support in a single cohesive ethnic group. Every one of the Ibo seats in the East had gone to the NCNC. The Yoruba had been less solid in their support of the Action Group, but a large majority had supported it, and the party that had begun as the political outlet of the Yorubas was still closely associated with them.

That the three parties had a strong ethnic and regional cast reflected the difficulty Nigeria was having in breaking down barriers between her people, and in turn made it more difficult to break the barriers down. Whether or not it is their intent to do so, such parties keep alive the fears of minority groups. Minority-group fear leads to agitation and accusations that in turn tend to make the majority more cohesive. The solid, seemingly unshakable, support that the Ibo gave the NCNC and that the Islamic Northerners gave the NPC were also responsible for the Action Group's desperate tactic of championing the cause of minorities in the North and East. The theoretical justification for that tactic was that after new regions were created ethnic jealousy would subside, but the Action Group agitation in the meantime added to ethnic fears and jealousies. The agitation did so when the new nation approaching independence particularly needed them to subside.

With independence won, the great question was whether the enthusiasm born of independence would give rise to a new cohesive spirit. A new problem was whether the nation would be able to agree upon a foreign policy that would bring it closer together. Or, if not that, could it change the emphasis from single-minded devotion to regional competition, or would the possibility of union with some tribal groups divided by Nigeria's frontier mean that tribal jealousies within Nigeria would even be accentuated by the acceptance of responsibility over foreign policy? In domestic politics the struggle between the governing coalition and the Action Group increasingly became the focal point.

Opposition or Treason

What is the role of an opposition party in a country that is not yet sure whether it is a nation? Is it inevitable that the opposition will be driven to support secession and sedition? What is the attitude toward opposition and criticism of a government of a newly freed colony that feels acutely the sting of its people being thought by many unfit to govern themselves? And in a country where the economy is undeveloped (and largely controlled by foreigners), so that the power of government is far, far greater than the power of any other indigenous institution, will the beneficiaries of all that power even contemplate their replacement?

All of those questions reflect problems in Nigeria. To none is the answer simple. They are the questions underlying the subject of this chapter: the increasingly rough struggle between the governing coalition and the Action Group during the first years after independence.

The Action Group Threat

After the 1959 election the Action Group made a concerted effort to capture the support of the country's impatient, emotional, discontented, and radical youth.

The party laid most stress on the charge that the Federal Government was soft on colonialism. In an ex-colonial country where those who have been awakened burn with desire to prove their independence, there is no more serious charge. Nigeria was derided by the Action Group for being too closely aligned with the Western world, particularly Great Britain.* She was said to be a "most faithful and pusillanimous train-bearer of Britain and her NATO allies."[1] Nigeria had signed a defense pact with Great Britain which gave Britain limited military training facilities and air-staging rights in Nigeria. The pact, Chief Awolowo claimed, had been extorted from Nigeria by the British, who had made it a condition for the granting of independence and used "bare-faced, unabashed and undue influence."[2] Several hundred students demonstrated in the streets of Lagos and broke for a moment into the Senate Building after the NPC and NCNC/NEPU members of the Federal Parliament approved the defense pact with England. Here clearly was a popular issue.

While Chief Awolowo did not abandon the distaste for the Communist world that he had shown during the 1959 campaign, he soon began to contend that Nigeria was too dependent upon the West economically and that therefore it should increase its trade with the Communist bloc. That would not be dangerous, he said, using the following analogy:

> When a Christian goes to the market or when a Mohammedan goes to the market and he wants to sell some goods, he does not go about asking about the faith of the buyer. He sells to the highest bidder — when he wants to buy he goes to the cheapest market. He does not go about asking whether the man he is buying from is a pagan or a Christian.[3]

At the same time as he was urging disengagement from England and increased contact with the Communist East, Chief Awolowo found much fault with the Western countries as he changed his focus from their democratic beliefs at home (which he had praised in the 1959 campaign) to their colonial policies. After the turmoil following the Congo's independence, he said that

> Belgium's economic enslavement has reasserted itself, [the] turmoil, famine, death and other evils which afflicted the young Republic were deliberately fomented and instigated by the Western imperialists as an essential prelude to the restoration and strengthening of their former economic stranglehold.[4]

Students had again demonstrated in Lagos when it was announced that Patrice Lumumba had been murdered, and once again it was clear that Chief Awolowo was telling many of the country's youth what they

---

*The foreign policy issues raised by the Action Group are discussed more extensively in Chapter 12; here they are merely mentioned to show that the Action Group was taking the popular side of every issue — doing so demogically, claimed the Government.

wanted to hear, what their emotions craved after long, degrading, and deadening years of colonialism.

In its policy for Africa, Nigeria was a stooge for the colonialists, the opposition charged; the Monrovia Conference of African Heads of State which Nigeria had cosponsored, and which had been boycotted by the more radical Casablanca powers, had been inspired and financed by the Western allies. The Government's advocacy of functional cooperation among African States instead of quick political union was contrary to the "climate of progressive opinion." When the Nigerian delegate at the United Nations in 1961 put forward a resolution calling for the ouster of colonial regimes from all of Africa, but made 1970 the terminal date for colonialism, it showed for certain, said an Action Group columnist, that Nigeria was the "pusillanimous stooge" of the colonial powers.[5] The praise which Nigeria received from many in Britain and America for being moderate was turned against the Government at home. It can be embarrassing to be called a good boy.

Perhaps more than in any other attack upon the Government the Action Group's attacks upon its foreign policy seemed to strike a popular response. The NCNC parliamentarian Dr. Kalu Ezera, author of the major work on Nigeria's constitutional history, said that he had also found "dissatisfaction in the whole country [and] . . . despondency in the rank and file of the youth," as he pleaded for a "dynamic and positive policy which will give leadership to this country, and the whole of the African continent."[6]

Dr. Ezera accurately reported the mood of much of the country when he spoke in the year after independence. And the voice of the Action Group became the loudest in calling for dynamism, boldness, and kick-the-heels-in-the-air-and-throw-off-the-wigs enthusiasm. Often, as when Chief Anthony Enahoro, Action Group shadow Foreign Minister, called for a more spirited foreign policy, the words had power of their own. Thus, he said:

> We want a guiding line, something to inspire us. The Americans speak of life, liberty and the pursuit of happiness. God gave us life, our leaders gave us liberty. We want the happiness of pursuit.[7]

The second major theme in the Action Group's appeal to radical opinion was that the country remained in "economic bondage" to foreigners.[8] The party's suggested remedy was nationalization, said to be with fair compensation, of industries such as the tin mining companies that were "basic" or "vital" but which were in foreign hands. It is a bit difficult to determine exactly what the Action Group would have taken over. Its ideological manifesto, entitled *Democratic Socialism*, which was agreed upon shortly before independence, advocated a planned economy with a public sector run by the state and a private sector open to free enterprise without suggesting what would be in the public and what in the private sector.[9] Later the party often seemed merely to be arguing in favor of the principle of nationalization without much attention to specific action.

Where the Action Group was in opposition (particularly in the Federal Parliament and in the Eastern House of Assembly), the strongest supporters of the nationalization policy were found. Being in opposition, those men were able to talk in general terms without having to clarify their position by action. In the Western Region, which the party controlled and where it could have acted, however, Chief S. L. Akintola, who replaced Chief Awolowo as Premier when Awolowo went to the Federal House, was opposed to the new policy. In Nigeria Chief Awolowo would demand nationalization of basic industries, and at the same time, Chief Akintola, the party's deputy leader, would be traveling in high style through Europe or North America assuring investors of his government's firm policy against nationalization.

In reply to Chief Awolowo's speeches, the Federal Government took a firm stand against nationalization beyond the extent to which "public utilities, shipping, airways, railways, power, communications and Marketing Boards are already nationalized."[10]* Chief Festus S. Okotie-Eboh, Federal Finance Minister, put forward the Government's case: to develop the local economy the country needs capital from outside; to attract capital it is necessary not to frighten investors; money spent to buy out existing businesses could be used to attract or aid new business; if the Government wastes its money it will not receive foreign aid.

Perhaps Chief Okotie-Eboh and the Government were winning the intellectual debate; it is certain that Chief Awolowo and the opposition were sounding emotional notes pleasant to the ears of many Nigerians. As in the debate on foreign policy, the Action Group had succeeded

---

*Before independence, the Governments of the three regions and the Federation had all taken a similar stand, saying that they had no plans for nationalization and did not foresee any, but that to remove all doubts they promised to pay "fair compensation, assessed by independent arbitration,"[11] if the occasion ever arose. All the ventures except for the small national shipping line which were mentioned as being already nationalized had been run by the Government when it was handed over by the British.

in taking a position that was more nationalistic than that of the government.

Some of Chief Awolowo's attacks on the Government, particularly his criticism of its close association with the West, seem surprising coming from a man who as recently as in the 1959 campaign had advocated outright alignment with the Western democracies. Many Nigerians have held that inconsistency against Chief Awolowo and have been highly cynical about his beliefs. There is no doubt that Chief Awolowo was deeply disappointed by the results of the 1959 election. (He has said he dreamed during the campaign that his prayers for victory had been granted and as a result, in his private diary, "Flashes of Inspiration," solemnly promised to assure justice for all, and thanked God "in advance for granting the object of my desire."[12]) A disappointed man, he turned to new radical policies which, irrespective of his own personal beliefs, he felt his party must support, in word at least, in order to attain the heights he had dreamt were near. It is not fair, however, to regard Chief Awolowo only as a cynical opportunist. Nigeria's greatest need as a nation was pride; as individuals the greatest handicap of many was their colonial mentality, which made them believe that things Nigerian had no good in them and things British were to be copied exactly. Chief Awolowo, spurred on perhaps by younger elements in his party, appreciated those national and individual needs and saw that the Government's early moderate policies were not placing primary emphasis on meeting those needs.

The third major theme in the Action Group's attempt to attract radical support was the charge that the nation was growing soft and corrupt. In his review of the first year of independence, Chief Awolowo found its most "outstanding feature" was a "dangerous decline in moral values" whereby "honesty is at a discount" and "there is a high premium on corruption and mediocrity."[13]

In a new nation with a new government anxious to disprove the belief of some that it was not ready for independence or that the Negro could not govern himself, Awolowo's remarks were considered disloyal. The Government newspaper, commenting on Awolowo's speech, editorialized:

> Maybe, it is right for the Opposition to say everything evil about the Government of the day; but it can hardly be described as wise for any man to destroy the throne — the people — on which he intends to sit in the grand manner in which Chief Awolowo has now done.[14]*

*The following day the paper followed with more criticism of the speech, the

Another speech by Chief Awolowo was even more galling. It contained nothing which had not been said before — the Government was "slavishly committed" to Britain in its foreign policy and economically;* wealth was not being fairly distributed; elections in the North were "neither free nor fair"; corruption was common.[16] What was new was that the speech was made in London, to a group of Nigerian students. To attack his country in the capital city of its former master was disloyal in the extreme, cried the government. The Federal House of Representatives voted to censure Chief Awolowo for making the "unbecoming" speech. Said Defense Minister Alhaji Muhammadu Ribadu, "Can anyone imagine Mr. Gaitskell coming to Nigeria to criticize the policy of the British Government? It is just unthinkable!"[17]†

It is hard to estimate what effect the Action Group's attempts to court radical opinion after the 1959 election had upon the governing coalition's desire to destroy it. For some, Chief Okotie-Eboh, for example, its economic program was anathema in itself. But there was a radical wing in both the NPC and the NCNC that would not have disagreed too much with the Action Group's general aims. The criticism by the NCNC's Dr. Ezera of the Government's moderate foreign policy has already been mentioned. The Action Group's support for nationalization found sympathetic listeners among the radical wing of the NCNC.[19] After the first year of independence, moreover, the Government moved somewhat toward the positions the Action Group was supporting. In its foreign policy it showed somewhat greater independence from Britain in ways that are set out hereafter; at home it demonstrated that it did not have a doctrinaire stand against governmental ownership of industry by announcing its plans to participate directly in the steel mill and oil refinery proposed under the 1962–1968 Development Plan.

The Action Group's efforts undoubtedly brought forth resentment from the radical wing of the NCNC, which saw that the Action Group was stealing its thunder — traditionally the NCNC had been the strong-

---

main point of which was that such a speech would not attract foreign investment.[15]

*Before making the speech attacking the government for being slavishly committed to Britain, Chief Awolowo and his family had spent a month's leave in England where three of his five children were attending school.

†Chief Awolowo of course had a constituency in England, a constituency of likely future leaders. At the time of his speech there were some 7,000 Nigerian students in England, more than from any other commonwealth country, even India.[18]

est advocate of the common man and Pan-Africanism and the strongest opponent of close association with Britain. There must also have been fear that the Action Group was becoming too popular with educated youth, though its new policy was certainly not bringing immediate electoral gains from the populace as a whole. Another important factor in developing resentment against the Action Group was the belief that its charges were too insulting and humiliating both to the nation, when it was said to be corrupt, and to the government, when it was said to be the colonialists' stooge. The very concept of opposition was questioned.

Particularly when it attacked the NPC for its policies in the North, the Action Group spoke with a sharp tongue of revolutionary impatience. Its magazine announced that "[i]t is the Action Group that is goading the teeming masses into protests against injustice perpetrated by feudal lords and undemocratic interpreters of the laws that are two hundred years behind time."[20] Some of those attacks were in poor taste. P. B. Olatunde, an Action Group Member of the Federal House for Ilorin, for example, charged in the House that whereas opposition members got "80 to 180" lashes for drinking beer in the North, "I know NPC Ministers who can even drink urine and get away unnoticed and unchallenged just because they are big NPC bosses."[21]* The reply of Usman Sarki, then an NPC Federal Minister, illustrates the angry contempt with which some NPC members regarded the opposition. The speech was "childish, insubstantial and disgruntled," he said. Thereupon there were interruptions. Then he said, "Mr. Speaker, if the dogs will keep quiet I will continue."[22]

More than because the Action Group had succeeded in appearing more nationalistic than the Government, more than because its unrelenting verbal attacks hit sensitive nerves, its continued support for minority movements in the Northern and Eastern Regions contributed to the governing coalition's desire to destroy it.

Shortly before independence the first serious disorder among a minority group occurred. It was among the Tiv, who had solidly supported the UMBC-Action Group alliance in the 1959 election.† The trouble began in March 1960 when the Tiv people defied the orders

---

*Mr. Olatunde, for all his vituperativeness on that occasion, crossed the carpet and joined the NPC two years later.

†Other minority movements have threatened violence. Thus, a supporter of the COR state in the East said: "If after independence we discover that war is a dire necessity, we shall be prepared to love war as much as we love peace."[23]

and tax assessments of the Tiv Native Authority, composed of chiefs and officials loyal to the NPC. At that point the Northern Government and Prime Minister Tafawa Balewa attributed the trouble, which led to at least five deaths when rioters were fired on by the police, to promises of UMBC-Action Group politicians that their election would mean the end of taxation.[24]

Immediately before independence more serious rioting broke out. Through the first week in October 1960, the week of independence, 16 deaths were caused by the rioters, and 4 by the police, and 4,800 persons were arrested (2,830 convicted) for rioting, house burning, and "going and causing fear."[25]

On that occasion the Northern Government charged that the UMBC-Action Group alliance had incited the Tiv to "wage war" in order to compel Great Britain to postpone independence until a Middle Belt State had been created. Several months later, at the start of a campaign for the Northern Region House of Assembly, Mr. J. S. Tarka and five other leaders of the alliance were indicted for treason. The timing of the Tiv riots lent weight to the charge that they were connected with the coming of independence, and the fact that palm branches (the palm being the symbol of the Action Group) were affixed to those huts that were not burned was a further indication that the riots had a political purpose. The Government was unable to prove, however, that Tarka and the others had inspired the rioting. The accused were all acquitted, with the English judge who tried them saying the case had been "bedevilled by politics" and that he could not say who was telling the truth.[26]

Shortly before independence, the Action Group took another step which the NPC may well have regarded as treasonable. After the defeat of Germany in World War I, a portion of the Cameroons, a German colony adjacent to Nigeria's eastern border, had been given to Great Britain to administer under the League of Nations. France administered the rest in the same way. The northern half of the British piece, known as the Northern Cameroons, was administered as part of Bornu and Adamawa provinces of Northern Nigeria.

During the 1959 campaign, a United Nations plebiscite was held in the Northern Cameroons with the voters given a choice between joining Northern Nigeria permanently and immediately, or postponing their decision as to what to do. To the surprise of most observers, they voted to postpone their decision.[27]

The Trusteeship Council of the United Nations met to consider what to do next and decided to conduct another plebiscite with the questions being whether the voters wished to achieve independence by joining the independent Federation of Nigeria (which would mean becoming part of the Northern Region) or by joining the independent Cameroon Republic, the portion which had been administered by France. The Council decided that those would be the only questions after hearing the protests of Action Group lawyer Ayotunde Rosiji, who urged the Council to give the voters an opportunity to postpone their decision again. It was clear that if the choice was between Nigeria and the Cameroon Republic, Nigeria would win: the Action Group wished to postpone that result because it felt that the NPC was so strong and so ruthless that it would succeed in eliminating any opposition if the Northern Cameroons was attached to Northern Nigeria without United Nations protection. To the NPC, however, the Action Group's attempt must have seemed an unpatriotic effort to diminish the size of Nigeria, not to speak of the North.

The plebiscite was eventually held in February 1961, and the North Cameroonians chose to join Nigeria. Thereafter they were added to Northern Nigeria, and their province was named Sardauna after the Premier. The Southern Cameroonians, on the other hand, voted to join the Cameroon Republic. The results of these two plebiscites, incidentally, increased the lead in population that the North had over the rest of the country, and with the addition of seven NPC representatives from the Northern Cameroons to the Federal House of Representatives, the NPC attained an absolute majority.

The Attacks upon the Action Group

After its defeat in the 1959 federal election, the Action Group quickly called an election to the Western Region House of Assembly in the hope of demonstrating that it still was a force to be reckoned with. The election was held in August 1960, and for the first time the Action Group trounced the NCNC in an election in the Western Region as a whole and matched it in the Midwest. Whereas in the 1959 federal election the Action Group won 53 per cent of the seats from the region as a whole and only 20 per cent from the Midwest, in the regional election eight months later it won 62 per cent of the seats in the region as a whole and half the Midwest seats.[28]

After that election, the NCNC intensified its efforts to create the

Midwest Region, believing that the election showed that as long as the Action Group could use the great power of the regional government to harass NCNC supporters in the Midwest, it would continue to eat into NCNC strength in that area. Thereafter the NCNC also constantly urged the Federal Government to take over the Western Region and "sack" the Action Group Government.

Almost immediately after the election, the NCNC — Dennis Osadebay, the leader of the Midwest State Movement, speaking first — argued, at the beginning apparently as an abstract legal point, that the Federal Government had the constitutional power to replace a regional government.[29] The Action Group disagreed. Prime Minister Tafawa Balewa seemed to support the Action Group, saying on a tour through the West that no government could dissolve another.

During the summer of 1961, when the Prime Minister was away visiting President Kennedy in the United States of America, the NCNC became less abstract. Law and order, it claimed, had broken down in the Western Region. In the beginning of August, R. A. Fani-Kayode, leader of the NCNC opposition in the Western House of Assembly, who as recently as the 1959 federal election had been an Action Grouper, led the NCNC members out of the Western House. He said they would not return until law and order were restored, and he called upon the Federal Government to declare a state of emergency in the West.

The Prime Minister then returned from the United States and said that he saw no breakdown of law and order in the West. Some of his NCNC ministers publically disagreed, and Dr. Michael Okpara, President of the NCNC, called upon his followers to fight if the Action Group did not stop harassing them. But after an emergency meeting called by the Prime Minister, Dr. Okpara and Chief Akintola issued a joint statement appealing to their followers "in the interest of the solidarity of the Federation of Nigeria and the unity of her people" not to take the law into their own hands.[30]

Prime Minister Tafawa Balewa was obviously acting as a restraining force. That was in character, for he is personally inclined toward moderation, in contrast to some of his more emotional colleagues. As a Northern leader, moreover, he was less concerned with the struggle for political supremacy in the South than were leaders of the NCNC. The reason he gave for minimizing the political strife in the Western Region is also an example of the surprisingly great effect that a concern for foreign opinion has had upon the political action of the Nigerian Government.

"My greatest concern," he said, "is the impression that we will give to the outside world. . . . People far away . . . really become frightened . . . they might say that such and such a country is turning into another Congo."[31]

In addition to alleging that law and order had broken down in the West, the NCNC charged that the Western Region Government was corrupt and that the Action Group had siphoned funds out of it in order to finance its 1959 federal election campaign. Pursuant to the last charge, the Federal Government appointed a Commission of Inquiry to examine the relationship between the National Bank of Nigeria and the Action Group during the 1959 campaign and the following year.

The bank (a private bank despite its name) was closely associated with the Action Group; it had been organized by patrons of the party and was associated with the company that published the party's newspapers and magazines; it had admittedly been helped by the Regional Government on the theory that the powerful foreign-owned banks discriminated against Nigerian businessmen, whereas the National Bank would not.

Faced with an investigation aimed at disclosing the relationship between bank, party, and government, the bank's directors, with the support of the party, turned to the courts to frustrate the inquiry. They succeeded until the declaration of emergency discussed in the next section of this chapter. The first Commission of Inquiry was dissolved by the Federal Government after the bank's lawyers found a technical mistake in the legislation which set up the Commission. The statute under which the Prime Minister convened the second Commission of Inquiry was held unconstitutional; the basic holding was a highly technical one which would not have prevented the Federal Government from trying again, but they did not immediately do so.*

The Action Group lawyers were having a merry and successful time with the Constitution. In Chief Rotimi Williams, the party legal adviser until the middle of 1962, they had quite possibly the best and probably the largest lawyer in the country. The Constitution was a complicated one, whose federal structure and fundamental rights provisions were relatively unfamiliar to the country's British-trained lawyers. One looking

---

*That, incidentally, was the first constitutional decision of the Federal Supreme Court against the Federal Government. It was accepted with apparent good grace by the Government. The reasoning underlying the decision is discussed in Chapter 11.

for mistakes, as was the Action Group, had the advantage. In the long run, however, the party's legal successes may have hurt it. In winning cases it hit some very sensitive nerves, as when it successfully established that under the Independence Constitution the Grand Kadi, a Muslim-trained Judge, was not eligible to sit along with English-trained judges on the Northern Nigerian High Court. Its successes in court undoubtedly contributed to attitudes like that of Mr. Fani-Kayode, who asked the Federal Government to declare an emergency in the West rather than appoint a Commission of Inquiry into the alleged breakdown of law and order, because, he said, Action Group lawyers would succeed in getting a commission declared unconstitutional and thereby "render the Federal Government futile."[32]

The governing coalition hit the Action Group hardest in the maneuvering over the excision of the Midwest area from the Western Region in order to create a new region. That maneuvering must be seen against the relevant Constitutional provisions. Under the Independence Constitution, five stages had to be passed to create a new region. First, two-thirds of the members of both houses of the Federal Parliament had to approve a resolution supporting the new region; second, both houses of the regional legislature in a majority of the existing regions had to approve the same resolution;* third, the Federal Parliament had to pass a more detailed bill providing for the creation of the new region; fourth, that bill had to be approved by resolutions of each legislative house in at least two regions; and fifth, 60 per cent of those entitled to vote in the proposed new region had to vote for its creation in a plebiscite.

That exhaustive procedure, translated into Nigerian realities after the 1959 election, meant (1) that the cards were stacked against the Action Group and (2) that the NPC could veto the creation of any new region.† The NPC and NCNC in combination had two-thirds of the members of both houses of the Federal Parliament. Together they controlled two (a majority) of the regional legislatures. Therefore, they could together do everything, except ensure success of the final plebiscite, to carve the Midwest Region out of the Action Group's home region. At the same time they could resolutely refuse to let their own regions be touched.

---

*This second step may also be accomplished by the approval of the region to be divided and one other.

†Because of the NPC's majority or near majority in the Federal House of Representatives, it could prevent the initial resolution from being passed.

That is just what they did. In April 1961 the constitutional machinery was set in motion by presentation to the Federal Parliament of a resolution for the creation of a Midwest Region. Chief Enahoro for the Action Group moved to amend by adding a reference to the proposed Middle Belt and COR Regions, but announced that the Action Group would support the Midwest resolution even if his amendment were defeated. After the amendment's defeat, and without a formal vote, the Midwest resolution was recorded as being passed without opposition.[33]

The Action Group was of course on the horns of a dilemma. After its improved showing in the Midwest in the 1960 regional elections, it had less reason to be glad to see the Midwest go than in 1955 when it first had given its formal approval to the creation of the Midwest. Furthermore, there had been indications that the area might produce oil. On the other hand, would the party lose its minority group support in the East and North and end forever its hopes of splitting those regions if it seemed to waver in its support for new states, including the one to be carved out of its stronghold?* In any event, the Action Group supported the Midwest resolution in 1961 and rationalized its action with the theory that once one new state was created irresistible pressure would build up for others.[34]

The resolution was reintroduced before the Federal Parliament in March 1962 because the Attorney General concluded that the failure to take a formal vote at its earlier passage might cast doubt upon whether it had been passed by the necessary two-thirds majority. It was decided, therefore, to begin the process anew. This time the Action Group opposed the resolution after the failure of three amendments offered by Chief Awolowo, including the proposal that the nation be reorganized into eleven new regions, five from the existing Northern Region.†

There are many reasons why the Action Group reversed its stand. In the first place, the regional elections in the Northern and Eastern

---

*The dissolution of the Northern Region House and the beginning of a campaign in the North was announced by the Sardauna of Sokoto on the day following the vote on the Midwest resolution, and the Action Group must have known that was soon coming.

†The two other amendments were that three areas should be excluded from the proposed Midwest region, and that prior agreements between the major parties concerning the new region's constitution, fiscal arrangements, time for the first election, and interim administration before the first election should be made and embodied in an act of Parliament.

129

Regions in which the party needed to appeal to minority groups had already taken place. In those elections, moreover, the party had done worse with the minorities then it had in the 1959 federal election. In the North in 1961, instead of the 25 of 174 seats it had won in the 1959 federal election it won 9 of 170 seats, holding only the Tiv solidly;* in the East, instead of 14 of 73 seats, it won 15 of 146. Thus, its policy of support for minority movements appeared to be producing less and less minority support. It was perfectly clear, moreover, that the NPC and the NCNC would oppose the creation of any more new regions after the Midwest.† Finally, the party feared that the Federal Government would use the six months given it by the Constitution between the time of a successful plebiscite and the emergence of the new region to make certain that the NCNC would form its first government.

In short order the Northern and Eastern regional legislatures approved the resolution and the Federal Parliament passed the detailed bill for the Region's creation. The Midwest Region was by no means yet created, however. The Action Group filed two cases attacking the constitutionality of the procedure used thus far. (One alleged that everything done by the Eastern Region Legislature since its election in November 1961, including its approval of the newest Midwest resolution, was invalid since it had been elected under an unconstitutional electoral law.) Chief Awolowo and Chief Enahoro, himself from the Midwest, threatened to have their supporters vote against the new region in the forthcoming plebiscite. That appeared to be a dangerous threat (though, as it turned out, all parties, including the Action Group, supported the creation of the new region at the plebiscite and there was an overwhelming affirmative vote‡). In December 1959 in the federal election the Action Group

---

*A special election held in Sardauna Province after the former Northern Cameroons became part of the Northern Region resulted in a sweep of all 7 seats by the NPC, leaving the Action Group with 9 of 177 seats in the Northern House of Assembly.

†The NCNC had continued to assert its general belief in the creation of new states but had specifically supported only the Midwest. In its election manifesto for the Western election of 1960, it stated "we are convinced that the North will awake to the need for more states just as . . . she awoke to the need for ministerial appointments and self-government. . . . To safeguard the unity of Nigeria, we feel we should take the North along with us as fast as she can appreciate the forces at work and adapt herself to those forces."35

‡At the plebiscite in July 1963, 579,077 out of 650,130 registered voters (about 90 per cent) voted in favor of the creation of the new region, and only 7,218 voted against. The surprisingly large favorable vote is support for the conclusion

had won 39 per cent of the Midwest vote and in August 1960 in the regional election it had won 46 per cent. It would by no means have to hold all its supporters to prevent the creation of the Midwest; the proponents of the new region had to receive in the plebiscite 60 per cent of the vote of those *eligible* to vote. The prospective difficulty of obtaining a 60 per cent majority of all eligible to vote was suggested by the fact that in the hard-fought 1959 election only 71.2 per cent of the eligible voters in the Western Region had gone to the polls.

The coalition — or really the NCNC, which was most concerned — had cause to be worried. Weakening the Action Group and gaining in the West was a necessity for the NCNC, the more so after the 1961 election to the Northern House of Assembly in which the NCNC-NEPU alliance won the grand total of one seat. Neither the NCNC nor the NPC, moreover, wished to forgo a peculiarly delightful way of humiliating the Action Group by turning its own policy against it so as to carve a new region out of its stronghold.

The Action Group Crisis

Suddenly the coalition was given by the Action Group a chance to humiliate the Action Group further. An internal split developed within the party between the supporters of Chief Awolowo, its leader, and Chief Akintola, its deputy leader and the Western Region Premier. Fighting between the factions broke out in the Western Region House of Assembly in May 1962. Thereupon the Federal Parliament declared a state of emergency pursuant to which the Federal Government deposed the Action Group-controlled Western Region Government and replaced it with a caretaker government under a federal administrator — the very move the NCNC had been working for since August 1960.

Most of the causes of the Action Group crisis are related in one way or another to the dangerously close association between each of Nigeria's political parties and the dominant ethnic or religious group of a particular region. One must conclude from the Action Group crisis that it will be extremely difficult to end that close association and develop political parties all of which are truly national, cutting across ethnic and regional lines. Until that close association is ended, however, political controversy will constantly exacerbate ethnic and regional tension.

---

that even if — as the Minorities Commission suggested — the desire for new regions in the minority areas of the North and East is slightly less than it was in the Midwest, it will remain a potent force.

One of the basic causes of the split within the party was a struggle for power between Chief Akintola and Chief Awolowo. Though Chief Awolowo had gone to the Federal Parliament after the 1959 election and turned over the Premier's office in Ibadan to Chief Akintola, he remained leader of the party and had no intention of losing control of affairs in Western Nigeria. The West after all remained the party's base, its only source of patronage, and the chief source of party funds. Chief Akintola was ambitious to replace the Party Leader. He was irked at having less power than the other two regional premiers, both of whom were presidents of their parties.[36]

Chief Akintola drew the wrath of Chief Awolowo and his supporters by taking several important steps — a reduction of head tax, an increase in the contribution local schools were expected to make to their own support, a reduction in the price of cocoa — without even informing, let alone consulting, the party leadership. When the crisis came to a head, the Premier attempted to remove some Awolowo supporters from the statutory boards that controlled much of the Region's spending. He also, it was charged, demanded overriding personal loyalty from his cabinet, and attempted to form his own party and to divert the party's 10 per cent levy upon the salaries of legislators from his division into a special fund.[37] Finally, the two leaders fought over the treatment of a local real estate corporation which had been a source of party funds.

Though Chief Awolowo was victorious over Chief Akintola in the struggle within the party, one lesson to be learned was that a party leader took a great risk by leaving the party's regional base to go to the Federal Parliament. The regional character of Nigeria's parties means that control of regional patronage and purse strings is of vital importance to party leadership. If for that reason party leaders stay in the regions, the regional character of the parties will be reinforced.

The other two causes of the Action Group crisis were directly connected with attempts to overcome its past as, on the one hand, a narrow party representing Yoruba ethnic interests and, on the other, a broad coalition of extremely diverse persons whose chief aim, the winning of independence, had already been achieved.

One of the charges against Chief Akintola was that he had tried to sabotage and ridicule the new party program of "democratic socialism." He would, said Chief Enahoro, spell out the new ideology

in incomparable Yoruba to elders and the right wing of the party [telling them] that the ideology means "if you have a buba, you must not have a pair of trousers, if you have more than one room it is a crime, and if you have a bicycle you must not aspire to own a car."[38]

The Action Group's espousal of "democratic socialism" — which, to be sure, was largely verbal — was an attempt to grapple with the problems of an independent Nigeria and to become a national party with appeal to the youth of all ethnic groups. The party's advocacy of nationalization in order to reduce the power of foreign economic interests and Chief Akintola's disapproval of nationalization has already been discussed. But "democratic socialism" meant more than nationalization. It also purported to aim to prevent the "South Americanization" of Nigeria — to guard against the development of an increasing gulf between rich and poor and to prevent the increasing concentration of political as well as economic power in the hands of a rich oligarchy mindless of the misery of their followers.* (Some inconsistencies between the Action Group's espousal of democratic socialism and the action of the Western Region Government, which it controlled, are discussed in the following section.) With the party itself being a coalition whose reason for existence had next to nothing to do with an economic or social program, it was inevitable that as soon as it focused its attention upon such a program, it would split. So long as the Action Group was a party of the Yoruba, or of the Yoruba plus minorities in the other regions seeking new states, so long as it was a party concerned primarily with the winning of independence or with the proper type of constitution for an independent Nigeria, it would hold together. When it attempted to pass beyond that it split. The lesson to be learned was that any existing party which attempted to become truly national through the adoption of an ideology that would appeal to an economic class from all ethnic groups would have to face an internal party upheaval.[39]

---

*One might have expected the Action Group to be the party of the new Nigerian upper class. It began as a party of the Yoruba and the Western Region; the Yoruba were the most successful Nigerian businessmen, and the West was Nigeria's richest region. Moreover, where the party failed to win the support of the Yoruba, as in Ibadan, it was because it supported the new class coming into the city against the poorer, traditional, indigenous settlers. But the party also attracted most of the radical intellectuals in the West (including most of the Marxist-influenced members of the United Working Peoples Party) and associated itself in the other regions with radical elements, notably Mr. S. G. Ikoku, leader of the opposition in the East.

The third difference between the Akintola and the Awolowo wings of the party was the Akintola wing's desire to cease support of the minority group movements in the North and East. Indeed the Akintola wing would have abandoned all compaigning outside the West. Its aim was to make a deal with the governing coalition to protect the West (and the Yoruba) against such attacks as the creation of the Midwest Region and the extension of the Federal Territory of Lagos into the Western Region. There was also some hope of being asked to join with the coalition in a national government, thereby sharing in the power (and the jobs) of the Federal Government.

The Akintola policy stemmed from discouragement born of defeats in the Northern and Eastern regional elections of 1961 and from belief in the primacy of Yoruba interests. Again, though Chief Awolowo's more courageous views were victorious within the party, the crisis and the attacks upon the party by the NCNC and the NPC show that a Nigerian party which tries to become truly national and fight elections hard in all regions invites serious trouble, if not destruction.

The party crisis came into the open at the annual party congress held in February 1962 at the African Games Club in Jos in Northern Nigeria. Chief Awolowo called attention to the "real and dangerous contradictions" within the party. After stating at length both sides of the issues — a rhetorical device common to himself and Dr. Azikiwe — Chief Awolowo reaffirmed his continued faith in "democratic socialism" and declared, "as for me and those who share my burning faith in the destiny of our great party, there can be no looking back. The Action Group of Nigeria as a country-wide political organization has come to stay."[40]

After that speech, while the Congress was still in session, Chief Akintola and Chief Ayotunde Rosiji, who had been the two Action Group ministers in the national government between 1957 and 1959, flew to Ibadan to meet with the Sardauna of Sokoto and thereafter boycotted the Congress. The meeting with the Sardauna was merely a courtesy between premiers, said Akintola; it was to discuss supporting the Sardauna as President when Nigeria became a republic and to sell out the West to the Fulani as had Afonja in Ilorin more than a century before, said the Awolowo wing.

After the Jos Congress, at which Chief Akintola's powers were reduced somewhat, the rift was publicly settled by the intervention of Action Group elders and chiefs. But it continued to simmer beneath

134

the surface and erupted again in May. On May 19, after hearing a five-hour speech from Chief Awolowo, the West and Midwest Executive Committees of the Action Group called upon Chief Akintola to resign as Premier of the West after finding him guilty of maladministration, antiparty activities, and indiscipline. Then in rapid succession came the events that brought shame on the West and gave the NPC and the NCNC a chance to move. Chief Akintola refused to resign and asked the Governor of the Western Region to convene the House to debate a motion of confidence in him; the Governor refused, whereupon Chief Akintola asked the Federal Prime Minister to revoke the Governor's appointment and sent his daughter flying to England to petition the Queen for the same purpose. The Governor immediately wrote to Chief Akintola revoking his appointment as Premier and appointed in his stead Alhaji D. S. Adegbenro.

On May 25, the Regional House was convened in order to approve Alhaji Adegbenro. Three words were spoken: "Mr. Speaker, Sir . . ." Then suddenly an Akintola supporter jumped on his bench and leapt through the room, shouting "fire, smoke, fire," or "fire on the mountain." Fighting immediately broke out, punches were traded, and chairs thrown; the speaker was nearly decapitated with the symbolic mace, and order was not restored until the police entered and cleared the room with tear gas. The evidence seems overwhelming that the riot was planned by the Akintola forces — both the timing and the histrionic slogan suggest planning — in order to prevent a vote from being taken and perhaps to provoke the response on the part of the Federal Government that in fact ensued.

The Awolowo faction wanted to reconvene the House so that they could complete the formalities of replacing Chief Akintola. Accordingly, they requested police protection from Prime Minister Tafawa Balewa. He replied that if police were present the Federal Government would not accept any decision reached.* The second meeting was broken up by more chair throwing followed by tear gas.

The Prime Minister spoke on the radio in the evening and summoned

---

*One would have thought that it was pre-eminently the duty of the Federal Government to use the police to enable a vote to be taken without disruption by rioting and then to accept the decision thus taken. Certainly there was no indication that the police would (or were being asked to) intimidate members to vote in one way or another. But the Akintola faction was favored by the NPC and the NCNC; one of its proposals, after all, was to cut down campaigning in the North and East.

Parliament, saying "no responsible government . . . could allow an explosive situation such as now exists in Western Nigeria to continue."[41]

On May 29, 1962, the Federal Parliament met and declared a state of emergency, pursuant to which a federal administrator was appointed to run the Western Region. The leading members of both factions of the Action Group, including Chiefs Awolowo and Akintola, were placed under restrictions and all political demonstrations were forbidden. It soon became apparent, however, that the emergency and the restrictions were to bear much harder upon the Awolowo supporters than upon the Akintola supporters. Akintola left the Action Group, was released from restriction, formed a new party known as the United Peoples Party, and at the end of the year when the emergency ended was restored to office by the Federal Government as Premier of the Western Region. Awolowo was sent under restriction to a remote fishing village, became the target of an investigation into corruption, and, along with a score of other opposition leaders, was convicted of treason.

Corruption and Treason

Soon after the declaration of emergency, the Federal Government appointed a commission under the chairmanship of Justice G. B. A. Coker of the Lagos High Court to investigate the financial and investment policies of six Western Region Government Statutory Corporations, including their relations with political parties. The six corporations included the Marketing Board, which had had at its disposal some £60 million derived from profits made upon the sale of cocoa and other export crops, and the Development Corporation, a recipient of funds from the Marketing Board and the Western Region Government, which was meant to use the funds to stimulate industrial development. The corporations, equivalents of which exist in the other regions, were run by directors appointed by the Government and removable at any time by the Government.

The Coker Commission concentrated upon the relationships between those two corporations and National Investment and Properties Co., Ltd., and the relations in turn between that company and the Action Group. In the best light, the dealings of the statutory corporations with National Investment were inconsistent with the Action Group's professed faith in socialism; indeed, they were inconsistent with any notion of equitable development. For the statutory corporations supplied at least £10 million to National Investment for use by its four wealthy owners on speculative real estate schemes. In fact the revelations were far more sensational because it appeared that National Investment financed the Action Group to the extent of some £3.5 million, and indeed may have been owned by the Action Group. The moneys of all the people, moneys which were designed for economic development and the protection of farmers, were diverted to the political ends of a party representing only part of the people.[42]

Before National Investment was even fully incorporated, it applied for and obtained in 1959 a loan of £750,000 from the Marketing Board, ostensibly for building projects. Of that money £660,498 was used to retire an Action Group overdraft with the National Bank of Nigeria.[*] In 1960, the Development Corporation obtained from the Marketing Board £3 million, purportedly for use by two corporations that were jointly owned by the Development Corporation and Israeli interests. In fact, only £.8 million was paid to the two corporations and £2.2 million was paid over to National Investment by Alfred Rewane, who was chairman of the Development Corporation and its two subsidiaries and a director of National Investment. Much of that money eventually went to the Action Group.[44]

Perhaps the most striking transaction uncovered by the Commission involved the Moba Estate — land on an island in the Western Region near to Lagos which was "subject to overflooding and most probably infested for the best part of year the with crabs."[45] In 1958 the Moba property was purchased for £11,000 by Dr. Akinola Maja, who has been called the father of the Action Group, and who was a leading figure in the National Bank and a director of National Investment, and Chief T. A. Doherty, a director of the National Bank. In 1961 National Investment sold the property to the Western Region Government for £850,000, having, the Commission found, paid £50,000 for it, though it made up documents showing that it paid over £700,000.[†]

---

[*]That was the bank that the Federal Government had earlier sought unsuccessfully to investigate concerning its relations with the Action Group. The Coker Commission investigation revealed that the National Bank kept three accounts for the Action Group, only one of which was kept in a name that would reveal the party's interest.[43] The bank made substantial amounts of money available to the Action Group without security and was the recipient of a great deal of money from the Western Region Government and statutory corporations, most of which the Commission found could not be repaid.

[†]In making the sale the Commission found that National Investment was aided

All of the money paid by the Government was paid over to the Action Group.

In all, the Commission found that the Action Group received £2.198 million in cash from National Investment, in addition to payment of its £660,498 overdraft with the National Bank, and that it benefited from National Investment's £686,262 investment in the corporations that published pro-Action Group newspapers. The cash payments were not disclosed on the Action Group's books and were hidden by a code name on National Investment's books. The Commission found that Chief Awolowo had instigated the scheme for financing the Action Group.[46]

In addition to its findings relating to devious schemes for supporting the party with government funds, the Commission found that several investments were made by statutory corporations for political reasons, that the advice of civil servants and economic experts was frequently disregarded, that directors and board members of the statutory corporations and private corporations such as the National Bank frequently dealt with themselves on better terms than the public. The Commission did not accuse Chief Awolowo of such conduct.

In September 1963, almost a full year after the trial began, Chief Awolowo and several other Action Group leaders were convicted of plotting to overthrow the Government, smuggling arms from Ghana, and training revolutionaries in Ghana. Chief Awolowo was given a ten-year prison sentence and Chief Enahoro, who was tried separately after having been extradited from England, was sentenced to fifteen years in prison. In view of the Action Group's attacks upon the Government for being too close to Great Britain, it is interesting that one of the vital issues in the early part of the Awolowo trial arose when Chief Awolowo asked to be represented by Dingle Foot, an English barrister and a member of the Nigerian Bar. The Government deported Foot shortly after his arrival in Nigeria, however.

The Government's refusal to permit Awolowo to be represented by his first choice of counsel, the long time between the end of the trial and the announcement of the verdict, and the common belief that some witnesses for the prosecution were political opportunists, are all reasons why many Nigerians who were supporters of Awolowo continue to believe that he was innocent. Moreover, even if he was

---

by an inflated valuation of the property prepared for the Government by a British firm of real estate experts.

guilty many will undoubtedly feel that he was driven to plan a coup by indications that the governing coalition intended to destroy the Action Group. On the other hand, supporters of the verdict and the fairness of the trial can point to the fact that several of the accused — including Chike Obi and J. S. Tarka — were acquitted, and others had their convictions reversed on appeal by the Federal Supreme Court.

The series of events from the emergency through Awolowo's conviction weakened the Action Group. But they by no means marked the end of opposition to the Government on the ground that it was too conservative in its economic and its foreign policy. The revelations about the internal workings of the party added to the cynicism of many people, particularly the young elite, about all the existing political parties. But they did not affect the strong appeal of many of the positions which the Action Group had begun to advocate after the 1959 election.

The Action Group crisis began a chain of events that culminated in a major realignment of Nigeria's parties, highlighted by an electoral alliance between two long-time enemies—the Action Group and the NCNC.

The 1964 Election:
Crisis Averted or Postponed

In 1953, at the time of the self-government-in-1956 motion, it was Northern fear of perpetual Southern domination that led to a crisis that culminated with a decision to decentralize through federalism. By 1964 the balance of power and the thinking of Nigerians had changed sufficiently so that Southern fear of perpetual Northern domination was a major factor contributing to the election-year crisis that included a partial boycott of the elections for the House of Representatives and a threat by the East to secede.

At the 1950 General Conference on the Constitution one of the more divisive issues had been the Northerners' demand that they be given 50 per cent of the seats in the Central House of Representatives. After the Conference they were. By the 1959 election, applying the figures of the 1952–1953 census showing the North with 16 million of the nation's 29 million persons, the North was allocated a majority of seats in the Federal House of Representatives (174 of 312). In 1959 the NPC won 134 of these 174 seats and in 1964, owing to carpet crossing and independents declaring for the party, the NPC had 165 of 174.

Northern, and NPC, power thus rested upon the results of the 1952–1953 census combined with the regional single-party trend. The single-party trend seemed to be getting stronger. But the 1952–1953 census was generally believed to be inaccurate for many reasons, including a belief by many Nigerians that head-counting was associated with tax collection. When it came time to take a new census after independence there was real doubt as to what the results would be.

A census was taken in May 1962. Its results were never officially announced. Each region accused the others of overcounting and a British official involved with the census suggested that there was substantial overcounting in Ibo provinces of the East. It was rumored that the 1962 census showed the North with less than half the country's population.

Because of the controversy concerning that census, another was taken in November 1963. As in 1962, persons who were living away from their ethnic homeland were urged to come home to be counted and as before there were accusations of overcounting.

The results showed enormous growth since the 1952–1953 census, lending weight either to the allegation that there had been undercounting in 1952–1953 or to the allegation that there had been overcounting in the current census, perhaps to both allegations. The total was up from 29 million to 55 million, but more significant than the total was the relative position of the regions.

The North retained a majority, though its share was down somewhat. Its current 29.8 million, translated into Parliamentary seats, meant 167 of 312 seats (instead of 174 of 312). The East, which many had thought to be the fastest growing region, was also shown to have lost ground compared with the other regions: its 1963 population of 12.4 million gave it 70 seats instead of the 73 previously assigned to it. The West, on the other hand, made great gains in relative terms. Now, with a population of 10.3 million, it was assigned 10 additional seats for a total of 57. The Midwest, with a population of 2.5 million, went from 15 to 14 seats and Lagos, at .6 million, went from 3 to 4 seats.

The results of the census were a great disappointment to many Southerners. The North, by which they usually meant the NPC, would, they feared, be perpetually in control of the Federal Government. Dr. Michael Okpara, leader of the NCNC and Premier of the East, led the political attack on the results of the census, charging irregularities and bringing suit to set the results aside.* In rejecting the census, he made the Sardauna of Sokoto the symbol of the threat of continual

*The Supreme Court dismissed the suit without reaching the merits.

Northern control by complaining about the "perpetual menacing threats of the Premier of Northern Nigeria and leader of the NPC that his forebears had always ruled Nigeria and that they would continue to rule forever."[1]

A common Southern reaction to the census figures and the prospect of continued NPC power was one of the principal factors bringing together the NCNC and the Action Group into an alliance for the 1964 election to the Federal House of Representatives. Another factor was the policy of Chief Akintola as Premier of the Western Region.

One of the reasons for Akintola's break with Obafemi Awolowo had been Akintola's desire to lead a political party that confined its efforts to the Western Region and its Yoruba inhabitants and that reached an accommodation with the NPC. After the Western Region emergency and Akintola's return to power as Premier, Yorubas in all political parties began to complain of discrimination, particularly in the Federal Government corporations whose chairmen were Ibos and members of the NCNC. Even T. O. S. Benson, then a First Vice President of the NCNC and Federal Minister of Information, felt called upon to "bring into the open . . . unfair and offensive practices against my people."[2]

In March 1964 a new political party was formed in the name of Yoruba and Western Region interests. Called the Nigerian National Democratic Party (NNDP),* it brought together in the Western House of Assembly Akintola's United Peoples Party and 14 NCNC members of the Assembly who resigned from the NCNC. Pointing to the strength of the NPC and the NCNC in the North and East, the announcement to the public of the new party complained that "notwithstanding our wealth and high social advancement, Western Nigeria has become a mere appendage in the community of the Federal Republic mainly because its people are disunited and disorganized." The announcement emphasized claims of job discrimination, asserting that Yorubas "have been superseded by relatives, tribesmen and clansmen of Eastern NCNC Chairmen, who shout the slogan of One Nigeria more than anyone else."[3]

As when Akintola opposed Awolowo, the NPC appeared to support the institutionalization of regionalism. The NPC party Secretary commented that it seemed as if "the Yoruba have come to realize their mistakes."[4] And for the election the NPC and the NNDP formed an alliance, known as the Nigerian National Alliance (NNA). Joined with

*The name was the same as Herbert Macaulay's Lagos-based party of the 1920's and 1930's.

those two parties in the NNA were Chike Obi's Dynamic Party,* the Republican Party and most elements of the Niger Delta Congress from the East, the Mid-West Democratic Front, and the Lagos State United Front.

Arrayed against the NNA was the United Progressive Grand Alliance (UPGA). It brought together the NCNC and the Action Group along with the Northern Progressive Front, an alliance of NEPU and the UMBC.

The UPGA advocated during the campaign a further restructuring of Nigeria's federal system in order, it said, to strengthen the bonds of Nigerian unity. It contended that "all efforts at unity are bound to fail until we have completely concluded the unfinished business of British administration in Nigeria. This is the perennial problem of the creation of more states in Nigeria."[7] If victorious, UPGA promised to create new states (specifying the Middle Belt, Kano, Calabar, and "all other states for whose creation there is popular demand"). It said it would do so at once and by way of constituent assembly rather than under the mechanism of the present Constitution.

The Nigerian National Alliance, on the other hand, said that "if there is real reason and necessity" to create any new states the provisions of the present Constitution should be followed.† Instead of new states, the NNA emphasized its promise to make every effort "to see that all ethnic groups are adequately represented in the [Federal Public Service]."[8]

In addition to the promise to create new states through a constituent assembly, Dr. Okpara of the NCNC and UPGA urged that the Federal Senate be given "concurrent power with the House of Representatives, instead of merely having the power to delay ordinary legislation."[9] (In the Senate, the North's population advantage would not be determinative because each region was given an equal number of seats.) UPGA

---

*In explaining his affiliation with the NPC in the NNA, after having supported both the NCNC and the Action Group and having accused both of being insufficiently progressive, Dr. Obi said that "even if it is true that the NPC is feudalistic [it] is not afflicted with corruption and squandermania — two incurable diseases which afflict the NCNC." He stated that most of the NCNC ministers were "greedy, avaricious men with a very high instinct for acquiring landed property."[5] He added, however, that following the census he had urged Dr. Okpara to boycott an election based upon the census and to secede if necessary.[6]

†As outlined in the previous chapter, the present Constitution as a practical matter gave the NPC (in the House of Representatives) and the North plus one other region (in the regional legislatures) a veto over the creation of new regions.

was placed in the position of claiming to be more progressive and democratic than the NNA, but at the same time seeking to curb majority rule.

Both UPGA and the NNA said in their manifestoes that their policies would protect Africa from danger. The nature of the danger as seen by the opposing alliances was somewhat different, however. UPGA stressed the continuance of foreign economic power (the strengthened "stranglehold of neo-colonialism on the national economy") and decried the "systematic frustration of the lofty aspirations of the people by the combined forces of reaction and neo-colonialism."[10]

The NNA, on the other hand, said that UPGA, "flying on the wings of dangerous doctrines which have never been tried in the African atmosphere," would destroy African institutions such as chieftaincy. In language reminiscent of the British advocates of indirect rule, the NNA said that its policy, in contrast to UPGA's, offered "progress through the traditional patterns of modernized African society. This modern society works through our traditional institutions; it modifies and improves them all the time."[11]

In their manifestoes both alliances used the word socialism to describe part or all of their program. The NNA, praising African tradition, stated that as part of that tradition Africa had "an indigenous socialism which is second to no other system in its humanity and brotherhood."[12] Dr. Okpara derided that reference to socialism as "timid and reluctant."[13] In its rhetoric, at least, UPGA was neither timid nor reluctant about espousing socialism: its choice, it said, was not to go "backward to the exploitation and corruption of the dying capitalist society" but to move "forward with progressive forces all over the world . . . to build a socialist society."[14] The alliance complained that the country's economy was neither capitalist nor socialist.[15] But despite that complaint and despite its militant rhetoric about socialism, scrutiny of the specific proposals made by UPGA shows that it envisaged the continuation of an economy that mixed free enterprise and socialism. It supported planning and it called for support of the private sector of the economy within limits set by the national economic plans. It promised to assist Nigerian businessmen but said that it would channel the growth of the business class to prevent huge concentrations of capital in a few hands.[16] It called for "all progressive forces . . . to rally around the banner of UPGA,"[17] but it refused to admit to the alliance Dr. Tunji Otegbeye's Socialist Workers and Farmers Party, a party that said it sought the "realization of a socialist Nigeria through the process of National Democratic Revolution."[18]

Another instance of where UPGA tempered strong language was in its attitude toward foreign business. On the one hand, it decried neo-colonialism and complained that industrialization was being frustrated by foreign capitalists. On the other hand, it promised to attract foreign capital (without discrimination as to its source) in order to support its program of industrialization.[19] The NNA was similarly ambivalent and pragmatic, stating that no real progress could be made until the economy was fully Nigerianized, but at the same time stating that it would vigorously encourage foreign investors through its liberal industrial policies.[20]

The NNDP, true to its origins, made the keynote of its campaign the promise that an NNA victory meant more Yorubas in the Federal Government and more favorable treatment for the Western Region.[21] Time and again Premier Akintola returned to the theme that since the Islamic peoples of the North and the Ibos of the East were united, the Yorubas should also unite to "fight for the progress and welfare of their race."[22]

As in the 1959 campaign, the question of whether or not the campaign was free and fair itself became a campaign issue. Again, though opposition politicians were harassed in all regions, the issue was highlighted by campaign tours of the NCNC leader, this time Michael Okpara instead of Nnamdi Azikiwe. Five days before Dr. Okpara was scheduled to speak at the University of Ife in the West, all outside politicians were barred from the University; he was barred from entering Premier Akintola's town, Ogbomosho, and forced to hold his rally on the outskirts of town.[23] On a tour in the North, his way to Katsina was barred by 100 cattle Fulani and he and Action Group leader Dauda Adegbenro were refused rooms in Kaduna's new hotel. Political violence, the use of party thugs, curfews, arrests, fighting, and even killings happened to an extent unmatched in 1959.

On the fourth anniversary of Nigerian Independence, as the election campaign was just beginning, President Azikiwe told the nation that it was at a fork of history with one path leading to a tolerant and united nation and the other to a "squabbling and disunited group of tribes."[24] In December, toward the end of the campaign, he again spoke on the radio complaining of tribal propaganda and incitement and accusing politicians of using their power to perpetuate their stay in office. He went on to suggest the possibility that the Federation might break up, saying: "if this our embryo Republic must disintegrate, then, in the name of God, let the operation be a short and painless one."[25]

A threat to secede did come from the East, whose Ibo residents, said Dr. Okpara in an election broadcast, had been singled out for vilification and destruction.[26] The secession threat was at first used by the Eastern leaders of the NCNC to bolster UPGA's contention that the election should be postponed. The postponement plea was based upon the allegation that the campaign had been neither free nor fair.* President Azikiwe accepted the allegations and sought to postpone the election. But Prime Minister Tafawa Balewa insisted that the election be held, and it was.

The UPGA leaders then asked their supporters to boycott the election. The UPGA boycott was totally effective in the East† and in three of the four Lagos constituencies. In both areas polling booths were destroyed and there was considerable disorder. In the Western Region the boycott was relatively effective — but very harmful to UPGA, particularly the Action Group. There was voting in all constituencies and the practical effect of the boycott was to increase the number of seats won by the NNDP (36 of 57) and reduce those won by the Action Group and NCNC. In the North the NPC solidified its position, winning 162 of the 167 seats at stake and thereby ensuring to itself a majority in the Federal House of Representatives. In the Midwest, NCNC leader Dennis Osadebay decided not to have his followers boycott the election and won for his party a smashing victory.

Following the partially boycotted election the East — with its vastly improved economic position based upon substantial strikes of oil — continued to threaten secession. It also appeared that President Azikiwe might refuse to appoint a government based upon the results of the election.[27] However, on January 4, 1965, five days after the election, President Azikiwe, saying that he was subordinating personal feeling to the Constitution, invited Abubakar Tafawa Balewa to form a government.‡

*One of the principal complaints was that many opposition candidates in the North had been harassed and obstructed so as to be unable even to be nominated. More than one-third of the seats in the North were awarded to NPC candidates prior to the election because they were not opposed.

†Nineteen supporters of the NCNC had already been returned unopposed in the East.

‡Azikiwe's action led R.A.B. Okafor, Parliamentary Secretary in the Ministry

Abubakar Tafawa Balewa
Courtesy of the Nigerian Consulate, New York City

Nnamdi Azikiwe
Courtesy of the Nigerian Consulate, New York City

Obafemi Awolowo
Courtesy of Africa Today

Parliament Building, Lagos
Photograph by C. Davis Fogg

Ahmadu Bello (Sardauna of Sokoto)
Courtesy of the United Nations

Michael I. Okpara
Courtesy of the Nigerian Consulate, New York City

Samuel L. Akintola
Courtesy of the Nigerian Embassy, Washington

Dennis Osadebay
Courtesy of the Nigerian Consulate, New York City

Lagos Demonstrators
Prior to 1964 Election
in Police Custody
Photograph by The New York Times

Northern Muslims Listening to Emir
Photograph by the Author

Northern City (Kano)
Courtesy of the Nigerian Consulate, New York City

Southern City (Ibadan)
Photograph by C. Davis Fogg

Trader, Kano Market
Photograph by C. Davis Fogg

Farm Couple,
Egedebe, Eastern Nigeria
Photograph by C. Davis Fogg

The reappointed Prime Minister followed with a speech in which he promised to form a " 'broadly based' government that would cater for all our people."[30] He also promised to call a conference to review the Constitution. The UPGA leaders shortly thereafter backed down from their threats.

Appointments to the Government pursuant to the Prime Minister's promise to make his government broadly based were completed after elections were held in March 1964 in the previously boycotted constituencies in the East and Lagos.* The Government was indeed broadly based — it included 54 ministers, double the number in the previous government.† The NPC took 22 of the ministries, 15 of those with cabinet rank. The NCNC and NNDP were assigned respectively 16 and 14 ministers (11 NCNC and 7 NNDP being of cabinet rank). The Action Group was not represented in the cabinet.

Nigeria did come through her most serious political crisis. Her leaders were able to compromise from increasingly hostile positions. But the political situation after the compromise does not suggest that the causes of the crisis had disappeared.

In 1965 politics were perhaps even more regionalized than in 1960. Not one of the major parties' leaders ran for election to the Federal House. To be sure, during the past elections there had been two national coalitions. But one, the NNA, was held together in large measure by a belief in regionalization. The other, UPGA, was formed largely because of Southern antipathy toward the North. During the crisis its senior partner, the NCNC, showed that it was willing to sacrifice the coalition, and perhaps the nation, for the interests of the NCNC, the East, and the Ibo people. Future moves toward less particularistic politics were scarcely made easier by the increased entrenchment of NPC and NCNC power in the North and East. The Midwest was also becoming increas-

---

of Justice, to resign from the Zikists, saying "our great philosophy developed cold feet."[28] The Secretary General of the Zikist movement commented that what failed was not Zikism as a philosophy but "the powerful mortal form on which . . . Zikism was hung."[29]

*UPGA candidates won 52 of the 54 seats at stake. The remaining two were won by independents.

†The enlargement of the cabinet in order to accommodate NCNC members of the UPGA coalition was somewhat ironic in view of the UPGA manifesto's claim that the number of existing ministers in the nation's various governments was "scandalous" and an "unpardonable drain" upon the nation's slender resources.[31]

ingly the bastion of a single party.* The West, after three years of turmoil, remained the one relatively open region, but regionalism and Yoruba nationalism became increasingly the dominant themes.†

As is discussed in the next chapter, the trend toward single-party control of Nigeria's regions and the regional characteristics of Nigeria's political parties has, for the short term, had some stabilizing effects and may, anomalously, have helped the early development of Nigeria's democratic system. But for the long term the trend and the characteristics of the parties are dangerous. The present party system and recent developments reflect *and* at the same time keep alive the ethnic divisions that could worsen to destroy the Nigerian federation. Time should be on the side of evolution toward greater national unity. But as the parties become entrenched in power in their respective regions there are dangers of a rigidity that will retard or prevent that evolution.

The principal solution to the crisis — an enormous increase in ministerial positions — was not itself particularly healthy for the future of Nigeria's political system. Many Nigerians, particularly young Nigerians, are already hostile to politicians, and to the political system, because of their belief that the politicians are selfish and greedy.

As Nigeria faces the problem of evolving away from its regionalistic politics — or at least avoiding increasing ethnic tension through party controversy — it at the same time faces the problem of a conflict between the generations. And it faces those problems in a context of frustration — frustration at the growing gap between rich and poor countries, frustration at the fact that independence has not done a great deal to bring a more abundant life to the people. Given its present and future problems, can Nigeria be expected to continue to develop as a democracy?

---

*In the spring of 1965 all but one of the opposition members of the Midwestern House of Assembly crossed the carpet to the NCNC.

†In the spring of 1965 one of the more controversial assertions of Yoruba nationalism occurred. The Vice-Chancellor (president) of Lagos University, Dr. Eni Njoku, was replaced by Dr. Saburi Biobaku. Both men were respected academicians, but Njoku was an Ibo and Biobaku was a Yoruba. The inference was strong that Yoruba nationalists were unwilling to tolerate two Ibos (Dr. K. O. Dike at Ibadan and Dr. Njoku at Lagos) as the heads of the two federal universities, both of which were in the Yoruba area. The *West African Pilot* saw Njoku as having been "shoed out to make room for a child of the bedchamber," which reflected a war against "the Jews of Nigeria for no other offense than that they are pushful and alert."[32] Opposition to the replacement, including opposition from Yoruba students, forced the closing of the University for three months.

Prospects for Democracy

Nigeria is a democracy. This chapter considers how Nigeria came to be a democracy and some factors bearing upon whether she is likely to remain one.

The Roots of Democracy

That Nigeria should be a democracy when she became independent was usually assumed. The only form of democracy seriously considered was the British parliamentary system. The prevailing view was expressed two years before independence by Jalo Waziri, a Northern member of the House of Representatives who later became its Speaker. "Western," he said, "and, in fact, the British democracy is the only type of government suited to this country."[1] It was not merely the British Parliamentary system that was chosen; it was twentieth-century British democracy with the vote extended to all adults (other than women in the North). There was, and is, no requirement that they be literate. Nigeria moved almost immediately to universal-suffrage democracy. It did not follow the historic pattern of Great Britain and the United States whereby the vote was first extended to classes limited by property or income qualifications and then gradually extended to other classes as — depending upon one's point of view — they became sufficiently aware of issues to vote upon them or sufficiently aware of their strength, and the strength of the democratic principle, to win their rights.*

The willingness of Nigeria's current rulers to skip stages and disregard historical patterns in the attainment of a democracy with universal suffrage contrasts with their reluctance to do so in order to attain a union of African states. As is further developed in Chapter 12, their position has been that the jumping-off place to African unity must be one of the intermediate steps — the nation state — and that the feet must remain firmly planted upon that step for some time before a successful jump can possibly be made. Yet at the same time they have, thus far, acted on the premise that all intermediate steps to the attainment of a democracy with universal suffrage can be skipped.

Conversely, some of those Nigerians who have been most enthusiastic about the immediate attainment of African unity have opposed full democracy and have opted instead for a more gradual, guided or tutorial democracy. Thus, Chike Obi, who views the union of West African States with "religious passion,"[2] also contends that the country must have an inspirational dictatorship for twenty years before becoming a parliamentary democracy.[3] Such a benevolent dictatorship, modeled after Kemal Ataturk's in Turkey, was, he wrote in his analysis of the "problems of the Negro peoples' struggling for true freedom," the only way "to succeed in persuading the illiterate, ignorant, lazy, individualistic, and undisciplined natives of Nigeria to make a great physical and mental sacrifice in military and labour camps for the defence of their country and the common good."[4]

Chike Obi's approach has heretofore been a distinctly minor theme. Most Nigerians were constant and fervent during the advance toward independence in affirming their faith in democracy. But some of their reasons for favoring democracy prior to independence are likely to lose their force and vitality as time passes.

The Nigerians favored democracy in part because they realized that doing so was a necessary tactic in their negotiations with the British for independence. The British could not have been expected to hand over power peacefully to some sort of totalitarian government. Nigerians believed, as Nnamdi Azikiwe said, that "it is a declared policy of Britain

---

*Lagos and Calabar, with their limited franchise seats on the prewar and immediately postwar Legislative Council, stand as a minor exception to this statement as does a very brief period of taxpayer suffrage in the regions.

that no colony can be considered ready for self-government unless it has made parliamentary democracy a political reality."[5]

Certain claimed justifications for colonialism made it particularly likely, moreover, that the Nigerian nationalists would seek to replace colonialism with a democratic form of government with universal, or near universal, suffrage. Colonialism rests upon an elitist philosophy of government. The colonial administrator, claiming to be more advanced, wiser, and fairer than "his people," would develop them to his level and was therefore entitled to rule them. Hostile to colonialism and to its tutorial justification, it would have been surprising if the nationalists had themselves put forward a similar elitist philosophy to justify their right to rule autocratically in the interest of the masses. Furthermore, though British rule was defended and justified by elitist and tutorial theories, the British opposed nationalist agitation for a more significant role on the ground that the agitators were unrepresentative of their fellow countrymen. Colonialism in its later stages was based upon the absurd proposition that a foreign elite should rule because it was an elite but an indigenous elite should *not* rule because it was an elite. As Lord Lugard said:

> It is a cardinal principle of British Colonial policy that the interests of a large native population shall not be subject to the will . . . of a small minority of educated and Europeanized natives who have nothing in common with them, and whose interests are often opposed to theirs. . . .[6]

Faced with that attitude, the nationalist politician could best overcome it by seeking a mandate from the people.

There is some power left to the idea that independent Nigeria should be a free society because colonial Nigeria was not. Thus, for example, the Northern Nigerian legislature repealed in 1962 some old colonial laws that gave the Government the right to imprison people without a trial, banish native authority officials without a hearing, and required deposits from newspapers before they could publish. The reason given was that those laws were unnecessary and "unsuitable in an independent Nigeria."[7]

Now that Nigerians have taken over from the British the difficult problems of governing a divided and underdeveloped country, however, the efficiency of the relatively autocratic colonial system is seen to have some advantages. The Federal Government newspaper made that point when it editorialized, "we must rule with the same efficiency with

151

which the British governed, we must be as firm as they in ensuring that . . . the obstructionist was crushed."[8]

To the extent that democracy was espoused as a tactic with which to persuade the British to grant independence or to undercut the theoretical justification for colonialism, much of the force behind democracy was weakened when the British relinquished power and Nigeria became independent. Though vastly oversimplified, the contrast between the use of democratic philosophy in colonial Nigeria's relations with Great Britain in the twentieth century and colonial America's relations with Great Britain in the eighteenth century tells something about the vitality of the democratic idea in each country after its independence. In America the democratic philosophy was an exciting revolutionary concept challenging British principle as well as British power; in Nigeria it was an established principle, espousal of which was necessary to win British approval of independence.

In addition to being a tactic with which to persuade the British to depart and a contrast with British colonial rule, the idea that Nigeria would be a democracy satisfied a deep longing among many of Nigeria's leaders. Ability to make a democratic system work was taken to be the hallmark of a mature people. Democracy was seen as a way to combat and overcome the bitterly resented assumption of some that Africans were inferior. "Parliamentary democracy," said Nnamdi Azikiwe, "has been used as a criterion to determine the political maturity of any people under the rule of others and we can be no exception."[9] To contend that Nigeria's citizens were not ready for democracy was to reveal the heart of a racist who "still regard[s] an African society as a group of inferior races," Obafemi Awolowo argued when he attacked the "new-fangled theory" that it is "inappropriate and hardly fair" to expect a newly emergent African nation to practice the democracy of Western Europe or America.[10]*

The appeal of liberal democracy as proof against assumptions of inferiority, as an answer to racial prejudice, still has force but will have less and less as time passes. As Nigerians continue to face the responsibilities of government, attention will be given more to whether democ-

---

*Chief Awolowo went on to discuss the idea of reaching universal-suffrage democracy by stages, saying that he was tired of the British "expatiating to the point of nausea" on the length of time it took them to advance from feudalism to democracy and adding that "it must always be remembered . . . [that] under existing conditions late-comers have the singular advantage of benefiting from the experiences and accomplishments of older nations."[11]

152

racy is in fact suited to Nigeria's needs and less to whether it satisfies some longing caused by the frustrations of colonial rule.

Indeed, in many African states, a system of government described as "African democracy" has been supported in part because it is different than the democracy practised in the leading Western democracies. "African democracy" permits only a single party without organized opposition outside the party or any centers of power other than the party and government. Opposition, insofar as it exists, is meant to take place within the party, which should be mass-based rather than, as the Communist party, an elite cadre. Under the ideal model, the party is to govern in the interest of the people rather than an elite, and the party, by referendum or election, is periodically to seek a new mandate from the people. Under the ideal model, there is also to be free discussion of alternative policies within the party until a consensus is reached, or a decision comes from the top, at which point the decision is to be carried out by strict party discipline.

"African democracy" is said to be consistent with African tribal traditions. It is said that while there might have been opposing camps when a chief was selected, the community fused after the choice was made. Various points of view might have been discussed at tribal councils, but the effort always was to reach a consensus. Never did the majority say that its solution must be accepted because it was the majority, and if, after the long discussion, there were losers, never did they carry their opposition further. Unanimity was almost a mystical necessity. (Traditional systems, however, have also been cited as supporting parliamentary or multiparty democracy. Thus the constitutional monarchies of the Yoruba and the individualistic tendencies of the Ibo have been said by Nigerians to prove that "all the materials for building sound foundations for parliamentary democracy are to be found in the ethnic composition of the country."[12])

Obviously "African democracy" rests upon forces more powerful than the desire to make African government unique, or to express the African personality and African traditions. Having a single party is on its face more consistent with the paramount aim of achieving national unity than having several parties, particularly if they tend to reflect regional or ethnic differences.* A single party is also consistent with

*A single party is perhaps also more consistent with quick Pan-African political union. It is difficult to reconcile several parties seeking power under a national constitution with a supranational ideal. Ghana's Kwame Nkrumah's desire for an

the premise that the poor, harassed African nations cannot afford to waste any of their limited talent in opposition parties. To have opposing ideas thrashed out quietly within the party instead of publicly in parliamentary or press battle is praised as less confusing to the people.*

Few Nigerians have converted the truth that there need not be an opposition in a democracy at any given time into the theory of "African democracy" that there should not be an opposition. Few have suggested that a one-party state would be suitable for Nigeria's needs.†

Nnamdi Azikiwe has been particularly outspoken against a one-party system. "Surely, this is an invitation to totalitarianism," he said in his annual birthday speech in 1962. On the second anniversary of Independence he spoke to the nation over the radio to "implore" all to "pledge anew our inflexible faith in liberal democracy as the system of government best suited to our present situation."[15] Azikiwe's remarks take on special significance since he is as *African* as any of the leading Nigerian politicians.

Azikiwe's shifting emphases on the subject of democracy are significant. On the third anniversary of Nigeria's independence he spoke of the manner in which Nigeria's respect for "the ideals of parliamentary democracy" have "distinguished us from the other emerging nations of the world," reflecting an increasing sense of national consciousness.[16] Whereas ten years earlier he had said that parliamentary democracy was a criterion of Nigeria's "political maturity" and had emphasized the need to meet Britain's standards, it is significant that in 1962 he described liberal democracy as "best suited to our present situation."

Whether liberal democracy is best suited to Nigeria's present situation

---

African continental government and his moves toward a single party state are related, though it is also true that either of the two attitudes can exist independently of the other.

*In the majority of the Ghanaian languages, for example, there is said to be no word meaning "opposition" other than the one meaning "enemy."[13]

†Dennis Osadebay is one Nigerian leader who since independence has come out in favor of a one-party system. He has referred to traditional tribal methods of government in Nigeria, but his principal argument has been that the multiparty system has been detrimental to the nation's unity, with parties based upon regions and ethnic groups within regions. "It has," he adds, "brought in its wake bitterness, enmity, hostility, violence, hatred, victimization, imprisonment and even death."[14] It may well be that his views have been influenced by his position as leader of the Midwest. The argument that a new, underdeveloped state cannot afford the duplication and waste of talent involved in a multiparty system is strongest in the Midwest Region, which is much less populated than other regions.

and whether it is likely to remain so is problematical. Discussion awaits consideration of the reasons why there has been an increasing trend toward a single party in each of the regions.

The Trend Toward a Single Party in the Regions

The underlying reason for the existence of extremely powerful parties in the North, the East, and (until the Action Group crisis) the West has been developed in earlier chapters. It stems from the political solidarity of the dominant regional majorities — Ibos in the East, Fulanis, Hausas, and the Islamic peoples generally in the North, and Yorubas in the West. The corollary to that solidarity has been oppositions within each region that are based primarily upon the fears and demands of minority ethnic groups. But after the Minorities Commission and the Constitutional Conferences decided not to create any new states and instead provided in the Constitution for an involved procedure by which new states could be created (which required, among other things, the consent of two regional legislatures) it became increasingly obvious to minority leaders in the North and East that their future lies in cooperating with the existing regional governments and in seeking to better their lot and that of their constituents from inside the majority party.

That analysis helps explain the increasing strength of the governing party in each of the regions. But it is by no means the complete explanation for any of the regions; for example, it has little relevance to the decline of the NEPU's strength in the North. It totally fails, moreover, to explain why the Action Group was able to increase its power in the Midwest in 1960 despite the fact that constitutional and political realities made it possible that a new state could be created in that area, as in fact it later was.

The trend toward single parties in the regions is due in part to the great strength of government relative to other centers of power and to opportunism, which has often been a feature of Nigerian politics.

Government has great control over the economy in Nigeria, and much of its power can be and has been used in a discretionary way to perpetuate existing governmental power. The Federal Government can control tariff rates and grant relief from income taxation to new (pioneer) businesses, and thus has some of this power. But the regions have more. Through Marketing Boards they determine the price that is to be paid for the major export crops and control the issuance of licenses permitting the holder to participate in the lucrative purchase of produce.* A major portion of agricultural and commercial credit comes from statutory boards or banks that are indirectly controlled by the regional governments. In the North the Government has even greater economic power than in the other regions because it owns all land and controls its use and occupancy.†

Of course neither the economic power of government nor the willingness to use that power to reward political friends and punish political enemies is unique to Nigeria. But Nigerian politicians have felt unusually free to say openly that, irrespective of merit, economic reward will come to those who are on the right side politically. Thus, campaigning in the COR area in the East, Regional Premier Okpara said, "I will give you all the amenities you require but first you must vote for me. Booty of war is always shared after war."[18]‡ If his party had not had an extremely secure majority it is doubtful whether a political leader in a democracy would have dared to imply that even simple amenities would be denied to his political opponents. The trend toward a single party in the regions is, obviously, reinforced by the existence of strong, secure majority parties.

In addition to their economic power, political parties once in power in a region have many tools with which to keep and increase their control. Among the more important are the regional governments' control over local government and chiefs, control which was inherited from the colonial regime.

The regional governments can dissolve local government bodies.§

---

*In the East, the produce-buying license of a Mr. Obioha, a leading businessman, was withdrawn after he had provided financial support to "Zik must go" rebels within the NCNC. Dr. Azikiwe was quite frank in saying that the license should be withdrawn because of that support.[17]

†An example of how that power can be used to harass the opposition is the order that the *Middle Belt Herald*, an Action Group newspaper located in Jos, shut down because it had no certificate of occupancy.

‡Such remarks do not always have their desired effect, however. In the 1959 federal election, for example, an Action Group leader, himself a former NCNC supporter, told the voters of Asaba East that the Action Group would remain in charge of the regional government and therefore responsible for providing "water, hospital, dispensary, maternity, loans and those immediate requirements of your everyday life." He then warned the voters that "if by any stroke of the misjudgment of the people of this constituency they cast their votes for a worthless NCNC candidate, the regret will be theirs and theirs for a long time."[19] The NCNC candidate won easily.

§There is a parallel between the statutory power of the regional governments

That is the equivalent of the Governor of New York State having the power to oust the Mayor of New York City. Whenever the power is exercised there are charges — which usually are not rebutted — of irresponsibility, inefficiency, or corruption.[20] But the power has been used so often against local bodies that happen to be controlled by the opposition that a strong suspicion is left that the regional governments use their power as a tool to curb the opposition as well as to keep local government responsible. Thus, in a period of one week in the West in 1960, NCNC-controlled councils in Ilesha, Ijesha, and Benin were dissolved. The Northern Government has dissolved the Ilorin local council controlled by the Action Group and Ilorin Talaka Parapo alliance and the UMBC-Action Group–controlled council in Jos.

In the East and the North the regional government also has the power to change the ratio between elected and appointed members in local governments. Because the appointed members are appointed directly or indirectly by the regional government, and the chiefs and others most likely to be appointed are usually supporters of the government, that also is a potent tool for perpetuating the power of the governing party. It can be used to convert a majority for the opposition among elected members to an overall majority for the government party by changing the ratio and injecting the necessary number of cooperative appointees. An example of where it was used was in Ilorin, where after the dissolution referred to above the number of elected members was reduced from 51 to 34 and the number of traditional members increased from 6 to 18.

The ability to control local government bodies and chiefs is extremely useful to the party in power at the regional center. It can be used to keep all patronage plums at the extremities as well as the center in its hands, and it can be used to deny the opposition an opportunity of showing their abilities on a small scale. It is a dangerous power in a

---

to dissolve a local government body and the constitutional power of the Federal Government to declare a state of emergency, remove the elected government of a region, and rule through an administrator. When the Federal Government did take over the Western Region in 1962, the writer was struck by the absence of comment from Nigerians who were politically uncommitted that, however shocking the fighting had been and however foul the corruption charged may have been, the Federal Government had gone further than it should have. One reason why such comment was not heard may have been that Nigerians, accustomed to regional power over local governments, had come to accept the principle that the larger government can always "sack" the smaller.

157

democracy for those reasons. It is also dangerous because when pushed too far it denies the people the opportunity of controlling their own local affairs which, since most easily understood, offer them the best training in self-rule. It is a reasonable hypothesis that central control in France of the local government system has been one of the reasons why the French have had such great difficulty in working their democracy.

Yet even the most ardent supporter of democracy would have to agree that it would be taking a great risk to dispense with the regional governments' powers and rely solely upon the good sense of the electorate, plus possible criminal sanctions. Local self-government is new; it is not certain how the electorate would react to corruption; the supply of skilled administrators is short and most go to the regional or the Federal Government; the underlying loyalty of some local units to their region, not to speak of the nation, is not assured. The regional governments have not been willing to take that risk. Their reluctance to do so is an example of the attitude earlier referred to whereby it was suggested that with independence won, the Nigerian rulers would see great advantages to the efficiency of the relatively autocratic system of colonial rule. For in their local government policy the Nigerian rulers, as their British predecessors, have opted for the security of efficient government rather than the risks of freedom. The continuing limitations upon the powers of local governments also illustrate that democratic elective politics were imposed rather suddenly upon the people from above rather than building up from below.

The regional governments also have complete constitutional power over chiefs. They either choose them directly or have a veto over the selections of traditional kingmakers. (Increasingly often, moreover, great chieftaincies, such as the Emirate of Bida in 1962, have been going to political leaders of the majority parties.*) In addition to the appointive power, the regional governments have the right to depose chiefs, determine their rank, and determine their salary.[22]

It seems anomalous even to suggest that democratically elected governments' power over chiefs could make the development of a healthy

---

*In 1962, Usman Sarki, an NPC leader, resigned his powerful position as Federal Minister of Information to become Etsu Nupe, with his palace located in Bida in Northern Nigeria. When during the following year he criticized President Azikiwe for deploring the area's abject poverty, the NCNC expressed resentment of his preference of a chiefly over a ministerial post and attacked him for leaving "civilization for the dark limbo of feudal lordship." The *West African Pilot* editorialized that he suffered from "Lugardism."[12]

democracy difficult. For the long term, reduction of the chiefs' power is an essential step toward a mobile society and the development of loyalties wider than the traditional tribal unit — necessary characteristics for the successful operation of Nigeria's democracy and the cementing of the Nigerian union. Indeed, the fact that the aristocratic elements still have such great local power in Nigeria without any great objection from the mass of the people makes one wonder how tenaciously the people would cling to their prerogative of selecting the more remote regional and Federal Governments. Nevertheless, for the short term the power of the democratically elected governments over the chiefs does tend to perpetuate the power of governments in power, which may or may not be desirable. Chiefs can often determine the result of elections. Since they know on which side their bread is buttered, most have favored the political parties in power without great regard to what kind of a job they were doing.

The party in control in a region has, therefore, many effective tools with which to check potential centers of opposition, and more or less subtly can put pressure on individuals or groups to support it. The other side of the coin is equally important in explaining the one-party trend in the regions. Many groups and institutions that could check governmental power are relatively weak in Nigeria. That reflects her status as an underdeveloped country just having emerged from colonial rule.

Of the educated elite a large percentage goes into the civil service. They do so for many reasons: the pay is relatively good, the job secure, and the prestige very high because traditionally these were the jobs of the colonialists.[23] Nigeria is lucky to have a competent civil service, but since, following in the British tradition, civil servants are forbidden to give any public opinions on politics or administration, the country is deprived of guidance from a very high proportion of its most capable and knowledgeable citizens.*

Of course that phenomenon will disappear as there are fewer openings in the civil service and more of Nigeria's capable young men seek jobs outside government. But thus far most such Nigerians, those who are free to speak out, have been very wary of criticizing governmental action. The explanation of columnist Tai Solarin is that Nigerians are too

---

*A recent survey taken in the Eastern Region suggests that civil servants believe they must be more aloof from politics than in fact is the case. Slightly over half the sample did not hold a party membership card because of their erroneous belief that civil servants could not do so.[24]

respectful of their government because the governments have inherited the prestige and pomp of the colonialists. "We are all slaves of colonial mentality," he said, "the ghost of a hundred-year old colonialism is marching triumphantly on. . . ."[25] Another Nigerian simply thinks his countrymen are overly concerned with their own security, writing:

> In Nigeria and in many African countries the intellectuals are in the grip of such a terrible lockjaw that all they do is crawl about in their cubicles fearful lest they lose their jobs. Most of us prefer to lose our freedom to the tyrant than to be without the material comforts of life. As a consequence it is difficult in Africa to maintain and sustain healthy public opinion.[26]

A further curb upon critical examination of governments is that criticism sometimes seems unpatriotic; when there are many prejudiced persons instinctively inclined to find fault, why give them fuel? Despite all those factors tending to curb criticism, however, many students, intellectuals, and much of the press has been highly critical of governmental action — often, however, in a region other than the critic's home base.

One must come back again and again to the great relative strength of government in Nigeria. With so few other sources of power it is hard indeed to be an independent, a rebel, or a reformer. This also helps to explain why so many politicians elected as members of an opposition party have switched sides — crossed the carpet — to support the majority.

A politician's seat is immensely valuable; a minister's pay is a fortune. An ordinary member of a legislature is paid approximately $2,800 per year plus allowances; a minister is paid approximately $8,400 plus allowances. Those are gigantic sums in Nigeria: a minister's salary alone is at least eighty-four times the average per capita income. (That is the equivalent of paying a United States Cabinet member $200,000.) Many politicians have managed to profit from their positions by means other than receipt of pay and allowances. An example is the number of politicians and politicians' relatives who obtained plots of the extremely valuable former Crown Lands in Lagos that were distributed shortly after independence.

To stand a chance of being a minister, to increase vastly one's chances of being elected at all, and to get all the advantages that go with being a member of the governing party, one must join it.* Chief Osadabay's

---

*The number of ministers is almost incredible. In October 1963, the West had

remarks that "ninety-nine percent of Nigerian political carpet crossers do so for personal gain rather than for ideological conviction" may be somewhat exaggerated in its proportion, but represents the general consensus among Nigerians, and is probably not far wrong.[28]

There are differences between the programs of the Nigerian political parties, but the ease with which some politicians have managed to switch sides does not suggest that they take those differences very seriously. As for the voters, there does not seem to have been any particular protest among those whose representatives have changed sides, which indicates either that they realize that to receive their share of amenities they must be on the winning side or that they really are not very concerned with what their representatives do.

The public media by which a healthy public opinion can best be molded — the press, radio, and television — are stronger and more independent in Nigeria than elsewhere in Africa, but there are, nevertheless, shortcomings. The radio and television stations, though owned in whole or in part by governments, are controlled by statutory boards somewhat protected against governmental interference. Nevertheless, the federal and regional ministers of information can give directions on matters of policy and public interest, and it would hardly be expected that stations owned by a government would serve as a very effective check upon its activity.*

There is a greater variety in the ownership of newspapers. There are some that are owned and run by quasi-governmental corporations such

---

thirty-one ministers, and a House of Assembly of ninety-four members. The North and East each had twenty-one ministers. The federal cabinet appointed after the 1964-65 election had fifty-four ministers. The democratic system itself becomes increasingly vulnerable to such wasteful and inefficient practices. The defense that large numbers of ministers are necessary to keep varying ethnic and local groups happy will not work among the new generation, which is economically frustrated itself and which talks more and more of the gap between the living standards of the masses and the elite.[27]

*The Federal Minister of Information was not given the power to give policy directives until the summer of 1961. When the House of Representatives was debating the change, he read letters from all four major political parties which suggested that news broadcasting was impartial only in that it was pleasing none of them. The NPC began the series by expressing its "grave concern over the continued discrimination." The NCNC, NEPU, and Action Group followed, complaining respectively of an "uncooperative and vexatious attitude," that "releases are being shortened or abandoned," and of "bias in favor of the NPC and its partners."[29]

as the *Nigerian Citizen*, and some that are owned by and run in the interest of a political party, such as the NPC's *Kano Daily Mail*. The *West African Pilot* (of the Zik chain) is closely associated with the NCNC, though not owned by it. Finally, some like the *Daily Times* are independent.

There are some weaknesses. The newspaper with by far the largest circulation and the only major independent, the *Daily Times*, is foreign-owned. Realization that it is therefore vulnerable may explain why it has sometimes avoided controversy. Without subsidies most Nigerian newspapers have a hard time surviving. Sales are held down because the literacy rate is low; the communal style of living means that a single copy of a newspaper is read by several persons — one of Nigeria's leading journalists guesses that the average copy is read by ten persons.[30] Since commerce and industry are underdeveloped, advertising is skimpy.*

For all its weaknesses, however, the press is probably the most potent institution supporting democratic freedom in Nigeria. There is a tradition of hard-hitting, fearless, and independent journalism which has carried over from the colonial days when the press was the spearhead of nationalism. Though most papers are intensely partisan, they have several times agreed with each other and opposed the authorities who sought to restrict freedom — of the press or individuals.† The most important occasion was during the summer of 1963, when all the regional premiers and the Federal Prime Minister said that, as a part of the con-

*It has been suggested, moreover, that as a disproportionate amount of commerce and industry is foreign owned so a disproportionate amount of advertising goes to foreign-owned newspapers.[31]

†During the Western Region emergency two pro-Action Group journalists, Lateef K. Jakande, then the only African on the International Press Institute's Executive Board, and V. Bisi Onabanjo, were placed in restriction because, or so it then appeared, of their blistering attacks upon the Federal Government's action and their threat to expose high federal officials as corrupt. The Nigerian Newspaper Guild, including editors strongly opposed to the Action Group, protested the restrictions as infringing upon press freedom. (Jakande was later convicted and Onabanjo acquitted in the Awolowo treason trial.)

How weak the tradition that the press should be free is outside the press, however, is suggested by the order issued later during the emergency which forbade newspapers even to refer to people held under restriction, or to the regulation forbidding them to do so, without the approval of a federal official. Hostility toward the press, and the belief of many politicians that Nigerian newspapers are irresponsible, underlay an amendment to the federal Newspapers Act passed in October 1964, which made criminal the publication of statements or rumors known to be false and placed upon the editor the burden of showing he took reasonable steps to verify the statement or rumor.

stitutional changes accompanying the transition to a republic, the various governments should be given power to imprison people without trial under a preventive detention law similar to that made famous by Ghana's Kwame Nkrumah. Most of the major newspapers denounced the proposal and it was withdrawn.

Most of Nigeria's largest businesses are foreign-owned. Because of the governments' great economic power, all business is under heavy pressure to conform, but there is extra pressure placed upon these that are foreign-owned. Their executives, particularly if foreign, must avoid any attempt to lead public opinion on controversial issues because their continued presence in the country depends in large measure upon their success in avoiding conflict with any group in the population, most of all the government of the day.*

Contrary to business, labor has felt quite free to engage in activity that challenges governmental power. A general strike that was threatened at the transition to a republic in the fall of 1963 and called in the spring of 1964 was effective to bring substantial benefits to workers, despite official discouragement. Indeed, the power of Nigeria's modern-sector labor force as compared with the power of the far more numerous but relatively unorganized peasant farmers is striking.

Many of the characteristics of Nigerian society that have contributed to the one-party trend in the regions make it difficult to operate a democracy and, incidentally, also are symptomatic of the difficulties of uniting the nation. In a sense Nigeria is underdeveloped politically in the same way as it is underdeveloped economically. The economic weaknesses are closely related to the political weaknesses. That is not to say that the country was not ready for self-government. To the contrary, it is clear that independence was essential to the further political development of the Nigerian people just as much as to the country's further economic development. But it does mean that the country will find it difficult to operate as a multiparty liberal democracy.

Asking observers not to draw racist conclusions if liberal democracy is cast aside in a newly independent country, Prime Minister Tafawa

---

*Similar forces tend to reduce the influence of the Christian Church, though Nigeria has had no incident like that in Ghana in 1962 when the Anglican Bishop was expelled because he criticized Ghana's Young Pioneers for their quasi-deification of Kwame Nkrumah. The Church's hierarchy is being increasingly Nigerianized but it too still has a strong foreign tinge. According to a Catholic Father teaching at Ibadan, moreover, the Church must also be wary of controversy because its flock's allegiance is new and largely untested.[32]

Balewa pointed out some of those difficulties when he said, "it is not possible . . . to wipe out illiteracy overnight or develop by legislative processes the degree of tolerance for the other man's point of view which can only come through years of practice and training."* It is hard to measure why that makes it difficult to operate as a liberal democracy, but it clearly does. (However, people in a largely literate country like the United States or Great Britain should be careful not to judge illiterates in a largely illiterate country like Nigeria by what they know of illiterates in their own country.) Probably even more important than limitations placed by illiteracy upon the flow and sources of information is that illiterates are more likely than literate persons to be parochial in their attitudes, prejudiced against strangers, and unable to weigh the views of strangers on their merits. As most of Nigeria's citizens are illiterate and thus have not been able to broaden their horizons through reading, so most live in the traditional ethnic homeland and thus have not broadened their horizons through contact with persons of a different sort than their ethnic, or even village, brothers. Similarly, Nigeria has only a small middle class — a class whose members are aware of interests they have in common with ethnic outsiders and desire change, but orderly change.

The fact that Nigeria *is* functioning as a democracy operates in some ways to change the characteristics of her society that make it difficult so to function. Governments which wish to retain the support of the Nigerian electorate must do one thing above all else — supply schools for the children of the voters.† The act of voting contributes more subtly toward changing traditional attitudes. The masses in an under-developed society are held back by a fatalistic state of mind; they lack conviction that much of man's destiny is in his own hands. Voting, and then observing the favorable or unfavorable results visited upon a

*The Prime Minister's remarks show the continuance of the previously mentioned feeling that a democratic system should be espoused so as to rebut racial prejudice. He vigorously asserted that no "racial group has a monopoly of dictatorial tendencies," and that "even in those climes where [democracy] is today firmly established, there had been long and bitter struggles against authoritarian or dictatorial tendencies." He also insisted that there is no evidence that "intelligent discussion . . . [or] tolerance is the exclusive heritage of any racial group."[33]

†The great emphasis upon education — particularly primary school education — however, also serves to create Nigeria's most explosive and revolutionary social problem. Each year thousands of boys leave primary school apparently destined for frustration. They will not go back to the family farm and they are not sufficiently educated to qualify for most of the jobs in the modern economy.

164

community because of its vote, is an object lesson in the power that man has to control his own future.

The Prospects

The strongest reasons for democracy in Nigeria and the strongest threats to democracy in Nigeria are closely linked. The more one considers why Nigeria's interest will be served by continuing to develop as a democracy, the more one realizes the pitfalls that lie ahead.

The newly free, underdeveloped, former colonial nations like Nigeria are in a period of profound communal crisis. They are changing in an awesome fashion. They seek to telescope into a few decades what was accomplished in the West in centuries. They want to move even faster away from their past than they did during the disrupting years of colonial control. Yet at the same time, particularly since their political independence, they want to retain and restore elements of their tradition. They desperately want to be like the developed world and yet they desperately want to be different from it. There is an enormous gap in education, in economic advantage, and in attitude between the elite and the great masses of the people. The strength of the ties that hold the nation together is uncertain.

It is that crisis that makes some form of democracy particularly desirable for a nation like Nigeria. It is, however, also that crisis that most threatens democracy.

It is not possible to tell what economic, social, and political institutions will emerge from the conflicting forces bubbling away in the world of which Nigeria forms a part. Nor is it possible to say what institutions will prove to be the most appropriate expressions of these societies' needs. It is this lack of prescience that renders democracy particularly suitable. With the road to the future so unclear, some form of democracy can best assure the evolution of appropriate institutions and best satisfy the need to express deeply-felt, changing desires. Democracy can best keep open the two-way communication between the leader and the led without which both begin to lose the ability to influence the other.

Yet as in any crisis situation, the simple, direct, apparently speedy solution increases in appeal. Democracy is not simple; its processes often seem slow. Thus, from out of the frustrations of a critical time can come the demand for a system, preferably with a single leader or guide, in which the rules are simply and directly laid down without contention, without press squabbles, without disruptive elections. Russian Communism's chief propaganda weapon in Africa is its claim that it succeeded in swiftly modernizing the economy and the society of a relatively backward nation.

Frustration is particularly dangerous to the new democracies. In most, democracy was something which the indigenous elite, in combination with the former colonial power, selected for the new nation. There was no popular ground swell from the grass roots pressing for the right to choose regional or national governments. Any system of government used after independence, moreover, would be vulnerable because of the frustrations of the crisis period, including the realization that political independence does not bring the economic bonanza that was hinted at by politicians prior to independence.

Another characteristic of the period of crisis in any new nation, and perhaps particularly in an African setting, is that criticism tends to be deeply resented. The new rulers are anxious to prove that they are as efficient and wise as the colonial administrators who preceded them. A few citizens have doubted that they can be.[34] Much of the outside world has doubted that countries like Nigeria were prepared to govern themselves. That doubt is made all the more provoking to Nigerians by its connection with racial prejudice. Given that background, criticism of the government is suspect for it is often looked upon as providing ammunition for the racists, and as unpatriotic in a time of national crisis. It is also looked upon as subversive where the government is not sure of the loyalty of the masses to the nation.

Thus the free flow of constructive criticism, which keeps a democracy alive, is hard for governments to swallow. Antipathy toward criticism in Nigeria is, moreover, reinforced by the rather narrow view of their role that members of the political opposition in all parts of the Federation have sometimes seemed to take. Often they have apparently opposed certain measures purely for the sake of opposing them.*

Related to distaste for criticism as subversive is a feeling that the nation cannot afford the luxury of opposition or the dispersion of talent into a government and an opposition. That that conception is not unique

---

*Perhaps they have done so by accentuating a tendency in British politics — that the opposition has a duty to put forward the reasons against a measure without much regard for the strength of those reasons. And perhaps that tendency is accentuated in Nigeria, as in Britain, by the parliamentary system, which reduces the freedom of individual legislators to vote for what they think is best.

to the African and Asian nations that have emerged since World War II — and is not necessarily inconsistent with democracy — is shown by George Washington's warnings against factions, against the very concept of political parties, in his farewell address as the first President of the United States.

Democracy helps the leaders of a nation in crisis meet and guide the wishes of its masses. But the leaders may so dislike the masses' wishes as to decide to discard the system. In a country like Nigeria, where the elite hold such power and the existing democratic system neither developed from the grass roots nor has clearly become a central tenet of the people's beliefs, the continued support of the elite for the country's democratic system is essential.

With government being so much the focus of power, with the pay and prestige of politicians so great, the prospect of defeat in an election may, if it becomes sufficiently realistic, simply not be swallowed. There are less selfish grounds for which the present elite might decide that the democratic system of government should be discarded.

The major political problem facing Nigeria, and most other new nations, is and will continue to be the problem of ensuring national unity. With differing degrees of enthusiasm, the elite from all ethnic groups are generally speaking, committed to unity. The next generation of the elite is more strongly committed to unity. But for the great mass of the people today the choice between tribe and nation is not even relevant. The tribe or subtribe is paramount; the nation, if known, is secondary.

It is not, moreover, completely clear that increasing sophistication among the masses will always bring about an increasing sense of national unity. It is significant that racial prejudice — a common reaction against which has been an important bond between the members of today's elite from different ethnic groups — will in the future be less important in the daily lives of Africans, at least in West Africa.

In any event, democracy can bring ethnic and regional jealousy to the surface. Election campaigns in Nigeria have as a dominant note calls to the children of the soil to band together to reject and defeat the stranger at the gate. The trend toward a single party in each region, with ethnic minorities within the regions forming the most significant countertrends, illustrates also how the democratic system reflects ethnic separatism.

There is much to be said for the theory (put forward with greatest influence in Nigeria's past history by the Minorities Commission) that democracy itself offers the best way to overcome ethnic jealousy and

167

separatism. To win elections political parties must broaden their base. They cannot afford to alienate large groups of voters. Also, as outlined above, the pressures of a democratic system tend to favor education, which can be a strong force against ethnic jealousy. But there are several factors in Nigeria which could render the theory academic. Impatience is one. That democratic campaigning has in fact for the short term brought to the surface, rather then glossed over, ethnic and regional jealousy is another. Finally, as discussed further below, the trend toward a single party in the regions may stagnate and distort the tendency toward widening the base of political parties, upon which the theory depends. In any event, it seems likely that if members of the elite become convinced that democracy is inconsistent with national unity, their desire for national unity is likely to triumph over their desire for democracy.

All the foregoing statements apply to any nation of the newly free, underdeveloped world just as much as to Nigeria. And most nations of that world have abandoned democracy for some form of autocratic rule. Nigeria has not. One searches, therefore, for differences between Nigeria and other members of that world.

History, the quality of her leaders, and a host of other reasons are relevant. But perhaps most relevant of all is Nigeria's federal system and the size and balance of power that produced that system.*

Federalism depends upon the existence of some of the elements of liberal democracy, most obviously acceptance of the rule of law. There must be an impartial, independent arbiter to determine the rights of the regions and the federal government under the written federal constitution. That arbiter, usually, as in Nigeria, a supreme court, holds governments to the limitations set out in the higher law of the constitution. In addition a successful federation engenders attitudes of restraint, accommodation, and compromise which are generally essential to the succesful operation of a democratic system.

Nigeria's federal system has also helped preserve the balance of power among competing groups that has been, and at least for the short term will be, the greatest safeguard for her democratic system. Under the present political setup no single group is strong enough to impose its will on the others. The federal system, which protects the regions as relatively autonomous bases for the power of different political parties,

---

*India has those same characteristics and has also remained a democracy. India, unlike Nigeria, has had a political party with truly national power.

has helped immeasurably to protect, preserve, and even create that balance of power.

Until the Action Group crisis, the balance was simple — three regions, three strongly entrenched parties, no one of which was sufficiently powerful to impose its will unilaterally all the time upon the others. The one-party trend in the regions kept alive diversity at the center. The secure regional bases of the major parties gave each a source of funds and publicity, as well as representatives.

The Action Group crisis will probably not, for the short run at least, alter the pattern too radically. In fact, to the extent that the Akintola faction with its new allies in the NNDP emerges triumphant, the trend will increase as the governing party in the West becomes more explicitly a regional party. Nor would a national or all-party coalition government change the pattern. There still would be need for accommodation, compromise, and explanations of policy. Each of the major parties of the coalition would retain the independence and strength given to them by their regional base.

Thus, at the federal center at least, the present and likely future balance of power serves to safeguard Nigeria's democratic system. And the longer that system is preserved, the more the habits, attitudes, and institutions that support democracy can take root and grow. But again, the more one analyses why democracy in Nigeria has a breathing spell, the more one sees a future threat to democracy.

The present balance of power, because it depends upon and institutionalizes regionalism and ethnic hostility, will come under increasing attack, even though one of its side effects is to keep alive democratic diversity and flexibility. The rigidity caused by the one-party trend in the regions makes it difficult for political parties to broaden their base as democratic theory would have them do. Perhaps more than any other, the crucial test for Nigeria's democracy will be whether her present political parties can evolve toward greater national emphases. One of the lessons of the Action Group crisis, which stemmed in part from a small step in the direction of that evolution, is that the evolution will not be easy.

Much of the future of Nigeria's democracy depends upon chance: good harvests or bad, the frustrations and ambitions of men who rise to power, the temperament of army officers,* the policies of other countries,

---

*Nigeria's armed forces have thus far appeared to be completely innocent of

and a host of other unpredictable factors will contribute to the development or to the destruction of democracy in Nigeria. The following two chapters deal with the relevance to democracy of institutions under Nigeria's Constitution — the choice of her head of state, her bill of rights, and her federal system.

Before discussing those particular institutions, it is useful to make the general comment that Nigeria's institutions are unique to Nigeria. They have much in common with the British system of government. They also have something of the American, Australian, Canadian, Swiss, Indian, and Malayan patterns. But Nigeria copies exactly no country. And no country copies it exactly.

The leader of the government is a prime minister chosen from the lower house of parliament by the head of state as the man most likely to command the allegiance of a majority of the house. The lower house, whose members are elected in single-member constituencies, sits for five years unless sooner dissolved. It must be sooner dissolved if the prime minister does not resign after it passes a motion of no confidence in the prime minister or his cabinet, who are collectively responsible to the house for their actions. In all these respects Nigeria follows closely the British (Westminster) pattern of parliamentary democracy.

But the powers of the Nigerian parliament are limited by Nigeria's federal Constitution. They are further limited by the Constitution's fundamental human rights provisions. In those matters Nigeria departs from the British pattern, borrows something from several countries, and ends with a new amalgam.

A further element of Nigeria's democracy is the combination of democratically elected legislative bodies with legislative bodies representing the traditional aristocracy. The regional houses of chiefs and to a much lesser extent the Federal Senate represent the chiefs. Their

---

political intrigue both at home and abroad, in the Congo where they were the mainstay of the UN forces, and in Tanganyika, where they were invited to replace British troops who had helped put down the short-lived mutiny of the Tanganyikan army in early 1964. The traditions of the modern British army — and for the short term a number of British officers are still serving with the Nigerian army — supports the nonpolitical traditions of Nigeria's army. But proof that the British tradition is not enough to ensure a nonpolitical and passive army is given by Pakistan's military government and the early 1964 mutinies in former British East Africa. The likelihood of any of the existing political parties being able to use the army extraconstitutionally is reduced by the fact that the great majority of Nigeria's officers are Southerners while the great majority of soldiers are Northerners.

powers are much less than those of the United States Senate, but substantially greater than those of the British House of Lords.

Most of the institutions of Nigeria's democracy can be found in one country or another. But as one looks closely at the details, a substantial number are unique to Nigeria. Examples are the provisions with respect to the dissolution of Parliament, the distribution of power with respect to the control of the police between the federal and the regional governments, and the specific provisions of the fundamental rights sections of the Constitution. And the combination of institutions is one that is found in Nigeria alone.

Obviously it is more important that Nigeria's democratic institutions be uniquely suited to Nigeria than that they be unique. But the uniqueness of Nigeria's democratic institutions, is, in and of itself, of some slight value in preserving democracy in Nigeria. Before independence, psychological and emotional pressures tended to make Nigerians want to copy established democratic forms, particularly British forms. Use of identical institutions then was proof of equal maturity and ability. After independence, psychological and emotional pressures have tended to push Nigerians in the opposite direction.* Equivalent institutions tend to show continued subservience. Uniqueness establishes independence and satisfies the desire to make that independence manifest.

*The pervasiveness of the desire to make the system of government unique is suggested by the program of the Nigerian Peoples' Party. As a Marxist Leninist party it might be expected to believe in some supposedly universal truth. It promises, however, to "enrich the international socialist pool by its originality and stand against the dogmatic and blind copying of politics and tactics of the Marxist Leninist parties of other countries." Instead, its program will "take cognizance and be based on the regard for Nigerian national peculiarities."[35]

Sacking the Queen
and a Bill of Rights:
The Constitution and Democracy

Nigeria remained a monarchy when she became independent. Elizabeth II, Queen of England, was its Head of State. The Governor-General was merely her representative, as were the regional governors. The Nigerian Parliament consisted of "Her Majesty" in addition to the House of Representatives and Senate. Of course she did not have real power in Nigeria any more than in England, and the ceremonial functions of the Monarch were performed by Nigerians — the Governor-General and the regional governors. Still, the formal power of the Queen was not wholly unobtrusive. Oaths of loyalty were sworn to the Queen. Chief Awolowo was charged with committing a treasonable felony against our Sovereign Lady the Queen. Ambassadors were accredited to foreign countries in the name of the Queen.

Nigeria changed from a monarchy to a republic on October 1, 1963, the third anniversary of independence; she decided to "sack the Queen," is the way that some have put it. That she did so is hardly surprising. All the nonwhite members of the Commonwealth that had become independent before Nigeria — India, Pakistan, Ceylon, Ghana, and Malaya — had become republics. Tanganyika, which became independent in 1961, a year after Nigeria, amended its constitution in 1962 so as to replace the Queen with an elected president. To have a woman, living thousands of miles away, as head of an independent nation populated by people of a different race who have no desire to be reminded of their subjection to her forebears is hardly an arrangement that could be expected to last long. It is more surprising that Nigeria took so long to make the change. The nature of the change made tells much about Nigeria's problems and prospects.

Prior to independence and for several months thereafter, the younger and more radical or nationally minded Nigerians were alone in advocating a republic. Columnist Tai Solarin, consistent in his belief that Nigeria must free herself of the symbolic reminders of the colonial past before she could have the pride and self-respect she needed to choose sensibly between that which came from her own past and that which Britain and other foreign countries could offer, supported a republic before independence. S. G. Ikoku, Amino Kano, and Kalu Ezera were all early supporters. Prime Minister Tafawa Balewa, however, twice told Parliament after independence that his government had no plans for supporting a change to a republic.[1]

The catalyst for the change was Nigeria's first great nationalist, Nnamdi Azikiwe, who in his annual birthday speech on November 16, 1961, called for a republican constitution. His speech concentrated on what the nature of the new constitution should be. Reviewing the recent history of other countries, he dealt primarily with the dangers of giving too much power to one man. To avoid those dangers, he suggested that a new constitution should divide power between an executive head of state chosen by a joint sitting of the Federal House and Senate and a Prime Minister who would continue to be the leader of the majority in the Federal House. The proposed new executive would have more power than the Governor-General under the present constitution (who of course was Azikiwe himself), and the proposed Prime Minister would have less than the existing one.[2]

Fourteen days later Prime Minister Tafawa Balewa, who appeared to have been somewhat surprised by Azikiwe's speech, announced his support for a change and called for general discussion of the form of the new constitution. He added, however, that if the new executive were to have any greater powers than the present Governor-General, he must be elected by popular vote.[3]

After the Prime Minister's announcement, the Sardauna of Sokoto

173

announced that he also approved changing to a republic. In doing so he came out with a statement which showed both his determination not to let the predominant position of the North disappear beneath some tricky constitutional change and the feelings that could be stirred up by a nationwide election. Women have not been allowed to vote in the North because, the Sardauna has said, the Islamic people would not tolerate it.[4] But if the president were to be popularly elected he would, he said, call upon the Northern women as well as men to vote. The Sardauna likened a nationwide election to a jihad, or holy war, fought for the preservation of the North, saying:

> [W]hen the wishes of the people are sought in this particular issue which amounts to Jihad, I will call upon all Northerners, men and women, to cast their votes. . . .[5]

By the fall of 1961 there was general agreement that Nigeria should become a republic.* The two-year delay in actually making the change is indicative of the difficulties inherent in devising a change that would not upset the country's balance of power. Even more significant is the nature of the change made.

When Ghana and Tanganyika became republics they made sweeping constitutional changes designed to institutionalize the concept of a one-party or dominant-party state. In both countries a popularly elected president rather than a prime minister selected by parliament was made the dominant figure. And the president was made powerful, on paper infinitely more so than the President of the United States, for example. In both countries the relationship between presidential candidate and candidates for seats in parliament assures the president of overwhelming support in parliament, and the president can, moreover, dissolve the parliament. In Ghana, the first president, Kwame Nkrumah, can promulgate legislation without the approval of parliament. On the other hand, when Nigeria became a republic most of the constitutional changes were designed to cut the symbolic ties to England. Nigeria avoided sweeping changes in her system of government and retained her parliamentary system as it was, except that a largely ceremonial President selected by

---

*There were a few dissenters whose chief argument was that republicanism meant a nationwide election for president that would drive Nigeria's ethnic groups apart, as candidates would appeal to tribal prejudice.[6] Some, but not all, of the dissenters were Action Group supporters who may have felt that the change should not be made until the party increased its strength.

the Parliament was substituted for the largely ceremonial Governor-General. Nnamdi Azikiwe changed his title from Governor-General to President, but the Prime Minister remained under the Constitution the nation's most powerful official.

Countries which adopt constitutions giving them strong elected presidents do not do so on the basis of pure political theory. There must be a leader ready for the post in whom the vast majority of the population would put their trust. George Washington, Kwame Nkrumah, Julius Nyerere, and Charles de Gaulle all illustrate this. Nigeria did not have any one leader who was generally revered above all others by all national groups as the father or savior of the country or as the embodiment of its glory.

The imperative in Nigeria has been to avoid institutional changes that would exacerbate the latent hostility between its ethnic groups and particularly between the North and the South. An election fought before the people for a presidency with power worth winning would almost certainly bring forth the sort of antagonism which Nigeria must put behind her; a strong president, however chosen, would quicken ethnic fear and exacerbate ethnic tension. One can have a coalition cabinet but not a coalition president.

Ensuring national unity has been Nigeria's greatest problem and the latent tension between her regional, ethnic, and religious groups, coupled with her size and the consequent power of those groups, explains many of her policies and why she shows differences from many of her less complex African neighbors. One of the notable differences is that Nigeria has been less likely to move toward single-party or one-man rule.

If one assumes that Nigeria's interests were served by the decision to retain a parliamentary or cabinet system of government instead of adopting a presidential form of government, either with or without checks and balances, one still must concede that a price was paid. Perhaps the most important and beneficial side effect of having a presidential system is that in order to increase their chance of winning the main prize, political parties must become national. Of course in a parliamentary system there is a corresponding pressure to become national in order to win as many seats as possible, but the pressure is probably not as great. In a parliamentary system coalitions are likely to be made after elections rather than as part of the election process itself. In a parliamentary system, where there are several parties, coalitions tend to be unstable because they are tested more often.

Formal Freedoms

Nigeria's internal divisions also help explain why her Constitution formally guarantees various "fundamental human rights" including a fair trial, freedom of speech and religion, and the right to be free from discrimination.[7] The reader will recall that a bill of rights was added to the Nigerian Constitution pursuant to the suggestion of the Minorities Commission that a bill of rights would help alleviate the fears of various minorities seeking new states. As was true in the United States of America, agreement that there should be a bill of rights was a part of the process of uniting disparate groups.

The liberties guaranteed in the Nigerian Constitution are an impressive list of those that have been thought most vital through the ages.*

Under Section 21 no person may be deprived of his personal liberty save in six specified cases, and then only when the deprivation is in accord with a procedure permitted by law.† Anybody who is arrested or

---

*In addition to the provisions discussed in the text, the following guarantees are included in the Constitution: *Section 18* — "No person shall be deprived intentionally of his life, save in execution of the sentence of a court in respect of a criminal offence of which he has been found guilty." Death resulting from reasonably justifiable use of legally permitted force in order to defend person or property, to affect an arrest or prevent escape, to suppress a riot, insurrection, or mutiny, or to prevent the commission of an offence by the person killed is excepted from the section. *Section 19* outlaws torture and "inhuman" or degrading punishment, but punishments that were lawful and customary on November 1, 1959, are excepted. (One of the chief consequences of the exception is to render immune from constitutional attack the supposedly symbolic whipping administered in Northern Nigeria for certain offences against Muslim law or analogous offences included in the new Penal Code.) *Section 20* provides that no one may be held in slavery or servitude or be required to perform forced labor. Forced labor, however, is said not to include labor required of prisoners or of members of the armed forces or conscientious objectors or labor required in an emergency that threatens the life of the community or labor that forms part of "normal communal or other civil obligations." *Section 31* provides that no property may be taken except under a law that requires the payment of adequate compensation and gives claimants a right of access to the High Court in the area. However, laws in existence as of March 31, 1958, or replacements that are no less favorable are not affected.

†The six specified cases are largely those that would be expected: a person may be deprived of his personal liberty when he is unfit to plead to a criminal charge or is found guilty of a crime or of contempt of court, when he is arrested upon reasonable suspicion of having committed a crime or to prevent him from committing a crime and to prevent unlawful entry into the country or to effect lawful expulsions from the country. In addition, a minor may be detained for "the purpose of his education and welfare" and drug addicts, alcoholics, vagrants,

detained unlawfully is entitled to compensation, and those who are legitimately arrested must be brought before a court "without undue delay." Despite the rather vague and possibly dangerous exception permitting detention "to secure the fulfillment of any obligations imposed upon [the detained] by law," Section 21 on its face is extremely significant in the setting in which Nigeria became independent. For it appears to prevent the enactment of a preventive detention act which could be used — as Ghana's has by Kwame Nkrumah — to keep political opponents in prison without trial.

Section 22 lays down the requirements of a fair procedure in civil and criminal trials. A "fair hearing" is required within a reasonable time in a court, or, in civil cases, in a court or other tribunal constituted so as to be independent and impartial. More specific elaborations of a fair hearing and of minimum procedural standards follow. Trials and the announcement of decisions must be public.* One accused of crime is entitled to be informed of the charge against him promptly and in detail, in a language that he understands. He also must be given adequate time and facilities for the preparation of his defense, allowed to defend himself and (except in a native or customary court where a law forbids legal representation, as is usually the case today) be represented by counsel of his choice. He is entitled to be given an interpreter without charge, to examine the prosecution's witnesses, to obtain witnesses on his behalf, and to obtain a transcript of the record of his trial (though a fee may be required of him). He may not be compelled to give evidence at his trial. In addition, every person charged with a crime is said to be presumed innocent until proven guilty, and no one may be retried after acquittal or conviction save upon the order of a superior court. Finally, Section 22 provides that no one can be convicted on account of an act that was not criminal when he acted or be given a greater penalty than was in

---

persons of unsound mind and persons suffering from infectious or contagious disease may be detained "for the purpose of their care or treatment or the protection of the community." Finally, any person may be detained by reason of his failure to comply with a court order or "to secure the fulfillment of any obligations imposed upon him by law."

*That guarantee could be undermined, however, by the provisions that (1) the court must hear a matter *in camera* if a federal or regional minister certifies that it is in the public interest to do so, and (2) the court may exclude everyone but the parties if it feels it to be necessary in the interest of defense, public safety, public morality, and so forth. (The Awolowo treasonable felony trial, however, was heard in public.)

force when he acted, and requires that all offences must be defined in a written law, *i.e.*, no one may be convicted of a customary crime.

There are also a series of provisions dealing with speech, religion, assembly, private life, freedom of movement, and freedom from discrimination. Section 23 guarantees respect for every person's "private and family life, his home and his correspondence." Section 24 states that every person shall be entitled to "freedom of thought, conscience and religion" and specifically guarantees the right in private and public to practice and propagate belief, either alone or with others. It is further provided that no person attending a school can be required to receive religious instruction or take part in a religious ceremony if the instruction or ceremony relate to a religion other than his own; no religious community, however, shall be prevented from providing religious instruction at a school maintained wholly by it.*

Article 25 states that every person is entitled to "freedom of expression" — the right to "hold opinions and to receive and impart ideas and information without interference." Article 26 guarantees to every person freedom of assembly and association, with trade union membership specifically included, and Article 27 guarantees to every citizen freedom to move freely throughout Nigeria. Finally, Article 28 provides that no citizen of a particular "community, tribe, place of origin, religion or political opinion" shall, expressly by any law or in the practical application of any law, either be discriminated against on the basis of such status or be accorded privileges or advantages on the basis of such status.

Procedurally the rights guaranteed are protected in a number of ways. In order to make perfectly clear that one who feels that his constitutional rights have been violated has a remedy, the Nigerian Constitution provides that he may apply to the high court of the relevant

---

*In terms of the United States Constitution, these are guarantees of the free exercise of religion. There is no equivalent in the Nigerian Constitution to the establishment clause (though the establishment of one religion can, of course, prevent the free exercise of another). Specifically, there is no prohibition of state aid to religious schools such as has been held to be implicit in the establishment of religion clause of the First Amendment to the United States Constitution. The difference reflects the fact that Nigeria's educational system has traditionally relied heavily upon mission schools aided by the government and the further fact that religious persecution caused by a close association between church and state has not been important in the past of the people. Moreover, the tradition of the strongest religion — Islam — calls for close association between church and state, indeed, in its pure form calls for amalgamation.

region, or of Lagos, for redress and that the high courts have jurisdiction to hear such applications and issue such orders, writs or directions as are appropriate to secure the applicant's rights.[8] The right to appeal constitutional decisions all the way up through the system from the lowest regional courts to the regional high courts, and from them to the Federal Supreme Court is also guaranteed.*

The Chief Justice and the associate justices of the Supreme Court can only be removed if a two-thirds majority of both Houses of Parliament finds them guilty of "misbehavior" or unable to discharge the functions of office.[9]† Finally, the constitutional guarantees of fundamental rights and the procedural provisions just referred to can only be changed by an amendment supported by two-thirds of the Federal House and of the Federal Senate and a majority of each legislative house of at least three regions.[11]

The rights guaranteed seem to be impressively broad. When compared with the first bill of rights, that of the United States, Nigeria's Constitution, moreover, enlarges the scope of protection in some significant ways. The United States Bill of Rights did not apply to the states until the post-Civil War amendments (the Thirteenth, Fourteenth, and Fifteenth) dealt directly with racial restrictions by the states and the due process clause of the Fourteenth Amendment was held to make applicable most of the original Bill of Rights to the states. In Nigeria, on the other hand, the constitutional guarantees apply from the outset

---

*When it became a republic, Nigeria eliminated the right to carry appeals beyond the Federal Supreme Court to the Judicial Committee of Her Majesty's Privy Council in England.

†There is one loophole in that provision which, presumably, is only as good as the good faith of the members of Parliament. A justice can be appointed as an acting justice and when so appointed can be removed simply by having his authority to act revoked.

Under the Independence Constitution, associate justices could be removed for the same reasons, but only after a tribunal composed of persons who had been or were judges of a Commonwealth court of unlimited jurisdiction had recommended their removal and the recommendation had been approved by the Judicial Committee of the Privy Council. The change from that procedure represented part of the process of throwing off the vestiges of British sovereignty that was dramatized by the change from a monarchy to a republic. Under the Independence Constitution associate justices were appointed by a nonpolitical commission. Under the Republican Constitution, however, it was provided that appointments of all the justices would be made by the President on the advice of the Prime Minister, except that four justices would be appointed on the respective advice of each of the four Regional Premiers.[10]

to the regions as well as to the Federal Government, though the tradition of local autonomy is no less strong than it was in the early days of the United States. Some of Nigeria's guarantees, such as the prohibition against compelling a student of one religion to receive instruction in another, appear, moreover, to forbid private action irrespective of whether a government is involved. An express right to receive as well as impart ideas is missing from the United States Bill of Rights. The Nigerian Constitution also makes explicit guarantees, such as the right to be free from discrimination in the practical administration of a law, which the United States Supreme Court had to strain to find implicit in the more general guarantees of the United States Constitution.*

But though the rights guaranteed are many, the exceptions to the guarantees, concise and prolix, specific and vague, could well render them symbolic rather than real protections and at the same time deprive them of much of their effect as symbols. What is given with one breath is taken with the next as broad right is followed by broad exception.

In a few cases, the exceptions are specific and are designed to protect interests which various Nigerians were not willing to risk for the sake of unity any more than the citizens of certain American states in 1789 were willing, for example, to abandon slavery for the sake of unity. Thus, the bar against discrimination on the basis of "community, tribe, place of origin, religion or political opinion" is said not to apply to discrimination with respect to the acquisition or use of land or other property. Nor does it apply to discriminatory rules determining who can be hired as a governmental employee. It seems extremely likely that those exceptions were in large measure intended to permit the Northern Government to continue to discourage people from Southern tribes from acquiring land in the North or positions in the Northern civil service.

---

*In addition to a ban against the establishment of religion, the following guarantees that are present in the United States Constitution are missing from the Nigerian Constitution: There is no due process clause, though some of the rights found implicit in the term "due process" by the United States Supreme Court are specifically covered in Sections 21 and 22 of the Nigerian Constitution and could be found implicit in Section 22's requirement of a "fair hearing." There is no jury trial requirement, no grand jury requirement, and no requirement that criminal trials take place in the district where the alleged crime was committed. There is no prohibition of excessive bail and no mention of the right to bear arms or the right not to have soldiers quartered in the home. In some other instances where the Nigerian Constitution has provisions similar to provisions of the United States Bill of Rights the protection is narrower. For example, freedom from discrimination applies only to citizens and to specified grounds of discrimination.

Similarly, there is a strong Northern flavor to the failure to mention discrimination on the grounds of sex. The failure to include foreigners among those protected against discrimination or within the class guaranteed freedom of movement, on the other hand, undoubtedly represents a more general feeling.

The specific exceptions or omissions represent specific and deeply felt political imperatives that overrode general principles of freedom. The general exceptions are more significant because they represent hesitancy about the very concept of guaranteed freedoms. The guarantees in Sections 23 through 28 — respect for private and family life, freedom of religion, freedom of expression, freedom of assembly and association, freedom of movement, and freedom from discrimination on the grounds of tribe, and so forth — are all undercut by a vague exception in similar form. The exception to the guarantee of freedom of expression is typical. After the first subsection, which says that everybody is entitled to "freedom of expression, including freedom to hold opinions and to receive and impart ideas and information without interference," the second subsection goes on to say:

> Nothing in this section shall invalidate any law that is reasonably justifiable in a democratic society —
> (a) in the interest of defense, public safety, public order, public morality or public health;
> (b) for the purpose of protecting the rights, reputations and freedom of other persons. . . .

Though there are minor differences in the wording of the exceptions to the other sections, all use the phrase "reasonably justifiable in a democratic society," and all but Section 28 (freedom from discrimination) tie that phrase to laws that are in the interest of "defence, public safety, public order, public morality or public health."*

*The differences are as follows: None of the other sections refer to laws protecting the reputations, as opposed to the rights and freedoms, of other people. Section 23 (private life) adds "the economic well-being of the community" to the list of defense, public safety, etc. Section 24 (religion) specifies that the "rights and freedom of other persons" includes their right to be free to practise their religion without the "unsolicited intervention" of members of other religions. Section 27 (freedom of movement) does not have a clause permitting reasonable laws in the interest of the rights and freedom of other persons and, as amended in the Republican Constitution, expressly permits laws excluding chiefs from their territory. Section 28 (freedom from discrimination) states that the guarantees shall not invalidate a law which "imposes any disability or restriction or accords any privilege or advantage that, having regard to its nature and to special

Does it make any difference that those general exceptions are spelled out, in contrast to the guarantees in the United States Bill of Rights which without exception say, for example, "Congress shall make no law . . . abridging the freedom of speech, or of the press" or "No State shall . . . deny to any person . . . the equal protection of the laws"? As the United States Constitution has been construed, those absolute and ringing pronouncements come quite close to meaning what the Nigerian Constitution says. The United States Supreme Court has held that speech can be punished or restricted if some vital interest, such as defense, public order, or public morality is sufficiently menaced by the speech to override the need in a democracy for opinion to be heard. Similarly, it has been held that classes of people can be treated differently if, considering the nature of the class and the nature of the distinction, it is reasonable to draw the distinction. If such qualifications would in any event be read in, is it not better to come out with them straightaway? Or, if not better, is it not true that spelling them out does not make any difference? Not quite.

Spelling out the exceptions in copious fashion makes the constitutional guarantees much less useful as an educative tool with which to imbue the people with the spirit of liberty. Laws can change attitudes, and none more so than constitutions. But to do so they should be simply expressed. The school child who is taught that the constitution says that free speech is guaranteed with no ifs, ands, or buts is bound to develop a different instinctive reaction toward restrictions of free speech than the school child who is told that free speech is guaranteed except in several enumerated situations.

Perhaps the greatest drawback to the way in which Nigeria's Bill of Rights is written is that it is dull. With all its carefully elaborated inclusions and the prolix and complicated exceptions, it becomes just another law. Lacking majesty, it is written for lawyers, not for the people.*

---

circumstances pertaining to the persons to whom it applies, is reasonably justifiable in a democratic society." Section 25 (freedom of expression) itself goes on to specify that the legitimate restrictions upon freedom of expression include laws preventing the disclosure of confidential information, protecting the courts, and regulating television, radio, film exhibitions, and telephony. The press is not specifically mentioned and thus can only be regulated under the language quoted in the text.

*The precise, legalistic way in which judges and lawyers trained in the British tradition have usually interpreted constitutions is likely to make it difficult for

Spelling out the exceptions, as is done in the Nigerian Constitution, also makes it easier for a legislature to justify a restriction and a little more likely that a court will uphold a restriction of liberty. The form of the guarantee makes at least some difference to its interpretation. Perhaps this can be illustrated by an analogy.[13] Suppose there were two fathers, one of whom proclaimed his resolve never to spank his child and another who promised not to spank his child unless it were reasonably justifiable in a harmonious family. It may be assumed that if sufficiently provoked and under certain circumstances even the father who had resolved never to spank his child would do so. Nevertheless, his child would feel less constrained than the child of the father who promised not to spank his child unless it were reasonably justifiable, and in fact would undoubtedly be given fewer spankings. A legislature

---

them to tie the constitution to life and history, as is necessary to make it meaningful. Dean Griswold of the Harvard Law School has proposed the theory that the prolixity of the Nigerian Bill of Rights stems from the British tradition of statutory interpretation and legislative drafting. Statutes are construed literally as if they have a "plain meaning" and constitutions, since they are regarded as statutes though they are written for the ages, cannot therefore be left with broad and sweeping language. He also points out that because of the nature of a constitution the attempt to be precise and certain would inevitably fail, as in fact it did. What exactly does "reasonably justifiable in a democratic society" mean?[12]

The British tradition can be influential in other ways. It tends to reinforce the fundamental rights provisions that deal with a fair criminal procedure because the tradition of fair trials and fair police practices have developed without a written constitution in British decisions and the Judges' Rules. In that regard, it is perhaps significant that the only Supreme Court decisions holding that the fundamental rights provisions had been violated — the Bank case discussed in the chapter on the Action Group crisis and the Ajayi case discussed in the footnote at p. 186 — involved the fair procedure provisions of the Constitution. On the other hand, Britain has a preventive detention law, and in the free speech field it has, despite general restraint in their use, extremly strict and repressive laws. The concept of restraints upon the supremacy of parliament is, moreover, alien to one trained in the British tradition.

The British tradition which prohibits the courts from relying upon cases or materials other than those cited by the litigants is particularly undesirable with respect to constitutional law (where interests far wider than those of the litigants are at stake) and in countries where the experience with respect to constitutional issues is minimal. Perhaps it was that tradition that led Justice Brett (concurring in the Chike Obi case, to be discussed, in which the Federal Supreme Court narrowly construed the free speech section of the Constitution) to quote a remark that the legislatures guard liberty and welfare to quite as great a degree as the courts (a comment which had been made by Justice Holmes in an economic regulation case) instead of referring to Justice Holmes' opinions in defense of free speech.

which has before it a bill restricting speech, or religious freedom, or movement, or a court which has before it the bill made law, has to overcome a lesser hurdle, and less moral and psychological resistance, when before it lies the inviting and reassuring lure of the multipurpose exceptions that are in the Nigerian Constitution.

Relatively few cases involving the fundamental rights provisions of the Constitution have come before the Nigerian Supreme Court. The courage and independence of the Court have been shown. One of the reasons why the Court held unconstitutional the Federal Government's attempt to investigate the relations between the National Bank of Nigeria and the Action Group was that the power of the investigators to imprison recalcitrant witnesses was contrary to the fundamental rights provisions; during the Western Region emergency, the Court ordered Rotimi Williams, then the Action Group lawyer and an extremely powerful advocate, released from restriction because the Government had not shown that it was reasonably justifiable to retain him."[14] Those were courageous decisions, for the Government was deeply committed to the actions it had taken and the feeling against the Action Group ran high. But despite those courageous decisions the Court has also indicated that it is not now going to construe the guarantees in a broad and liberal fashion any more than they were written in a broad and liberal fashion.

Dr. Chike Obi, the advocate of an inspirational dictatorship to modernize the country, had distributed, and perhaps written, a pamphlet entitled "The People: Facts That You Must Know" whose subtitle stated, "Down with the enemies of the people, the exploiters of the weak and the oppressors of the poor!" The pamphlet was largely devoted to an attack upon the high salaries and high living of the politicians and ministers, and their "squandermania" compared with the squalor and poverty that enveloped the common man. It was capped by the prediction that

> The days of those who have enriched themselves at the expense of the poor are numbered. The common man in Nigeria can no longer be fooled by sweet talk at election time only to be exploited and treated like dirt after the booty of office has been shared among the politicians.

For distributing the pamphlet, Dr. Obi was arrested and charged with sedition under a section of the Nigerian Criminal Code which made it a crime to distribute a seditious publication with the intent, among other things, to "bring into hatred or contempt or to excite disaffection against the person of her Majesty . . . or the Government . . . of Nigeria." After deciding that a violation of the law had been proved, the Lagos High Court asked the Supreme Court if it would be contrary to the constitutional guarantee of freedom of expression to convict Dr. Obi. The Supreme Court held that the Constitution did not prevent his conviction.[15]*

There was no evidence that what Dr. Obi said was untrue; indeed the Supreme Court eventually held that the truth of the pamphlet was not relevant. There was no evidence that the pamphlet had led to violence or that the government was in any way threatened by a conspiracy to overthrow it or by a restless mob waiting for stirring language to ignite compressed fury. The pamphlet did not directly call upon its readers to overthrow the government by other than constitutional means and did not even imply that that should be done unless one strains to find that meaning in the words "down with the enemies of the people." Indeed, the Federal Supreme Court eventually held that the absence of an incitement to violence was irrelevant.

The heart of the Court's decision was the Chief Justice's statement that though a person can criticize the government he must keep within "the limits of fair criticism" and that "what is not permitted is to criticize the government in a malignant manner . . . for such acts by their nature tend to affect the public peace." That is a sound rule of manners, but it hardly seems to carry out the spirit of the promise that people can speak freely. Governments in a "democratic society" should be thick-skinned enough to withstand a bit of malignant criticism. On the particular facts, if it is criminal to say that the ministers are enemies of the people or oppress the poor or to imply that politicians are corrupt in that they share booty of office, exactly what can be said without fear of punishment?†

*That Chike Obi was the first Nigerian to assert his constitutional right to free speech in the Supreme Court is somewhat ironic in view of the following passage from his book *Our Struggle:*
For the fools who would rather die for their democratic freedom of speech in a colonial country than LIVE and help in paying the price in personal restraint and personal discipline for the upliftment of their backward RACE and for the guarantee of REAL DEMOCRATIC FREEDOM for their descendants and probably for themselves — for such fools no amount of light is bright enough for them to see.[16]
†Other decisions involving the fundamental rights provisions include the following:
R. v. *Amalgamated Press Ltd.* (1961) 1 All N.L.R. 199 (Federal Supreme

Court). Decided on the same day as Chike Obi's case, relies upon it, and holds it is not unconstitutional to convict newspaper of publishing false news likely to cause fear and alarm. The Court commented that the fundamental rights provisions guarantee "nothing but ordered freedom."

Olawoyin v. *Attorney-General of the Northern Region* (1961) 1 All N.L.R. 269 (Federal Supreme Court). Father who asserted desire to involve his children in politics and feared he could be punished for doing so lacks standing to seek declaratory judgment testing the constitutionality of law prohibiting political activity of children and young persons or inducing such activity.

Ojiegbe v. *Ubani* (1961) 1 All N.L.R. 277 (Federal Supreme Court). The claim was that holding an election on a Saturday violated the right to freedom of religion of Seventh-Day Adventists and that therefore election in a constituency where there were six to seven thousand Seventh-Day Adventists should be set aside. The claim was denied, on the grounds that no harm was shown, since complaining candidate lost by twenty thousand votes.

Ibeziako v. *Commissioner of Police* (1963) (Federal Supreme Court, 329/1962). In criminal trial, after hearing prosecution's witnesses, magistrate, acting pursuant to Northern Nigeria Criminal Procedure Code, framed a formal charge against the accused, accused pleaded not guilty, a few more witnesses were heard, and the magistrate found the accused guilty. Held that that procedure was not inconsistent with constitutional guarantee of presumption of innocence. The Court suggested that perhaps the fundamental rights provisions do not mean anything more than the requirements of fair procedure required in the colonial days, saying objection to a procedure chosen by the legislature is not sound unless the procedure is "repugnant to natural justice, equity and good conscience." It also cited with approval a case that stated "It must be presumed that the court followed the right procedure. . . . It differs from the English procedure but that is not enough for attacking it."

Ajayi v. *Zaria Native Authority* (1963) (Federal Supreme Court, 113/1962). Complaint that criminal accused were not granted the services of an effective interpreter at their trial. Conviction reversed on ground that a reasonable person at the trial might have thought that the interpretation was defective in trial of Yoruba speaker by Hausa-speaking native court.

Cheranci v. *Cheranci* (1960) N.R.N.L.R. 24 (High Court, Northern Region). Upholding law referred to above in Olawoyin as applied to one convicted under it. Presumption that legislature acted constitutionally.

Arzika v. *Governor, Northern Region* (1961) 1 All N.L.R. 37 (High Court, Northern Nigeria). Restriction on freedom of movement of former district head upheld. Presumption that Governor acts constitutionally when he exercises powers conferred upon him by Legislature on the advice of Executive Council.

Aoko v. *Fagbemi* (1961) 1 All N.L.R. 400 (High Court, Western Nigeria). Conviction of adultery in a customary court held unconstitutional because did not constitute a violation of any written law.

Gokpa v. *Inspector-General of Police* (1961) 1 All N.L.R. 423 (High Court, Eastern Nigeria). Conviction reversed because trial judge had denied defendant's request for adjournment until his counsel could be present. Burden put on prosecution to show refusal to adjourn did not deny defendant a fair hearing and the defendant knew of trial date or had sufficient time to obtain counsel.

The "reasonably justifiable in a democratic society" exceptions indirectly make it easier for a legislature to justify passing a law which restricts liberty. The Nigerian Constitution contains one further exception which explicitly permits the Federal Parliament to undercut certain of the constitutional guarantees. During a "period of emergency," Parliament is permitted to provide for the disregard of certain guarantees so long as the provision is "reasonably justifiable for dealing with the situation that exists during that period of emergency."[17] The guarantees that can be so disregarded are those included in Section 18 (deprivation of life), Section 21 (which limits to six the situations in which a person can be deprived of his personal liberty), Section 22 (which gives the right to a "fair hearing," specifies some of its elements and adds certain other requirements such as that all criminal offences must be contained in a written law)* and Section 28 (freedom from discrimination on the ground of tribe, etc.). Contrary to the exceptions previously discussed, such emergency restrictions need only be "reasonably justifiable" and not "reasonably justifiable in a democratic society."†

A "period of emergency" is defined as existing whenever Nigeria is at war, or when each House of Parliament has declared by a two-thirds vote that democratic institutions in Nigeria are threatened by subversion, *or,* as during the Action Group crisis, when each House of Parliament has by a simple majority passed a resolution declaring that a state of emergency exists.[19] Such resolutions cannot remain in force

---

Olawoyin v. *Commissioner of Police* (1962) N.N.L.R. 29 (High Court, Northern Nigeria). Defendant has burden of showing that procedural errors caused such prejudice as to deny him fair hearing.

*An exception to the exception provides that a period of emergency cannot be used to justify laws making criminal acts not criminal when done.

†For one whose restriction or detention during a period of emergency has been upheld as "reasonably justifiable" (and where there has been no emergency declared, for one the restriction of whose movement has been challenged under Section 27 and upheld as "reasonably justifiable in a democratic society") the Constitution holds out one further solace of uncertain value but which still stands in favorable contrast with Ghana, whose use of preventive detention has been mentioned before. Within one month of his detention or restriction and thereafter at six-month intervals, he may refer his case to a tribunal constituted so as to "ensure its independence and impartiality," with the chairman appointed by the Chief Justice of the Federal Supreme Court from among legal practitioners. The tribunal may make recommendations to the executive concerning the "necessity or expediency" of continuing the detention or restriction. But its recommendations do not have to be followed; it is not required that its recommendations be publicized, though that seemingly sensible practice could, of course, be followed voluntarily.[18]

for longer than a year but at the end of a year a new resolution declaring an emergency can be passed. Thus, using all the democratic and constitutional forms, a simple majority of the Parliament can resolve that an emergency exists and give the executive power to lock up without trial the unpopular, the weak, the defenseless, and the supposedly dangerous. There is then a recourse to the courts, but by that simple act of power the courts are told no longer to rest their judgment upon what is reasonable in a democracy but rather upon what is reasonable under some other, undefined, system.

The first reaction to the Nigerian fundamental rights provisions of one trained in the American tradition is to stress the negative — the dullness of the prolix language, the breadth of the exceptions, the ability of Parliament to change the rules of the game, and the somewhat hesitant attitude of the courts. And that has been the reaction of others, Nigerians included.[20] But Nigeria has much more in the way of constitutional guarantees of liberty than most countries. The requirement that laws be "reasonably justifiable in a democratic society" (or even that they be "reasonably justifiable"), moreover, can when used by the right men at the right time help freedom along. It cannot do more; for more than on courts and more than on constitutions the future of freedom depends upon the people and their representatives.

Constitutions do not exist in a vacuum. The most airtight, ringing constitutional guarantees of liberty will not prevent repression if the people are apathetic and the political leaders are determined to ignore the restraints that keep their people free. Courts can hear only a few cases; courts lack force. Without any constitutional restraints, on the other hand, customs can develop that make it unthinkable for a government to act arbitrarily against those suspected of crime or to punish its opponents for their criticisms.

There are forces that favor and forces that threaten Nigeria's Bill of Rights. Since it was part of the bargain under which Nigeria's disparate groups agreed to live together as one nation, it would risk exacerbation of those tensions to excise the fundamental rights provisions from Nigeria's Constitution. But Nigeria's constitutional history also has elements that undercut her bill of rights.

Prior to its addition to the Constitution, there had been only sporadic Nigerian support for a bill of rights. Eyo Ita was alone in proposing a bill of rights at the 1950 General Conference on the Constitution. Before the 1953 Constitutional Conference a short-lived Action Group–NCNC alliance advocated constitutional protection of a few fundamental rights. And at the 1957 Conference which appointed the Minorities Commission there was agreement in principle that some sort of bill of rights should be adopted. The decision of the Commission to recommend a bill of rights, however, was its own; it was not a demand of the Nigerian groups that appeared before it.[21]

Britain was very influential in persuading the Nigerians to include a bill of rights in their Constitution. That is ironic, because Britain herself has no constitutional guarantees of fundamental rights. Thus, Nigeria's Bill of Rights is open to attack as having been imposed, based upon the degrading and patronizing principle that, contrary to the British themselves, Britain's former subjects were incapable of being fair without formal restraints upon their freedom of action.

The Bill of Rights was formally added to the Constitution in a way that makes it further vulnerable because when added it appeared primarily to be a weapon aimed against the North. During the 1959 election, both the NCNC and the Action Group demanded, with eventual success, that the Governor-General bring the Bill of Rights into force. Their chief contention was that their campaigns in the North were being disrupted by repressive and discriminatory tactics.[22] A hint of Northern resentment was revealed, in a slightly different context, when the Northern Minister of Information replied to criticism of the Northern penal reforms by exclaiming: "[in his] defensive action against the forces of Northern Nationalism . . . [the critic] does not realize that he is fighting a losing cause, . . . the perpetration of British imperialism in a subtle way, in the name of safeguarding fundamental human rights."[23]

Since their adoption, most cases in which the fundamental rights provisions have been put in issue have involved an Action Group member or have been financed and argued by the Action Group. Of course the very purpose of the constitutional guarantees is to protect unpopular minorities, and thus reliance upon the Bill of Rights by the Action Group carries out its purpose. Nevertheless, in considering the likelihood of continued support for the fundamental rights provisions, it is unfortunate that so many of the cases have involved the political minority.

The driving force underlying Nigerian nationalism during the struggle for independence and today after independence is not one which particularly supports the Bill of Rights, if one looks upon the Bill of Rights as primarily designed to protect the individual against the state.* The idea that gave Nigerian nationalism its dynamic force was not the primacy of individual rights but the collective right of a people, indeed a race, to be free from alien domination. With independence won, the paramount aim is to consolidate the state, establish the authority of its leaders, and uphold the dignity of the nation and the race. Dissenters and critics are seen as real dangers to those aims. Similarly, where governments are not sure — as they are not in Nigeria — that the nation's system of government and the nation's need for unity are unquestionably accepted by the overwhelming majority of its citizens, it is extremely difficult for governments to accept a decision striking down their action as contrary to a constitution.†

Looked upon slightly differently than as a device through which to protect the individual against the state, however, the Bill of Rights becomes much more closely aligned with the driving forces underlying Nigerian nationalism. The section of the Constitution which prohibits discrimination or favoritism on the basis of tribe illustrates that point well. It is a legal expression of the desire that a nation develop based upon loyalties which are wider than the tribe. (It also builds upon the desire for group security that is a strong element in the African tradition.) A similar right is the guarantee of freedom of movement which prohibits rules such as often obtained during the British era limiting

---

*Neither, speaking very generally, do traditional African mores emphasize individual rights. While there was a tradition of discussion before decision and law was conceived of as a method for achieving a just result rather than forcing adherence to rules, the pressure to conform was great, and the individual was not thought to have the right to (or be likely to wish to) dissent from the community's decision once that decision had been made.

†A disloyal opposition — any group which wishes to break up the country or fundamentally alter its system of government — puts a bill of rights to its severest test. Witness the disregard of the United States Supreme Court by President Lincoln during the Civil War and the bending of the First Amendment's guarantees of free speech and free association to cope with the American Communists. Disloyalty in Nigeria is a substantial threat, not because disloyal movements are particularly powerful but because the consensus that the nation should be united is so fragile.

Speaking generally, moreover, the changing function of the state throughout the world makes it increasingly difficult for a bill of rights' emphasis upon the individual above the state to take hold today. The state increasingly has become the arbiter and provider of everything. For all that the state is thereby able to do to increase opportunity for individuals and to prevent their exploitation, the trend toward increased state power obviously presents obstacles to the development of support for the rights of the individual against the state.

movement of persons from one area of the country into other areas or segregating Northerners and Southerners from each other in certain towns.*

Law suits in which those sections of the Constitution are relied upon still will, if successful, present great problems of acceptability to governments in the current and likely future atmosphere of Nigeria where the need to establish the prestige and authority of government is felt so desperately. Nevertheless, they are infinitely easier to accept than, say, a decision holding unconstitutional a sedition conviction of a vituperative critic of the government. That is so because they can readily be supported by reference to the nationalistic desire to cut down tribalism. For that reason, it is likely that Nigeria's Bill of Rights can best take root if it first has dramatic decisional effect in such cases.

Conversely, taking a long view, there is something to be said for Nigeria's courts, as exemplified in Chike Obi's case, having declined to be very bold in enforcing the more political guarantees. For though the Federal Government accepted the adverse decision of the Bank case with extremely good grace, it is unlikely that either the Federal Supreme Court or the Bill of Rights itself could withstand much judicial boldness in the political field.†

But that goes for the decisions of the courts and not their language

---

*Stressing those sections of the Nigerian Constitution is not to suggest that other sections of the Constitution are inconsistent with Nigerians' developing wider loyalties. For the long run, stress upon the rights of the individual is highly consistent with the development of wider loyalties.

†Perhaps the most explicitly political case decided by the Nigerian courts was *Akintola* v. *Adegbenro*, arising out of the Action Group crisis. After he had been removed as Premier by the Governor of Western Nigeria, who acted upon a petition signed by a majority of the members of the Western House of Assembly, but without there having been an adverse vote in the House, S. L. Akintola brought suit against the new Premier, claiming that he could only be removed after a vote on the floor. The Federal Supreme Court (one Justice dissenting) agreed with Chief Akintola. The Supreme Court's decision was reversed by Her Majesty's Privy Council.[24]

Certainly by the time the case was decided in the Privy Council it was moot, because Akintola was back in office with a clear majority. While appeals to the Privy Council would undoubtedly have been ended under the Republican Constitution in any event, the Privy Council's decision may have made that change more likely. The Federal Supreme Court might also have concluded that questions as to the division of responsibility between Governor, Premier, and Legislature were "political questions," in the sense used by the United States Supreme Court, and hence not fit for judicial resolution. Those United States Supreme Court decisions were not called to the attention of the Nigerian Court.

191

or approach. Through today's language in defense of liberty the courts can do much to make possible tomorrow's decisions in defense of liberty. It is also extremely important that future Nigerian courts do not rigidly apply notions of *stare decisis* so as blindly to follow the early decisions that reflected considerable caution in applying many of the fundamental rights provisions of the Constitution.

For more than survival, for life to be breathed into the Nigerian Bill of Rights, three changes must take place. The Bill of Rights must become part of Nigeria's history, not a transplant from the West. The resistance by Nigeria's press, by many of its politicians and by prominent figures, such as the Federal Chief Justice, to the suggestion by governmental leaders in the summer of 1963 that they be given the power of preventive detention is worth countless recitations of the Barons at Runnymede winning the Magna Carta, of John Otis in Boston defending against the British the right to speak freely, or of the Founding Fathers of the United States adding a Bill of Rights to their constitution. A great judge, or a great politician must persuade the people that African history and African tradition as applied to modern conditions support free speech and support a fair procedure.

The second and third changes point in what appear to be quite different directions. On the one hand, governments must become more confident of the basic loyalties of their peoples. On the other hand, the people, through continual struggle for their own individual rights, must overcome the aftermath of the colonial mentality whereby governmental power and prestige are not questioned. All three changes which must occur before the Bill of Rights can become an effective force have one common element: they are part of the still continuing process of emerging from colonialism.

Federalism and National Unity

Being a federal nation has been and will continue to be of enormous importance to Nigeria. It is doubtful whether in view of the deep-seated differences between Nigeria's various powerful groups — highlighted by the conflict between North and South over the timing of self-government — that she could have become independent as one nation unless the major groups had been given the security that stems from their dominant position in the regions of a federal system. But making the major groups relatively secure by giving them power to control a region has meant that other groups within each region have felt their security menaced. Thus arose the demand of minorities for new regions that has been such a strong undercurrent in Nigeria's politics.

One of the great advantages of federalism is often said to be that it keeps diversity alive. As one example of that effect in Nigeria, federalism has had much to do with keeping viable the nation's multiparty political system. But to many Nigerians today the diversities that are kept alive are what the nation must be rid of to prosper — tribal jealousies, superstitions, and ignorance. Thus to some nationalists the system itself is suspect though the system should probably be credited with enabling Nigeria's 50 million people to form a nation.

The significant question to ask is not whether Nigeria is better off with or without a federal system. The significant questions are two. First, does Nigeria's federal system tend to accentuate or to mute the jealousies between the country's groups, large and small? Second, is its federal constitution capable of growing with the nation? If, for example, there is an increase in national sentiment and in the need for national action, will Nigeria's federal constitution hold the country back so that change must be accomplished by violent revolution rather than constitutional evolution?

For the short term, the political test of Nigeria's federal system is in how well it siphons off ethnic and religious discord into the separate regional pools and whether the domination that each of the major ethnic groups has over its own pool gives it confidence to cooperate with the others or becomes its singleminded concern. The economic test is whether the national government will be able to mix and stir the pools and thereby prevent stagnation.

The short-term political and economic tests point in differing directions. Politically, the emphasis is upon the adequacy of the protection afforded to the regions, though it is also important to know what power the Federal Government has to prevent a region from disregarding the national interest. Economically, the emphasis is upon the adequacy of the powers given to the Federal Government, though it is also important to know whether the federal system gives the regions power to solve their differing economic problems in their own way.

That divergence in emphasis is likely to occur in any federation. For federations are formed precisely for the reason that while the people are not prepared to live in the same room politically, they nevertheless realize that there will be great advantages — especially economic advantages — in living in adjoining rooms of the same house. Nevertheless, the difference in emphasis in Nigeria may be particularly acute and the ensuing strain upon her Constitution particularly great.

In this respect, a useful contrast can be drawn between Nigeria at the time of the formation of her federation and three earlier federations at their formation: the United States of America, Canada, and Australia. Nigeria is more divided politically. What could put greater strain on a federal system than the existence of political parties each of which is basically representative of only one of the constituent units of the federation? In Nigeria, moreover, the distinctions between the regional units under the federal system are reinforced by ethnic, religious, educational, and, to a lesser extent, economic differences to an extraordinary degree.

Contrary to the other federations, moreover, the decision to make Nigeria a federation represented a step away from rather than toward

194

formal unity (as is also true for India). Nigeria had been governed by the British under a unitary, though decentralized, system and became a federation because the people and leaders of the various regions decided that they wanted to loosen the ties. The United States, Canada, and Australia, on the other hand, all became federations because the people and leaders of the smaller units decided that a tighter union was desirable. Thus, the emotional attitude of nationally-minded Nigerians to her federal system tends to be lukewarm as compared with that of the nationally minded in the other federations to their federal systems at the outset.

Economically, the contrasts run in the other direction. Nigeria is probably both more united economically and faced by greater pressure for national economic action than were the other federations at their formation. Here the fact that she had been ruled by the British as a unity is significant, for, while the political institutions of a unitary state did not survive colonialism, the unitary economic institutions built up by the colonialists have for the most part been transferred to the Nigerian national government. Before independence Nigeria had a common external tariff and no internal tariffs, a common currency, some central government taxation, and a national transportation system controlled in large measure by the central government. Unified, but alien, political institutions can be broken up relatively easily compared with the iron tracks of a national railway system crossing the land.

Nigeria became a federation at a time when national economic power was much more important than when the other federations were formed in 1789, 1867, or 1900. Attitudes as to the proper role of government had also changed. That government must play a major role in regulating economic activity and in bringing the unfortunate up toward the level of the fortunate is generally accepted today in Nigeria. Both functions inevitably involve the national government to a large extent. Economic activity overlaps regional lines. The most noticeable gap between the fortunate and the unfortunate may be between peoples of different regions (as between the educational opportunities in the North and the South of Nigeria), the overcoming of which is likely to require federal taxation. The very growth of governmental activity and the consequent increase in the cost of government puts special emphasis on the national government because many of the available taxes can best be imposed by it. Furthermore, though the Nigerian economy is probably less developed than the economies of the earlier federations when they were formed, those aspects of it that are national in scope are, because of advances in technology, more significant and more obvicus.

National economic power would be emphasized in any federation setting forth today. There is at least one further difference from the earlier federations that reflects Nigeria's position as an underdeveloped nation. Foreign aid is both available and necessary. Efforts to obtain foreign aid and foreign private investment put a premium on foreign policy and thus on the federal government. They also call for a national approach rather than the confusion and conflicts and disruption of the national balance of payments policy that could arise if each region sought its own foreign aid and bore primary responsibility for negotiating the terms under which foreign private investment would be made. Under the Nigerian Constitution, without regard to whether the money is to be used for federal or for regional purposes only the Federal Government can borrow overseas, either in the private market or from a foreign government.[1] As the sole channel for foreign aid and loans from foreign private sources, the national government becomes infinitely more important and powerful. As a rule — but perhaps particularly for new nations anxious to be noticed and to be known to be free — foreign policy, which emphasizes the national government rather than regional (or state) governments, has become more significant today than when the United States, Canadian, and Australian federations were formed.

Legislative Power

In its division of legislative power between the national and the regional governments, the Nigerian Constitution reflects the modern tendency toward a strong national government that has also been the trend of development under the constitutions of the United States and Australia.

Under Nigeria's constitution (as in the United States, Australia, and India), the constituent units, the regions, are given power to legislate with respect to residual matters; all powers not specifically delegated to the Federal Government are reserved to the regions. There are some very significant powers that are not specifically mentioned as coming within the federal sphere and which therefore appear to be reserved for regional control. Agriculture, education (other than higher education), health, housing, and local government are among them.

Nevertheless, the powers given to the Nigerian Federal Government by the Constitution are very many, and its legislative power on paper is very great, far greater, for example, than is the power of the Federal Government in the United States. If Nigeria has had a weak Federal Government, as many people have said with some truth, it is not primarily because of the Constitution but rather reflects the fact that the people's representatives have not chosen to use all the power given them. A remark such as that of the Federal Minister of Economic Planning that "our Constitution is such that we cannot carry out a central planning as many members would have liked us to do" could only have been made on the basis of bad legal advice or for political purposes.[2]

Many of the Federal Government's powers concern Nigeria's relations with the outside world.* It has exclusive power over foreign policy, defense, immigration, exchange control, import and export duties, borrowing overseas, and trade with foreign nations.[4] But the striking thing about the power of Nigeria's Federal Government is the breadth of its mandate to deal with the domestic economy. In addition to its exclusive power to regulate interregional trade and some other powers directly tied to an interregional interest, it has a host of further powers that do not depend upon proof that more than one region is involved. It has all the economic power that the United States Supreme Court has so tortuously found to be implicit in the interstate commerce clause of the United States Constitution and much more besides.

It has exclusive power over mines, minerals, and nuclear energy, and concurrent power over industrial development, labor, waterpower, and electricity.[5] All those powers it has whether or not there is any demonstrable relationship to interregional commerce. In transportation, Parliament has exclusive power to regulate the railways,† aviation, and

---

*In formal terms, the Federal Parliament is given exclusive power over forty-three items in an Exclusive Legislative List and power concurrent with the regions with respect to twenty-seven items in a Concurrent Legislative List. (Where a power is concurrent the regions may act, as long as their law is not inconsistent with a federal law; if it is inconsistent, the federal law prevails.) The Federal Parliament also has power over any matter that is "incidental or supplementary" to the items on the legislative lists, and there are several federal powers set forth in the body of the Constitution itself.[3]

†Where the Constitution provides that the Federal Government shall have exclusive power over a particular industry, it does not mean that the Federal Government must own the industry. Rather, it means that it can own it if it wishes, or it can regulate it when in private hands. Thus, it owns the railways but merely regulates the mining industry.

shipping on tidal waters and the River Niger and its branches; Parliament can, if it wishes, bring any road within its control, regulate any port that it declares to be federal, and regulate shipping on any waterway that it declares to be an international or interregional waterway.[6]

The national government's powers over commerce and finance are extremely wide. In addition to its power to control the currency and regulate exchange control, it has exclusive power to regulate banks and banking and to determine the law applicable to checks and notes.[7] It has exclusive power to regulate business corporations, corporate issues of securities, indeed any capital issue, and "insurance" other than a regional government's insurance within its region.[8] It has concurrent power over commercial and industrial monopolies and combines and over scientific and industrial research.[9] Only the Federal Government can impose taxes upon the "income and profits" of corporations ("companies"), enact an excise tax, or, with certain exceptions mentioned in the next sections, impose a sales tax.[10]

Nigeria's Constitution goes to great lengths to ensure that business will not be inconvenienced by the fact that hers is a federal system. It goes even further than other constitutions which her framers examined, the Canadian, Australian, and Indian, all of which also sought to avoid some of the problems that have arisen under the United States Constitution.

Even with respect to some matters apparently within the residual powers of the regions, the Federal Government could probably take action in the economic sphere under the powers granted to it. It probably could regulate or supply housing for workers or for anyone around industrial estates under its powers over labor or industrial development, since adequate housing is closely related both to the welfare of workers and to industrial development. It presumably could regulate agricultural production for interregional sales under its power over "trade and commerce among the [regions]."

There is a possibility, however, that Nigeria's courts will construe the specific federal powers narrowly, because, paradoxically, there are so many of them. Where scores of specific powers are listed, it becomes harder to argue, for example, that the power to regulate housing for workers is incidental or supplementary to the power over labor or industrial development; housing itself is a category which could easily have been included on the legislative lists. A conclusion that Parliament lacked the power would seem erroneous — it is after all a perfectly reasonably constitutional intent that housing should be within the federal sway only when related to one of the powers specifically granted to the Federal Government. But the specificity and number of powers listed can give rise to many negative implications and, if interpreted woodenly by the courts, confound the prediction that Nigeria's Constitution is well equipped to grow with the country.

In its first decision that tested the extent of federal power under the Constitution, the Federal Supreme Court took a rather narrow view of federal power. The case was the so-called Bank case,* in which a Western Region bank sought to prevent a federal investigation into its relations with the Action Group and the Western Region statutory corporations. The Federal Government instituted the investigation under a Commissions of Inquiry Act, which gave it power to inquire into matters "within . . . Federal competence." Banks and banking were of course matters that the Federal Parliament had exclusive power to regulate. The Court reasoned, however, that a *general* power to investigate matters within Federal competence was not "incidental or supplementary" to the federal powers, even though the words "incidental or supplementary" were defined in the Constitution as including "the establishment and regulation of tribunals of inquiry." A more wooden interpretation of a constitution can scarcely be imagined.

Outside the economic sphere, the Federal Parliament has very wide powers in addition to those already mentioned. It has, for example, exclusive power over such varied subjects as meteorology and marriage and divorce, unless the marriage took place "under Muslim or other customary law."[11] It has concurrent power over the control of the voluntary movement of persons between the regions, over the legal and medical professions, and over prisons.[12] In the communications field it has exclusive control of the posts, telegraph, telephone, and radio and television, except that a region can have its own radio and television station.[13]

Moreover, even if regulation of a matter is reserved to the regions, Parliament is explicitly permitted to appropriate federal money for it.[14] The crucial question, of course, is whether it can use that power as a carrot with which to "persuade" the regions to perform their functions in a way desired by the Federal Government. It would seem that the power to give money away includes the power to give money away

*Its formal name was *Chief Doherty and the Western Nigeria Development Corporation* v. *Tafawa Balewa et al.*

upon a condition, but if the Federal Supreme Court is unimaginative it could conceivably decide that Parliament was legislating upon a residual matter if it made a grant of money for primary education conditional, for example, upon the teaching of French or a particular indigenous language.

Finally, the Constitution provides for the expansion of federal power by act of either a regional legislature or the Federal Parliament. The regional legislatures are authorized to give the Federal Parliament power to act upon all matters, such as primary education, which would otherwise be reserved to the region.[15]* More importantly, the Federal Parliament by majority vote can declare that an emergency exists and thereby give itself power to enact laws dealing with matters reserved in normal times to regional control.

The legislative powers of the Federal Government are very great. The existence of a federal system in Nigeria is not likely substantially to add to the complications of business operations in the country. The likelihood of conflict between the regions is reduced by limiting their legislative power. Of course the fact that power exists does not mean that it must be exercised, and the Nigerian Federal Government has heretofore barely scratched the surface of federal power. But, if the sentiment for national action grows, the Constitution's division of legislative authority between the Federation and the regions should not serve to frustrate that sentiment.

Interlocking Powers

The division of power between the regions and the Federal Government in Nigeria does not follow any simple pattern. Frequently there is no sharp demarcation between regional and federal power but rather interlocking power, or checked and balanced power.

*Under Ghana's constitution, the Ghanaian Parliament is empowered to surrender sovereignty to a union of African states. The comparison between Nigeria's provision for a temporary surrender of power by the regions to the nation and Ghana's provision for a permanent surrender of national sovereignty to a supranational body is illustrative of the two nations' differing attitudes toward Pan-Africanism and, perhaps, even more of the greater difficulty of attaining a unified community in Africa's giant, Nigeria, as compared with Ghana, one of Africa's medium-sized countries. (The preamble to Nigeria's Republican Constitution takes note of Pan-African as well as national aspirations by stating, "Having firmly resolved to establish the Federal Republic of Nigeria, with a view to ensuring the unity of our people and faith in our fatherland, for the purpose of promoting inter-African co-operation and solidarity. . . .")

As in any federal constitution a requisite number of states or regions (three out of four in Nigeria) must consent to significant amendments to the federal constitution. But in Nigeria it is also true that the Federal Parliament must consent to significant amendments to the regional constitutions.[16]

In several instances the regions are given a right of veto with respect to federal legislation. Parliament can, for example, pass laws relating to matters outside the Legislative Lists if it is necessary to do so to implement a treaty, convention, or international agreement. But such laws only apply in a region if its governor consents.[17] Other instances of regional veto power include the necessity of consent from all the regions for Parliament to have the right to regulate professions other than law and medicine.[18]

With respect to the police, on the other hand, the Federal Government has, in effect, a veto upon each region's control of the federal police located within its territory. The Commissioners of Police in each region — who are federal officials appointed after consultation with the respective regional premiers by a commission whose members are appointed by the President acting on the advice of the Prime Minister — are to comply with the directions of the regional premier or his deputy unless those directions are vetoed by the Prime Minister or his deputy.[19]

With respect to legislative power to impose a tax upon the sale of "produce," the Federation and regions acting together can without amendment change the division of power set out in the Constitution. The Constitution gives the Federation exclusive power to impose such a tax. But it provides that the regions can acquire the exclusive power to impose such a tax as to any kind of produce that the Federal Government designates with the consent of the governments of all the regions.[20] It has already been mentioned how the Constitution gives each region power unilaterally to add to federal legislative power and how the Federal Parliament through declaring an emergency can unilaterally expand its own power.

The Nigerian judicial system is a further indication of the interlocking nature of federal and regional power. The Federal Supreme Court has great powers. But the regional premiers are each given the right to control the appointment of one of the court's associate justices.[21]

The Federal Supreme Court's power includes the right to decide cases that involve the Federal Constitution or federal legislation. But it is also empowered to decide cases involving the interpretation of a regional constitution, of regional statutory law, and of the common law or tribal law relating to matters within the legislative jurisdiction of the regions.[22]* Though Parliament is empowered to establish inferior federal courts, there are in fact none; all the courts beneath the Federal Supreme Court are regional (except for the courts in the Federal Territory of Lagos). Thus Nigeria has a unified if not unitary judicial system with the ultimate authority on all significant questions resting with the Federal Supreme Court.

The advantage of giving the Federal Supreme Court the last word on the interpretation of regional statutory law and the common law is obvious. The confusion caused by conflicting interpretations or decisions can be avoided. That is particularly significant in Nigeria, where the regions inherited identical legislation from the colonial central government when jurisdiction over various matters already legislated upon came within their sway. It will also ensure that if the regions want to pass new identical legislation in the future, their aim will not be frustrated (as sometimes has been the case in the United States where two state courts, each with the last word, have interpreted identical language in different ways.) An eventual disadvantage is that the Federal Supreme Court will become overburdened and unable to devote sufficient time to the constitutional cases upon which its considered judgment is absolutely vital. When that problem arises, it can be solved by amending the Constitution so as to make more nonconstitutional cases appealable by permission instead of by right.

With all its history of regionalization and with its reputation of being a loose federation, it is somewhat surprising that Nigeria should in fact have a relatively centralized judiciary and a federal parliament with extremely wide powers. But historically there was a unified court system and, in the economic field, for example, a unified railway system owned by the central government. The forces of inertia, therefore, favored a continuation of power at the center. The British — though they may have realized that the transition to independence could best be accomplished as a federation — were often strong supporters of continued power at the center. Examples are the opposition of the British colonial judiciary to the degree of judicial regionalization that in fact occurred and the insistence of the very influential fiscal commissions (entirely British) upon

---

*Under the Republican Constitution jurisdiction over chieftancy questions is removed from all Nigerian courts of law.[23]

structuring the constitution so as to prevent conflicting or overlapping regional taxes or economic regulation.[24] To a certain extent, moreover, the power of Nigeria's Federal Government stems, paradoxically, from the very ethnic antagonism and ethnic fear that led to the decision to decentralize through federation. The federal power over the police, for example, stems directly from the fear of ethnic minorities within the regions that a police force responsible to a regional government dominated by a particular ethnic or religious group might prove to be an instrument of repression and political aggrandizement.[25] The power of the Federal Government is, furthermore, in many instances only latent, as where its power is concurrent or concerns a matter such as nuclear energy. Other powers, such as that of the Federal Supreme Court to decide cases interpreting regional law, have a relatively tenuous and subtle relationship to the desire for regional power, prestige, and security that contributed to the history of regionalization. Where power is clearly at stake and the issue is immediate, such as with respect to the division of revenue between the Federal Government and the regional governments, Nigeria's Constitution is far more solicitous of the regions.

Money and Power

Without money, the broadest legislative powers are unlikely to prove significant. Nigeria's Constitution limits the money available to the Federal Government. In that respect, the Constitution fits the notion that Nigeria's is a loose federation. But even in that respect the Constitution is rather well designed to change with the country if the need for national action increases.

It was previously mentioned that the Federal Government has exclusive power to impose certain taxes — import duties, export duties, excise taxes, income taxes upon the profits of business corporations, royalties upon the extraction of minerals, mineral rents, and most sales taxes[26] can only be imposed by the Federal Government. Though the residual taxing power lies with the regions, the taxes that the regions impose today are much less lucrative than the exclusively federal taxes. During the fiscal year 1960–1961, the Federal Government collected over £85 million under its taxing power while the total revenue collected by the then three regions was only slightly over £14 million. Estimates for the fiscal year 1962–1963 show a similar relationship, the figures being £93 million for the Federal Government and £19.6 for the regions. Yet despite the fact that the Federal Government collects most of the taxes, the regional governments are doing most of the spending. They spend several times what they collect in taxes. Thus, in 1962–1963 the regions' recurrent expenditure of over £67 million was more than £7 million more than the Federation's recurrent expenditure.[27]

The regions are able to spend several times what they collect in taxes because the Constitution compels the Federal Government to turn over to the regions large portions of its revenue from specified taxes. Since independence it has turned over to the regions each year approximately 40 per cent of its yearly revenue. Thus, though the Federal Government is given wide taxing powers so as to ensure uniformity and avoid conflicting and overlapping regional taxes, the regional governments eventually have the power to decide how to spend much of the revenue collected by the Federal Government.

There are a number of rational methods by which federal revenue could be allocated to the regions. One is to return tax revenue to the region from which it can best be estimated that it came. A second possibility is to give each region a share equal to its share of the country's population. A third method is to ensure balanced development between the regions by helping the backward more than the advanced. The Constitution reflects all these principles — derivation, per capita distribution, and balanced development. Though the ratio varies from year to year, approximately two-thirds of the money is distributed according to the principle of derivation and the remainder is distributed under a formula which was designed to take into account "population as a broad indicator of need" and the "balanced development of the Federation."[28]

Of the taxes that must, under the principle of derivation, be returned to the region from whence they came, the most important has been the export duty on produce (basically agricultural commodities) and hides and skins.[29] For the fiscal year 1960–1961, the regions collectively received over £14 million from the return of that tax, approximately as much as they collected from all the taxes they themselves were able to impose. (Table 11.1 sets forth the amounts the various regions received from the various taxes returned to them.) Import duties from tobacco, diesel oil, and gasoline, and the excise duty on tobacco go to the region of consumption.[30] Finally, 50 per cent of the royalties and rents received from mining enterprises are also returned to the region in which the mining was done.[31] With the discovery and increasing production of oil in the South, particularly the East and Midwest, that should prove an extremely significant source of revenue. The Eastern Region's 50 per cent share of the royalties on Eastern Region oil jumped from £492,476 in 1960–1961 to an estimated return of £2,276,100 in 1961–1962. Because the North appears to have no oil, and because the nation's oil revenue may move as high as £100 million in the relatively near future, it is highly likely that some day there will be political controversy about the distribution of oil revenue.

The money that is distributed according to a formula that reflects population and the policy of balanced development comes from two sources. Thirty per cent of all import duties (other than the few mentioned above, which are transferred in their entirety to the regions, and the duty on beer, spirits, and wine, which is kept by the Federal Government) goes into a "Distributable Pool Account." So does 30 per cent of the royalties and rents received from mining enterprises, including oil wells. Then the money in the "Distributable Pool" is transferred to the regions in the ratio of 40 to the North, 31 to the East, 18 to the West, and 6 to the Midwest.[32]

In assessing the revenue allocation provisions of the Nigerian Constitution, there are a number of questions to be answered. First, how do they affect the balance between the Federal Government and the regions? Second, how do they affect the relations between the regions themselves and how will they affect the nature of Nigerian political parties? Third, will they hold back or encourage the development of a sense of national unity?

The conclusion — based upon examination of the wide scope of its legislative powers — that the Federal Government is unusually powerful, at least potentially, must be adjusted somewhat upon examination of its constitutional duty to hand over some 40 per cent of its revenue to the regions without having any control over how the money is spent. Though much regulation can be done with little money, the Federal Government, even if it wanted to act, might well be unable to support some more ambitious programs because of the automatic transfers to the regions. Here, moreover, its emergency powers are not a complete answer to frustration. During a period of emergency it could impose taxes, like the personal income tax, which in normal times are reserved to the regions; indeed that was one of the chief reasons for including the emergency powers in the Constitution.[33] But the existence of a state of emergency does not

TABLE 11.1
AMOUNTS RECEIVED BY THE REGIONS FROM THE FEDERATION (IN POUNDS)

		1959–1960	1960–1961	1962–1963 (est.)
Import Duty	N.	516,347	515,731	479,600
(Tobacco)	W.	1,142,413	1,068,845	1,002,010
	E.	1,564,862	1,429,868	1,243,070
Import Duty		759,878	679,385	759,850
(Gasoline)		1,350,459	1,179,871	1,988,350
		772,917	880,344	982,800
Import Duty		496,659	655,597	858,600
(Diesel Oil)		402,759	611,270	802,950
		410,562	525,785	667,800
Export Duties		4,451,466	4,078,298	3,354,800
(Produce, Hides, Skins)		8,447,011	7,488,591	5,658,710
		2,684,841	2,457,199	1,883,600
Excise Duty		1,449,433	1,522,640	1,881,890
(Tobacco)		1,619,285	1,708,743	2,116,470
		500,601	388,956	479,600
Mining Royalties		414,255	529,454	689,720
and Rents		79,247	114,919	1,326,200
		415,717	492,476	2,951,350
Distributable Pool			282,983	982,960
(Mining)			169,983	589,780
			219,180	761,790
Distributable Pool		3,654,671	4,993,662	5,431,580
(General Imports)		2,192,802	2,999,060	3,259,950
		2,832,370	3,868,119	4,209,470
Total Rounded Off	N.	12,124	13,775	15,504
To Nearest Thousand	W.	15,417	16,250	16,307
	E.	9,413	10,629	13,390

(A small amount of income tax was also transferred in 1959–1960 and 1960–1961 so that the sum of the listed figures is somewhat less than the totals.)

Percentage of Regional Revenue Derived from Constitutionally Required Payments from the Federal Government

	1959–1960	1960–1961	1962–1963 (est.)
N.	69.2	78	71
W.	78.3	79.1	73
E.	63.8	63.2	64.8

free the Federal Government from its constitutional duty to transfer to the regions the revenue received from the various taxes described above.

Though the transfers to the regions are automatic and compelled by the Constitution, the Federal Government is not completely powerless with respect to those taxes the revenue from which must be transferred. It retains the right to determine how high or low those taxes should be. That power could be used to influence the policy of a region that is particularly dependent upon a given tax. Furthermore, the economic effect of one tax, the revenue from which is kept by the Federal Government, may well be the same as the economic effect of another tax, the receipts from which are transferred to the regions. That would be true for duties on imported goods, a major portion of which goes to the regions, and sales taxes on imported goods, the entire receipts from which are kept by the Federal Government. The Federal Government could substitute the tax that favors it for the economically equivalent tax that favors the regions.

As the country develops economically and the need and sentiment for federal action increases, moreover, the percentage of the revenue collected by the Federal Government which is available for its own use without automatic distribution to the regions is likely to increase. Thus, in this respect the revenue allocation provisions are capable of growing with the country just as are the provisions for the division of legislative authority. If the economy develops industrially and Nigeria begins to produce locally some and eventually many of the goods she now imports, the revenue from the tax upon corporations ("companies"), all of which is retained by the Federal Government, will become relatively more important, and the revenue from various import duties, some or all of which is automatically passed on to the regions, will become relatively less important. Almost all taxes that are built upon an industrial base are kept by the Federation; the regions receive most taxes which rest upon an agricultural base. In addition to the income tax on corporations, only the Federal Government can impose sales taxes on industrial products (other than gasoline and diesel oil used for nonindustrial purposes) or excise taxes and export duties on industrial products. The Federal Government keeps all the revenue from such taxes.

One qualification should be made, however, to the thesis that the revenue allocation provisions will favor the Federal Government as the country develops economically. As the country develops, the personal income tax will become infinitely more lucrative. The Federal Government has no power to impose a personal income tax except during an emergency.*

As for the relations between the regions themselves, one weakness is that the revenue allocation provisions were not devised so as to give each region a greater stake in the success of the others. It might have been sensible, for example, to provide that while most of the export duty on an agricultural product went to the region where it was grown, a substantial portion would be distributed among the other regions. That would make more obvious the interest of the Northerner in Western cocoa or the Easterner in Northern cotton and thus highlight regional interdependence.

It is frequently said of Nigeria, moreover, that it is better off than most tropical countries because the diversity of its agricultural products would save it from disaster should the world market price of any one product tumble. That is true when the focus is on the country as a whole, but the individual regions, each of which relies heavily on one or two export crops, are in a far more precarious position. The revenue allocation system increases their risk, for as a region gets 100 per cent of the export duties on its crops, so it bears all the loss if duties must be reduced to compete when prices fall.

The regions depend for their success and survival on their share of the automatic transfers of money from the Federal Government. Unfortunately, that may tend to keep Nigeria's political parties regional rather than national and therefore help keep alive ethnic and regional tension. Where a region must depend for its very lifeblood upon transfers from the Federal Government and where the regions must compete for the limited funds available, citizens of each region are almost certain to look at the issue in regional rather than national terms. Even assuming that the ethnic and regional-religious jealousies which have been the major shaper of Nigerian political parties subside, the need for a region's citizens to unite to get more Federal revenue will continue. And that of course makes the circle vicious, because the regional nature of the parties is not only caused by ethnic antagonism, fear, and jealousy but also causes those feelings to arise.

*Consistent with other efforts to ensure that Nigeria's federal system does not cause economic hardship to those who operate in more than one region, the Federal Parliament is empowered to ensure that there will be no double taxation under regional personal income or estate tax laws. Parliament also has power to enact uniform principles for the computation of income and for the treatment of depreciation and losses.[34]

The fault is not in the system of revenue allocation. Rather it is in the need for the payments. Indeed, the system, by making the payments automatic under the Constitution instead of subject to annual political strife, makes the issue somewhat less obviously controversial and therefore should mute regional conflict. But the Constitution can be amended. Considering how the revenue needs of the regions and the benefits each gets from various transferred taxes could change so substantially as Nigeria and its economy changes, those provisions will have to be amended if they are not to distort the nation's development. Fights over Constitutional amendments can be just as bitter as fights over legislative appropriations. However, in the summer of 1965 the various Nigerian governments agreed upon recommendations for constitutional amendments, presented by an Australian expert, the principal aim of which was to increase the money going from the Federal Government to the regions, particularly the North.

A struggle between the regions over their shares of the money transferred from the Federation to the regions is one of the rocks on which the Nigerian ship of state could most easily founder. Given the regional nature of Nigeria's political parties, a purely political change would produce lasting hostility from the region that was harmed. But there are so many variables, so many systems that would be rational, that there is no sound objective test by which to support the fair or expose the unfair. One of the crucial tests of statesmanship in Nigeria will be the way in which the country handles adjustment of its revenue allocation provisions.

The Balance of Power

Structurally, Nigeria's federal system is somewhat unusual in two respects. It has only four regions, and of course had only three until the Midwest was created in July 1963. One of its regions — the North — is larger in area and more populous than the rest of the regions combined. These two factors are likely to have a great impact upon developments under the Nigerian Constitution, and to cause results which would not necessarily be foreseen from the earlier examination of federal as opposed to regional power, which was made without regard to the number and relative size of the regions.

As is true of all federal constitutions, the Nigerian Constitution compromises between the principle that the Federal Government as the voice of all the nation should be controlled by a majority of the people without regard to the separate existence of the regions or states and the principle that those regions or states should be given equal representation without regard to differences in population. The House of Representatives is based upon population. The Senate gives equal representation to each region and has some additional members as discussed below. Significant amendments to the Constitution had, until the creation of the Midwest Region, to be agreed upon by two out of the three regional legislatures and after the addition of the Midwest must be agreed upon by three out of the four regional legislatures. The Senate and the amendment process, therefore, are designed to protect regional interests.

The Senate, however, is a somewhat uncertain shield. It can only delay ordinary legislation.[35] In this respect, it is like the British House of Lords rather than the United States Senate.* The Senate is, however, given power equal to the House of Representatives with respect to two matters that are likely to affect the regions vitally — the declaration of an emergency (majority of both houses required) and the amendment of the Constitution (two-thirds vote of both houses required for first step).[36] But because of its composition the value of the Senate to a dissenting region is reduced.

Each region selects twelve Senators,† and two Lagos Chiefs are ex officio members. Two others come from Lagos, selected in a manner determined by Parliament. Finally, the Prime Minister, through the Presi-

*The United States pattern is somewhat incompatible with a parliamentary system of government. Where the executive is responsible to Parliament, a senate that could require a dissolution or change in government by defeating a government proposal that had passed in the lower house (where the representatives chosen according to population clearly support the government) would be an anomaly. Perhaps that explains why in Australia, Canada, and India — all, like Nigeria, federations with a parliamentary system — the senate does not serve the federal principle to the same extent as in the United States. Either the senators are nominated by the national cabinet (Canada) or the senate is given only powers to delay or to require a joint sitting in which it will be vastly outnumbered by the lower house (Australia, India).

The needs of a parliamentary system also help explain why the Nigerian Prime Minister is entitled to select four Senators from anywhere in the country. Cabinet Ministers have to be members of Parliament. And it may well be that no person suited to run certain ministries will run for the House of Representatives or be elected to it. The Prime Minister would then be able to appoint his choice for minister to the Senate.

†They are selected at a joint sitting of the two houses of various regional legislatures. It had been contemplated that the opposition in each region would be given a number of Senators proportionate to its strength in the particular regional house of assembly. That has not happened.

dent, can select four additional Senators.[37] In some cases, therefore, the deciding votes in the Senate may be made by the appointees of the representative of the majority in the House where population (not regional interest) is determinative.

The amendment process is also less of a shield to the regions than might be expected from the fact that three out of four regions must concur in amendments. Declaration of an emergency—which can be done by an ordinary majority of the House and Senate without any participation of the regions—is in most respects the equivalent of power to amend the Constitution. Furthermore, because of the relatively few regions in Nigeria, the amendment process probably is less of a shield for the group that fears change than it would be in a federation which also required 75 per cent of the constituent units to approve amendments but had more constituent units. The fewer the constituent units, the easier it should be to form a coalition for change. (Similarly, the fewer the constituent units the more likely it is that the interests of the constituent units will be given precedence over national interests.) The way in which the North and the East, the NPC and the NCNC, combined to carve the Midwest out of the West was almost brutally simple.

Probably the most significant balance of political power created under the Nigerian Constitution is not that between national and regional power but that between North and South. Because of its size, the North can protect its interests against even a coalition of all the other regions. With more than half the nation's population, it has more than half the seats in the House of Representatives. Therefore, if at any time its interests seem menaced, its representatives could (even if the NPC's majority disappears at some time) band together in the House of Representatives and prevent a bill from being passed or the amendment process from even beginning. On the other hand, the three Southern regions, if they act together, can use their combined strength in the Senate (36 — plus the 4 from Lagos and any Southerners appointed by the Prime Minister — of a total of 56) to prevent the amendment process from starting or an emergency from being declared. (But they can only delay ordinary legislation favored by the House.) Any two of them could also prevent final passage of a constitutional amendment that required the consent of three of the four regions.

*   *   *

The federal aspects of Nigeria's Constitution must be rated as very successful. Striving for an abstractly perfect constitution might result in there being no nation under the constitution. In constitution-making, perhaps more than anything else, the best can be the enemy of the good. Though there may be serious fights over amendments, particularly of the revenue provisions, and the few regions may make exploitation of a minority region overly simple and tempting, the Nigerian Constitution is a compromise under which often jealous and sometimes hostile groups agreed to live together, remarkably closely. The powers of the national government are flexible and capable of growing with the country and with sentiment for their use.

The success of Nigeria's federal system is of importance to all Africa. As the most populous and ethnically diverse of Africa's nations, Nigeria is a test case of whether greater African unity is possible. African unity, Pan-Africanism, is one of the key subjects of the following chapter on Nigeria's foreign policy.

Foreign Policy

The foreign policy choices facing Nigeria must be seen against the highlights of Africa's recent history.

Africa was carved up according to the whim and fancy of the rival European colonial powers so that its nations make sense neither geographically, nor economically, nor from the point of view of the peoples who are included. Consider, for example, the strip of West African coast between Nigeria and Ghana. The frontier between Nigeria and Dahomey splits the Yoruba tribe, the frontier between Dahomey and Togo splits the Fon and Adja-Ouatchi tribes, and the frontier between Togo and Ghana splits the Ewe tribe; none of the frontiers is based on a geographical dividing line, and the narrow fingers that are Togo and Dahomey are too small for sensible economic development.

The different colonial powers created some real differences among the artifical blocks into which they divided African soil. They did so by tying the colonies' economies to the metropolitan countries, ignoring intra-African communications while building roads and railroads from the interior to the sea, and by introducing their own educational systems and languages. But in no case had the internal unity of the new African nations been assured when the colonialists departed. The paramount importance of developing wider loyalties, loyalties beyond the traditional tribal unit, which has been emphasized throughout this analysis of Nigeria, is paralleled in all the other African states.

By the time of Nigeria's independence in October 1960, most of Africa was either free or scheduled for independence at an early date. Exceptions were the Portugese and Spanish colonies and those British and French colonies which had a substantial white settler minority (Algeria, the Rhodesias, and Kenya being the most important). Most of these were in the southern third of the continent, at the tip of which lay South Africa, which was independent from Europe but which had enshrined white supremacy as a principle of government.

Most of the former colonies had become independent peacefully. The colonialists had surrendered peacefully, partly because they did not feel that a struggle to put down actual or threatened insurrectionary movements would be worth the effort, partly because they felt they could best retain the friendship of and advantageous economic relations with their former colonies by doing so, partly because of the exigencies of the Cold War, and partly because of the pressure of progressive public opinion at home and abroad.

Though independent, the new nations of Africa were weak. Indeed, it is highly doubtful whether those nations could have succeeded in winning their independence through a revolution fought against determined opposition. (The Algerian nationalists, who really only barely survived a long bloody stalemate, were better equipped to fight a revolution than counterparts in countries south of the Sahara in terms of the availability both of numbers of skilled soldiers and of military aid from outside.) In any event, it is clear that after gaining their independence the new nations of Africa were militarily weak, still dependent economically upon their former colonial masters, and in need of massive infusions of capital and educational and technological aid.

The final important fact about Africa's history is that Africa, particularly black Africa, had been victimized and exploited unmercifully for a long time.* The rape of slavery had been followed by the leech of colonialism. More significant than physical exploitation had been the psychological assault upon the African's human dignity. He was told that biology

---

*Perhaps more important than the fact that Africa has been exploited is the fact that Africans feel that it has been and will continue to be exploited unless extraordinary steps are taken. The feeling and the consequent fear are well illustrated by the remark of a member of the Nigerian Parliament who saw the main purpose of the European Common Market as being the spoilation of Africa and who went on to say, "Africa is their target . . . not only for the six nations but also for Britain, America, and the Soviet Union. The question of how the booty will be shared after the Scramble [for] Africa is as yet unsettled."[1]

and the Bible proved that he was fit only to be a hewer of wood and the drawer of water. Ethnocentric bearers of Western civilization derided all his customs, saw no culture, and then laughed at him for aping their ways.

This background has an important, but often conflicting, bearing upon the foreign policy choices that face Nigeria and other African nations. Irrationality of the national frontiers, particularly when they split ethnic groups, has traditionally been a major cause for conflict between neighboring countries, but common revulsion against the colonialism that produced Africa's irrational frontiers tends to bring Africa's nations together. Their weakness makes it imperative that they join together in larger unities. Yet because they are weak (and the territory of many is guaranteed by the former colonial power), and because of the Cold War and the shrinking world (which helped bring about their independence), larger unities are not likely to be attained by force. Union through consent is possible, but it is not easy for the fortunate individuals who lead new nations to surrender the power structure received intact from the colonialists. To develop loyalties wider than the tribe, leaders emphasize the glory of the nation, but doing so tends to drive it apart from neighboring nations with whom it should unite. For psychological reasons it is necessary to loosen the ties with the former colonial master, yet the former master is well equipped to give a major portion of the vast amount of technical and financial aid that is needed.

*   *   *

Nigeria's reaction to the use by France of Algeria's Sahara sands as a testing ground for atomic weapons is an example of the conflicting pressures upon the framers of her foreign policy.* When the tests began, Nigeria protested them; when they continued, she broke diplomatic relations with France and proclaimed an embargo on French shipping and goods. The tests did not in fact deposit radioactive material upon Nigeria.[3] The serious counteraction that was nevertheless taken is an example of a continental rather than a national approach to foreign policy issues, though Nigeria was in fact the only African country to take such action against France despite much talk by others, such as Ghana.

---

*Chief Akintola's ridicule of France for trying to assert her national glory was phrased in a way that United States or British statesmen might recently have wished themselves free to match. His comment was: "The bloated bladder of a frog which pretended to be as big as an elephant would burst in the end, and so be it with arrogant France."[2]

There is a close parallel between African opposition to manifestations of power on the African continent by the European nations and the American opposition to similar manifestations in the Western Hemisphere that led to the Monroe Doctrine. The African reaction is, moreover, overlaid by a feeling of racial solidarity in the face of attack. Thus, Mr. R. A. Fani-Kayode saw the French tests as a gesture of contempt for the black man and, speaking in the Nigerian House of Representatives, said,

> This is the opportunity we have been looking for to show that black men all over Africa must stand or fall together. I have said it often and often in this house that blackism is the answer to our problems.[4]

The aftermath of the embargo placed by Nigeria upon French goods and shipping shows one of the difficulties of combating a European power with a solid African front and is an example of the economic dependence of African nations upon the colonial powers — a dependence so great that many believe political independence is thereby rendered meaningless. The boycott caused an economic crisis in Nigeria's neighbors, Dahomey, Niger, and Chad, which depended upon French ships and Nigerian harbors for much of their export and import trade and for the supply of capital goods such as those being used to build a major seaport for Dahomey.[5] Four months after it was instituted the boycott was called off.

Nigeria has also treated distant South Africa's policy of racial discrimination as a threat and has participated in joint African efforts to isolate South Africa diplomatically and to bring the pressure of world opinion against her.* She has instituted a boycott against South African goods and sought to have South Africa ousted from various world bodies, such as the International Labor Organization. Prime Minister Tafawa Balewa took a leading part in the condemnation of South Africa at the Commonwealth Prime Minister's Conference in March 1961 that led to the withdrawal of her application for readmission to the

---

*When installed as Governor-General, Nnamdi Azikiwe generalized about racial prejudice and Nigeria's foreign policy, saying:
We cannot concede that it is in our national interest to fraternize with such nations which practice race prejudice and we must not acquiesce in such an outrageous insult to the black race. In fact, we must regard it as a mark of disrespect and unfriendly act if any country with whom we have friendly relations indulges in race prejudice in any shape or form, no matter how it may be legally clothed.[6]

Commonwealth after having become a republic. This he did after the Sardauna of Sokoto, using a rather inept simile, or perhaps with tongue in cheek, had supported South Africa's expulsion by saying "The Commonwealth is a family affair, and we do not expect to find a black goat among the white ones."[7]

As described, Nigeria's policy with respect to French atomic testing in the Sahara and apartheid in South Africa has been little different from the aggressive, insistent policy that a reader of the daily papers expects to come out of Africa. Closer analysis reveals, however, some distinctly Nigerian views, in which the moderate style and tone of the Prime Minister has been very significant. During a Parliamentary session when speakers vied to make the most vituperative attacks upon South Africa for the Sharpesville massacre, it was typical of Alhaji Abubakar Tafawa Balewa to remark that, unless the independent nations of black Africa govern themselves objectively and well, "we shall only make the conditions of the black race in South Africa more difficult."[8] It was also typical of the Prime Minister to announce that, for all his distate for her policy, he would if asked exchange ambassadors with South Africa, and if invited would visit South Africa to help make the country change its apartheid policy.[9]*

Nigeria's position as an African moderate, which is suggested by the Prime Minister's statements, is most clearly revealed by her policy on the timing of independence for those African countries which remain under colonial rule. While insisting that colonial rule must end in all of Africa, Nigeria's governmental spokesmen have not accepted the frequently voiced African view that the lack of political, social, and economic progress is no excuse for continued foreign control.[11] Little talk about the raising of armies of liberation has come from official Nigeria, and when Foreign Minister Jaja Wachuku† put forward before the United Nations in the fall of 1961 a target date for the termination

---

*A similar statement was made by the Prime Minister at a 1962 meeting of the Commonwealth Prime Ministers' Conference when he said he would not oppose the Rhodesias' Roy Welensky coming to Nigeria because he was not a racist and Africans in the Rhodesias, contrary to South Africa, could hold political meetings. That somewhat surprising statement was described in a telegram to the Prime Minister from a leading Rhodesian political party as "shocking, disturbing and unbefitting an African Prime Minister."[10]

†In the new cabinet appointed after the 1964 election, Prime Minister Tafawa Balewa kept the foreign affairs ministry for himself and appointed Mr. Wachuku as Aviation Minister.

of all colonial rule in Africa, it was one surprisingly far in the future — 1970.

There are a number of possible explanations why Nigeria's policy on the liberation of colonial Africa has been cautious and moderate. Nigeria's own history of careful preparation for independence and her many years of constitutional conferences designed to create governmental institutions that would reduce intergroup tension proved to many Nigerians the wisdom of slow but steady progress.* The chaos in the Congo, on the other hand, said Jaja Wachuku, proved the folly of sudden freedom.[12] What was necessary in racially-mixed Southern Rhodesia in 1962 was not, according to Mr. Wachuku, the usual African principle of representation proportionate to population but, as an interim solution, an equal number of seats for members of both races (with the United Kingdom having the deciding vote) so that, as had been true in Nigeria, the Africans "will learn to govern by governing."[13]

On the assumption that the colonial powers remaining in Africa all planned to guide their colonies to freedom as Britain had guided Nigeria to freedom, Nigeria's history would perhaps support the wisdom of Nigeria's cautious approach to the liberation of colonial Africa. But the assumption cannot be supported. The Portugese and the white settlers of southern Africa are repressing their Africans' drive toward independence rather than guiding it and laying the groundwork for success. A cautious course cannot, therefore, legitimately claim the support of Nigeria's history.

Foreign Minister Wachuku also supported the independence-by-1970 resolution by pointing out that South Africa and the Portugese colonies in the south were far away and blessed with strong armies. Force could not possibly challenge them until free African nations on their borders could serve as sources of arms and places of refuge — as the Congo has at times done for Angola. Given their strength and intransigence, the most realistic policy to assist their African subjects is, said the Foreign Minister, "to go through those who have trodden their paths."[14] In other words, it was necessary to win the support of their friends or associates like the United Kingdom and the United States which could not be expected to support immediate independence.

---

*A particularly relevant aspect of Nigeria's own history that may help to explain Nigeria's moderate position on the timing of African independence is that the senior party in her coalition government, the NPC, had itself sought to delay Nigeria's independence.

The Nigerian Foreign Minister expressed an extremely realistic view of the power structure in Africa and the world. One wishes that his analysis of how to persuade the United States or the United Kingdom to act was equally realistic. But it is at least doubtful whether they are likely to act reasonably — or the way in which Nigeria would want them to — unless subjected to great, perhaps unreasonable, pressure, the most likely source of which is Africa in which Nigeria by virtue of her size is looked upon for leadership.

Nigeria's moderate position on the liberation of colonial Africa has threatened her status as a leader in Africa. In Nigeria's relations with Great Britain and her allies moderation has also been a dominant note. But Nigeria's leaders have increasingly tended to demonstrate their independence.

Nigeria's official policy has been one of nonalignment with either the Communist world or the Western world. As phrased by the Prime Minister before his Parliament and before the United Nations, Nigeria would not "associate itself as a matter of routine with any of the power blocs."[15] True to the policy, Nigeria has supported both East and West on various Cold War issues. It has, for example, supported the admission of Communist China to the United Nations (though advocating the two-China solution whereby Nationalist China would remain a member as well); on the other hand, the Prime Minister supported the United States' series of nuclear tests in 1962, after the Russians had broken the testing moratorium, on the grounds that while all testing was unfortunate, the American tests were necessary to keep the balance of power that ensured world peace.[16] Though nonaligned, Nigeria has not accepted the neutralist principle that a primary requirement of her foreign policy is to avoid taking a position on Cold War issues. Thus, when most African nations were conspicuously silent about or minimized the seriousness of Communist China's attack on India in 1962, Prime Minister Tafawa Balewa extended his strong support to India's Nehru.

Though the Government had promised not to associate itself as a matter of routine with either East or West, there were signs after independence that suggested that association with Great Britain was going to be extremely intimate even if not automatic. At the United Nations immediately prior to his matter-of-routine statement, Alhaji Abubakar Tafawa Balewa promised, "we shall not forget our old friends," meaning Great Britain. The Sardauna of Sokoto showed no desire to make new, Russian, friends when he brushed off the possibility of accepting a low-interest Russian loan by saying, "That is not our policy. We have to work with those we are accustomed to."[17]*

Shortly after independence, the Nigerian government signed a mutual defense pact with Great Britain. From the time it was first mentioned, public feeling against entering into such a pact was strong, and Awolowo and his Action Group supporters made much of the assertion that the British had made their agreement to grant independence in 1960 conditional upon a defense pact.† As a result, the Prime Minister promised not to sign the agreement until he obtained the consent of the House of Representatives after independence. Accordingly, the proposed treaty was presented to the House in November 1960. By a straight party vote, with the NPC and NCNC members all voting in favor and the Action Group members (plus Chike Obi) all voting against, the treaty was approved.

The agreement provided generally that the two countries would furnish to each other "such assistance as might be necessary for mutual defense."[20] More specifically, Britain agreed to assist in the training of the Nigerian armed forces both in Nigeria and in Britain, to provide personnel, and to make efforts to ensure an adequate supply of modern weapons. For her part, Nigeria agreed to give British military aircraft unrestricted rights to fly over and land in Nigeria,‡ and to make her airfields available for trials of new military aircraft in a tropical climate.

The agreement was a serious embarrassment to the Government. On the day it was signed, students rioted and poured protesting into the Parliament buildings. A people's conference called by the Government a year later unanimously called for its abrogation. It symbolized

---

*In a similar vein, the Chinese Communists were not invited to Nigeria's independence day celebrations, and the Russians, who were invited, were told that they would have to wait in line to open an embassy. The Prime Minister also publicly complained that Jacob Malik, Russian delegate to the celebrations, had tried to bully him into speeding up the embassy opening.[18]

†The Prime Minister denied that allegation, saying: "It is not in the nature of the British to force people in the manner that the leader of opposition says."[19] Awolowo admitted that he (along with the Sardauna, Tafawa Balewa, and Azikiwe) initialed at the 1958 Constitutional Conference a defense pact broader than the one eventually signed. He later said he initialed the draft agreement only because he thought it would be broken as soon as publicized in Nigeria.

‡The then nonexistent Nigerian Air Force was given reciprocal rights which prompted J. S. Tarka of the UMBC to ask: "Are we going to carry our mosquitoes and flies over to Britain? Are we going to carry our tsetse flies over to Britain?"[21] (In 1963 it was revealed that the West German government had agreed to assist Nigeria in setting up an Air Force).

Nigeria's close ties to Great Britain when symbolic demonstrations of its independence were what the country wanted and needed. It reduced Nigeria's influence in Africa and among all those nations that call themselves uncommitted. Because Nigeria had given Great Britain certain military rights, Ghana succeeded until the very last minute in keeping Nigeria from being invited to the Belgrade Conference of non-aligned states held in the summer of 1961 even though Ghana, without any treaty but merely as a member of the Commonwealth, relied heavily upon British support for its army.*

The defense pact was finally abrogated by mutual consent in January 1962, on the eve of a Conference of African Heads of State held in Lagos. The timing of the abrogation strongly suggests that Nigeria's leaders had come to realize that the treaty limited their opportunities for leadership in Africa.

The trend toward increased emphasis upon leadership in Africa and decreased emphasis upon ties with "old friends" continued. It was manifested in Nigeria's decision not to accept Associate Membership in the European Common Market if Great Britain became a member, as it was assumed she would. There were strong economic arguments, at least in the short run, for accepting. Of Nigeria's total exports, 48 per cent went to Great Britain and 30 per cent went to the six existing members of the Common Market† Under existing conditions Nigeria's exports benefited from the Commonwealth preference system that applied to goods of Commonwealth countries entering the British market. If Britain entered the Common Market, the preference would end. If Nigeria did not accept Associate status, her products would in addition face a discriminatory tariff favorable to those of competing countries, such as most of the ex-French African colonies, which were to be Associates. On the other hand, if she did accept, her cocoa, for example, would be given preference over Brazilian cocoa. Associate status would also have entitled the country to aid from a special Common Market development fund.

*When an invitation to the Belgrade Conference finally came it was declined because, said Jaja Wachuku, "Nigeria is not going to beg for a thing she is entitled to."[22] Earlier, Prime Minister Tafawa Balewa had said Nigeria would not attend because she was opposed to all blocs, including blocs of neutralists.

†For some of her major export products the ratios were even higher. Fifty-seven per cent of her palm kernel exports went to Great Britain, and 91 per cent to Great Britain plus the six; 27 per cent of the groundnuts exported went to Great Britain and 87 per cent to Great Britain plus the six.[23]

The economic arguments were not controlling, however, and Abu-bakar Tafawa Balewa told the Commonwealth Prime Minister's Conference in London in 1962 that Nigeria would not accept Associate Membership.[24] He told the Nigerian Parliament that acceptance would have prevented Nigeria from making "her full contribution towards promoting African unity."[25] Too obvious an association with the colonial powers would have reduced Nigeria's influence in Africa as had her defense agreement with Great Britain. Since some African nations (Ghana, for example) were obviously not going to accept and others (Liberia, for example) would not be asked, association with the Common Market might lead to new and perpetual differences between Common Market and non-Common Market African countries.

Associate membership in the Common Market was also criticized as a neocolonialist device aimed at keeping Africa economically weak and at the mercy of Europe. It was felt that it was intended to keep Africa as a mere European greenhouse and to prevent her from advancing her wealth and status through industrialization.[26] Finally, the word "associate" was a foolish choice bound to be resented by peoples terribly sensitive concerning their independence.* The intensity of the Nigerians' emotional drive to rid themselves of humiliating reminders of their colonial status is illustrated by the praise heaped about the Prime Minister for the decision.†

While cutting down upon her formal ties with Great Britain, Nigeria began to increase her contacts with Russia and the other Communist countries. In 1962, the first scholarship students officially sponsored by Nigeria (16) went to Russia.‡ About the same time a few trade agreements were signed. Earlier, the Prime Minister had cancelled a ban which the Colonial Government had placed upon the importation of Communist literature, saying that he believed that the people had the "maturity and self-confidence not to be misled by literature of this sort."[29] The movement toward increased contact with the East, however, has been cautious. The spirit with which the ban on literature

---

*In January 1964 Nigeria began negotiations with the Common Market, seeking a trade agreement without formal ties. By the summer of 1965 it appeared quite likely that an agreement would be made.

†On his return from England, the leading independent newspaper, the Lagos *Daily Times*, covered half of its front page with a picture of The Prime Minister surrounded by Hausa greetings and placed on the other half a laudatory editorial.[27]

‡Earlier, some students had gone without the Government's sponsorship, and usually without its consent on Ghanaian passports.[28]

was cancelled was typical. The aim was not to embrace the Communist world and certainly not to run the risk of substituting a Communist master for a colonial master. Rather it was to remove intellectual or economic blinders put on by the colonialists, which were particularly distasteful because they were not applicable in Great Britain.

Despite the trend toward greater emphasis upon African affairs and the increased attention paid to disengagement from Great Britain and her allies, Nigeria is still generally regarded as a moderate in Africa. Her cautious policy on the timing of the liberation of colonial Africa has already been described. Equally significant has been her policy on the union of independent Africa.

The desire that Africa's nations should unite is one aspect of the Pan-African movement. That movement stems from and seeks to build a bond of blackness between all Africans and persons of African descent. Centuries of contempt and discrimination made the race itself appear to be the basis upon which its members' political loyalties should be founded. The early leaders of the Pan-African movement, moreover, were West Indian and American Negroes who were cut off from any particular African territory and naturally thought in continental or racial terms. But early African nationalists often thought in the same way. They usually had rejected the tribe as a political unit, and the pieces of African soil carved out by the colonial powers were not natural objects of loyalty. It was, after all, to the renascent *African* that Nnamdi Azikiwe had written that the future belonged, and it was the God of *Africa* that he said had chosen his people to lead the children of *Africa* from the bondage of the ages.

Pan-Africanism has been seen as an almost magical solution to Africa's needs. Through Pan-Africanism, wrote a Nigerian student in the United States during World War II, Africa would find that "all embracing myth that can arouse whole communities of men into action" and would be redeemed from "social wreckage, political servitude, and economic impotency."[30]

The deep feeling that Africa is still under attack and that political union is the only road to safety is shown by the remark of Tanganyika's President Julius Nyerere that

> As long as there remain separate African nations there will remain too a danger that other states will exploit our differences for their own purposes. Only with unity can we ensure that Africa really governs Africa. Only with unity can we be sure that African resources will be used for the benefit of Africa.[31]

Economically, union, at least in regional federations, would clearly be advantageous. With union, competition in the production of agricultural produce for export could best be rationally controlled. With union, the larger markets necessary for industrialization would be available. With union, wasteful duplication of ports, roads, steel mills, world economic tours, and so forth might be avoided.

Despite the emotional support and all the good reasons for it, the past years have seen few concrete steps toward political union.* There are many reasons. The economic infrastructure for it is largely absent. Independence has forced African leaders to concentrate upon the problems of governing their own states. Power held by the leaders of sovereign states, no matter how small and weak those states may be, is not easy to surrender. With independence won, African personalities sometimes overshadow the "African personality." For groups, as well as leaders, union might mean an apparent loss of power vis-à-vis other Africans, for all that it would do to increase the power of Africa as a whole.

The differences between African nations on the question of African unity are now differences of emphasis rather than principle. There is general agreement that greater unity is desirable. The conflict arises over whether political union should come immediately ("seek ye first the political kingdom," says Ghana's Kwame Nkrumah) or whether it should be a long-term goal which must be preceded by gradual steps, functional cooperation, and the development of the existing nation states.

In addition to general agreement on the desirability of greater African unity, there are certain issues which almost all African nations look upon in Pan-African terms even after independence. Thus, South Africa's racial discrimination or French testing in the Sahara can readily be said to call for a policy of "blackism" and to prove that "black men all over Africa must stand or fall together." But when a question of surrendering sovereignty arises it is harder to keep cold-blooded notions of national advantage out of the mind. Africans' ability to do so is usually directly proportionate to the intensity of their belief that Africa remains

---

*Indeed, there have been steps in the other direction, as when Mali and Senegal split apart or, for special reasons related to the white settler problem, Nyasaland and Northern Rhodesia (now Malawi and Zambia) left the Central African Federation. The future of the Union of Tanganyika and Zanzibar (now Tanzania) is, at the time of writing, problematical, and Kenya, Uganda, and Tanganyika have not taken the steps toward East African Federation that had been thought quite possible when they achieved their independence.

in mortal danger of exploitation, and needs, more than anything else, to restore her pride.

The feasibility of early union in Africa is seen by African leaders to depend upon the nature of African nationalism. A dilemma arises because an immediate enemy is tribalism, and exaltation of the existing nation state is a natural way to attack tribalism. But doing so makes the people of one nation feel that they are different from their neighbors and thereby makes union more difficult.

Is union in Africa possible without going through stages of excessive nationalism? Some leaders say it is. Thus, Julius Nyerere (adding a wish to his assertion) has said, "the role of African nationalism is different — or should be different — from the nationalism of the past."[32] Nnamdi Azikiwe, on the other hand, has expressed a far more doubtful view, saying that it would be "capital folly" to expect politicians to surrender "newly-won political power" in the interest of a socially and economically "alien" "political leviathan . . . [i]t has not been possible in Europe or America, and unless Africa can show herself different from other continents, the verdict of history on this score will remain unchallenged and unaltered."[33]

Nigeria's Government has been a leading advocate of functional cooperation and the development of the existing nation state as necessary steps to African unity. The reasons given by Jaja Wachuku shortly before he became Foreign Minister reveal the persistence of racial concern even as immediate union founded upon racial sympathy is rejected. His argument was:

> For internationalism, there must be *nationalism* before you can have the "inter" between nations. . . . You cannot have inter-racialism unless our racial stock is respected by the world. And we will gain this racial respect only after we have established strong and thriving nations in Africa, created mutual respect among these nations, and, consequently gained the respect of other nations for Africa. Once we attain that respected status in the world community of nations, then there will be no black man anywhere who will be treated with lack of dignity.[34]

A major premise of advocates of quick political union has been that the frontiers of the various African states should be done away with because they are artificial and divide ethnic groups. Thus, the Fifth Pan-African Congress, meeting in London in 1945 with Kwame Nkrumah as a principal rapporteur, deplored the colonial frontiers as "deliberate steps to obstruct the political unity of the West African peoples."[35]

Similarly, the First All-African Peoples Conference held at Accra in Ghana in 1958 resolved that frontiers which cut across ethnic groups are "unnatural and are not conducive to peace or stability" and called for "the abolition or adjustment of such frontiers at an early date."[36]

After African states became independent, continued rhetoric about the need to abolish colonial frontiers occasionally appeared to mask simple expansionist ambitions. Had Nigeria sought to expand by seizing territory of her small neighbors (particularly Dahomey, which contains a number of Yoruba, and Niger, which contains a number of Hausa and Fulani and which the Sardauna of Sokoto, recalling the Fulani Empire, has referred to as "once ours,"[37]) there would, therefore, have been substantial ideological backing for her action. But in his speech to the United Nations shortly after independence, the Prime Minister stated in almost his first words that Nigeria had no "territorial or expansionist intentions."[38] Action has in no way belied those words.

Beyond Nigeria's own frontiers, the Prime Minister has insisted that throughout Africa the colonial frontiers and the sovereignty of each new nation must be "respected" until "the peoples concerned decide of their own free will to change or to merge into one unit." Furthermore, Nigeria has stated she would "discourage" any attempt "by force" or "undue pressure" to influence people to change.[39]

In 1961 a division appeared between two groups of African states known as the Casablanca* and the Monrovia† powers. From the point of view of the Monrovia group, in which Nigeria was a leader, the vital difference was their greater respect for the sovereignty and frontiers of the existing African states. Noting that on the average the Casablanca powers were more radical at home, more aggressively neutralist in their foreign policy, and, on specific issues, such as recognition of the Algerian rebels, more likely to risk offending a Western power, some Western observers have seen the division between the two groups in Cold War terms as a split between states likely to favor the Communists and states

---

*The Casablanca powers, named for a conference in Casablanca in January 1961, included Ghana, Guinea, Mali, the United Arab Republic, Morocco, Libya, and the Algerian rebels (plus Ceylon).

†The Monrovia powers, named for a conference in Monrovia in May 1961, included Nigeria, Liberia, Togo, Sierra Leone, Ethiopia, Somalia, Libya, Tunisia, and the twelve Brazzaville states (all former French colonies) — Ivory Coast, Senegal, Mauritania, Upper Volta, Niger, Dahomey, Chad, Gabon, the Central African Republic, Cameroon, the Malagasay Republic, and the Congo (Brazzaville).

tending to favor the West. But to the extent that differences in those respects were important to the Casablanca powers, they were primarily so because of a belief that Africa's fundamental need was economic and psychological disengagement from the West and not because of a desire to see Communism triumph over the West.

The Monrovia Conference Communiqué began by "noting with deep regret the absence of some of our sister states" and then adhered to the principles for inter-African relations of which Nigeria had been a leading exponent.[40] In its first four principles the Communiqué demanded respect for the territorial integrity and sovereignty of the existing African states: "Absolute equality . . . whatever may be the size of their territories, the density of their populations, or the value of their possessions" was to be the rule; each has an "inalienable right to existence and development of its personality"; interference in the internal affairs of states and support of subversion were unqualifiedly condemned.

Though the Casablanca powers were not mentioned by name, the Monrovia Communiqué was aimed against them. Ghana had claimed Togo, and Morocco had claimed Mauritania. (During the conference, the Monrovia powers cabled the Security Council asking for Mauritania's admission to the United Nations.) Guinea and the UAR were accused of supporting rebels in the Cameroon Republic and Tunisia. Much of the alleged subversion was directed against ex-French colonies which had extremely close economic and political ties with France. Added to reasons of national aggrandizement or personal enmity for supporting subversion, deep commitment to militant Pan-Africanism implies support for the overthrow of African governments closely tied to the colonial powers, because those ties render inter-African unity more difficult.

The Monrovia powers, with a few additions, met again in Lagos in January 1962. Intensive efforts to persuade the Casablanca powers to attend foundered over the failure to invite the Algerian rebels.[41] Again the differences concerning respect for sovereignty were stressed. In his welcoming speech, Nnamdi Azikiwe said that the vital difference between the two groups was the "conspicuous absence" of a specific declaration by the Casablanca powers of their belief in the right of African states to legal equality and freedom from externally supported subversion. Without that, he warned of "spectres to haunt the conscience of those who would rather pay lip service to the Charter of the United Nations while secretly they nurse expansionist ambitions against their smaller and perhaps weaker neighbors."[42]*

The Monrovia powers went out of their way to stress their disagreement with Ghana's view that African states should immediately join together in political union. "The unity that is aimed to be achieved at the moment is not," they said, "the political integration of sovereign African States, but unity of aspirations and of action considered from the point of view of African social solidarity and political identity." Promotion of cooperation throughout Africa based upon "tolerance, solidarity and good-neighbor relations" was an aim, but it was to be based upon the "non-acceptance of any leadership." At the Monrovia and Lagos Conferences emphasis was laid upon functional cooperation to build economic, cultural, and linguistic links which in time might form the basis for political union.[44]

The principle of gradual steps toward union, as the principle of respect for boundaries, followed the policies which the Nigerian Government had already enunciated. Given the differences between African countries, the lack of communications between them, and their lack of knowledge about each other (the Prime Minister once said that he knew "more about the history of Europe and the geography of Australia than I do of Africa and I think this is a shameful thing"[45]), the Nigerian belief has been that political union is premature.

Nigeria's hesitancy in espousing the political union of African states must also be evaluated in light of the fact that Nigeria herself represents a giant step toward union. One out of every four Africans south of the Sahara is a Nigerian. She is a test case of whether "multi-tribal Africa can fuse its diverse elements into a purposeful union."[46] In addition to the ample problems of putting her own house in order, her great size means that she has an opportunity to be a leader among the existing sovereign states of Africa. Furthermore, the desirability of union with some of her neighbors, Niger and Chad particularly, is sharply reduced by the fact that they would, initially at least, be economic liabilities. A possible explanation of why Nigeria has been so adamant in insisting that national frontiers must stand even though they split ethnic groups is that to say otherwise would be inconsistent with the NPC's insistence that the boundary between Northern and Western Nigeria must stand even though it splits the Yoruba.

*At this point Togo's President Sylvanus Olympio — since assassinated by

Nigeria's own history has been called forth by Nigerian leaders to support a slow pace toward unity. Warning against "coercion or precipitate action," Eastern Region Premier Okpara referred obliquely to the North's slow acceptance of independence and said "the cardinal point . . . is that the voyage to African union will be made at the pace of the slowest boat. This is the lesson of Nigerian unity."[47]

The concept that African union can best be arrived at through the functional cooperation of the existing African nation states was the consensus of the conference of African Heads of State held at Addis Ababa in May 1963. At that meeting, when the Casablanca and Monrovia groups were dissolved, the leaders of Africa's independent states* resolved to create a number of common institutions as part of the "Organization of African Unity." The organization was founded, however, upon the principles of respect for the sovereignty and territorial integrity of each member and of noninterference in the affairs of others which Nigeria and the Monrovia group had consistently supported.[48]

Addis Ababa was further proof that the desire for African solidarity is a potent political force in every African country. But events since Addis show that an organization of unity does not suddenly create unity either of view or of organization.† Addis was also symbolic of

---

disgruntled soldiers and replaced by a regime somewhat more favorable to Ghana — joined demonstratively in the applause by clapping his hands above his head.[43]

*All were present except Togo and South Africa. Morocco was the only state present which was not represented by its Head of State.

†Moise Tshombe's accession to power in the Congo revealed conflicting pressures upon the foreign policies of African states. Having led a secessionist movement and having been accused of being the tool of white businessmen and the murderer of Patrice Lumumba, he was anathema to many African states and not popular in any. Conflict over whether to shun him or to help the Congolese rebels overthrow him brought forth some of the conflict as to the relative importance of sovereignty and ideology in the form of anticolonialism that had divided the Casablanca and Monrovia groups. Nigeria remained consistent with its previous position, opposing the exclusion of Tshombe from the Cairo conference of nonaligned states in October 1964 and defending the Belgian paratroop drop on Stanleyville in November 1964 on the ground that the paratroopers had been requested by the Congo Government.

Some of the other events since Addis are: eighteen African governments (mostly ex-French colonies) entered into a second convention tying their economies to the European Common Market, and President Nkrumah told his National Assembly that African governments closely tied to Europe were a menace and those who sought to bring them down were freedom fighters deserving a refuge in Ghana as much as those who fought colonial regimes. Algeria and Morocco fought a brief war disputing the border between them. The fighting was stopped through the efforts of the OAU. The Committee of Nine formed

increased militancy about freeing colonial Africa. A fund for support of revolutionary movements and a promise to help train revolutionaries were agreed upon. But events since Addis also show a continued difficulty in translating militant rhetoric into action. Nevertheless, the organization created at Addis can become an important factor in the efforts of Africans to solve their own problems and make their influence felt.

*   *   *

All African governments, including Nigeria's, oppose colonialism. All African governments, including Nigeria's, have been fearful that the West (including the United States) retains too much control over their affairs. All African governments, including Nigeria's, emphasize African problems. That has been increasingly true for Nigeria, as illustrated by the scrapping of the defense pact for the Lagos conference. At times Nigeria has been more militant than any other African government, as when it broke diplomatic and trade relations with France after a Saharan atomic bomb test. By its refusal to become an Associate Member of the Common Market, Nigeria indicated that it was willing to place the political ideal of independence from neocolonialism above immediate economic advantage. Where Nigeria has apparently let her position as a poor nation dependent upon foreign aid influence her foreign policy — as in the refusal to recognize East Germany for fear of losing West German aid under the Hallstein doctrine — it has done so in the company of other African states, like Ghana, who accuse Nigeria of being a stooge for the colonialists.

Nevertheless, there has been widespread dissatisfaction with the country's foreign policy by many who find it to have been insufficiently militant, insufficiently "African," and insufficiently aware of the threat of neocolonialism. At times the foreign policy of Ghana has been held up by the critics as an ideal, though recently, for reasons mentioned later in this chapter, Ghana has been less favored. Of course the critics' antagonism has been highlighted by reaction to specific incidents such as the independence-in-1970 proposal or the defense pact with Great

---

by the Organization of African Unity — to which Nigeria belonged but Ghana did not — was attacked by Ghana's *Spark* as a "real danger" to liberation movements and Ghana was accused in July 1964 by Tanganyika's Nyerere of undercutting the Committee's efforts. Tanganyika was humiliated by having to ask Britain for help in quelling a military mutiny. Nigeria later supplied soldiers to replace the British. The most promising liberation movement at the time of Addis — Holden Roberto's in Angola — lost ground thereafter.

Britain. But the antagonism has been directed as much against the general tone and philosophy of Nigeria's foreign policy as against specific incidents.

The Government's critics have exaggerated the differences between Nigeria's foreign policy and, say, that of Ghana and most of the other members of the former Casablanca group. Nevertheless, there are real differences of degree. Nigeria has been more likely to support Great Britain, the United States, and the West. It has done less to increase contact with the Communist world. In strictly African matters the differences are more complex. But on many issues — the timing of the termination of colonialism, the role of the United Nations in the Congo, respect for sovereignty regardless of differences of opinion, for example — Nigeria has taken a position that can be called, without too much oversimplification, more moderate than militant.

How does one account for the fact that Nigeria has been a moderate African state? A simple explanation would be that the Government decided cynically to adopt the foreign policy which would be most likely to obtain economic aid from Western sources. Foreign aid is immensely important to Nigeria. Its 1962–1968 development plan was based upon the hope that at least half of the capital investment planned would be paid for by foreign aid and foreign private investments. But that explanation does not really hold up. Nigeria has disagreed with all the Western nations on matters important to them. In addition, it is not clear that the way to get foreign aid from the United States is to follow a foreign policy line generally appreciated in the United States. Countries which threaten to "go Communist" have often done rather well. Nor is there anything that indicates that Nigeria's leaders would have had a markedly different foreign policy if there had been no need for foreign assistance.

Only slightly more satisfactory is the opinion that Nigeria would have had a more militant foreign policy if she were not a federation with a coalition government and competing political parties. It is true that Nigeria's turbulent political situation means that her leaders are not as free to focus on foreign affairs as the leader of a one-party state. But Africa has one-party states whose foreign policies are more conservative than Nigeria's as well as some that are more radical. It is also true that compromise between opposing views is required by Nigeria's federal system. But there is nothing inevitable or built into the system that would require one of those views to be conservative.

Indeed, Nigeria is unusual politically in Africa in that it has an opposition, and the fact has been that the opposition has moved the Government toward a more militant, "African," foreign policy. Perhaps there is something to the idea that the spirit of compromise necessary to operate a federation at home has made it more natural for Nigeria's leaders to propose compromise, moderate, solutions abroad.

History has been quite influential. The foreign policies of African states depend in part upon how traumatic the colonial experience was, with the more traumatic experience generally leading to the more radical foreign policy. For Nigeria the colonial experience was extremely traumatic, but it was less so than for many African countries. Independence came with less hostility and more preparation than in practically any other African country. The Northerners, though they did not benefit from colonialism nearly as much as did the Southerners, also were less humiliated and uprooted by the colonial experience, and the Northern influence upon Nigeria's foreign policy has been significant.

African foreign policies are also a function of the confidence with which Africans face the world. Nigeria's size has unquestionably given her confidence, and quite possibly has cut down upon the appeal of political union with other states and the fear of continued Western European domination. But the question of confidence is a far more complex one than whether or not the nation is lucky enough to have, or have potentially, some of the traditional elements of international power.

Prime Minister Tafawa Balewa told the Heads of State at Addis Ababa that to call for a foreign policy based on the "African personality" betrayed an inferiority complex. He added that he believed in the human personality, not the African personality.[49] Earlier, to his own Parliament, in replying to criticism that Nigerian foreign policy did not sufficiently express an African personality, he said

> The Africans I regard as human beings, like any other race in the world and when I speak of "a personality" for the Africans I speak of a human personality, and whatever we project, we in Nigeria are to express a human personality.[50]

Emphasis upon the virtues of the African personality does not necessarily produce a militant, relatively anti-Western foreign policy. Senegal, led by Senghor, a poet of negritude, has had a moderate, relatively pro-Western, foreign policy. Nevertheless, there is some correlation between emphasis upon the African personality and belief that radical measures must be taken to combat neo-colonialism.

The Prime Minister's personality and philosophy have had a profound influence upon the tone of Nigeria's foreign policy. He is a calm and moderate man, with a knack for compromise. His expressed aversion to even an African bloc, in the sense of a group automatically voting together at, say, the United Nations, is illustrative of his belief that issues should be judged on their merits on a case-by-case basis. At times he seems to believe that attempts to lead others, or militancy in general, are immoral. Thus in his efforts to reassure the surrounding countries that Nigeria would not engulf them, he solemnly promised that "we in Nigeria will not impose ourselves on other people . . . we are not going to ask to give assistance."[51] So he commented, in reaction to criticism that Ghana was robbing Nigeria of leadership by being more radical, that

> I regard it as shameful for Nigeria to try to compete with Ghana in any way. It is shameful. That is how I feel and we should not show the slightest sign of being in competition at all. If it is football, sports — yes — but on these issues I think it is very wrong and I feel very shameful.[52]

Prime Minister Tafawa Balewa's foreign policy has been brilliant in avoiding issues that would drive Nigeria's tenuously united peoples apart. A foreign policy which advocated alteration of Nigeria's boundaries so as to unite tribal groups split by the colonialists would have intensified tribal jealousies. If the Hausa from Niger were added, for example, other groups would fear that the balance of power had been tipped against them, and the same fear and resentment would arise even if all divided groups were reunited because some, like the Ibo, would gain nothing, or next to nothing.

The Prime Minister has been as skillful in avoiding intensification of religious differences as of tribal ones. In 1960, Israel offered Nigeria technical assistance and a loan of over three million pounds. The Principal Organizing Secretary of the NPC immediately condemned the Federal Government's efforts to obtain aid from Israel and called for the ouster of the Israeli consul. The Northern Regional Government followed with another attack based upon its sympathy with the Arab Muslims in their controversy with Israel. Southerners, on the other hand, had often expressed their admiration for Israel's phenomenal economic success and immediately made it clear that the loss of any money or technical aid because of the Northerners' religious scruples would be bitterly resented.[53] The Prime Minister, who, of course, is a Muslim, found a neat solution which enabled the North to save face, while at the same time letting the South benefit from the aid. The Federal Government would accept the aid, but any region could disassociate itself from it. The North did so, and the East and West benefited from the aid. At the same time the Prime Minister stated emphatically that the Federal Government would not get involved in Middle East politics and warned against letting religion affect Nigeria's political decisions.

A side effect of the Government's foreign policy is that it has intensified a rivalry with Ghana which has had some effect in bringing forth national solidarity. The rivalry stems in part from disagreement concerning the liberation of colonial Africa and the union of independent Africa — Ghana taking the radical and Nigeria the moderate position. Jealousy has played a part as well. Because Ghana became independent first, and took more radical and flamboyant positions than Nigeria, it received attention that the larger country believed should properly go to it.[54] Nigerians, on the other hand, often have been contemptuous of Ghana's small size, as when Michael Okpara asked: "How can an ant and an elephant be rivals?"[55]* Newspapers and politicians of each country have made provocative and insulting remarks about the leaders of the other. Kwame Nkrumah has been called a false Messiah and likened to Adolf Hitler. Nnamdi Azikiwe has been called "the voice of London," and Prime Minister Tafawa Balewa has been dismissed as a "dark-skinned Englishman."[57] Ghana has been accused of trying to reduce Nigeria's influence in neutralist and African councils and of supporting subversion in Nigeria.[58]

One effect of the rivalry with Ghana is that it has persuaded a group of NCNC backbenchers led by Dr. Kalu Ezera to mute their complaints that the Government was not offering a "dynamic and positive policy which will give leadership to this country, and the whole of the African continent."[59] After Ghana had referred to Ezera's idol, Azikiwe, as the "voice of London" in an attack "we vehemently protest and we vehemently condemn," Ezera confessed that he had had a change of

---

*Resentment at greater attention paid to Ghana and confidence in Nigeria based upon her size were coupled in Nnamdi Azikiwe's attack upon the Bandung Conference for inviting Ghana but not Nigeria. He said that any decision concerning Africa that does not take into account that every sixth person in Africa is a Nigerian "is bound to be like a flower that 'is born to blush unseen and to waste its sweetness in the desert air.' "[56]

heart as he introduced a parliamentary motion congratulating the Government for its handling of the Lagos Conference, saying: "We get irritated certain times ourselves, and say that we want some dynamism. But it appears that in the path of wisdom it is often the case that compromise may be the better judge."[60]

The discontent of the radicals has by no means disappeared. It may create differences among Nigerians, but it does in a sense make easier the task of overcoming narrow loyalties. The differences created cut across the more basic and destructive ones of region, tribe, and religion.

But the differences created are themselves rather explosive. They are not based simply upon differing calculations of national interest. Rather they are based, in the critics' minds, upon differing views of the national character. They raise questions of spirit and motive. For that reason differences over foreign policy, as differences over domestic policy, are basic, deeply felt, and conceivably even sources of subversive movements.

The great failing of Nigeria's policy is that despite increased attention to Africa and an increased awareness of the dangers of automatic association with Great Britain, it has done little to inspire the Nigerian people or to restore the pride which colonialism sucked away. Whatever the very real practical difficulties of Pan-Africanism or the immediate liberation of colonial Africa, placing faith in African solidarity and militancy would do much to develop a sense of unity and a sense of purpose which Nigeria's moderate course does not.

Tafawa Balewa's strengths and virtues as a man and as a citizen of the world are in some ways weaknesses for a politician leading a newly independent African nation. Loyalty to old friends is an admirable trait, and the Prime Minister must be deeply respected for not dealing in the cheap currency of hatred in his relations with Great Britain. Still, to attain national responsibility and individual self-reliance, Nigeria must do more to free herself from the stifling vestiges of colonialism.

The Prime Minister is of course correct that excessive nationalism and racism are dangers in the Africa of tomorrow. There must be men who prize humanity more than race. He is one when he asks for belief in the human personality instead of the African personality. His beliefs are both refreshing and a cry of good sense for the next great cold war — that between the rich white peoples and the poor colored peoples. But it is hard to ask a Nigerian to work an extra hour by asking him to express his human personality. And where a great crisis of confidence stems from centuries of assault upon the African, it may be that the African cannot take his place in a world community of individuals until that crisis has been defeated by turning inward to explore and extoll his own virtues.

The Mind of Africa
and the Western World

Both unity, national or supranational, and power are attained by intangibles as well as tangibles. A nation is held together as much by its songs and shared myths, by its memories of common peril and common struggle, as by calculations of mutual advantage. Power cannot be gained through resources alone; desire must be joined to them.

For Africa, with Nigeria being no exception, it seems likely that her myth (myth in the sense of the emotional ideal or faith for which she will struggle) will be emphasis upon the uniqueness and virtue of the Negro race and African society — yesterday's and today's. That ideal is summed up by the vague statement that the African personality must be fulfilled. At the same time, the struggle will be against the Western world; disengagement from the West will be a paramount aim.

There is nothing particularly controversial about those observations. The tendencies are what would be expected from societies which had been dominated — but not destroyed — by Western colonialism. To assert that it is to the West's own interest that Africa emphasize its differences from the West may be more controversial and so may be the assertion that the coming concentration upon the virtue of Africa and of black people is one necessary step toward reducing the importance of race in human affairs.

The fact that African nations have achieved their political independence does not mean that they have yet become free. Because their economies are underdeveloped and still excessively dependent upon the colonial powers, they are not free economically. Because the years of colonial patronizing left their mark and because of their continued need for technical aid, they are not completely free in spirit. Having attained political independence, they will fight a long battle for economic and spiritual independence. This battle will lack the drama and heroic quality of a classic political revolution and to the outside observer will often seem silly, or nasty, or immature.

The fight will often center upon such things as firing faithful foreign teachers. Some Africans will claim to be fighting the battle, but in fact will become stuffy caricatures anxious only to appear to be dignified. But the aim of the battle remains true independence, pride, and self-confidence.

Nigeria, as is true with most of Africa, attained her independence without a revolutionary struggle. Individual Nigerians and groups such as the Zikists fought and suffered, but the people as a whole did not. The people were not asked to die a little and in one mighty shrug throw off the colonial master. The British gave in before a nationalist revolution had to be mounted, the skirmishes were fought with the pen and not with the sword, and the final victories were won in conference rooms of capital cities and not on a battlefield.

No one would wish upon a people the bloodshed and misery that are the lot of those who have to die for their freedom. Yet it is clear that such a common struggle can bring a divided people together as can nothing else. And in the future the memory of the common peril, magnified by myth and kept alive in song and story, holds them together. A successful common struggle is significant also in that it is symptomatic of greater power with which the new country can begin its national existence.

Nigeria's problems are the greater because she was blessed by a peaceful transition to independence. Mr. R. A. Fani-Kayode, in a speech to the House of Representatives calling for independence in 1960, described the peaceful transition as a challenge. He said:

We face the tranquil and peaceful transmutation of our State from slavery to freedom, constructive nationalism without the forcible destruction of the old imperialistic order by the collective efforts of a subject people. Without heat, without rancour, without the age-worn rallying cry to nationhood of death to the oppressor . . . without blending of our peoples through the fire, the furnace and the forge of the common struggle for freedom against the common enemy. Without the inspiration and the brotherhood born of common sufferings, common risks and dangers faced together in the fight for a common cause and the common satisfactory exhilaration and thanksgiving of achievement in the attainment of freedom together into a solid and indivisible whole, into a nation, we will find all these old formulae useless in our attempt to build a nation. For we are faced with freedom without tears, a new product of the twentieth century — the British challenge to history, to the civilized world and to us.[1]

The use that Nnamdi Azikiwe has made of the peaceful transition to independence is illustrative of the increasing tendency to argue that the African is different from and better than the Western peoples. He contended that:

The continent of Europe set a pattern for bloodshed in the attainment of liberty . . . but we in forgotten and neglected Africa know better. We are so steeped in religiosity and humanitarianism, and we are so cultured and civilized that we have often trodden the path to freedom bloodlessly. . . .[2]

For several reasons, Nigeria has been relatively moderate about mounting an emotional battle against the West. Its own internal divisions provide one explanation for its moderation. In the North, foreigners are preferred to Southerners in positions of responsibility for which Northerners are not formally qualified. The entire Northern Nigerian High Court is composed of foreigners, though the South has so many qualified lawyers that some are sent to other African countries as a form of foreign aid. (A Southern Nigerian recently became Chief Justice of Uganda, for example.) Beyond the relevance of the Northerners' lag, the existence of tension between ethnic groups means that a European in a sensitive post has the one advantage of appearing to be neutral as between the competing indigenous ethnic groups.

The balanced, restrained views of Prime Minister Tafawa Balewa have been influential in this respect just as they have been influential in shaping Nigeria's foreign policy. His emphasis upon the human personality as opposed to the African personality has already been mentioned. He frequently has sought to tone down what he regarded to be the excesses of nationalistic emotion. For example, a few months after independence, he defended his retention of an Englishman as his chief assistant by telling a heckling audience of Nigerian students in London "you don't kick people out for emotional reasons."[3] He has returned again and again to the theme of national responsibility rather than national rights. Shortly before independence he remarked:

> I remember it being said in a previous debate that it is better to govern ourselves badly than to be governed well. Perhaps it is better for those who do the governing, but we must think of those who are going to be governed by us.[4]*

It is also tempting to explain Nigeria's often moderate position on the need to assert the African personality as reflecting the psychology of the Northerners who play a dominant role in her government. Because Northerners were left more alone by the British than the Southerners and because their civilization (grounded in Islam) better withstood the shock of the powerful Western civilization, colonialism was less of a traumatic experience for them than for the Southerners and the rulers of many other African nations. Having retained more of their confidence, they have less of an emotional need to take drastic steps to restore their confidence.

For many Nigerians, however, the easy victory of the powerful colonialists, the disruptive effect of the years of tutorial colonial rule, patronizing contempt for their indigenous values, and their continuing need for outside aid have produced a crisis of confidence which has been described as a "colonial mentality." That crisis, which could also be called an inferiority complex, is manifested by an attitude that standards can be maintained only by copying the British, that things African are necessarily inferior, or at least that strangers would think so and that their approval is vitally important.†

---

*The Prime Minister's remarks were reminiscent of Governor Richards' speech to the Legislative Council thirteen years before, except that the Prime Minister when he spoke believed the Nigerians could govern themselves well while the Governor did not. Governor Richards said:
A Philippino politician is reported to have said that he would prefer to go to hell with a government of his own than to heaven under alien guidance. Possibly so. But there are silent millions of the people to be considered and the reply to him was that if premature independence were to be hell it would be little consolation to tell the victims that the fire had been lit by their own countrymen.[5]

†India's Jawaharlal Nehru commented upon the same phenomena in India, saying
We developed the mentality of a good country house servant. Sometimes we were treated to a rare honor — we were given a cup of tea in the drawing room. The height of our ambition was to become respectable and to be promoted individually to the upper regions. Greater than any victory of arms or diplomacy was this psychological triumph of the British in India.[6]

That attitude is responsible for many small things — the prestige of imported goods, wigs on the heads of the lawyers, formal garden parties on national occasions, no Nigerian food in the Government resthouses. It is the attitude which made a Government Minister, himself an ardent nationalist, begin an article describing postindependence accomplishments by referring to the praise ("the remarkably frank admission") of a "well known expatriate who has been in this country for over four decades."[7] The loss of confidence caused by colonialism explains why the newspapers care so desperately about the opinions of the British press concerning Nigeria. As one Nigerian journalist explains,

> We sensationalize [British opinions] because we the Editors accept in the first place that the British journalist must of necessity know more than we do about our own country and about our own affairs. And being still unconsciously colonial, we publicize these comments to strengthen our arguments and prove to readers that the press of the "bigmaster" sitting in London agrees with our point of view.[8]

Many of these attitudes are insignificant in themselves, though indicative of a lack of confidence that itself is serious. But the results are sometimes more significant. For one thing it has made it hard for many to derive the pride that they should from their own cultural heritage.

It was loss of respect for their roots that Ulli Beier referred to when he wrote that most educated Nigerians were "indifferent or hostile" to "their most important cultural heritage," their vital, vibrant, and expressive traditional wood carving. As he explained it:

> The present generation of Nigerians is in the process of a social revolution. They are trying to build for themselves a new life and a new society, and anything which reminds them of the old way of life which they are trying to leave behind is therefore suspect. . . . In the average primary school the child is taught to look at traditional Nigerian art as crude and "primitive". . . . Art teaching suffers from the same failing from which the whole of Nigerian education suffers: it is foreign-orientated.[9]

The most serious consequence of the colonial mentality is that it distorts the career choices of Nigerians. Far too few are willing to become technicians or farmers as compared to the many who seek a liberal arts education and a civil service career.* Economic realities do not explain this fact.[10] Rather, the source is psychological. The colonial adminis-

---

*Eastern Region Premier Okpara has recently been putting forward a scheme to force one segment of the Nigerian elite to participate in agriculture. He has said that those who want to run for office under the NCNC banner should establish a farm in their local area.

trators who came to Nigeria were themselves trained in that way and filled those positions. "And so," said the Ashby Commission Report on Higher Education in Nigeria, "the literary tradition and the university degree have become indelible symbols of prestige in Nigeria; by contrast technology, agriculture, and other practical subjects . . . have not won esteem."[11] A Nigerian put the distorting desire to emulate Europeans more pithily, saying that it was the colonial mentality which made his countrymen "take things easily, enjoy some booty . . . [in order to satisfy] the urge to live and behave big so that our people can notice they are now more important than the Europeans."[12]*

A further example of the tendency to overemphasize the British way of doing things and to find differences humiliating can be found in the reasons given for an amendment to the Federal Constitution in 1962. The amendment eliminated the provisions designed to isolate the Federal Director of Public Prosecutions from political control. In urging the Federal House of Representatives to begin the amendment process, the Attorney-General pointed out that the equivalent official in Great Britain and the United States is subject to political control and vigorously asserted that no other "civilized country" had a completely independent prosecutor.[13] The implication was that by isolating the prosecutor from politics the Nigerian Constitution suggested that Nigerians were less to to be trusted than Englishmen or Americans and that it was therefore derogatory. A good case can be made for precisely the opposite proposition, i.e., that the Constitution before amendment showed rather that Nigeria in this respect was more civilized than either the United States or Great Britain and that devices to ensure that prosecutions are not based on partisan politics are desirable reforms everywhere rather than insulting to the first country that makes the reform. But it is harder to maintain this position when one finds security in doing things in the same way as Great Britain and is acutely sensitive to anything that might be construed as either an admission or an accusation of inferiority.†

---

*Of course, one of Nigeria's vital needs is that her people realize that Nigerians are now more important than Europeans in the sense that they govern the country. Another disadvantage of not having had a dramatic transition to independence, particularly since so many of the familiar colonial administrators remained, is that it was not clearly brought home to the people that the country was theirs to make of it what they could.

†To make the record complete, it should be noted that the presentation of the amendment to the House was delayed because of possible opposition and that the independent press opposed the amendment as a "dangerous proposal."[14]

A somewhat different consequence of the crisis of confidence caused by colonialism is an acute sensitivity to foreign criticism, which produces a tendency to respond in ways so extreme that without knowledge of the background the response would often appear ludicrous. After a British ex-magistrate in Northern Nigeria, who had no connection whatsoever with the British Government, had written an article calling the Northern criminal reforms a "retrograde step," the Northern Minister of Information concluded his heated reply by saying "we must reconsider the connection between our country and the United Kingdom [if this attitude continues]."[15] Similarly, after the *Manchester Guardian* had speculated in an editorial that Nnamdi Azikiwe sought to return to partisan politics from his position as Governor-General, the Student Union at the University of Nigeria threatened to call on the Federal Government to sever diplomatic relations with Great Britain unless she disassociated herself from the *Guardian* editorial.[16]* Azikiwe's own reaction reflects the deep frustrations underlying Nigeria's relations with the West and suggests one direction that those frustrations might push her. He denounced the "regular tendentious references" of the "Anglo-Saxon" press to African political leaders as examples of its "congenital racial snobbery," remarked that neither *Pravda* nor *Izvestia* have been so "insolent" or "boorish," and finished by saying that though the older generation has held on to the British connection because of its belief in liberal democracy "in spite of regular doses of insults and gibes from the Anglo-Saxon press . . . I cannot guarantee that our children will stomach your continued irreverent attitude toward Africans and their political leaders."[17]

The most celebrated case of Nigerian hypersensitivity to foreign criticism was the Margery Michelmore incident. Miss Michelmore, one of the first Peace Corps volunteers in Nigeria, wrote her impressions of Ibadan on a postcard which was seen and quickly publicized at the University of Ibadan. Her view was one-sided and exaggerated as she graphically sought to portray squalor — "We really were not prepared for this squalor and absolutely primitive living conditions both in the city and the bush. Everyone except us lives in the street, cooks in the street, sells in the street and even goes to the bathroom in the street." There

---

*Nigerian sensitivity to what appear to be slights from Englishmen should not surprise Americans, who in the latter part of the nineteenth century, approximately a century after their own independence, would react hypersensitively to disparaging remarks about American society by Englishmen such as Charles Dickens.

was not a balancing word about the beautiful and respected university at which the volunteers were staying or of the hopes and successes of the people.

The first reactions in Nigeria after Miss Michelmore's post card was publicized were quick and angry. A campus rally organized by the Ibadan Student Union called upon Nigeria to oust the Peace Corps; even the conservative NPC newspaper hotly decried the insult to those who have fought beside the "pig-headed" and "dollar-flowing" Americans.[18]

Some second thoughts in Nigeria give a foretaste of the more balanced reaction to criticism that will become general only after the confidence lost during the colonial years has been restored. As the Federal Government newspaper editorialized:

> There is the danger of our paying all the attention to all the wrong things which Miss Michelmore said, rather, to the clumsy way in which she said them; of forgetting the truth which the little American girl told.
> We feel we owe it as a moral duty to ourselves to face the facts of our country and to reply to the critics, not in demonstrations, but in doubling our relentless efforts to ensure that we quickly remove the things which distress both our eyes and our hearts.[19]

*　　*　　*

An unnatural predilection for things British without thought to their suitability for Nigeria and a hypersensitive reaction to foreign criticism are both aspects of the crisis of confidence caused by colonialism, race prejudice, and the powerful sweep of Western civilization through Africa. They are the emotional or mental part of the whole complex of weaknesses that, despite political independence, constitute the relationship between Africa and the West. In its search for a force to overcome those weaknesses, and in frustration at their existence, Africa will turn more and more to exhalt the African way, the "African personality," or "negritude."

A Westerner's assessment of exaltation of the African way or the African personality must depend in the final analysis upon his opinion of Western civilization. If all its values are universals, if man has reached his peak here and now in the West, then of course only fools worship at a different shrine. But even if one doubts that the West has reached the peak, should not the ethnocentrism of Africans be attacked as much as the ethnocentrism of Westerners?

The answer to the question, considered in the abstract, is yes. But to consider it in the abstract is to ignore the vital facts. Those are that the years of Western mastery and racial prejudice have deprived the African of much of the pride and self-confidence needed to pick and choose judiciously those elements from Africa and those elements from the West and other parts of the world that together are suited to his present situation. That is the aim of the exponents of finding an African way: they do not want to return to primitive Africa, and they do not want to become carbon copies of the Western world; they believe that their own society has values and institutions which could enrich the world community and which, at the least, are more suited to their own development than standards or institutions which evolved in quite different social settings.

A synthesis must be struck, a balance. But before that can be done the scales must be evened by shoring up the previously scorned and ignored African side.

Many of those in the West who react to assertions of African uniqueness by crying out that all men are individuals can be disregarded because they earlier justified colonial rule by the statement that the colored man was the white man's inferior. Others cannot be so dismissed, and the danger of racist heresy in Africa is great. But is it not true that the African will never come to the table as an individual until he comes with pride and is met with respect? Both pride and respect will arrive sooner if the African comes not as a blurred copy of the Western white man but with his own individualistic style.

Black racism — or more precisely hatred and intolerance of the white man, particularly Western whites — is a very real danger in Africa. Past injustices, present prejudice inside and outside Africa, insults and slights real and imagined — those are the things, all intensified by frustration at Africa's weakness, that create the danger.

The danger of racism directed against the white man is not going to disappear because of efforts of the wealthy, largely white, Western nations to aid Africa. Though aid is absolutely necessary to end the weakness upon which black racism feeds, aid, even when given with only good intentions and good will, takes place in a context of superiority and inferiority, calls attention to weakness, and thus for the short term can magnify the frustrations that underly racism. The recipient nation, moreover, will constantly feel pressure to assert its independence from the donor nations.

The danger of black racism will not disappear until the African no longer feels menaced by white racism and, apart from that, until he has become genuinely self-confident. That he will not become without emphasis upon the African way. That is not to say that the danger of racism can only be met by indulgence in racism, for seeking to develop an African way is not the equivalent of some doctrine of black superiority. Rather it is a continuing quest for independence, based upon acceptance of cultural diversity, a desire for development, and a belief that the powerful nations of the world have not yet found the key to the good life.

Accompanying exaltation of the African way will, of course, be attacks upon the Western way. Disengagement from the West will be the keynote. To the West this will often be distasteful in the extreme: sad acts of disloyal ingratitude the African's course will often appear to be. But apart from the short-term interests of some Western countries that profit from Africa's present weakness, this trend should be seen as in the interest of the West.

It is, in the first place, in the interest of the West to have strong rather than weak African countries. When weak they create a power vacuum which is a threat to the stability in which the West today has the greatest stake. Their present emotional and economic dependence upon the West is their greatest weakness. They cannot develop unless the energy of development is tied to institutions, ideals, and desires to which the people naturally respond. Second, those aspects of Western civilization which are of universal value must, to prosper in Africa, be rid of the incidental baggage with which they came. The right of the people periodically to choose their government must, for example, be winnowed from less universal values. Even such matters must be found to have roots in indigenous thought and action rather than being solely the gift of the munificent West.

The most common question asked of an American who returns from Africa is: Is it we or the Communists who are winning? The question proceeds on an assumption of Western superiority and on the *tabula rasa* theory of the African mind — that it is empty and waiting to choose either the West, the embodiment of virtue, or the Communists, the embodiment of evil.

If that is the right question to ask, then the answer is likely to be that the Communists will ultimately win. For the emotional drive to become independent of the West is so strong that if the only alternative to the West were the Communists that alternative would probably be taken. It would have, moreover, the advantage of enabling the African to attain many Western comforts (which he by no means has ceased to want) and of still appearing to oppose the West.[20] If that is the right question, Africans will be driven into the arms of Communism, and Communists will ride the backs of African nationalism to victory. Furthermore, if the West assumes it to be the question then the danger of Communist domination can become a self-fulfilling prophecy. Because if it is the question, then the West will intervene in Africa and if it does so Africans will turn to the enemies of the West.*

But it is not the right question. Africa has another alternative, which is to develop the African way and move toward a synthesis of that way, the Western way and perhaps a bit of the Communist way.

Thus, even from the point of view of the West's struggle against Communism, Africa's disengagement from the West to develop the African way is desirable. George Padmore, a West Indian Negro who became a leading advisor of Ghana's Kwame Nkrumah on African affairs, saw the future well several years ago when he wrote that Africa's choice was between the two parts of the title of his book — *Pan-Africanism or Communism.*[21]

The West is far better equipped than the Communist world to understand and appreciate the new African philosophy and for that reason — but for its lingering racial prejudice — far more likely to retain the friendship of Africa after it has won its true freedom. The African way is a threat to any system which believes it has found the universal truth. Communism is such a system. The iron laws of Communist ideology will not readily bend to accommodate a pluralistic world, and if they do much of the threat is gone.

The West — led by countries like the United States, one of whose most deeply held ideals or myths has been that it has prospered from its own pluralism — can welcome a pluralistic world. Though much of its power has been built upon ethnocentrism, of which the white man's burden approach to colonialism is a classic example, its ability to adapt to change and to live with and learn from differences, is more relevant to its continuing strength today. That is one ability that enables a civilization to grow with the world, and the West, just as Africa, will grow by mixing its own values with what it can learn from other parts of the world.

*This is not to suggest that the Communists are not a threat to Africa. They are. All African governments are fragile. Frustration is great and will become greater. But the strongest defense against Communism is African nationalism and the West has to be careful not to push Africans, particularlry young Africans, into an alliance with Communism.

Notes

Chapter 1

1. See *Language and Communication in the Commonwealth,* a Report of the Commonwealth Education Liaison Committee (H.M.S.O., London, 1965), estimate: 150; and James S. Coleman, *Nigeria: Background to Nationalism* (University of California Press, Berkeley and Los Angeles, 1958), p. 15, estimate: 248.
2. Obafemi Awolowo, *Path to Nigerian Freedom* (Faber and Faber, Ltd., London, 1947), pp. 47–48.
3. Hugh Clifford, address to the Nigerian Council, Dec. 29, 1920 (typed copy), Macaulay Papers, quoted in James S. Coleman, *Nigeria: Background to Nationalism, op. cit.,* p. 194.
4. *The Constitution of the Federal Republic of Nigeria,* Sec. 28.
5. "Hail, the Alake," *Morning Post,* Sept. 2, 1963, p. 5.
6. Thomas Hodgkin, *Nigerian Perspectives: An Historical Anthology* (Oxford University Press, London, 1960), p. 2.
7. The first quotation is from Lady G. Cecil, *Life of Robert, Marquis of Salisbury,* Vol. IV (London, 1933), p. 323. The second appears in J. R. V. Prescott, "Nigeria's Boundaries: A Colonial Heritage," *1958 Proceedings of the Nigerian Institute of Social and Economic Research,* p. 144.
8. Quoted in Hodgkin, *op. cit.,* p. 87, from the Kano Chronicle as translated by H. R. Palmer in his *Sudanese Memoirs,* Vol. III.
9. Quoted in translation in Hodgkin, *op. cit.,* p. 102.
10. H. F. C. Smith, "A Neglected Theme of West African History: The Islamic Revolutions of the Nineteenth Century," *Journal of the Historical Society of Nigeria,* Vol. II, No. 2 (Dec. 1961), p. 175.

11. *Debates,* House of Assembly, Northern Nigeria, Sept. 30, 1961, col. 343.
12. *Legislative Council Debates,* Mar. 24, 1947, p. 212.
13. *Parliamentary Debates,* House of Representatives (hereafter abbreviated as H. of R.), Jan. 14, 1960, p. 61.
14. Quoted in translation in Hodgkin, *op. cit.,* pp. 199, 201.
15. The particular Emir of Kontagora is described, among other places, in Margery Perham, *Lugard: The Years of Authority* (Collins, London, 1960), pp. 43–47, and in K. O. Dike, ed., "Umoru and Ibrahim Nagwamase," in *Eminent Nigerians of the Nineteenth Century* (Cambridge University Press, Cambridge, 1960), p. 71.
16. Quoted in Charles H. Wesley, "The Changing African Historical Tradition," *Journal of Human Relations,* Spring-Summer 1960, p. 324.
17. J. T. Bent. *The Ruined Cities of Mashonaland* (Longmans, Green & Co., London, 1892), quoted in K. O. Dike, "History and African Nationalism," *1952 Proceedings, West African Institute of Social and Economic Research* (printed 1957) and *West Africa,* Feb. 28, 1953.
18. Margery Perham, "The British Problem in Africa," *Foreign Affairs,* July 1951, p. 638.
19. Nnamdi Azikiwe, "Let us Build a New Africa" (or "I Speak of a New Africa"), reprinted in *Solidarity in Africa, A Record of the Conference of the Heads of African and Malagasay States held in Lagos from January 25–30, 1962* (Federal Ministry of Information, Nigerian National Press, Apapa, 1962).
20. Hilaire Belloc, *The Modern Traveller.*
21. Quoted in *West Africa,* Apr. 4, 1959, p. 317.
22. *See,* for example, K. O. Dike, "History and African Nationalism," *op. cit.;* cf. J. C. Anene, "Towards a National History," *Ibadan,* No. 16 (June 1963), p. 7.
23. *The Times,* Jan. 8, 1897. *See also* A. H. M. Kirk-Greene, "Who Coined the Name 'Nigeria,'" *West Africa,* Dec. 22, 1956, p. 1035.

Chapter 2

1. The figures are based upon the 1952–1953 census, updated in the *Annual Abstract of Statistics,* 1961 (Federal Office of Statistics, Lagos, 1961), Table 3, pp. 9–10. For the North, the figures for the Northern Cameroons, now Sardauna Province, are not included. The 1963 census revealed that the 1952–1953 census had substantially undercounted Nigeria's population.
2. See *Federal Government Development Programme, 1962–1968* (Sessional Paper No. 1 of 1962, Federal Printing Division, Lagos), p. 19.
3. Frederick D. Lugard, *The Dual Mandate in British Tropical Africa* (W. Blackwood & Sons, London, 1922), p. 618.
4. Frederick D. Lugard, *Annual Report, Northern Nigeria, 1902.* Quoted in Margery Perham, *Lugard, The Years of Authority, op. cit.,* pp. 113–114.

5. Awolowo, *Path to Nigerian Freedom, op. cit.*, pp. 73, 48.
6. *See* Margery Perham, "Some Problems of Indirect Rule in Africa," *Journal of the Royal African Society*, May 18, 1934.
7. G. I. Jones, *Report of the Position, Status and Influence of Chiefs and Natural Rulers in the Eastern Region of Nigeria* (Government Printer, Enugu, 1957), pp. 10–11. The Eastern Region Government, despite the report, created a House of Chiefs, but its reasons for acting did not suggest that it disagreed with Mr. Jones' analysis of political decision making among the Ibo.
8. *See* Perham, *Lugard, op. cit.*, p. 499.
9. *Reports, Northern Nigeria, 1902*, p. 106, quoted in Perham, *Lugard, op. cit.*, p. 497.
10. M. M. Mahood, "Joyce Cary in Borgu," *Ibadan*, June 1960, pp. 22, 23.
11. *Annual Abstract of Statistics, 1963* (Federal Office of Statistics, Lagos), Table 145, p. 66. In each region there are also students of secondary-school age at teachers training and technical or vocational schools. See also *Investment in Education: The Report of the Commission on Post-School Certificate and Higher Education in Nigeria* (The Ashby Report. St. Clements Press, Ltd., London, 1960). Comparative figures on nonexpatriate physicians and surgeons further illustrate the North's lag: the North has 9, the East 74, and the West 91 (Lagos has 101). *Annual Abstract of Statistics, 1963*, Tables 107–109.

Chapter 3

1. *See* Naresh Chandra Roy, *Federalism and Linguistic States* (Firma, K. L. Mukjopadkyay, Calcutta, 1962) and Selig S. Harrison, *India: The Most Dangerous Decades* (Princeton University Press, Princeton, N.J., 1960).
2. Joseph Stalin, *Marxism and the National and Colonial Question* (Foreign Language Publishing House, Moscow), pp. 5–6. Stalin wrote the book in 1913.
3. Tai Solarin, "English Language and Ourselves," *Daily Times*, Feb. 4, 1961, p. 5.
4. In this regard, *see* Shehu Malami, "The Claims of Hausa," *West Africa*, May 6, 1961, p. 483, and a letter in response in *West Africa*, May 27, 1961, p. 578, discussing the difficulties of modernizing Hausa. *See also* the long discussion of the same subject in the Foreword to the Hausa translation of the Northern Region Penal Code Law, 1959.
5. Frederick Harbison, "High-Level Manpower for Nigeria's Future," a special report for The Ashby Report, *op. cit.*, pp. 52, 60.
6. *Ibid.*, p. 63.
7. *Parliamentary Debates*, H. of R., Nov. 21, 1961, cols. 3156–3157.
8. *Ibid.*, col. 3161.
9. *Proceedings of the General Conference on Review of the Constitution Held at Ibadan*, January 1950 (Government Printer, Lagos, 1950).

10. *Resolutions* of the Conference of Heads of States and Governments of Africa and Malagasay meeting at Monrovia, May 8–12, 1961: Resolution on the means of promoting better understanding and cooperation toward achieving unity in Africa and Malagasay, Paragraph D(4). The Monrovia Conference resolutions can be found in Appendix 17 of Colin Legum, *Pan-Africanism: A Short Political Guide* (Pall Mall Press, London, 1962).

11. *See* Republic of Ghana: Civil Service Act, 1960, Sec. 39; Standing Orders of the National Assembly, Sec. 6; Act No. 78 of 1959, Sec. 4(1); Leslie Rubin and Pauli Murray, *The Constitution and Government of Ghana* (Sweet and Maxwell, London, 1961), Secs. 47, 57, 120, 184.

12. *See* Ulli Beier, "Nigerian Literature," *Nigeria Magazine*, Oct. 1960, p. 211.

13. *Cf. Christianity in Africa as Seen by the Africans*, edited by Ram Desai (Alan Swallow, Denver, 1962).

14. *Speech*, Accra, Gold Coast, Jan. 12, 1937, reprinted in *Zik: A Selection from the Speeches of Nnamdi Azikiwe* (Cambridge University Press, Cambridge, 1961), p. 57.

15. NPC Charter, reprinted in *Report on the Kano Disturbances, 16th, 17th, 18th, 19th of May, 1953* (Northern Regional Government, Kaduna, 1953), p. 45.

16. For a discussion of his statement, *see* "The Important Jihad," *Morning Post*, Dec. 5, 1961, p. 5. For a discussion of the amendment, *see* the explanation of it by the Northern Nigerian Minister of Justice, Muhammed Nasir, in the *Nigerian Citizen*, Mar. 14, 1962, p. 12.

17. *See* J. N. D. Anderson, *Islamic Law in the Modern World* (New York University Press, New York, 1959).

18. J. N. D. Anderson's "Criminal Law Reform in Northern Nigeria: A Major Advance," *Modern Law Review* Vol. XXIV (1961), p. 616, has a brief description of the Maliki criminal law as it applied in Northern Nigeria prior to the reforms. Professor Anderson was on the panel that recommended changes. For a more complete description of Maliki law in Nigeria, *see* his *Islamic Law in Africa* (H.M.S.O., London, 1954).

19. *Report of the Commission Appointed to Enquire into the Fears of Minorities and the Means of Allaying Them* (Minorities Commission Report. H.M.S.O., London, 1958), Cmnd. 505, pp. 66–70.

20. "Statement by the Government of the Northern Region of Nigeria on the Reorganization of the Legal and Judicial Systems of the Northern Region" (White Paper, laid upon the table of the Legislative Houses of Northern Nigeria, Dec. 1958).

21. J. N. D. Anderson, "Criminal Law Reform," *op. cit.*, p. 617.

22. *Daily Service*, Oct. 13, 1957, quoted in Minorities Commission Report, *op. cit.*, p. 26.

23. Ahmadu Bello (the Sardauna of Sokoto), *My Life* (Cambridge University Press, Cambridge, 1962), p. 131.

Chapter 4

1. Margery Perham, ed., *Ten Africans* (London, 1935), pp. 323–325.
2. J. F. Ade Ajayi, "Nineteenth Century Origins of Nigerian Nationalism," *Journal of the Historical Society of Nigeria*, Vol. II, No. 2 (Dec. 1961), pp. 196, 209.
3. Samuel Johnson, *The History of the Yorubas*, edited by O. Johnson (Routledge & Kegan Paul, London, 1921). The book was not published until twenty-four years after it had been written.
4. Akiga, *Akiga's Story*, translated by Rupert East (Oxford University Press, London, 1939), pp. 2–4, quoted in Thomas Hodgkin, *Nigerian Perspectives: An Historical Anthology, op. cit.*, p. 328.
5. A. Creech Jones (later Labour Party Secretary of State for the Colonies), *Parliamentary Debates*, House of Commons (hereafter abbreviated as H. of C.), June 6, 1944, col. 1250.
6. Awolowo, *Path to Nigerian Freedom, op. cit.*, p. 18.
7. *West African Pilot*, Aug. 28, 1944 and June 28, 1944.
8. *Enquiry into the Cost of Living and the Control of the Cost of Living in the Colony and Protectorate of Nigeria*, Colonial No. 204 (H.M.S.O., London, 1946).
9. *See* Nnamdi Azikiwe, *Assassination Story: True or False* (Onitsha, 1946).
10. Anthony Enahoro, *Nnamdi Azikiwe: Saint or Sinner* (Lagos, n.d.), p. 16.
11. Coleman, *Nigeria: Background to Nationalism, op cit.*, p. 291, quoting from quotation in Obadia Adegboyega Sobande, *Notes and Comments on the Life of Mr. H. Macaulay* (Lagos, n.d.).
12. *West African Pilot*, Aug. 3–8, 1947.
13. *West African Pilot*, quoted in Coleman, *op. cit.*, p. 298.
14. *Ibid.*
15. *West African Pilot*, Mar. 2, 1946.
16. *Report of the Commission of Enquiry into the Disorders of the Eastern Provinces of Nigeria, November, 1949.* Colonial No. 256 (H.M.S.O., London, 1950).
17. *West African Pilot*, July 7, 1950.
18. Nnamdi Azikiwe, *Inaugural Speech on Installation as Premier of Eastern Nigeria*, Oct. 1, 1954, reprinted in *Zik: A Selection from the Speeches of Nnamdi Azikiwe* (Cambridge University Press, Cambridge, 1961), p. 90.
19. See *Report of the Commission Appointed by His Excellency the Governor to make Recommendations about the Recruitment and Training of Nigerians for Service Posts in the Government Service*

of Nigeria (Lagos, 1948), p. 17, and Kenneth Mellanby, *The Birth of Nigeria's University* (Methuen and Company, London, 1958).

20. Oluwole Alanija, *Egbe Omo Oduduwa Monthly Bulletin*, 1 (Dec. 1944), p. 4. Quoted in Coleman, *op. cit.*, p. 346.
21. Minutes of the First Inaugural Conference of the Egbe Omo Oduduwa, June, 1948 (typed copy), quoted in Coleman, *op. cit.*, p. 346.
22. *West African Pilot*, Aug. 30, 1948.
23. *West African Pilot*, July 6, 1949.
24. Obafemi Awolowo, *Awo: The Autobiography of Chief Obafemi Awolowo* (Cambridge University Press, Cambridge, 1960), p. 20.
25. *Ibid.*, p. 101.
26. Obafemi Awolowo, *Path to Nigerian Freedom, op. cit.*, p. 47.
27. *Ibid.*, p. 32.
28. *Ibid.*, p. 35 and p. 53. The last quotation is the end of a sentence which begins, "[b]ut so long as every person in Nigeria is made to feel that he is a Nigerian first and a Yoruba or Ibo, or Hausa next, each will be justified to poke his nose. . . ."
29. *Constitution of the Egbe Omo Oduduwa* (Ijebu-Ode, 1948).
30. Action Group Minutes, Nov. 12, 1950. Quoted in Richard L. Sklar, *Nigerian Political Parties: Power in an Emergent African Nation* (Princeton University Press, Princeton, 1963), p. 104.
31. Kalu Ezera, *Constitutional Developments in Nigeria* (Cambridge University Press, Cambridge, 1960), p. 210.
32. *Gaskiya Ta Fi Kwabo*, Feb. 18, 1950. Quoted in *Report on the Kano Disturbances, op. cit.*, p. 43.
33. *Legislative Council Debates*, Mar. 4, 1948, p. 227.
34. *Report of the Drafting Committee on the Constitution* (Lagos, 1950), p. 16.
35. *Proceedings of the General Conference on Review of the Constitution Held at Ibadan, January 1950* (Government Printer, Lagos, 1950), p. 218.
36. *Ibid.*, pp. 244 ff. (*see particularly* Minority Report No. III).
37. *Ibid.*, pp. 16 (Eyo Ita), 39 (Mbonu Ojike), 142 (Sardauna of Sokoto).
38. *Daily Comet*, Dec. 29, 1949.
39. *See* Northern House of Assembly, *Official Report*, Aug. 1950, pp. 91–98.
40. *NPC Charter*, quoted in *Report on the Kano Disturbances, op. cit.*, p. 45.
41. Quoted in *Report on the Kano Disturbances, op. cit.*, p. 45.
42. Compare the NPC 1952 Aims and Objects in *Report on the Kano Disturbances, op cit.*, with the *Nigerian Citizen*, Oct. 4, 1951.
43. *See* Richard L. Sklar, *Nigerian Political Parties: Power in an Emergent African Nation, op. cit.*, pp. 518–520, Tables 1 and 2 and Kenneth W. J. Post, *The Nigerian Federal Election of 1959* (Oxford University Press, London, 1963), p. 279, Table X.
44. *Parliamentary Debates*, Mar. 31, 1953.

45. *Ibid.*, Apr. 1, 1953.
46. *Ibid.*, Mar. 31, 1953.
47. Ahmadu Bello (the Sardauna of Sokoto), *My Life, op. cit.*, p. 111.
48. *Report on the Kano Disturbances, op. cit.*, p. 21.
49. The phrase is that of the Sardauna of Sokoto in his autobiography *My Life, op. cit.*, p. 135. Writing in 1962, with Nigerian unity an accomplished fact, he does not try to conceal his feeling that secession was tempting.
50. *Debates*, Northern Region House of Assembly, May 23, 1953.
51. *Parliamentary Debates*, H. of C., May 22, 1953

Chapter 5

1. Obafemi Awolowo, *Path to Nigerian Freedom, op. cit.*, pp. 54, 48.
2. Nnamdi Azikiwe, *Political Blueprint of Nigeria* (Lagos, 1943), p. 11.
3. NCNC, *Freedom Charter* (Lagos, 1948), p. 2.
4. *Proceedings of the General Conference on Review of the Constitution Held at Ibadan, January, 1950* (Government Printer, Lagos, 1950), p. 244; *Legislative Council Debates*, Apr. 3, 1950, p. 510.
5. *Proceedings, op. cit.*, p. 244.
6. NCNC, *Forward to Freedom and Progress* (Yaba, 1951).
7. *Debates*, Western Region House of Assembly, June 14, 1955, pp. 58–73.
8. *Daily Times*, Jan. 29, 1957 and Mar. 13, 1957.
9. *Daily Times*, Oct. 29, 1957.
10. Minorities Commission Report, *op. cit.*, p. 57.
11. *Report by the Nigerian Constitutional Conference, held in London in May and June, 1957* (H.M.S.O., London, 1957), para. 24.
12. *Ibid.*
13. Minorities Commission Report, *op. cit.*, pp. 1–2.
14. *See* capsule biographies in *West Africa*, Aug. 23, 1958.
15. Philip Mason, "Prospects of Permanence," *West Africa*, Nov. 22, 1958, p. 1115.
16. *See* the Citizen's Committee for Independence, *Forward to Freedom* (Ibadan, 1957); *The Case for More States* (Ibadan, 1957).
17. Minorities Commission Report, *op. cit.*, p. 47.
18. *Ibid.*, p. 48.
19. *Ibid.*, p. 30.
20. *Ibid.*, pp. 32, 49, and 72.
21. *Ibid.*, p. 51.
22. *Ibid.*, p. 72.
23. *Ibid.*, pp. 74–86.
24. *Ibid.*, pp. 87–88.
25. "Democratic Socialism: Being the Manifesto of the Action Group of Nigeria for an Independent Nigeria," Action Group Bureau of Information (Amalgamated Press of Nigeria, Lagos, 1960), pp. 12–13.

26. Minorities Commission Report, *op. cit.*, p. 89.
27. See *Report by the Resumed Nigerian Constitutional Conference, held in London in September and October, 1958* (H.M.S.O., London, 1958), Cmnd. 569, Secs. 44–50.
28. *Ibid.*, Sec. 51(c).
29. *See*, for example, the speeches of COR advocates in the Federal House of Representatives on the question of whether to support the motion for independence in April, 1960. *Parliamentary Debates*, H. of R., Aug. 5, 1958, cols. 2054–2058, 2060.
30. "These Men are Dangerous," *West African Pilot*, June 11, 1958, p. 2.
31. See *Report of the Resumed Nigerian Constitutional Conference, 1958, op. cit.*, Sec. 52; *Report on the Activities of the Midwest Advisory Council together with Statements of Government Action in the Midwest*, Sess. Paper 3 of 1960, Western Region Legislature (Government Printer, Ibadan, 1960); *Proposals for the Declaration of a Minority Area for the Midwest Area of the Western Region and the Establishment of the Midwest Minority Council*, Sess. Paper 14 of 1960 (Government Printer, Ibadan, 1960).
32. *Report by the Nigerian Constitutional Conference, 1957, op. cit.*, Sec. 30.

Chapter 6

1. Niger Delta Congress, "Policy Paper," *Daily Times*, Dec. 7, 1959, p. 5.
2. *Daily Times*, Oct. 13, 1959, p. 2.
3. *Daily Times*, Oct. 29, 1959, p. 16.
4. *Daily Times*, Oct. 19, 1959, p. 2 (Isa Kaita).
5. Northern Peoples Congress, "Election Manifesto," *Nigerian Citizen*, Sept. 19, 1959, p. 6, and *Daily Times*, Dec. 4, 1959, p. 12.
6. Dennis Osadebay, "Why I Shall Vote NCNC," *Daily Times*, Dec. 1, 1959, pp. 12, 13, 19.
7. NCNC-NEPU, "Joint Manifesto," *Daily Times*, Oct. 5, 6, and 7, 1959. The quote is in the October 5 issue.
8. Action Group of Nigeria, "Facts and Figures on the Provision of Welfare Services in the Three Regions (VI) Electricity," Advertisement, *Daily Times*, Nov. 23, 1959, p. 2. This was one of a series of advertisements on different welfare services.
9. These quotations come from his autobiography, *Awo, op. cit.*, pp. 310–311. The book was written shortly after the campaign and its discussion of issues raised during the campaign was based on Chief Awolowo's campaign speeches and followed them very closely.
10. *Ibid.*, p. 311.
11. NPC, "*Election Manifesto*," *op. cit.*
12. *Awo, op. cit.*, p. 309.
13. NCNC-NEPU, "Joint Election Manifesto," *Daily Times*, Oct. 5, 6,

7, and 9, 1959 — Foreign Policy on Oct. 9 at p. 10; "The Policy Papers of the National Council of Nigeria and the Cameroons; Foreign Policy," *Daily Times*, Oct. 23, 1959, pp. 9, 10, 11.

14. *Daily Times* (advertisement), Dec. 10, 1959, p. 7.

15. In addition to the NCNC-NEPU Manifesto and policy paper cited in note 13, *see* the separate manifesto of the NEPU in the *Daily Times*, Oct. 3, 1959, p. 6.

16. NCNC policy paper on foreign policy, *op. cit.*

17. *See*, for example, *Daily Times*, Oct. 13, 1959, p. 1.

18. See *Nigerian Citizen*, Dec. 12, 1957 and Dec. 21, 1957.

19. *See* the reversal of these convictions in *S.E. and Seven others* v. *Ilorin Native Authority* (High Court of Northern Nigeria, 1962).

20. "Will the North and South Meet?" *The Service*, Vol. II, No. 60 (Nov. 11, 1961), p. 13.

21. The assault occurred before the campaign. The man convicted, Mallam Shehu Cigari Alhassan, was re-elected to the Northern House of Assembly in May 1961. In his capsule biography in the *Northern Nigeria Legislature: Who's Who* (Gaskiya Corporation, Zaria, 1961), p. 102, he is identified as having been a "political prisoner" during 1959–1961. The man who convicted him, Magistrate Justin Price, soon left Nigeria and showed his pique by writing an article which offhandedly and unfairly described the Northern Nigerian Criminal Law Reforms as a "retrograde step." Justin Price, "Retrograde Legislation in Northern Nigeria?" *Modern Law Review*, Vol. 24 (1961), p. 604.

22. The articles appear in the *Daily Times* of 1959: Oct. 12, 19, 22; Nov. 5, 25, 26, 28, 30; Dec. 5, 7.

23. *General Report and Summary on the Nigeria Police Force for the Year 1959* (Federal Printing Division, Lagos, 1961), pp. 10–13.

24. Obafemi Awolowo, "Action Group 14 Point Programme" (Ibadan, 1959); *Daily Times*, Oct. 13, 1960, p. 2.

25. NCNC-NEPU, "Joint Election Manifesto," *op. cit.*, Oct. 5, 1959. "We Will Extend the Federal Territory," Policy Paper of the National Council of Nigeria and the Cameroons, *Daily Times*, Oct. 17, 1959, pp. 10–11.

26. NCNC-NEPU, "Joint Election Manifesto," *op. cit.*, Oct. 5, 1959.

27. Dennis Osadebay, "Why I Shall Vote NCNC," *op. cit.*

28. *Daily Times*, Oct. 24, 1959, p. 2; *Daily Times*, Oct. 23, 1959, p. 2. Speech of Alhaji Ahmadu Fatiba, Parliamentary Secretary to the Northern Nigeria Ministry of Finance.

29. *Daily Times*, Nov. 2, 1959, p. 2. What he meant by that remark was probably shown by his following remark, which was that his people in Kabba were opposed to merger with the West.

30. *Kano Daily Mail*, May 2, 1961, p. 1.

31. By far the most complete coverage of the results and all that led up to them is in Kenneth W. J. Post's *The Nigerian Federal Election of 1959*, *op. cit.*

32. *Sunday Post*, Mar. 4, 1962, p. 1.
33. Ahmadu Bello (The Sardauna of Sokoto), *My Life, op. cit.*, p. 227.
34. *Sunday Post, op. cit.* During the 1959 campaign the Sardauna made a similar statement when asked if he would become Governor-General. *Daily Times*, Nov. 28, 1959.
35. *My Life, op. cit.*, p. 135.
36. *Ibid.*, p. 229.
37. See *Final Report of the Parliamentary Committee on the Nigerianization of the Federal Public Service*, Sess. Paper 6 of 1959 (Lagos, 1959), pp. 22–23.
38. The figures for the end of 1960 and the end of 1961, by which time the Federal Public Service was 2 per cent Northern, were given by the Parliamentary secretary to the Ministry of Establishments in answer to a Parliamentary question. *Parliamentary Debates*, H. of R., Apr. 4, 1962, cols. 815–816. In 1963 the Chairman of the Nigeria Railway Corporation announced the tribal origin of his corporation's senior staff. There were only two from Northern tribes (one Hausa and one Tiv) as compared, for example, to 149 Yorubas and 120 Ibos.

Chapter 7

1. Obafemi Awolowo, "Twelve Months of Independence," *The Service*, Vol. II, No. 59 (Nov. 4, 1961), p. 28.
2. *Parliamentary Debates*, H. of R., Nov. 19, 1960, col. 97.
3. *Ibid.*, Nov. 24, 1960, col. 378.
4. Obafemi Awolowo, "My Plan for Africa," *The Service*, Vol I, No. 41 (July 1, 1961), pp. 6, 20.
5. "John West," "The Devil's Advocate," *The Service*, Vol. II. No. 61 (Nov. 18, 1961), p. 13. John West is the pen name for Lateef Jakende, who was one of the Action Group leaders convicted of treason in 1963.
6. *Parliamentary Debates*, H. of R., Aug. 26, 1961, cols. 2283–2284.
7. *Ibid.*, Sept. 4, 1961, col. 2810.
8. *Ibid.*, Nov. 29, 1961, col. 3528.
9. *Democratic Socialism: Being the Manifesto of the Action Group of Nigeria for an Independent Nigeria* (Amalgamated Press of Nigeria, Lagos, 1960).
10. *Parliamentary Debates,* H. of R., Nov. 29, 1961, col. 3535.
11. "Opportunities for Overseas Investment in the Federation of Nigeria," July 19, 1958, reprinted as Appendix VIII-B to *Economic Survey of Nigeria, 1959* (Federal Government Printer, Lagos, 1959).
12. The diary was read at his trial for treason and was quoted in the *Daily Times*, Nov. 27, 1962, p. 1.
13. Obafemi Awolowo, "Twelve Months of Independence," Speech at the National Press Club of Nigeria, Lagos, Nov. 3, 1961. Reprinted in *The Service,* Vol. II, No. 59 (Nov. 4, 1961), p. 28.

14. "Awolowo and Nigeria. An Open Rebuke," *Morning Post*, Nov. 6, 1961, p. 5.
15. "Advertising Nigeria. Awolowo Does It in Poor Fashion," *ibid.*, Nov. 7, 1961, p. 5.
16. Obafemi Awolowo, "Philosophy for Independent Nigeria," Lecture to Nigerian students at Conway Hall, London, Sept. 3, 1961 (mimeographed).
17. *Parliamentary Debates*, H. of R., Nov. 29, 1961, col. 3589; Nov. 30, 1961, col. 3629.
18. *West Africa*, Oct. 21, 1961, p. 1159.
19. *See*, for example, *Daily Times*, Oct. 19, 1960, p. 1. But *see* the speech of Dr. Michael Okpara, successor to Dr. Azikiwe as President of the NCNC and Premier of the Eastern Region, saying that while he supported socialism he opposed nationalization because the country needs capital and "ordinary common sense dictates that it can only come from outside since it is not here." *Ibid.*, Oct. 20, 1960, p. 3.
20. *The Service*, Vol. II, No. 83 (April 21, 1962), p. 15; *ibid.*, Vol. I, No. 9 (Nov. 19, 1960), p. 16; *ibid.*, Vol. I, No. 7 (Nov. 5, 1960), p. 3.
21. *Parliamentary Debates*, H. of R., Apr. 12, 1960, col. 1122.
22. *Ibid.*, col. 1123.
23. *Ibid.*, Jan. 14, 1960, p. 39.
24. *The Times* (London), March 29, 1960, p. 13; *Daily Times*, Apr. 21, 1960, p. 3; *Daily Times*, May 2, 1960, p. 3, letter of the Prime Minister to the Secretary of the UMBC.
25. David Williams, "The Tiv Are in Turmoil," *Daily Times*, Oct. 20, 1960, p. 5. This is a reprint of the article in *West Africa*, Oct. 15, 1960, pp. 1157–1158.
26. *Daily Times*, June 30, 1961, p. 1; *The Service*, Vol. I, No. 42 (July 8, 1961), p. 3.
27. *See* "Cameroon Dress Rehearsal," *West Africa*, Dec. 5, 1959, p. 1049. The Sardauna of Sokoto blamed the result on the "subversive activities of British officers who organized the plebiscite," *Daily Times*, Nov. 11, 1959, p. 20.
28. *See* the discussion of the Action Group's gains in the West in J. P. MacIntosh, "Electoral Trends and the Tendency to a One Party System in Nigeria: (1) The Action Group in the West," *The Service*, Vol. II, No. 81 (Apr. 7, 1962), p. 12.
29. *See* the *Daily Times*, Oct. 10, 1960, p. 20, report of Osadebay's statement in the Western House; *ibid.*, Oct. 13, 1960, p. 1. Chief Akintola disagrees and in "How Powerful is the Federal Government?" *The Service*, Vol. I, No. 5 (Oct. 22, 1960), p. 16, "John West" does likewise. Prime Minister Tafawa Balewa's statement is in the *Daily Times*, Nov. 7, 1960, p. 1.
30. Joint statement, *Daily Times*, Sept. 18, 1961, p. 1.
31. *Parliamentary Debates*, H. of R., Aug. 29, 1961, col. 2495.
32. *Daily Times*, Aug. 5, 1961, p. 7.

33. *Parliamentary Debates,* H. of R., Apr. 4, 1961, cols. 755–803.
34. "Nigeria's Fourth Region," *The Service,* Vol. I, No. 30 (Apr. 15, 1961). Another argument was Chief Enahoro's that a third region in the southern portion of the country would reduce NPC strength in the Senate, where each region had equal representation.
35. *Daily Times,* Aug. 2, 1960, p. 13.
36. *See* Chief Akintola's defense to the charges in the *Daily Express,* May 23, 1962, p. 5.
37. *See* Bola Ige (Action Group Federal Publicity Secretary), "The Action Group Crisis," *The Service,* Vol. II, No. 88 (May 26, 1962), pp. 12–14; Anthony Enahoro, "Statement," *Daily Express,* May 17, 1962, p. 7.
38. "Statement," *op. cit.*
39. *See* the views of S. G. Ikoku in "The Action Group X-Rays Itself," *The Service,* Vol. II, No. 70 (Jan. 28, 1962), pp. 18, 19, 23.
40. Obafemi Awolowo, "Presidential Address," Eighth Annual Congress of the Action Group of Nigeria, held at Jos, Feb. 2, 1962.
41. *Morning Post,* May 26, 1962, p. 16.
42. *See* the *Report of Coker Commission of Inquiry Into the Affairs of Certain Statutory Corporations in Western Nigeria* (4 vols.) (Printing Division, Federal Ministry of Information, Lagos, 1962).
43. *Ibid.,* Vol. II, pp. 2 ff.
44. *Ibid.,* Vol I, pp. 25–69, Vol. II, pp. 31–40.
45. *Ibid.,* Vol. III, pp. 24–35. The reference to flooding and crabs is on page 35.
46. *Ibid.,* Vol. I, pp. 37–40, 43, 59, 69–73. The Federal Government's *Comments* on the Coker Commission Report are in Sess. Paper No. 4 of 1962. It places primary emphasis upon derogatory comments concerning Chief Awolowo.

Chapter 8

1. *Daily Times,* Mar. 4, 1964, p. 5.
2. *Daily Times,* Dec. 13, 1963.
3. *Daily Times,* Mar. 11, 1964, pp. 1, 11. *See* the Western Nigerian Government's white paper charging Ibo tribalism in the administration of the Nigerian Railway Corporation, which is printed, along with Chairman Ikejiani's reply, in the *Daily Times* of Apr. 2, 1964.
4. *Daily Times,* Mar. 13, 1964, p. 3.
5. *Morning Post,* Nov. 17, 1964, p. 5.
6. *Morning Post,* Nov. 19, 1964, p. 9.
7. *UPGA Manifesto, Morning Post,* Nov. 11, 1964.
8. *NNA Manifesto, Morning Post,* Nov. 1, 1964.
9. *Morning Post,* Nov. 16, 1964, p. 3.
10. *UPGA Manifesto, op. cit.*
11. *NNA Manifesto, op. cit.*

12. *Ibid.*
13. *Morning Post*, Nov. 16, 1964, p. 3.
14. *UPGA Manifesto, op. cit.*
15. *Ibid.*
16. *Ibid.* For analyses of "African socialism" in general and in various countries (not Nigeria), see *African Socialism*, edited by William H. Friedland and Carl G. Rosberg, Jr. (Stanford University Press, Stanford, Cal., 1964).
17. *UPGA Manifesto, op. cit.*
18. *Manifesto of the Socialist Workers and Farmers Party*, *Morning Post*, Oct. 28, 1964.
19. *UPGA Manifesto, op. cit.*
20. *NNA Manifesto, op. cit.*
21. See *Daily Times*, Oct. 15, 1964, pp. 8–9; Nov. 21, 1964, p. 3; Dec. 3, 1964, p. 1; and Dec. 29, 1964, p. 6; and *Morning Post*, Nov. 1, 1964, p. 2; Nov. 3, 1964, pp. 8–10; and Nov. 19, 1964, p. 3.
22. *Morning Post*, Nov. 19, 1964, p. 3.
23. *Daily Times*, Nov. 20, 1964, and Nov. 27, 1964.
24. *Morning Post*, Oct. 1, 1964, p. 8.
25. *Daily Times*, Dec. 11, 1964.
26. *Daily Times*, Dec. 24, 1964.
27. For what is apparently President Azikiwe's version of events during the crisis, see *Sixteen Days of Political Crisis from the State House Diary* (Federal Ministry of Information, Nigerian National Press, Apapa, 1965).
28. *Daily Times*, Jan. 8, 1965, p. 7.
29. *Nigerian Outlook*, Jan. 11, 1965, p. 8.
30. *Morning Post*, Jan. 5, 1965.
31. *UPGA Manifesto, op. cit.*
32. *West African Pilot*, "Dirty Tale," Mar. 2, 1965 and "Dr. Njoku, "Mar. 1, 1965.

Chapter 9

1. *Parliamentary Debates*, H. of R., Aug. 5, 1958, col. 2060.
2. *Ibid.*, Nov. 25, 1960, col. 399.
3. Chike Obi, *I Speak for the People* (Dynamic Party, Department of Propaganda and Spiritual Education, Times Press, 1960), pp. 11, 13. Part 3 of this pamphlet contains the "Protocols of the Dynamic Party"; *cf.* Tai Solarin, "Ten Years Labour Drive: A Dictator's Manifesto," *Daily Times*, July 14, 1962, p. 5.
4. Chike Obi, *Our Struggle, A Political Analysis of the Problems of the Negro Peoples' Struggling for True Freedom* (John Okwessa and Co., Yaba, 1955), p. 30.
5. Presidential Address to the National Executive Committee of the

National Council of Nigeria and the Cameroons at Port Harcourt on Oct. 3, 1952. Reprinted in *Zik, A Selection from the Speeches of Nnamdi Azikiwe, op. cit.*, p. 85.

6. *Report on the Amalgamation of Southern and Northern Nigeria, and Administration, 1912–1919,* Cmnd. 468 (H.M.S.O., London, 1920), p. 19.

7. A Bill for a Law to Amend the Peace Preservation Ordinance (Objects and Reasons), *Northern Nigeria Gazette,* Vol. XI, No. 41 (July 26, 1962), Supplement Part C, pp. 187, 189.

8. "Times Have Changed," *Morning Post,* Apr. 13, 1962, p. 5.

9. Nnamdi Azikiwe, *Zik: A Selection from the Speeches of Nnamdi Azikiwe, op. cit.*, p. 85. (Speech to NCNC National Executive Committee in 1952.)

10. Obafemi Awolowo, *Awo, op. cit.*, pp. 302–303.

11. *Ibid.*, p. 303.

12. H. O. Davies, *Nigeria: The Prospects for Democracy* (Weidenfeld and Nicolson, London, 1961), p. 119. Chief Davies completes his analysis of how the traditions of the major ethnic groups support democracy by saying the Northern peoples are very disciplined with a sense of deference to authority and that their emirate governments were "greatly tempered by the precepts of the Holy Prophet."

13. *What are the Problems of Parliamentary Government in West Africa?* (Printed for the Hansard Society for Parliamentary Government by the Chiswick Press, London, 1958), p. 48.

14. "Nigeria Needs a One Party System," *Daily Times,* Nov. 18, 1960.

15. *Morning Post,* Dec. 6, 1962, p. 8; *Daily Times,* Oct. 1, 1962, pp. 10, 11.

16. *Daily Times,* Oct. 2, 1963, p. 8.

17. *West African Pilot,* July 26, 1958.

18. Quoted in J. P. MacIntosh, "Electoral Trends and the Tendency to a One Party System in Nigeria: (2) The National Convention of Nigerian Citizens," *The Service,* Vol. II, No. 82 (April 14, 1962), p. 13.

19. *Daily Service,* Sept. 4, 1959.

20. *See,* for example, *Statement of the Government of the Northern Region of Nigeria on the Report of the Committee of Inquiry Appointed to Investigate Allegations About Ilorin N. A.* (Government Printer, Kaduna, 1958). The relevant legislation permitting removal is: *North,* The Native Authority Law, 1954, N. R. No. 4 of 1954; *East,* The Local Government Law, 1960, E. R. No. 17 of 1960; *West,* The Local Government Law, Cap. 68 of the *Laws of the Western Region of Nigeria,* 1959.

21. *West African Pilot,* Dec. 11 and 12, 1963.

22. In the North, under Section 74 of the Constitution, a Council of Chiefs is established whose instructions the Governor must follow with respect to the appointment, grading, and deposition of a chief. The Council consists of the Premier, any Regional Ministers who were

appointed from the House of Chiefs, and up to four members of the House of Chiefs appointed by the Premier. The Premier is given formal power with which to control the Council if he wishes because he chooses which chiefs shall be Regional Ministers and because he can decide whom to add from the House of Chiefs. In the West under the Chiefs Law, Chap. 19 of the *Laws of the Western Region of Nigeria, 1959,* the Governor in Council (which means the Regional Government) can set aside the choice of the kingmakers or competent council and may suspend or depose a chief if satisfied it is necessary.

23. S. A. Aluko gave this explanation for the prestige of the civil service: "the young graduate who would normally have wished to lend his services to the press prefers the civil service which can provide him with a beautiful car for evening trips and fanfare." *The Problems of Self-Government for Nigeria: A Critical Analysis* (Arthur H. Stockwell, Ltd., Ilfracombe, England, 1955), p. 42.

24. Dr. E. O. Awa and Richard L. Sklar, *The Voting Behavior and Attitudes of Eastern Nigerians* (Aba, 1961).

25. Tai Solarin, "Speak Out, Public Men," *Daily Times,* June 30, 1962, p. 5.

26. H. A. Oluwasanmi, "Government by Stealth," *Sunday Express,* Nov. 19, 1961, p. 7.

27. *See* for example, "Cut it Down," *Daily Times,* Oct. 5, 1963.

28. Dennis Osadebay, "Nigeria Needs a One Party System," *op. cit.*

29. *Parliamentary Debates,* H. of R., Aug. 8, 1961, cols. 2408–2409.

30. Lateef K. Jakande, "Towards a More Virile West African Press," *The Service,* Vol. I, No. 37 (June 3, 1961), p. 6. Reprint of paper read at Editor's Conference in Lagos.

31. *Ibid.* Mr. Jakande estimates that out of Nigeria's national income of over £800 million less than £1 million goes into newspaper advertising.

32. Father James O'Connell, "The Changing Role of the State in West Africa," *The Nigerian Journal of Economic and Social Studies,* Vol. III, No. 1 (Nov. 1961), p. 1.

33. *Foreword* to Davies, *Nigeria, The Prospects for Democracy, op. cit.,* p. xi.

34. *See* Obafemi Awolowo, *Path to Nigerian Freedom, op. cit.,* pp. 31–32. ["Given a choice from among white officials, Chiefs, and educated Nigerians, as the principal rulers of the country, the illiterate man, today, would exercise his preference for the three in the order in which they are named. He is convinced, and has good reason to be, that he can always get better treatment from the white man then he could hope to get from the Chiefs and the educated elements."] *See also* S. A. Aluko, *The Problems of Self-Government for Nigeria, op. cit.,* pp. 16–17. [Says is strong feeling (at that time) of both peasants and educated persons that would be more fairly treated if matters such as promotion and scholarships determined by a European.]

35. "The New Nigerian," Program of the Nigerian Peoples' Party (Yaba, 1961), p. 4. For a general discussion of "Afro-Communist" parties

in other parts of tropical Africa, *see* Walter Z. Laquer, "Communism and Nationalism in Tropical Africa," *Foreign Affairs*, Vol XXXIX, No. 4 (July 1961), p. 610. For a discussion of adjustments of Marxist thought and language in Africa, *see* Thomas Hodgkin, "A Note on the Language of African Nationalism," in *African Affairs* (St. Anthony's Papers No. 10, Southern Illinois University Press, Carbondale, Ill., 1961).

Chapter 10

1. *Parliamentary Debates,* H. of R., Apr. 13, 1961, col. 1426; *ibid.,* July 20, 1961, col. 111.
2. Dr. Azikiwe's speech is reprinted in the *Daily Times* for several days beginning on November 18, 1961.
3. *Daily Express,* Dec. 1, 1961, p. 1.
4. *See,* for example, Ahmadu Bello (The Sardauna of Sokoto), *My Life, op. cit.,* pp. 232–233.
5. *Nigerian Citizen,* Dec. 2, 1962, p. 1.
6. *See* S. A. Aluko, "Forget it for Ten Years," *Morning Post,* Dec. 7, 1962, p. 9 (Dr. Aluko also contended that the nation should not become a republic since its people are "essentially and traditionally monarchical"); Ebenezer Williams, "May I Repeat All My Known Heresies," *Morning Post,* Dec. 9, 1961, p. 6; Nduka Eze, "No Need to Change to a Republic," *Daily Express,* Nov. 27, 1961, p. 4; Oke Osanyimtolu, *Daily Times,* Jan. 14, 1961, p. 5.
7. *The Constitution of the Federal Republic of Nigeria* (hereafter cited as *Constitution*), Chap. III (Fundamental Rights), Sections 18–33.
8. *Ibid.,* Sec. 32.
9. *Ibid.,* Sec. 113.
10. *Ibid.,* Sec. 112.
11. *Ibid.,* Sec. 4(1).
12. Erwin N. Griswold, "Two Branches of the Same Stream," Third Maccabaean Lecture in Jurisprudence, British Academy, London, Oct. 18, 1962, pp. 12–14 (mimeographed).
13. The analogy is based on one used in C. L. Black, Jr., "Mr. Justice Black, the Supreme Court and the Bill of Rights," *Harper's,* No. 222 (Feb. 1961), p. 63.
14. *Williams* v. *Majekodonmi,* F.S.C. 166/1962, July 7, 1962.
15. *In re The Director of Public Prosecutions* v. *Chike Obi,* F.S.C. 56/1961, April 6, 1961.
16. Chike Obi, *Our Struggle, A Political Analysis of the Problems of the Negro Peoples' Struggling for True Freedom, op. cit.,* p. 36.
17. *The Constitution of the Federation of Nigeria, op. cit.,* Sec. 28.
18. *Ibid.,* Sec. 30.
19. *Ibid.,* Sec. 70.

20. Among the Nigerians who have queried the worth of their constitutional guarantees are C. Ogwunike in his helpful thesis, *The Federation of Nigeria*, submitted for a Ph.D. at the University of London, Institute of Advanced Legal Studies, pp. 292, 437, and Aliyi Ekineh in "Our Human Rights Provisions," *Daily Times*, June 28, 1961, p. 5.

21. *Minorities Commission Report, op. cit.,* p. 77, para. 37.

22. *See* T. O. Elias, "The New Constitution of Nigeria and the Protection of Human Rights and Fundamental Freedoms," *Journal of the International Commission of Jurists*, Vol. II (1959–1960), p. 30.

23. Ibrahim Biu, *The Service,* Vol. II, No. 61 (Nov. 18, 1961), p. 11.

24. *Adegbenro* v. *Akintola* [1963], A.C. 614. *See* H. H. Marshall, "Interpretation of the Constitution of Western Nigeria: A Privy Council Decision," *International and Comparative Law Quarterly*, Vol. XIII, p. 280.

Chapter 11

1. *Constitution of the Federal Republic of Nigeria* (hereafter cited as *Constitution*), Exclusive Legislative List (E.L.L.), Item 5. See *Nigeria: Report of the Fiscal Commission* (H.M.S.O., London, 1958), Cmnd. 481 — saying in "light of the competing demands for loans in all Nigeria, the creditworthyness of all Nigeria is the best basis for borrowing." As a minor exception to Item 5, a region may borrow overseas for a period of less than a year using the security of its own assets held outside Nigeria.

2. *Parliamentary Debates*, H. of R., Nov. 17, 1961, cols. 2984–2985.

3. *Constitution, op. cit.,* Sec. 69.

4. *Ibid.*, E.L.L., Items 15, 11, 18, 14, 10, and 5; Sec. 77.

5. *Ibid.*, E.L.L., Items 25 and 28; Concurrent Legislative List (C.L.L.), Items 11, 12, and 27; Sec. 79.

6. *Ibid.*, E.L.L., Items 37, 3, 22(*a* and *b*), 40, 22(*d*), and 22(*b*).

7. *Ibid.*, Sec. 78 (with the proviso that Parliament's exclusive power to regulate banks and banking does not preclude a region from having its own bank and regulating it in ways that are not inconsistent with federal law); E.L.L., Item 4.

8. *Ibid.*, E.L.L., Items 19, 7, and 20.

9. *Ibid.*, C.L.L., Items 6 and 21.

10. *Ibid.*, Sec. 76(i); E.L.L., Items 10 and 38.

11. *Ibid.*, E.L.L., Items 24 and 23.

12. *Ibid.*, C.L.L., Items 7, 13, and 16.

13. *Ibid.*, E.L.L., Items 32 and 43.

14. *Ibid.*, Sec. 73.

15. *Ibid.*, Sec. 72.

16. *Ibid.*, Secs. 4, 5.

17. *Ibid.*, Sec. 74.

18. *Ibid.*, C.L.L., Item 13. *See also* Items 14 and 15, which provide for the consent of a region to federal control of national monuments and parks within the region.
19. *Ibid.*, Secs. 105–110.
20. *Ibid.*, E.L.L., Item 38; Sec. 164.
21. *Ibid.*, Sec. 112. That provision was new in the Republican Constitution. Previously the Associate Justices had been appointed by a nonpolitical Judicial Service Commission, upon which the regional Chief Justices sat, along with four others.
22. *Ibid.*, Secs. 115, 117; *cf.* Sec. 119. Under Sec. 115 substantial questions of law involving the interpretation of the Federal or regional constitutions may be referred to the Federal Supreme Court by a regional High Court before that court passes upon the question, and they must be referred if a party so requests. Similarly, lower regional courts can (must, if requested) refer such questions to the regional High Court, and the High Court must refer them on to the Federal Supreme Court if it regards the question as substantial. This procedure seems highly undesirable. It deprives the Supreme Court of the thinking of lower courts and may result in overburdening the court. It probably will artificially isolate constitutional issues from their factual setting.
23. *Ibid.*, Sec. 161(3).
24. Memorandum of Chief Justice John Verity, submitted to the Resumed Conference on the Nigerian Constitution held in Lagos, January and Febuary 1954. *See also Fiscal Commission Report, op. cit.*, and reports of other fiscal or revenue allocation commissions cited in the bibliography.
25. See *Minorities Commission Report, op. cit.*, pp. 90–94.
26. The sales taxes excepted are on "produce" (defined as animal or vegetable products other than tobacco, hides, or skins, designated by the President with the consent of the governments of the regions, Constitution, *op. cit.*, Section 165[1]), hides and skins, motor spirit, and diesel oil for road vehicles or nonindustrial use. *Ibid.*, E.L.L. Item 38.
27. *See* Regional and Federal annual *Estimates* and the Federal *Digest of Statistics.*
28. *Fiscal Commission Report, op. cit.*, p. 32.
29. *Constitution, op. cit.*, Sec. 139.
30. *Ibid.*, Secs. 137 and 138.
31. *Ibid.*, Sec. 140.
32. *Ibid.*, Sec. 141.
33. *Fiscal Commission Report, op. cit.*, p, 21.
34. *Constitution, op. cit.*, Sec. 76(2).
35. *Ibid.*, Sec. 64. A "money bill" can only be delayed for thirty days by the Senate. A bill other than a money bill which is passed by the House and sent to the Senate more than thirty days before the end of one session and not approved by the Senate will, if repassed by the House in the next session (but no sooner than six months after first passed by

the House) and then sent to the Senate at least thirty days before the end of the session and not passed by the Senate, become law at the end of the session. (Technically, it will be "presented to the President for his assent" before it becomes a law.)

36. *Ibid.*, Sec. 70 (declaration of emergency) and Sec. 4 (amendment of Constitution). Amendments to certain sections of the Constitution can be made by a majority vote of Parliament and without the assent of three regions which is required for amendments which must be initiated by a two-thirds vote of both houses of Parliament. The fundamental rights provisions and all provisions relating to the division of authority between the regions and the federation are among those provisions that can only be amended by more rigorous procedure. The provisions that can be amended in the simpler fashion are as a rule those dealing with matters such as citizenship and naturalization that are often handled by ordinary legislation, others where Parliament has complete discretion in any event under the Constitutional provision, and still others relating to details of executive or parliamentary administration.

37. *Ibid.*, Sec. 42.

Chapter 12

1. A. B. U. Nzeribe, *Parliamentary Debates*, H. of. R., Aug. 21, 1962, col. 2496.
2. *West Africa*, Jan. 7, 1961, p. 18.
3. See *Report by the Joint United Kingdom-Nigerian Scientific Committee on the Monitoring of Radioactivity* (Lagos, Government Printer, 1960).
4. *Parliamentary Debates*, H. of R., Aug. 11, 1959.
5. See *Daily Times*, Jan. 16, 1961, pp. 1 and 2; Jan 20, 1961, p. 16.
6. Nnamdi Azikiwe, *Respect for Human Dignity*, Nov. 16, 1960.
7. *Daily Times*, Oct. 14, 1960, p. 1.
8. *Parliamentary Debates,* H. of R., Apr. 5, 1960, col. 698.
9. *Morning Post*, Apr. 10, 1962, p. 16.
10. *Daily Times*, Aug. 27, 1962, p. 10; Aug. 30, 1962, p. 16.
11. Compare paragraph 3 of the resolution on colonialism of the 1960 General Assembly with Sir Abubakar Tafawa Balewa, "Nigeria Looks Ahead," *Foreign Affairs*, Vol. XLI, No. 1 (Oct. 1962), p. 138.
12. *Parliamentary Debates*, H. of R., Nov. 20, 1961, cols. 318–319.
13. *The New York Times*, June 21, 1962.
14. *Parliamentary Debates*, H. of R., Nov. 20, 1961, cols. 3119–3121.
15. *Ibid.*, Aug. 20, 1960, col. 2670; United Nations General Assembly, Fifteenth Session, 893rd Plenary Meeting, Oct. 2, 1960.
16. See *The New York Times*, July 28, 1961, p. 4 and *Morning Post*, Mar. 6, 1962, p. 6.

17. *Daily Times,* Jan. 19, 1960, p. 16.
18. *The Times* (London), Nov. 3, 1960, p. 10.
19. *Parliamentary Debates,* H. of. R., Nov. 19, 1960, col. 106.
20. *Defense Agreement Between the Government of the United Kingdom of Great Britain and Northern Ireland and the Government of the Federation of Nigeria,* Sess. Paper No. 4 of 1960 (Federal Government Printer, Lagos, 1960), printed as an appendix to Claude S. Phillips, Jr., *The Development of Nigerian Foreign Policy* (Northwestern University Press, Evanston, 1964).
21. *Parliamentary Debates,* H. of R., Nov. 24, 1960, col. 414.
22. *Ibid.,* Sept. 4, 1961, col. 2858–2859.
23. The figures are for 1960 and are rounded off to the nearest whole number from statistics in Tables 53, 54, and 64 in the *Annual Abstract of Statistics, 1961* (Federal Office of Statistics, Lagos).
24. His speech to the Conference is reprinted in the *Daily Times,* Sept. 14, 1962, p. 5.
25. *Daily Times,* Sept. 25, 1962.
26. *See,* for example, Barbara Ward Jackson, "Free Africa and the Common Market," *Foreign Affairs,* Vol. XL, No. 3 (Apr. 1962), p. 419.
27. *Daily Times,* Sept. 20, 1962, p. 1.
28. See *West Africa,* Aug. 5, 1962, *Parliamentary Debates,* H. of R., Apr. 12, 1962, col. 1501.
29. *Parliamentary Debates,* H. of R., Nov. 22, 1961, col. 3232.
30. A. A. Nwafor Orizu, *Without Bitterness: Western Nations in Postwar Africa* (Creative Age Press, New York, 1944), pp. 304–306.
31. Julius K. Nyerere, "A United States of Africa," *The Journal of Modern African Studies,* Vol. I, No. 1 (1963), pp. 1–3.
32. *Ibid.,* p. 6.
33. Nnamdi Azikiwe, address delivered in London under the auspices of the London Branch of the NCNC on July 31, 1958. Reprinted in *Zik: A Selection from the Speeches of Nnamdi Azikiwe, op. cit.,* pp. 70, 72.
34. *Pan-Africanism Reconsidered,* edited by the American Society of African Culture (University of California Press, Berkeley and Los Angeles, 1962), p. 371.
35. Resolutions, Pan-African Congress, Manchester, 1945. Resolution I(e). This can be found in Legum, *Pan-Africanism,* Appendix 2, p. 135.
36. Resolution No. 2 (3). Found in Legum, *Pan-Africanism, op. cit.,* Appendix 22, p. 223.
37. The Sardauna's remark was in *West Africa,* Oct. 22, 1960, p. 1186. For sentiment for union with Dahomey *see* the articles by "John West" in the *Daily Service,* March 11–14, 1960.
38. United Nations speech, *op. cit.,* n. 15.
39. *Parliamentary Debates,* H. of R., Aug. 22, 1960, col. 2670.

40. The communiqué is printed as Appendix 17 in Legum, *Pan-Africanism, op. cit.*
41. *See* (Ghana's) *Voice of Africa,* Vol. III, No. 43 (Feb. 8, 1962), p. 4.
42. The speech is reprinted in its entirety in the *Daily Times,* Jan. 26, 1962, p. 3.
43. *The New York Times,* Jan. 26, 1962, p. 3.
44. The proceedings of the Lagos Conference can be found in *Solidarity in Africa: A Record of the Conference of the Heads of African and Malagasy States Held in Lagos from January 25–30, 1962* (Nigerian National Press, Apapa, 1962).
45. *Parliamentary Debates,* H. of R., Apr. 19, 1960, col. 1430.
46. H. A. Oluwasanmi, "Africa's Hour of Triumph: Yet Shrouded in Uncertainty," *Daily Times,* Aug. 29, 1960, p. 8.
47. M. I. Okpara, "The Responsibilities of Independence," Presidential Address to delegates to the NCNC convention at Port Harcourt, January 1962. The speech is reprinted in the *Morning Post,* Jan. 17, 1962, pp. 8, 9, 13, and Jan. 18, 1962, pp. 8, 9, 13.
48. The Addis Charter and some other proceedings of the Addis Conference can be found in *Dawn of Africa: Nigeria and African Unity* (Nigerian National Press, Apapa, n.d.).
49. *Daily Times,* May 25, 1963, p. 2.
50. *Parliamentary Debates,* H. of R., Apr. 19, 1960, col. 1439.
51. *Ibid.,* Nov. 24, 1960, col. 371.
52. *Ibid.,* Apr. 17, 1961, col. 1782.
53. *See,* for example, Kalu Ezera, "Nigeria in Middle East Politics," *Daily Times,* Aug. 8, 1960.
54. *See,* for example, the comment of Bello Dandago in *What are the Problems of Parliamentary Government in West Africa?, op. cit.,* p. 26.
55. *Daily Times,* Sept. 8, 1962.
56. *Zik, A Selection from the Speeches of Nnamdi Azikiwe, op. cit.,* pp. 63–65.
57. A. K. Barden, "Balance Sheet of Lagos Talks," *The Ghanaian Times,* Feb. 2, 1962, reprinted in the pro-Action Group *Daily Express* on Feb. 15, 1962, p. 4, "Copying Ghana the Wrong Way," *Ghana Evening News* quoted in the *Daily Express,* June 7, 1962, p. 2. The *Evening News* added that "Balewa and his friends" are jealous of "the historical position of Ghana with foolish references to the size of Nigeria."
58. *See,* for example, *Parliamentary Debates,* H. of R., Sept. 4, 1961, cols. 2858–2859; Chief Enahoro's report upon his return from the All African Peoples' Conference at Tunis in January 1960: a conspiracy to deny Nigeria its proper place in African affairs—a clique formed by certain independent West African States; *Sunday Times,* June 10, 1962, p. 16; reports of the Awolowo Treason Trial.
59. *Parliamentary Debates,* H. of R., Aug. 26, 1961, cols. 2283–2284.
60. *Parliamentary Debates,* H. of R., Apr. 3, 1962, cols. 777–778.

Chapter 13

1. *Parliamentary Debates*, H. of R., Aug. 5, 1959.
2. Address to NCNC members of the Eastern House of Assembly and officers of the NCNC at Enugu, January 1952. Reprinted in *Zik: A Selection from the Speeches of Nnamdi Azikiwe*, p. 54.
3. *The Times*, (London), Mar. 13, 1961, p. 8. (A Nigerian now holds the post.)
4. *Parliamentary Debates*, H. of R., Jan. 14, 1960, p. 28.
5. Quoted in Joan Wheare, *The Nigerian Legislative Council* (Faber and Faber, Ltd., London, 1950), p. 251.
6. Jawaharlal Nehru, *Towards Freedom* (John Day, New York, 1941), p. 264.
7. Ibrahim Biu, "Northern Nigeria," *Daily Times,* Oct. 2, 1961.
8. "Peter Pan" (pen name for Peter Enahoro), "When Zik Spoke," *Daily Times,* Aug. 5, 1962, p. 5.
9. Ulli Beier, *Art in Nigeria, 1960* (Cambridge University Press in collaboration with the Information Division, Ministry of Home Affairs, Ibadan, Nigeria, 1960), pp. 5 and 24.
10. *See,* for example, Archibald Callaway, "School Leavers and the Developing Economy of Nigeria," *The Nigerian Political Scene,* ed. by Robert O. Tilman and Taylor Cole (Duke University Press, Durham, N.C., 1962), pp. 220 ff.
11. *Investment in Education, The Report of the Commission on Post-School Certificate Education in Nigeria* (The Ashby Report) *op. cit.,* p. 5.
12. S. A. Aluko, "A Nation in Need of Ideals," *The Service,* Vol II, No. 67 (Dec. 30, 1961), p. 15.
13. *Paliamentary Debates*, H. of R., Mar. 23 and 24, 1964, cols. 128–142 and 143–184.
14. *Daily Times*, Nov. 23, 1961, p. 5.
15. *Morning Post*, Nov. 9, 1961, p. 11.
16. *Daily Times*, Aug. 14, 1962, p. 1.
17. "Nigeria's Struggle," *The Manchester Guardian*, July 31, 1962, p. 6; letter by the Governor-General, *ibid.,* Aug. 10, 1962, p. 7.
18. "Not an Unhappy Ending," *Morning Post,* Nov. 21, 1961, p. 5.
19. *See* a similar thesis put forward by Francis X. Sutton in "Authority and Authoritarianism in the New Africa," *The Nigerian Political Scene, op. cit.,* pp. 271, 283–284.
20. George Padmore, *Pan-Africanism or Communism? The Coming Struggle for Africa* (Dobson, London, 1956).

Selected Bibliography

What follows is broken down into two sections. The first mentions or describes some sources of material about Nigeria. The second lists various books, articles, and documents, which are classified according to subject matter, and occasionally followed by a description, a significant excerpt, or a comment.

Neither section of this bibliography is by any means a complete listing of all material about Nigeria; some of the material cited in the text is not even mentioned. The bibliography is intended to list some of the more important material covering Nigeria and to help the reader find other material. To facilitate that end, the first section concludes with a brief list of other bibliographies.

I. SOURCES OF MATERIAL ABOUT NIGERIA

A. Newspapers

Nigeria's newspapers are more useful in helping one to get a feel for the country than for recording news. Opinion pieces — editorials, columns, and letters to the editor — take up much of the papers' space. From those opinion pieces a foreigner can acquire a sense of what makes Nigerians angry; what they hope for; where they are realistic; where they are dreamers. From what is said and from what is left unsaid, a foreigner can begin to understand anti-colonialism and the colonial mentality, the fear of neocolonialism, and the desire for economic development, tribalism, and Pan-Africanism.

The Nigerian newspapers perform another very useful service to the student of politics by reprinting the full text of the lengthy party manifestoes prepared for elections, and of major speeches at party conventions, at international conventions, and other important occasions.

In their news reporting, however, the Nigerian papers are limited both in the subjects they cover and in the treatment given to the subjects covered. Only two types of news are consistently covered: politics and criminal justice. In a sense the Nigerian newspapers are quite complete in their political coverage. However, they seldom seem to go beneath the surface for news. They concentrate on the pronouncements and the squabbles of the major political figures. One gets the feeling that while the opinion pieces might predict a major upheaval, the news reporters would not get out and uncover the facts about a popular ground swell.

If one could read only a single Nigerian paper, the *Daily Times,* and its companion the *Sunday Times,* should be chosen because it is the leading independent. But one would also do well to read at least the *Morning Post* (supported by the Federal Government), the *West African Pilot* (traditionally NCNC, Azikiwe's first Nigerian paper) and the *Daily Express* (which at least through the 1962 crisis was pro-Action Group). In addition to those four national dailies (which since May 1, 1963, sell for 3 *d.*), there are a great many other newspapers which supplement them with news, or more often with the views of the party or government that supports them. Some of these are the *Kano Daily Mail* (supported by the NPC), *The Nigerian Citizen* (supported by the Northern Region Government), *The Nigerian Tribune* (supported by the Action Group), the *Eastern Outlook* (supported by the Eastern Region Government).

Some discussions of the Nigerian Press can be found in Increase Coker, *Seventy Terms of the Nigerian Press* (Times, Lagos, 1952) and "The Nigerian Press" in *The Press in West Africa; Report Prepared for the Dakar Conference on the Press, 1960* (Ibadan, 1960); Ernest Ikoli, "The Nigerian Press," *West African Review,* June 1950, p. 625; Lateef K. Jakande, "Towards a More Virile African Press," *The Service,* Vol. I, No. 37 (June 3, 1961), p. 6; and *The Press in Africa,* edited by Helen Kitchen (Ruth Sloan Assoc., Inc., Washington, 1956), which includes an article by the editor of the *Sunday Times* entitled "A Nigerian Journalist Looks at African Newspapers." James S. Coleman's *Nigeria: Background to Nationalism* (University of California Press, Berkeley and Los Angeles, 1958) includes some discussion of the nationalist press, including its early days during which British administrators sought ways of curbing what one called its "monstrous freedom." An attack upon press suppression in the colonial days is in Nnamdi Azikiwe's *Suppression of the Press in British West Africa* (Onitsha, 1946). Mass media in fifteen African countries, including Nigeria, are described and analyzed in Arno G. Huth, *Communications Media in Tropical Africa* (The International Cooperation Administration, Washington, D.C., 1961). The report lists priorities for further development.

British newspapers — the *Observer,* the *Times,* the *Guardian,* and the *Telegraph,* as the leading examples — carry a fair amount of news and interpretative material about Nigeria. They are sometimes a bit patronizing and preachy and are often deeply resented by Nigerians. But they are sources of relatively steady reports that do give extensive and well-written background to crises. In contrast to most of the American press, moreover, when they do go beyond political crises they concentrate on the Africa of the university graduate and the primary school leaver rather than the Africa of the witch doctor.

American newspaper and mass-magazine reporting about Africa is generally facile, misleading, and extremely incomplete, as it darts in and then quickly away from crisis spots. There are some exceptions, such as Mario Rossi's articles in the *Christian Science Monitor* and an occasional impressionistic background piece in *The New York Times*.

B. *Periodicals*

1. Coverage Wider than Nigeria but with Substantial Material on Nigeria

African Abstracts, a quarterly published by the International African Institute, London, abstracts ethnographic, social, and linguistic studies appearing in current periodicals.

West Africa, a British weekly magazine specializing in West Africa with emphasis upon Britain's former West African colonies, particularly Nigeria in recent years, does not purport to be scholarly or profound, but because of its coverage is essential reading. It covers political and economic (and, to a lesser extent, cultural) news. It has an occasional analytical article and frequent profiles. Its style is occasionally rather fussy but is perfectly readable. Contemporary African opinion fills its correspondence columns, though the correspondence columns perhaps overemphasize African student politics in England and are too ready to print somewhat pompous personal posturings of self-styled leaders of that student community.

Sometimes it appears that *West Africa's* writers are diplomats more than they are reporters. They bend over backwards not to say anything nasty about or critical of any African personality or government. They almost always succeed in finding a sunny side to events. They are obviously extremely conscious of the sensitivity of Africans toward the foreign press. Sometimes the line between sympathetic understanding and patronizing concern is a bit blurred.

Other periodicals written in English likely to have material on Nigeria are

Africa (quarterly, journal of the International African Institute, London).
African Digest (six issues a year, African Publications Trust, London).
Africa Today (monthly, American Committee on Africa, New York).
African Affairs (quarterly, Royal African Society, London).
African Report (monthly, African-American Institute, Washington).
Black Orpheus: a Journal of African and Afro-American Literature (three
    issues a year, Ibadan University).
Freedomways: A Quarterly Review of the Negro Freedom Movement (New
    York).

Journal of African Administration (quarterly, edited by African Studies Branch of the Colonial Office).*

Journal of African History (three issues a year; editors at School of Oriental and African Studies, University of London; published by Cambridge University Press).

Journal of African Law (three issues a year; published by Butterworth & Co., London, for the International African Law Association).

Journal of Modern African Studies (quarterly, Cambridge, England, and Dar es Salaam, Tanzania).

Presence Africaine: Cultural Review of the Negro World (English edition; quarterly, Paris).

The West African Review (monthly, British commercial interests, Liverpool; ceased publication in November 1962).

2. Specializing in Nigeria

Ibadan (three issues a year, Ibadan University).

Journal of the Historical Society of Nigeria (irregular, Ibadan University). The Society's *Bulletin* lists current historical publications relating to Nigeria.

Nigeria Magazine (quarterly, Federal Government Printer, Lagos). Mostly art, archeology, and style of life throughout the country.

The Nigerian Journal of Economic and Social Studies (three issues a year, The Nigerian Economic Society).

The Nigerian Law Journal (annual, African Universities Press, Lagos).

Proceedings of the Nigerian Institute of Social and Economic Research (annual, Ibadan).

The Service (weekly, Action Group militancy). Until shortly prior to independence, a daily newspaper was published under the same name.

C. *Parliamentary Reports*

Special mention should be made of the verbatim reports (Daily Hansard) of the two houses of the Federal Parliament and the regional legislatures. Particularly in the Federal House of Representatives the members are out-spoken and frank in speech — the intellectual quality of which varies enormously — even though on votes party discipline is invariably kept. Parliament and the legislature do not play a particularly important role in the decision-making process, but next to the newspapers, the Hansards are the best single printed source for developing a feeling for the country. In addition, the various ministries' answers to parliamentary questions occasionally supply information not available elsewhere. Since the legislatures are in session for relatively few days each year (in 1961 the Federal House met on only forty-two days) the reports are not very long. The

*Succeeded in January 1962 by the *Journal of Local Administration Overseas*.

Hansard has descriptive headings which enable a reader to scan until reaching subjects relevant to him.

D. *Other Bibliographies and Sources*

Among other bibliographies at least the following deserve special note:

Coleman, James S., *Nigeria: Background to Nationalism* (University of California Press, Berkeley and Los Angeles, 1958), pp. 481–496.

Coleman, James S. "A Survey of Selected Literature on the Government and Politics of British West Africa," *American Political Science Review*, Vol. XLIX (Dec. 1955), pp. 1130–1150.

Conover, Helen F., *Nigerian Official Publications, 1869–1959: A Guide* (Reference Department, Library of Congress, Washington, D.C., 1959).*

Harris, John, *Books About Nigeria: a Select Reading List* (University College Press, Ibadan, 1959).

O'Connell, James, "A Survey of Selected Social Science Research on Nigeria since the End of 1957." Appendix to Robert O. Tilman and Taylor Cole, *The Nigerian Political Scene* (Duke University Press, Durham, N.C., 1962). Organized by topic with evaluations.

Perry, Ruth, *A Preliminary Bibliography of the Literature of Nationalism in Nigeria* (International African Institute, London, 1955).

Sklar, Richard L., *Nigerian Political Parties: Power in an Emergent African Nation* (Princeton University Press, Princeton, N.J., 1963), pp. 535–559. The bibliography is particularly useful in its listing of the internal documents and publications of Nigerian political parties and where they can be found.

Ibadan University (formerly University College Ibadan) is under the Publications Ordinance (Act) the official depository of all material printed in Nigeria. The University Library annually publishes *Nigerian Publications*, which lists material received each year. For sources of Africana, *see* Helen F. Conover, *African Libraries, Book Production and Archives* (Reference Department, Library of Congress, Washington, D.C., 1962). Stanford University publishes, for the African Studies Association, *Africana Newsletter* (semi-annually) and the *African Studies Bulletin* (three times a year). Both publications have helpful bibliographies, notes, and information on sources and archives.

II. *SPECIFIC PUBLICATIONS*

The following material is classified by subject matter under the headings of history, the land and the people, domestic politics, foreign policy, and the Constitution. Several of those headings are further subdivided. Obviously some publications are relevant to more than one heading, but they are

---

* English governmental publications relating to Nigeria are listed by Her Majesty's Stationery Office—H.M.S.O.

placed under the heading to which they seem most pertinent, sometimes with a comment that material on another subject is covered. Under each heading the more general works are covered first. It is worth repeating that what follows is not all-inclusive and is designed to be most helpful to the amateur, the student beginning to study Nigeria, rather than the specialist already expert on the subject. To that end general works and secondary sources are given more emphasis than would be the case in a more conventional bibliography.

A. *History*

Two recent general histories of Nigeria are Thomas Hodgkin's *Nigerian Perspectives: An Historical Anthology* (Oxford University Press, London, 1960) and Michael Crowder's *The Story of Nigeria* (Faber and Faber, Ltd., London, 1962). Hodgkin's anthology includes selected historical documents ranging from legends of origin of various Nigerian groups and the coming of Islam to the nineteenth and early twentieth centuries. Writers of the documents run the gamut from Arab chroniclers of West Africa to Portuguese and English merchants and travelers, freed slaves, leaders of the Fulani jihad, African traders, and so forth. The documents are preceded by a fairly lengthy historical introduction which includes references to the sources available with respect to various peoples and various periods. The introduction's major contention is that

> . . . the study of Nigerian history is [not] essentially an inquiry into the past of a conglomeration of peoples, whose associations with one another are purely "artificial," the product of the colonial epoch. In one sense all human associations are artificial in that they are man-made. But it will be clear, I hope, from the extracts which follow that a variety of links existed between the various states and peoples which were the predecessors of modern Nigeria. . . . These relationships sometimes took the form of war and enslavement. But they expressed themselves also through diplomacy, treaties, the visits of wandering scholars, the diffusion of political and religious ideas, the borrowing of techniques, and above all trade. These passages are full of references to the impact of Ife on Benin; of Benin on Iboland; of Ibo society on the Delta States, of the Hausa peoples on Yorubaland; of Kanem-Bornu on the Hausa system.

The documents in the anthology bear Mr. Hodgkin out. However, he is also careful to caution the reader,

> None the less, one reason why it is difficult to present a coherent picture of the Nigerian past — of the various pasts of its constituent peoples — is that it is necessary to pursue several themes at the same time. And, though these themes frequently run together and interlace, each is distinct: each culture has its own particular qualities, its proper history.

Two more cautionary points should perhaps be made. First, the historical associations between various Nigerian groups brought out in Mr. Hodgkin's book do not establish that all of the groups brought together in Nigeria were historically associated in any meaningful sense. Second, some Nigerian groups had their closest historical ties with groups outside Nigeria.

Crowder's *Story* is a popularly written history of Nigeria covering indigenous history, the slave trade, European exploration and colonization, and Nigerian nationalism through the attainment of independence.

A somewhat less complete and less sympathetic general history is M. C. English's *An Outline of Nigerian History* (Longmans, Green & Co., London, 1959). *An Introduction to the History of West Africa* by J. D. Fage (Cambridge University Press, Cambridge, 1959) is a compact general history designed for secondary schools. It covers all of West Africa with little attention to events after the establishment of colonial control. It has a short, topical, descriptive bibliography.

Each of those books reflects, to a greater or lesser extent, the recent tendency, prompted by African independence and emotional support for it, and by new research, to seek to disprove the old belief that Africa was a continent "without history" before the European coastal contacts, which, reflecting the outsiders' view with which "African" history was written, were universally referred to as "discoveries." (For histories of Nigeria weakened by their overemphasis upon Europe's role, *see* the books of two long-time colonial administrators: C. R. Niven, *A Short History of Nigeria* (Longmans, Green & Co., London, 1937) and Alan Burns, *History of Nigeria* (Allen & Unwin, Ltd., London, 1958, fifth ed.), which includes advice on how to live in the tropics — "keep away from strong drink until after exercise has been taken".)

K. Onwuka Dike, perhaps the leading Nigerian historian, reacts against the theory that there was no indigenous African history in "History and African Nationalism," *Proceedings of the First Annual Conference of the West African Institute of Social and Economic Research, Held at University College, Ibadan, 1952*, p. 31. Starting with the thesis that since "every nation builds its future on its past . . . the African must not only instinctively have faith in his own inheritance, but must also satisfy himself by scientific inquiry that it exists," but also warning against "unwarranted claims for the African past often based on slender evidence," Dike, now principal of Ibadan University, points out some significant accomplishments of the African past and gives reasons for Africa's lag in some fields. *See also* his "African History and Self-Government," *West Africa*, Feb. 28, 1953, p. 177. And *see* generally J. C. Anene, "Towards a National History," *Ibadan*, No. 16 (June 1963), p. 7, and Charles H. Wesley, "The Changing African Historical Tradition," *Journal of Human Relations*, Spring-Summer 1960, p. 323.

An example of a general work on indigenous African History is Basil Davidson's *The Lost Cities of Africa* (Little, Brown and Company, Boston, 1959) in which the author — quite like Dr. Dike — states that his aim is to steer between "the rock of prejudice and the whirlpool of romance."

There has also been a reaction against the theory that Nigeria throws together an "unnatural" grouping of ethnic groups. *See*, for example,

Okoi Arikpo, "Who are the Nigerians?" (1957 Lugard Lectures, Published by the Ministry of Information, Lagos). Making the point that if one goes back far enough all nations could be called unnatural geographic expressions, the author points out many similarities between Nigeria's ethnic groups. *See also* his "Is There a Nigerian Nation?," *West Africa Review.* Feb. 1960, p. 53.

With respect to the period when the British were becoming influential, some recent histories of the period have greater interest in and insight into how events affected the Africans and what motivated Africans to act. The best example is Dike's *Trade and Politics in the Niger Delta, 1830–1885: An Introduction to the Economic and Political History of Nigeria* (Clarendon Press, Oxford, 1956), a highly readable account of commercial and political intrigue of Africans and Europeans in the Niger delta area. *See also* G. I. Jones, *The Trading States of the Oil Rivers* (Oxford University Press, London, 1963).

Examples of more specialized writing are G. I. Jones, "Native and Trade Currencies in Southern Nigeria during the 18th and 19th Centuries," *Africa*, Vol. XXVIII, No. 1 (1958), p. 43, and Daryll Forde, *Efik Traders of Old Calabar* (Oxford University Press, London, 1956). A brief, general, analytical, treatment of the period can be found in J. F. Ade Ajayi, "Nineteenth Century Origins of Nigerian Nationalism," *Journal of the Historical Society of Nigeria*, Vol. II, No. 2 (Dec. 1961), p. 196, which contends that the driving force of nineteenth-century nationalism was "racial consciousness as Africans." Capsule biographies of several nineteenth-century Nigerians, none of whom, however, were nationalists in the sense of advocates of a Nigerian nation state, are in K. Onwuka Dike, ed., *Eminent Nigerians of the Nineteenth Century* (Cambridge University Press, Cambridge, 1960).

A great many histories concern particular ethnic groups in Nigeria. The first of these was Samuel Johnson's *The History of the Yoruba* (Routledge & Kegan Paul, London, 1921, reprinted by Northwestern University Press, Evanston, Ill., 1964). Some other histories of Southern groups are

Biobaku, S. O., *The Origin of the Yorubas* (Lagos, 1955).

Biobaku, S. O., *The Egba and their Neighbors, 1842–1872* (Clarendon Press, Oxford, 1957). The second volume of Margery Perham's biography of Lugard describes in Chapters 21 and 22 the strength of the Egba State at Abeokuta which remained independent until 1914.

Egharevba, J. U., *A Short History of Benin* (Ibadan University Press, Ibadan, 1960, third ed.).

Obio-Offiong, U. E., *A First Step to the Study of Ibibio History* (Aba, 1958).

The written sources for histories of Northern groups (other than in the Middle Belt) are more numerous than for Southern groups because Muslim Northerners could write (in the Arabic script) and several traveling Arabs recounted what they had seen in the North. *The Golden Trade of the Moors*, by E. W. Bovill (Oxford University Press, London, 1958), is an absorbing account of the desert, slaves, gold, salt, camels, kingdoms, and battles, and of the links between North Africa and sub-Saharan West Africa down through the north of Nigeria (the area known as the Western Sudan). There is a topical bibliography at the end. A less readable, but perhaps more scholarly, book on the Muslim kingdoms of the Western Sudan is J. Spencer Trimingham's *History of Islam in West Africa* (Oxford University Press, London, 1962). Questions left unanswered by both books and some other related material, including much that is pertinent to Northern Nigeria, are discussed in Thomas Hodgkin's "Islam, History, and Politics," *Journal of Modern African Studies*, Vol. I, No. 1 (Mar. 1963), p. 91.

Some of the Arab sources for the history of the North are described in A. D. H. Bivar's "Arabic Documents of Northern Nigeria," *Bulletin of the School of Oriental and African Studies,* Vol. XXII, No. 2, 1959. Sources relating to the Fulani around the time of their jihad are mentioned in M. Hiskett's "Material Relating to the State of Learning Among the Fulani Before Their Jihad," *Bulletin of the School of Oriental and African Studies,* Vol. XIX (1957) and H. F. C. Smith's "Source Material for the History of the Western Sudan," *Journal of the Historical Society of Nigeria*, Vol I, No. 3 (1958). H. F. C. Smith's "A Neglected Theme of West African History: The Islamic Revolutions of the Nineteenth Century," *Journal of the Historical Society of Nigeria,* Vol. II, No. 2 (Dec. 1961) has a good deal on Usuman dan Fodio's Jihad and relates it to other Muslim revolutionary movements in the Western Sudan around the same time.

Many of the books mentioned later under the heading "The Land and the People" include historical background.

The first Europeans to explore Nigeria, particularly its hinterlands, were prolific journal keepers. Many of their works are cited or quoted in the books referred to in the preceding paragraphs. A readily available example is A. H. M. Kirk-Greene's *Barth's Travels in Nigeria: Extracts from the Journal of Heinrich Barth's Travels in Nigeria, 1850–1855* (Oxford University Press, London, 1962). *West African Explorers*, edited by C. Howard (Oxford University Press, London, 1961) has excerpts from the writings of several explorers of Nigeria.

The British influence was of course immense. A new, comprehensive analysis of the motives behind colonialism is in Ronald Robinson and John Gallagher, with Alice Denny, *Africa and the Victorians: The Official Mind of Imperialism* (The Macmillan Company, London, 1961). The thesis is that

> . . . the British colonies and protectorates in tropical Africa had not been claimed originally because they were needed as colonial estates. Rather, they had been claimed for strategic reasons, and they had to be developed as colonial estates to pay the costs of their administration. Their economic development was more a consequence than a motive of the "Scramble." As an explanation of European rule in tropical Africa, the theory of economic imperialism puts the trade before the flag, the capital before the conquest, the cart before the horse.

In dealing with West Africa, however, the authors place more stress upon economic motives than they do for the rest of Africa. As they put it, the Chamberlain regime called a halt to the "policy of trading the strategically worthless west for the economically worthless east."

The British colonial record and legacy are discussed by a sympathizer, who nevertheless presents some of the reasons why Africans are often resentful of the record and bitter about the legacy, in Margery Perham, *The Colonial Reckoning* (Collins, London, 1961). The British colonial service, particularly its selection, is discussed with hindsight and compared with that of Belgians, French, and others in Robert Heussler's *Yesterday's Rulers: The Making of the British Colonial Service* (Syracuse University Press, Syracuse, 1963).

The spirit of the British colonial advance is best appreciated through reading the biographies of some of the men on the spot. Examples are: Roland Oliver, *Sir Harry Johnston and the Scramble for Africa*, (Chatto & Windus, Ltd., London, 1957) and John E. Flint, *Sir George Goldie and the Making of Nigeria* (Oxford University Press, London, 1960). Johnston was, among other things, a British Consular official in the delta area. Goldie was the founder and leader of the Royal Niger Company (originally the National African Company which governed much of what became of Nigeria under a Royal Charter granted in 1886 after the company had entered into treaties with a number of African states and become the leading commercial power on the lower Niger. For a brief picture of John Holt, another commercial giant who mostly stayed at home in Liverpool, *see* C. Gertzel, "The Early Days of an African Trader," *Ibadan*, No. 10 (Nov. 1960), p. 12.

Undoubtedly the most influential colonial administrator was Frederick L. Lugard, whose Nigerian career is the major subject of Margery Perham's *Lugard (II): The Years of Authority* (Collins, London, 1960). Lugard was the first Governor of Northern Nigeria and, as Nigeria's first Governor-General, amalgamated Northern and Southern Nigeria. He conquered much of the North and was responsible for the use of indirect rule, though the book makes a case for the proposition that he would not have been as rigid in its application in the North, particularly in holding back Muslim educational opportunities, as were some who followed him. The book combines an easy style with a great deal of information. One of its interesting sidelights is its glimpses of Winston Churchill in the Colonial Office — for example, Churchill's memorandum to Lugard in 1906 saying "I see no reason why our occupation should be immediately effective up to the French frontier line, or why these savage tribes should not be allowed to eat each other without restraint, until some more suitable opportunity than the present shall arise for 'pacifying' them." The book has a bibliography at the end which includes an extremely comprehensive list of Lugard's published writings and a listing of official and other published material relating particularly to Britain's expansion into Nigeria and elsewhere and to colonial administration during the Lugard era.

Of Lugard's own many writings, perhaps the most famous and comprehensive is *The Dual Mandate in British Tropical Africa* (William Blackwood & Sons, London, 1922) which takes its title from his contention that the benefits of colonialism "can be made reciprocal and . . . it is the aim and desire of civilized administration to fulfil this dual mandate." His *Report on the Amalgamation of Northern and Southern Nigeria and Administration, 1912–1918* (H.M.S.O., London, 1920) is also extremely important

Lugard's wife, who as Flora Shaw had previously been colonial editor of *The Times* — and probably then coined the name Nigeria; *see* A. H. M. Kirk-Greene, "Who Coined the Name 'Nigeria,' " *West Africa*, Dec. 22, 1956, p. 1035 — contributed her impressions, views, and quite a bit of history in Flora L. S. Lugard, *A Tropical Dependency* (J. Nisbet & Co., London, 1905). An Englishman who wrote about amalgamation of North and South with slightly different views than Lugard was E. D. Morel, *Nigeria: Its Peoples and Problems* (The Macmillan Company, London, 1912). Among other things Morel had proposals for the way to end extreme separateness of North and South, including redrawing of boundaries so as to create four provinces.

Some comments on indirect rule can be found in Donald Cameron, *The Principles of Native Administration and their Application* (London, 1935); Margery Perham, "Some Problems of Indirect Rule in Africa," *Journal of the Royal African Society*, May 18, 1934, p. 12, and *Native Administration in Nigeria* (London, 1937); Peter C. Lloyd, "Lugard and Indirect Rule," *Ibadan*, No. 10 (Nov. 1960), p. 18.

A picture of a British colonial institution perhaps as well known as that of indirect rule is in Joan Wheare, *The Nigerian Legislative Council* (Faber and Faber, Ltd., London, 1950).

Though (pursuant to the theory of indirect rule) the chief colonial officers in the provinces were called residents to indicate that they were advisers, almost diplomats, rather than administrators, in fact they and their subordinates, the district officers, had and exercised a great deal of power. One district officer was Joyce Cary before he won acclaim as a writer. His experience in Northern Nigeria is reflected in *Mr. Johnson, Aissa Saved, An American Visitor*, and *The African Witch*. M. M. Mahood, in "Joyce Cary in Borgu," *Ibadan*, June 1960, p. 22, refers to Cary's view when in Nigeria that Northern Nigeria was a paradise compared to Lagos and his opinion twenty-five years later that the social ferment of Lagos made the dignity of the North "an anachronism, though very nice to look at." Some other relevant Cary writings are collected in *The Case for African Freedom and other writings on Africa*, with an introduction by Christopher Fyfe (University of Texas Press, Austin, Texas, 1962).

B. *The Land and the People*

1. Primarily Geography

A study of the haphazard historical basis for Nigeria's boundaries is in

J. R. V. Prescott, "Nigeria's Boundaries: A Colonial Heritage," *1958 Proceedings of the Nigerian Institute of Social and Economic Research*, p. 140. *See also* Prescott's "The Evolution of Nigeria's Boundaries," *Nigerian Geographic Journal*, Vol. II, No. 2 (Mar. 1959). T. C. Anene, in "The Nigeria-Southern Cameroons Boundary," *Journal of the Historical Society of Nigeria*, Vol. II, No. 2 (Dec. 1961), p. 186, suggests that while it was true that indigenous groups were split by the European colonial boundary makers, it is misleading to contend that for all areas that fact remains a source of friction and irredentism.

An analysis of the geographical basis for the minority new-state movement in Northern Nigeria is given in Keith M. Buchanan, "The Northern Region of Nigeria: The Geographical Background of its Political Duality," *Geographical Review*, Vol. XLIII, No. 4 (Oct. 1953), p. 451.

Several of the books dealing with colonial history cited in the preceding section and general descriptions of Nigeria cited in the following section cover the same themes — for example, Flint's *Goldie* for colonial origins of boundaries and Buchanan and Pugh's *Land and People* for the geographical basis for new-state movements.

W. A. Perkins and Jasper H. Stembridge, *Nigeria: A Descriptive Geography* (Oxford University Press, London, 1957) is designed for secondary school students.

2. Geographic and Ethnographic

Two comprehensive general works on Africa are George H. T. Kimble, *Tropical Africa* (Vol. I: *Land and Livelihood;* Vol. II: *Society and Polity*, The Twentieth Century Fund, New York, 1960) and Lord Hailey's *An African Survey, Revised 1956* (Oxford University Press, London, 1957). Both survey politics as well as geography, the people, economics, etc.

An attempt to classify the multitude of African languages is in Joseph Greenberg's *Studies in African Linguistic Classification* (Compass Publishing Co., New Haven, 1955) and *The Languages of Africa* (Indiana University Research Center in Anthropology, Folklore and Linguistics, Bloomington, Ind., 1963). *See also* Diedrich Westerman and M. A. Bryan, *Languages of West Africa* (Oxford University Press, London, 1952). *Language in Africa*, edited by John Spencer (Cambridge University Press, Cambridge, 1963) contains papers on African language studies and lists conferences held on the subject from 1950–1962. In 1964 Cambridge University, in association with the University of Ibadan, began to publish *The Journal of West African Languages*.

An extremely informative and useful general study of Nigeria is K. M. Buchanan and J. C. Pugh, *Land and People in Nigeria* (University of London Press, London, 1955).

Reflecting influence upon a publisher by the sharp administrative division between Northern and Southern Nigeria are C. K. Meek, *The Northern Tribes of Nigeria* (Oxford University Press, London, 1925) and P. Amaury

Talbot, *The Peoples of Southern Nigeria* (Oxford University Press, London, 1926).

The International African Institute is publishing an Ethnographic Survey on particular ethnic groups and peoples that includes

Bohannan, Laura and Paul, *The Tiv of Central Nigeria* (International African Institute, London, 1953).

Bradbury, R. E., *The Benin Kingdom and the Edo-Speaking Peoples of South-Western Nigeria,* with a section on the Itsekeri by Peter C. Lloyd (International African Institute, London, 1957).

Forde, Daryll, Brown, Paula, and Armstrong, Robert G., *Peoples of the Niger-Benue Confluence* (International African Institute, London, 1950).

Forde, Daryll and Jones, G. I., *The Ibo and Ibibio-Speaking Peoples of South-Eastern Nigeria* (International African Institute, London, 1950).

Forde, Daryll, *The Yoruba-Speaking Peoples of South-Western Nigeria* (International African Institute, London, 1951).

Gunn, Harold D., *Peoples of the Plateau Area of Nigeria* (International African Institute, London, 1953).

Gunn, Harold D., *Pagan Peoples of the Central Area of Northern Nigeria* (International African Institute, London, 1956).

Gunn, Harold D. and Conant, F. P., *Peoples of the Middle Niger Region, Northern Nigeria* (International African Institute, London, 1960).

The Ethnographic Survey gives comparatively great attention to the minority ethnic groups of Nigeria — the Edo-speaking peoples being a minority until the creation of the Midwest Region in 1963. One minority group that has been given a good deal of attention is the Tiv, who are of great political interest today because of their continuing resistance to inclusion in the Northern Region and their opposition, sometimes violent, to the NPC Regional Government and the NPC-controlled native authorities in their area. J. G. Wallace, in "The Tiv System of Election," *Journal of African Administration*, Vol. X, No. 10, p. 63, stresses a Tiv tradition against the concentration and perpetuation of political power or personal power, as does the chapter on the Tiv by Laura Bohannan in *Tribes Without Rulers*, edited by John Middleton and David Tait (Routledge & Kegan Paul, London, 1958). *See also* Paul Bohannan's *Justice and Judgment among the Tiv* (Oxford University Press, London, 1957).

Another Northern minority group's concept of politics is discussed in T. M. Baker, "Political Control among the Birom," *Fifth Annual Conference Proceedings of the West African Institute of Social and Economic Research* (Ibadan, 1956), p. 111.

There is a great deal of material on the Ibo, the Yoruba, the Hausa, and the Fulani.

The material on the Ibo includes

Green, M. M., *Ibo Village Affairs* (Sedgwick and Jackson, London, 1947).

Jones, G. I., *Report of the Position, Status and Influence of Chiefs and*

Natural Rulers in the Eastern Region of Nigeria (Government Printer, Enugu, 1957).

Leith-Ross, Sylvia, *Beyond the Niger* (Butterworth & Co., London, 1951).

Meek, C. K., *Law and Authority in a Nigerian Tribe* (Oxford University Press, London, 1937).

Ottenberg, S. O., "Ibo Receptivity to Change," in *Continuity and Change in African Cultures*, edited by William R. Bascom and Melville J. Herskovits (University of Chicago Press, Chicago, 1959), p. 130.

Works on the Yoruba include

Bascom, William R., "Urbanization among the Yoruba," *American Journal of Sociology*, Mar. 1955, p. 446.

Biobaku, S. O., "An Historical Sketch of Egba Traditional Authorities," *Africa*, Jan. 1952, p. 35.

Idowu, Bolaji, *Olodumare — God in Yoruba Belief* (Longmans, Green & Co., London, 1962).

Lloyd, Peter C., *Yoruba Land Law* (Oxford University Press, London, 1962).

Lloyd, Peter C., "Sacred Kingship and Government among the Yoruba," *Africa*, Vol XXX, No. 3 (July 1960), p. 221.

Lloyd, Peter C., "The Yoruba Town Today," *Sociological Review*, Vol. VII (1959). Special issue on Urbanism in West Africa.

Lloyd, Peter C., "The Traditional Political System of the Yoruba," *South-Western Journal of Anthropology*, Winter 1954, p. 366.

Lloyd, Peter C., "The Yoruba Lineage," *Africa*, July 1955, p. 235.

Schwab, William B., "Kinship and Lineage Among the Yoruba," *Africa*, Oct. 1955, p. 352.

Material about the Hausa and Fulani includes

Dry, D. P. L., "The Hausa Attitude to Authority," *Proceedings of the First Annual Conference of the West African Institute of Social and Economic Research*, University College, Ibadan, 1952 (reprinted Mar. 1957).

Hogben, S. J., *The Muhammedan Emirates of Nigeria* (Oxford University Press, London, 1930).

Hopen, C. Edward, *The Pastoral Fulbe Family in Gwandu* (Oxford University Press, London, 1958).

Smith, Mary F., *Baba of Karo* (Faber and Faber, Ltd., London, 1954). The autobiography of an elderly Hausa woman with an introduction on Hausa social structure by Michael G. Smith, the husband of the author.

Smith, Michael G., *The Economy of the Hausa Communities in Zaria* (H.M.S.O., London, 1955).

Smith, Michael G., "The Hausa System of Social Status," *Proceedings of the Nigerian Institute of Social and Economic Research, 1958*, p. 180.

Smith, Michael G., *Government in Zazzau, 1800–1950* (Oxford University Press, London, 1960). Particularly interesting for the native authority's accommodations to indirect rule as well as for indigenous institutions of and attitudes toward government.

Yeld, E. R., "Islam and Social Stratification in Northern Nigeria," *The British Journal of Sociology,* Vol. XI, No. 2 (June 1960). Replied to by Michael G. Smith in "Kebbi and Hausa Stratification," *ibid.,* Vol. XII, No. 1 (Mar. 1961).

Studies of Northern groups that have been influenced or conquered by the Hausa-Fulani are in

Nadel, S. F., *A Black Byzantium, The Kingdom of Nupe in Nigeria* (Oxford University Press, London, 1942) and

Kirk-Greene, A. H. M., *Adamawa Past and Present* (Oxford University Press, London, 1958).

Bornu was the leading Islamic area of what is now Northern Nigeria to resist successfully the Fulani jihad, and it is described in detail in A. Schultze, *The Sultanate of Bornu,* translated by P. A. Benton (Oxford University Press, London, 1913).

Islam has been the most influential social force in the northern portion of the Northern Region. Two books which deal, among other things, with the influence of traditional Africa upon Islam in Africa are

Trimingham, J. Spencer, *Islam in West Africa* (Oxford University Press, London, 1959) and

Anderson, J. N. D., *Islamic Law in Africa* (H.M.S.O., London, 1954).

Recently Islam again has adjusted to a new social situation — this time the needs of a modern, secular, multireligious state —as reflected by the new Northern Penal Code, discussed in Chapter 3 of the text. There are three articles on the penal code in *Modern Law Review,* Vol. XXIV (1961): Justin Price's "Retrograde Legislation in Northern Nigeria?" p. 604; Olu Odumosu's "The Northern Nigerian Codes," p. 612; J. N. D. Anderson's "A Major Advance," p. 616. Professor Anderson was a member of the Panel of Jurists that recommended the charges, and his article gives a succinct analysis of Muslim criminal law and the changes in Northern Nigeria. Professor Anderson also discusses the changes in "Conflict of Law in Northern Nigeria: A New Start," *International and Comparative Law Quarterly,* Vol. VIII (1959), p. 442. *See also* Samuel Richardson's book on the criminal procedure code passed as part of the reforms: *The Criminal Procedure Code of Northern Nigeria* (Sweet & Maxwell, Ltd., London, 1963).

Some description of and thoughts about African law can be found in

Allott, Antony N., *Judicial and Legal Systems of Africa* (Butterworth & Co., London, 1962). The first major publication of the restatement of African customary law being undertaken at the School of Oriental and African Studies at the University of London. *See* William Twining, "The Restatement of African Customary Law: A Comment," *Journal of Modern African Studies,* Vol. I, No. 2 (1963), p. 221.

Allott, Antony N., *Essays in African Law* (Butterworth & Co., London, 1960).

285

Elias, T. O., *Nigerian Land Law and Custom* (Routledge & Kegan Paul, London, 1953, second ed.).

Dr. Elias, who is the Nigerian Federal Attorney General, has also written on *The Impact of English Law on Nigerian Customary Law* (Ministry of Information, Lagos, 1960). *See also* J. F. Ade Ajayi, "The Interaction of English Law with Customary Law in Western Nigeria," *Journal of African Law,* Vol. IV, No. 1 (1960), pp. 40, 98.

3. Economic

Buchanan and Pugh's *Land and People* is one of the books mentioned in the preceding section in which the domestic economy and internal trade of Nigeria are discussed, as they are in parts of *The Native Economies of Nigeria,* edited by Margery Perham (Faber and Faber, Ltd., London, 1946). An early work on the nonagricultural domestic economy is Margery Perham, *Mining, Commerce and Finance in Nigeria* (Faber and Faber, Ltd., London, 1948).

Exports of primary agricultural products have become the key to the Nigerian economy and its development. P. T. Bauer's *West African Trade: A Study of Competition, Oligopoly and Monopoly in a Changing Economy* (Cambridge University Press, 1954) is, among other things, critical of the produce-marketing boards which (since 1954 as regional instrumentalities) purchase the produce from the farmers and sell it on the world market. Originally their function was said to be to cushion the farmer from fluctuations in the world market price, but increasingly their profits and reserves have been used as a source for general developmental purposes. *See,* for example, William P. Mott, "Nigeria's Experience in Internal Financing of Development Plans," in Warren H. Hausman, ed., *Managing Economic Development in Africa* (The M.I.T. Press, Cambridge, Mass., 1963). Through their power to license buying agents and in other ways they have been an important vehicle for Nigerianization and commercial and political patronage. *See also* F. Kuiper, "Some Aspects of the Operations of Marketing Boards," *Proceedings of the Nigerian Institute of Social and Economic Research, 1958,* p. 43.

General studies and reviews of the Nigerian economy are in

The Economic Development of Nigeria; Report of a Mission Organized by the International Bank for Reconstruction and Development at the Request of the Governments of Nigeria and the United Kingdom (Federal Government Printer, Lagos, 1954; Johns Hopkins Press, Baltimore, 1955).

Nigeria: The Political and Economic Background, prepared by The Royal Institute of International Affairs (Oxford University Press, London, 1960). A compact review of historical and political developments through 1959 combined with a summary of economic resources and prospects.

Stapleton, G. B., *The Wealth of Nigeria* (Oxford University Press, London, 1958).

Economic Survey of Nigeria, 1959 (National Economic Council, Lagos, 1959).

The International Bank's report influenced the 1962–1968 Development Plans, some of the emphases of which are reflected in the *Economic Survey* and in *The Role of the Federal Government in Promoting Industrial Development*, Federal Parliament Sess. Paper No. 3 of 1958. The Federal and regional development plans can be found in *National Development Plan, 1962–1968* (Ministry of Economic Development, Lagos, 1962). *The Nigerian Journal of Economic and Social Studies* has many comments on the plans, their premises, and the Nigerian economy.

For the public sector of the economy prior to the development plan a useful article is A. H. Hanson, "Public Enterprise in Nigeria: I, Federal Public Utilities [and] II, Development Corporations," *Public Administration, Vols.* XXXVI and XXXVII (1958 and 1959), p. 366 and p. 21.

A rather optimistic study of the possibilities of economic development in the tropics, which at the same time presents all of the disadvantages of a tropical climate, is D. K. H. Lee, *Climate and Economic Development in the Tropics* (Harper & Row, Publishers, published for the Council on Foreign Relations, New York, 1957).

One of the difficulties of planning for development in Nigeria is the unreliability of some statistics and the slowness with which most statistics are compiled. The most significant example of unreliability is with respect to the number of persons in Nigeria. The 1963 census revealed phenomenal increases in population, many millions more than would have been expected by applying the assumed 2 per cent annual growth in population to the population figures of the 1952 census. If the figures can be accepted, it means that the Development Plan was designed to cope with a population over 10 million short of the actual number. A rather theoretical analysis of the problem of the "Malthusian trap" as population growth sponges up economic development is Joseph J. Spengler, "Population Movements and Economic Development in Nigeria," in *The Nigerian Political Scene*, edited by Robert O. Tilman and Taylor Cole (Duke University Press, Durham, N.C., 1962).

Some of the difficulties of being sure that economic statistics are accurate are outlined in Pius N. Okigbo's *Nigerian National Accounts, 1950–1957* (Government Printer, Enugu, 1962), a statistical survey which follows upon A. R. Prest and I. G. Stewart, *The National Income of Nigeria, 1950–1951* (H.M.S.O., London, 1953). The statistical difficulties and sources are also discussed in D. Nicholas G. Carter, "An Application of Input-Output Methods to the Nigerian Economy," in *Managing Economic Development in Nigeria, op. cit.*

The *Annual Abstract of Statistics* and the *Quarterly Abstract* published by the Federal Office of Statistics (Federal Government Printer, Lagos) are a potpourri of statistics ranging from domestic commodity prices and external trade to the number of children in schools and the punishments imposed for slave dealing. Barclays Bank's monthly *Overseas Review* is a helpful source for current economic information about Nigeria, among other places.

Detailed reports on the revenue and expenditures of the Governments of Nigeria are in the Annual *Estimates* of the Federal and Regional Governments. For a rather detailed report on the Federal Government's financial record and proposals, *see* the annual budget speeches of the Federal Minister of Finance given in Parliament in the budget sessions (early spring) and printed in the Hansard and separately in pamphlet form.

Some other sources of economic statistics are the *Annual* (and *Monthly*) *Trade Summary*, the *Journal of Commerce and Industry*, and the *Nigerian Trade Journal*.

Despite the fact that Nigeria's economy is still overwhelmingly agricultural, her labor force showed at the transition to a republic in October 1963 and in the spring of 1964 (when it mounted a successful general strike in support of a substantial wage increase) that it can be an extremely powerful force *if* it forgets its feuding and acts together. Labor's power, despite the low degree of industrialization and the oversupply of workers for the jobs available, is illustrative of the fragility of the state and the power vacuum that exists. Discussions of wages are in *Review of Salaries and Wages, Report by the Commission Appointed by the Governments of the Federation, the Northern Region, the Eastern Region and the Southern Cameroons* (Federal Government Printer, Lagos, 1959) and *Report of the Commission on the Review of Wages, Salary and Conditions of Service of the Junior Employees of the Governments of the Federation and in Private Establishments, 1963–1964* (Lagos, 1964). Studies of the labor movement and employee-employer relations are in J. I. Roper, *Labour Problems in West Africa* (Penguin Books, London, 1958) and T. M. Yesufu, *An Introduction to Industrial Relations in Nigeria* (Oxford University Press, New York, 1962). Colin Legum, *Pan-Africanism: A Short Political Guide* (Pall Mall Press, London, 1962), has a chapter written by his wife, entitled "Africa's Divided Workers," which deals with splits within African labor movements over the issue of outside affiliation. *See* generally *Bulletin: A Quarterly Review of Labour Problems in Africa,* published by the Inter-African Labour Institute, now under the auspices of the O.A.U., formerly under the auspices of the Commission for Technical Co-operation in Africa.

Farmers and peasants, though they are infinitely more numerous than workers, have not become a potent, united national force. Those Nigerians who have come into contact with the modern world through education are extremely reluctant to return to traditional farming. That reluctance and the general problem of finding jobs for primary school leavers is increasingly being recognized as Nigeria's most pressing social and economic problem. *See*, for example, Archibald Callaway, "School Leavers and the Developing Economy of Nigeria," in *The Nigerian Political Scene, op. cit.*

An introduction to the social and economic problems and opportunities with respect to Nigerian agriculture is H. A. Oluwasanmi, "The Agrarian Situation in Nigeria," *Journal of Human Relations*, Vol. VIII, Nos. 3 and 4 (Spring-Summer 1960), p. 657.

4. Some New Forces

Education is the password to life more abundant and is the great demand of many Nigerian parents for their children, as is graphically illustrated each year at registration time by the newspaper pictures of sleepy mothers and children queued up for hours. In Helen Kitchen, ed., *The Educated African: A Country-by-Country Survey of Educational Development in Africa* (Frederick A. Praeger, New York, 1962), there is a chapter on education in Nigeria during the colonial period and at the time of independence.

Major questions with respect to education in Nigeria are education for what sort of jobs and how much emphasis should be placed on primary, secondary, and university education. Both subjects are considered in *Investment in Education, the Report of the Commission on Post-School Certificate and Higher Education in Nigeria*, called the Ashby Report (St. Clements Press, Ltd., London, 1960). The Federal Government's comments on the Ashby Report are in *Educational Development 1961–1970* (Lagos, 1961). Another comment is Ian Espie, "Decade of Decision," *Ibadan,* No. 11 (Feb. 1961), p. 9.

Frederick Harbison wrote a report for the Ashby Commission entitled "High-Level Manpower for Nigeria's Future," which concluded that intermediate education should be given precedence over both university and primary education. *See also* his "Human Resources and Economic Development" in *The Nigerian Political Scene, op. cit.* T. M. Yesufu's "Nigerian Manpower Problems: A Preliminary Assessment," *The Nigerian Journal of Economic and Social Studies*, Vol. IV, No. 3 (Nov. 1962), p. 207, is more complete than its title suggests. A theoretical discussion of manpower planning with attention to specific Eastern Region problems is C. Davis Fogg's "Manpower Planning" in *Managing Economic Development in Africa, op. cit.* For a more general discussion, *see* Harbison's "Human Resources Development Planning in Modernizing Economies," *International Labour Review*, May 1962, p. 1.

Because of the prestige of the British civil servants, and the relative paucity of non-civil-service modern sector jobs, education in Nigeria has been typified by the liberal arts university education preparatory for a civil service career, or perhaps the law. The prestige of the civil service, combined with nationalism and the continued return from the United Kingdom and the United States of liberal arts trainees, made Nigerianization of the civil service one of the major issues prior to and at the time of independence. *See* the *Final Report of the Committee of the House of Representatives on the Nigerianization of the Federal Public Service* (Sess. Paper No. 6 of 1959; interim Report issued as Sess. Paper No. 72 of 1958. The Federal Government's more cautious comments on the Interim Report are in Sess.

Paper No. 7 of 1958 and on the Final Report are in Sess. Paper No. 2 of 1960). Earlier reports on the same subject are in the *Report of the Commission to Make Recommendations about the Recruitment and Training of Nigerians for Service Posts in the Government Service* (Government Printer, Lagos, 1948) and in Sidney Phillipson and S. O. Adebo, *Nigerianization of the Civil Service* (Sess. Paper No. 4 of 1954. *See also* the Annual Reports of the Federal and Regional Public Service Commissions).

An approach to Nigerianization which tempers nationalist resolution with caution is S. O. Abedo, "The Civil Service in an Independent Nigeria," *The New Nigerian: Journal of the Nigeria Society*, Aug. 1961, p. 16. Chief Adebo, now Nigeria's permanent Representative at the U.N. and previously head of the Western Region Civil Service, said that "accelerated Nigerianization is bound to involve a temporary lowering of efficiency. This is not a point against accelerated Nigerianization."

A general study of the civil (public) service in new nations is Kenneth Younger, *The Public Service in New States* (Oxford University Press, London, 1960).

Except in the North, where Nigerianization conflicts for the short term with Northernization, the problem of Nigerianization of the civil service is fast disappearing though the influx of relatively young men into the civil service at around the time of independence itself creates a problem. Younger men will be shut off from jobs as those now in them grow old. The problem now is Nigerianization of the economy, the creation of new jobs for the elite, and the education of the right kind of skilled worker. An early article to connect criticism of governments and failure by young, educated Nigerians to find jobs is Hugh H. Smythe, "Nigeria's Marginal Men," *Phylon*, Vol. XIX, No. 3 (1958), p. 268. It characterizes the young elite, educated abroad, as "nurtured in the traditional past, trained in the scientific present, and unable to fit into either; they are Nigeria's marginal men." The article anticipates the frustrations that began to be written about generally several years later, pointing out, in addition to the connection between failure to find jobs and criticism, the frustrations caused upon returning home from education abroad and seeing that social and economic change has not been as great as political.

Some of the thoughts and habits of 156 Nigerians (including five women) — selected as an elite group from the frequency of their mention in "high-status roles" in the press, the Nigerian *Who's Who*, and names suggested by Nigerians and persons interested in Nigeria — are presented in a sociological study by Hugh H. and Mabel M. Smythe entitled *The New Nigerian Elite* (Stanford University Press, Stanford, California, 1960). The notes include a full listing of published material on some topics such as urbanization in Africa.

Essays and biographical sketches of Africans which give a moving, sympathetic insight into the effect of change upon personality are in Colin M. Turnbull's *The Lonely African* (Simon and Schuster, Inc., New York, 1962), which, though not at all about Nigeria, has much that is generally applicable. A more scholarly and comprehensive book dealing with the same subject is Melville J. Herskovits, *The Human Factor in Changing Africa* (Alfred A. Knopf, New York, 1962).

Chinua Achebe's first and third novels, *Things Fall Apart* (William Heinemann, Ltd., London, 1958) and *Arrow of God* (William Heinemann, Ltd., London, 1964), also tell of the destructive effect upon the personality of a tribal leader of the new forces brought by the British. His second novel, *No Longer at Ease* (William Heinemann, Ltd., London, 1960) tells the sad story of a young educated Ibo civil servant whose promise is dashed by the temptations of Lagos life and the confusion between traditional and modern life.

The tension caused by the meeting of Africa and Europe, by the attempt to take something from both and lose neither, is a theme, and sometimes the dominant theme in the novels of Nigerians Cyprian Ekwensi (*People of the City* [Dakers, London, 1954]; *Jagua Nana* [Hutchinson & Co., London, 1961]; *Burning Grass* [William Heinemann, Ltd., London, 1962]; *Beautiful Feather* [Hutchinson & Co., London, 1963]) and Onuoka Nzekwu (*Wand of Noble Wood* [Hutchinson & Co., London, 1961] and *Blade Among the Boys* [Hutchinson & Co., London, 1962]). Amos Tutuola writes fantasies out of Yoruba folklore in a style that some critics say reflects ignorance of English grammar and others say is rhythmical and exciting. Among his books, all published by Faber and Faber, Ltd., London, are *The Palm Wine Drinkard* (1953), *My Life in the Bush of Ghosts* (1954), *Simbi and the Satyr of the Dark* (1955), *The Brave African Huntress* (1959), and *Featherwomen of the Jungle* (1962).

C. *Political Developments*

Of the books that have been written about Nigerian politics, three stand head and shoulders above the others. They are James S. Coleman's *Nigeria: Background to Nationalism*, *op. cit.*, Richard L. Sklar's *Nigerian Political Parties: Power in an Emergent African Nation*, *op. cit.*, and Kenneth W. J. Post's *The Nigerian Federal Election of 1959* (Oxford University Press, London, 1963). Each book concentrates on political developments, Coleman's through 1954 with some attention to developments through 1957, Sklar's through 1957 and 1958 with some reference to events as late as 1962, and Post's on 1959, as indicated by its title.

The books are different in scope; their titles are fairly descriptive of the differences. Coleman places more emphasis than Sklar on the reasons for the development of nationalism in Nigeria — the effects of the church, of education, of developments in Britain's colonial policy, and so forth. Sklar concentrates more than Coleman on the details of party development and structure. Coleman tends toward the general conclusion; Sklar to the use of statistics. Post is more limited in coverage, though he has some interesting thoughts on matters such as the trend toward a single party in the regions. He focuses more attention on the parties' efforts to win public support and upon administration than Sklar, who emphasizes the parties' structure and their internal struggles for power. The books are well written. They are stimulating to the nonspecialist — Coleman's perhaps the most so because of its wider scope. All are essential for the specialist.

Coleman and Sklar are Americans. It is worth speculating as to whether Americans have any advantage over Nigerians or Englishmen in writing about Nigerian politics. Events in Nigeria are fast moving; the issues are basic. Nigerians with the training and talent to write political studies are in demand to participate more directly in the political process. Nigerians, therefore, tend to write political polemics rather than political studies. There is nothing surprising about that: in America's revolutionary period few detached and detailed political studies were written.

One weakness of almost all the foreign writing about Nigerian nationalism, including even Sklar's, Coleman's, and Post's, is that the studies are a bit dry. The books have generally failed to describe with understanding the strength of various psychological and emotional forces that are highly significant to Nigeria's political development, past and future. A true picture of politics in Nigeria, as in any country, must have something of the poet's or novelist's insight into human motives and emotions. Nigerians themselves are best equipped to add those more subtle qualities to writings about their country.

Compared with British writers about Nigeria, Americans have some advantages, despite Britain's long and close connection with Nigeria. Ethnic politics are well known to Americans. Even white Americans grow up in a society where they can in their daily lives acquire some understanding of the effect of racial prejudice upon the attitudes of colored people. Federalism and a bill of rights are institutions with which Americans live every day. Americans have not entirely forgotten their own colonial revolution. All those aspects of the American experience are highly relevant to Nigeria. All of them must be learned by Englishmen in schools instead of life.

There are a staggering number of books about government, nationalism, democracy, and politics in the underdeveloped world. Two of the best are Gabriel A. Almond and James S. Coleman, eds., *The Politics of the Developing Areas* (Princeton University Press, Princeton, 1960) and Rupert Emerson, *From Empire to Nation: The Rise to Self-Assertion of Asian and African Peoples* (Harvard University Press, Cambridge, 1960). Professor Emerson's book seeks "uniformities on the grand scale" and has the excitement of sweeping generalities, most of which seem to hold up when tested against particular cases. Its notes include references to many books on nationalism and the development of national unity. The Almond-Coleman book, which has a section on sub-Saharan Africa written by Professor Coleman, is given to placing, sometimes almost forcing, political systems in various underdeveloped nations into particular categories.

Among the useful general works confined to Africa are the prolific Thomas Hodgkin's *African Political Parties* (Penguin Books, London, 1961) and his more searching *Nationalism in Colonial Africa* (Frederick Muller,

London, 1956). And *see* Martin L. Kelson, Jr., "The Rise of Nationalist Organizations and Parties in British West Africa" in *Africa from the Point of View of American Negro Scholars* (published by *Presence Africaine*, Dijon, 1958). James S. Coleman's "Nationalism in Tropical Africa," *American Political Science Review*, Vol. XLVIII (1954), p. 404, "The Emergence of African Political Parties" in C. Grove Haines, ed., *Africa Today* (Johns Hopkins Press, Baltimore, Md., 1955) and "The Character and Viability of African Political Systems" in *The United States and Africa* (The American Assembly, Columbia University, 1955) all are stimulating, although a bit formalistic as compared with his great work on Nigeria. Immanuel Wallenstein in *Africa, the Politics of Independence* (Random House, Inc., New York, 1961) has some interesting thoughts on the relationship between multiparty democracy and national unity.

Harvey Glickman's "Introducing Political Africa," *The Journal of Modern African Studies*, Vol. I, No. 2, p. 229, finds fault with most and praises a few of the many books which seek to introduce the reader to politics in Africa.

Extremely valuable for an understanding of political developments and prospects in Africa in general and Nigeria in particular are some of the studies which focus upon a particular attribute of society related to political development. An example is *Development of a Middle Class in Tropical and Sub-Tropical Countries*, Record of the XXIXth *Session of the International Institute of Differing Civilizations Held in London*, Sept. 13–16, 1955, one of the contributions to which was Sylvia Leith-Ross, "The Development of a Middle Class in the Federation of Nigeria." On the same general subject *see* Peter C. Lloyd, "Cocoa Politics and the Yoruba Middle Class," *West Africa*, January 17, 1953. J. Donald Kingsley focuses upon the relation between the bureaucracy and political development in *Bureaucracy and Political Development*, ed. Joseph La Palombara (Princeton University Press, Princeton, 1963).

See also *Tradition and Change — Problems of Progress: An International Conference on Representative Government and National Progress* held at University College, Ibadan, March 16–23, 1959, one of the more interesting contributions to which is Ayo Ogunsheye's "The Traditional Order and Modern Society." For a provocative review of that conference, particularly the similarities and differences between the thinking of delegates from former French and former English colonies, *see* Herbert Passim's "The Ancient Jar of Dahomey," *Encounter*, Vol. XIII, No. 3 (Sept. 1959), p. 33.

Tribalism is the attribute of Nigerian and African society related to political development which has received more comment than any other, with most comments emphasizing its divisive effect upon national unity and its tendency to make democratic elections unthinking battles for survival dominated by appeals to ethnic prejudice. An article which takes a somewhat different view is Richard L. Sklar, "The Contribution of Tribalism to Nationalism in Western Nigeria," *Journal of Human Relations*, Vol.

VIII, Nos. 3 and 4 (Spring and Summer 1960), p. 407. Sklar questions the assumptions that ethnic group loyalty necessarily undermines loyalty to a multitribal state and that loyalty to traditional rulers is necessarily incompatible with social change. With respect to the first assumption he states that "millions of tradition-bound people were drawn through the medium of communal partisanship into the mainstream of political activity where they accepted the leadership of progressive nationalists." Sklar should be read along with Peter C. Lloyd, "The Development of Political Parties in Western Nigeria," *American Political Science Review*, Vol. XLIX, No. 3 (Sept. 1955), p. 693.

The relationship between democracy and African society, history and aspirations, is the prime focus of the sometimes formalistic articles in *What Are the Problems of Parliamentary Government in West Africa, Report of a Conference Held by the Hansard Society for Parliamentary Government in Oxford in September 1957* (The Chiswick Press, London, 1958). A brief study of some of the reasons why democracy might thrive in Nigeria and others why it might not is H. O. Davies, *Nigeria: The Prospects for Democracy* (Weidenfeld and Nicolson, London, 1961). The book, which has a foreword by Prime Minister Tafawa Balewa, spends perhaps an inordinate amount of time in a slightly superficial account of the failures of democracy in other countries of the underdeveloped world, sometimes with comparisons between those countries and Nigeria. One of the more interesting conclusions of Chief Davies, an early Nigerian nationalist who has had a tendency to join dissenting movements, is that the failure of self-government in Africa is likely to be attributed to an inherent incapacity in the African for self-rule, and that therefore African leaders are "ruthless in combatting any forces which they think to be a barrier to success." Chief Davies makes somewhat different comparisons in "The New African Profile," *Foreign Affairs*, Vol. XL, No. 2 (Jan. 1962), p. 293. There he concludes that because of its federal system and the personality of Prime Minister Tafawa Balewa, a "thoroughbred democrat," Nigeria is different from other African countries where a system of democratic elections "lends itself to bribery and corruption on a large scale, and encourages hooliganism, and the invocation of tribal, racial and religious propaganda."

Pendleton Herring's "The Future for Democracy in Nigeria" in Robert O. Tilman and Taylor Cole, *The Nigerian Political Scene, op. cit.,* is of greatest interest for its attack upon the proposition that there are necessary preconditions to the development of healthy democracy. The article agrees with Obafemi Awolowo's thesis in the final chapter of *Awo: The Autobiography of Chief Obafemi Awolowo* (Cambridge University Press, Cambridge, 1960), that most writers who discuss democracy in the underdeveloped world err in assuming that the historical pattern of the development of democracy in the Western world is the only pattern. Quite another bias is thought to distort writings about democracy in Africa in the opinion of Henry C. Bretton. His *Power and Stability in Nigeria: The Politics of Decolonization* (Frederick A. Praeger, New York, 1962) contends that most books about African politics suffer from an "overwhelming love and concern" for Africans and from too much attention to official reports. His book is a devastating critique of Nigerian institutions, private and public. A substantial portion of the book is devoted to the thesis that Nigeria's present leaders serve and represent the interest of expatriates and indigenous groups who depend upon the perpetuation of conditions increasingly unacceptable to the masses. A further thesis is that moderation and compromise with respect to those conditions only serves the political Cold War interests of the West in the narrowest possible sense and postpones "unrest, riot, and a general showdown among the principal contenders for power."

Less attention has been paid to local government than it merits. Two books on the subject are Phillip J. Harris, *Local Government in Southern Nigeria* (Cambridge University Press, Cambridge, 1957) and L. Gray Cowan, *Local Government in West Africa* (Columbia University Press, New York, 1958).

The trend toward single-party states has been one of the most significant in Africa. Differences among single-party systems are illustrated by the examination of six countries in *African One-Party States*, edited by Gwendolen M. Carter (Cornell University Press, New York, 1962). *See also* Ruth Schachter, "Single Party Systems in West Africa," *The American Political Science Review*, Vol. LXV (June 1961), p. 294.

The tendency toward a single party in Nigeria's regions and the reasons for that tendency are discussed, among other places, in J. P. MacIntosh, "Electoral Trends and the Tendency to a One Party System," *The Service*, Vol. II, Nos. 81–83 (Apr. 7–21, 1962). "The Changing Role of the State in West Africa," by James O'Connell, in *The Nigerian Journal of Economic and Social Studies*, Vol. III, No. 1 (Nov. 1961), p. 1, contains a concise description of some of the reasons for the tendency. Ways in which a political party in power in a region can surreptitiously supply government funds to the party it represents are suggested in the Coker Commission report (*Report of Coker Commission of Inquiry into the Affairs of Certain Statutory Corporations in Western Nigeria* (Lagos, 1962) and the Foster-Sutton Tribunal Report (*Tribunal to Inquire into Allegations of Improper Conduct by the Premier of the Eastern Region of Nigeria in Connection with the Affairs of the African Continental Bank Limited and other Relevant Matters, Proceedings; with the Minutes of Evidence Taken before the Tribunal, August–November, 1956* (Lagos, 1957). (For a wider study of corruption which concentrates upon Nigeria, see *Corruption in Developing Countries* by Ronald Wraith and Edgar Simkins [W. W. Norton & Company, New York, 1964].)

Two of the earlier elections establishing the single-party trend are discussed in Philip Whitaker, "The Western Region of Nigeria, May, 1956," and J. H. Price, "The Eastern Region of Nigeria, March 1957," in *Five Elections in Africa,* edited by W. J. M. Mackenzie, and Kenneth Robinson (Clarendon Press, Oxford, 1960).

The Cambridge University Press showed its impartiality among members of the Nigerian establishment by publishing *Zik: A Selection from the Speeches of Nnamdi Azikiwe* (1961); Obafemi Awolowo, *Awo, op. cit.* (1960); and Ahmadu Bello (The Sardauna of Sokoto), *My Life* (1962). The Sardauna's and Chief Awolowo's autobiographies are interesting not only for their political history and their political philosophy (before his more radical postindependence period for Chief Awolowo) but also for their pictures of early life in two quite different societies. The very influential early thinking of Obafemi Awolowo on federalism is set forth in *Path to Nigerian Freedom* (Faber and Faber, Ltd., London, 1947). Some of Nnamdi Azikiwe's many early writings are *Liberia in World Politics* (London, 1934); *Renascent Africa* (Accra, 1933); "My Odyssey," *West African Pilot* installments from July 1938 to June 1939; *Political Blueprint of Nigeria* (Lagos, 1943); *The Development of Political Parties in Nigeria* (London, 1957). The latter work should be read with NCNC official Fred Anyiam's *Men and Matters in Nigerian Politics 1934–1958* (Yaba, 1959).

Some of the many books by Nigerian politicians that give an insight into the country's problems and aspirations are Adelabu Adegoke (the leader of Ibadan's Mabolaje), *Africa in Ebullition* (Ibadan, n.d.); S. A. Aluko, *The Problems of Self-Government for Nigeria: A Critical Analysis* (Arthur S. Stockwell, Ltd., Ilfracombe, England, 1955). Professor Aluko, an economist, recently has been closely associated with the Action Group. His remark that "we may be less capable now, but given time, we are equal to any race in the world" is typical of the book's approach. Other such books are Kolawole Balogun, *My Country Nigeria* (Lagos, 1955); K. O. Mbadiwe, *British and Axis Aims in Africa* (W. Malliet, New York, 1942); Mbonu Ojike, *My Africa* (John Day, New York, 1946); A. A. Nwafor Orizu, *Without Bitterness: Western Nations in Postwar Africa* (Creative Age Press, New York, 1944); Chike Obi, *Our Struggle, A Political Analysis of the Negro Peoples' Struggling for True Freedom* (John Okwessa and Co., Yaba, 1955).

The Ibadan University depository of all pamphlets published in Nigeria contains many that are political, quite often polemics.

D. *Foreign Policy*

The only book on Nigerian foreign policy is Claude S. Phillips, Jr., *The Development of Nigerian Foreign Policy* (Northwestern University Press, Evanston, Ill., 1964). L. Gray Cowan has an article entitled "Nigeria's Foreign Policy" in *The Nigerian Political Scene,* ed. Tilman and Cole, *op. cit.,* which concludes that "the rising generation of younger Nigerian leaders may well be prepared to sacrifice a continuing relationship to the

West if this relationship appears likely to threaten Nigeria's potential position of leadership in African politics." Douglas G. Anglin in "Nigeria: Political Non-alignment and Economic Alignment," *The Journal of Modern African Studies*, Vol. II, No. 2, p. 247, considers the extent to which economic self-interest has influenced Nigeria's foreign policy, shows instances where it has and has not, and concludes with "the somewhat unfashionable view that, in most cases, Nigerian leaders pursue the policies they do because, rightly or wrongly, they happen to believe in them."

Prime Minister Tafawa Balewa's "Nigeria Looks Ahead," *Foreign Affairs*, Vol. XLI, No. 1, p. 131, gives some insight into the philosophy underlying Nigeria's foreign policy.

The foreign policy subject about which there is undoubtedly the most talk is Pan-Africanism. The economic advantages of closer cooperation tend sometimes to get swamped in the rhetoric of racial mysticism. Those economic advantages, and the difficulties caused in attaining them by the colonial era, are persuasively presented by Barbara Ward Jackson in "Free Africa and the Common Market," *Foreign Affairs*, Vol. XL, No. 3 (Apr. 1962), p. 419. That should be read with H. M. A. Onitiri, "Nigeria's International Economic Relations: A Survey," *The Nigerian Journal of Economic and Social Studies*, Vol. III, No. 1 (Nov. 1961), p. 13, and Gerald K. Helleinner, "Nigeria and the African Common Market," *The Nigerian Journal of Economic and Social Studies*, Vol. IV, No. 3 (Nov. 1962), p. 283, which contends that Nigeria, primarily because of its already large internal market, would gain less than any other country from an African common market, and the "Symposium on West African Integration" in the March 1963 issue of the *Journal*. Arnold Rivkin, in *Africa and the European Common Market* (University of Denver Press, Denver, 1964), discusses developments with respect to the subject covered by his title after the Addis Ababa Conference.

A collection of speeches, papers, and comments on Pan-Africanism by a conference of Africans (including several Nigerians) and American Africanists can be found in *Pan-Africanism Reconsidered,* edited by the American Society of African Culture (University of California Press, Berkeley, 1962) — often sparkling and insightful; ideas and theories more than events. Colin Legum, *Pan-Africanism: A Short Political Guide, op. cit.,* is a compact account of Pan-Africanism from its West Indian and American roots through the Casablanca and Monrovia Conferences, with attention to cultural as well as political links. The book has a lengthy appendix of the documents of Pan-Africanism (conference resolutions and speeches) for the period covered. The appendix of Pan-African documents in Legum should be supplemented by *Solidarity in Africa, A Record of the Conference of the Heads of African and Malagasy States held in Lagos from January 25–30, 1962,* Federal Ministry of Information (Nigerian National Press, Apapa, 1962) and *Dawn of Africa: Nigeria and African Unity,* Federal Ministry of Information (Nigerian National Press, Apapa, n.d.). The latter is a review of Nigerian foreign policy through the Addis Conference of Heads of State and includes the Charter of the Organization of African Unity which was promulgated at Addis.

The Spring-Summer 1962 issue of *International Organization* is devoted to "African and International Organization," edited by Norman J. Padelford and Rupert Emerson (also published as *Africa and World Order* (Frederick A. Praeger, New York, 1963). In addition to articles on Pan-Africanism, the Congo, Africa at the United Nations, and so forth, there is a good bibliography, pp. 449–464. Thomas Hovet, Jr., in *Africa in the United Nations* (Northwestern University Press, Evanston, Ill., 1963) has more on the relations between African states in the United Nations through 1962 than can be found elsewhere. *See also* Vernon McKay, *Africa in World Politics* (Harper & Row, Publishers, New York, 1963).

Some thoughts on communism in Africa are Zbigniew Brzezinski, ed., *Africa and the Communist World* (Stanford University Press, Stanford, 1963); Kalu Ezera, "Apartheid, Multiracialism, or Communism in Africa," *Journal of Human Relations,* Vol. VIII, Nos. 33 and 34 (Spring and Summer 1960), p. 568, and George Padmore, *Pan-Africanism or Communism? The Coming Struggle for Africa* (Dobson, London, 1956).

E. *The Constitution*

Kalu Ezera's *Constitutional Developments in Nigeria* (Cambridge University Press, Cambridge, 1960) is the only complete account of Nigeria's constitutions (prior to the Independence Constitution), their terms, background, and effect upon party positions. The author, in addition to teaching at the University of Nigeria at Nsuka is an NCNC member of the House of Representatives and often a critic of the Government for not being sufficiently dynamic; the book occasionally reflects NCNC partisanship. It includes a bibliography which stresses works on federalism, both general and in Nigeria.

Oluwole Idowu Odumosu's *The Nigerian Constitution, History and Development* (Sweet and Maxwell, London, 1963) covers much of the same historical ground as Ezera and adds some analysis of Nigerian federalism. Odumosu also has a chapter on the Western Region crisis of 1962 through the arrest of Awolowo. He is one of many Nigerian writers who refers to K. C. Wheare's remark in *Federal Government* (Oxford University Press, London, 1953, third ed.), p. 52, that "it is undesirable that one or two units should be so powerful as to be able to override the others and bend the will of the federal government to themselves." The remark is used to support the contention that the Northern Region is too big and powerful for healthy federalism. Eme O. Awa, in *Federal Government in Nigeria* (University of California Press, Berkeley, 1964), concentrates on the structure of Nigeria's federal system.

Useful comparisons can be found in *The New Commonwealth and Its Constitutions* by S. A. de Smith (Stevens, London, 1964).

The following is a chronological list of documents relating to the Constitution:

Proposals for the Revision of the Constitution of Nigeria (H.M.S.O., London, 1945), Cmnd. 6599. Governor Richards' proposals which led to the Constitution of 1946 — *Nigeria (Legislative Council) Order-in-Council, 1946.*

Review of the Constitution — Regional Recommendations (Lagos, 1949).

Proceedings of the General Conference on Review of the Constitution Held at Ibadan, January 1950 (Lagos, 1950). Includes extracts from the speeches and remarks of Nigerian leaders of the time, including many (other than Azikiwe, who boycotted the conference) who still are prominent. Often very revealing with respect to differing attitudes of representatives of North and South and the three regions. Most important decision of the conference was to recommend increased regional autonomy.

Report of the Drafting Committee on the Constitution (Lagos, 1950).

Review of Constitutional Proposals by Colonial Secretary, Sess. Paper No. 20, 1950. Colonial Office Official Dispatch, Nigeria, No. 464A.

Legislative Council Debates, Sept. 16, 1950. Resolution of certain outstanding issues, including giving North seats in central legislature equal in number to other regions.

Nigeria (Constitution) Order-in-Council, 1951, S. I. No. 1172 of 1951.

Report by the Conference on the Nigerian Constitution Held in London, July and August 1953 (H.M.S.O., London, 1953), Cmnd. 8994.

Report by the Resumed Conference on the Nigerian Constitution Held in Lagos, January and February 1954 (H.M.S.O., London, 1954), Cmnd. 9059.

The Nigerian (Constitution) Order-in-Council, 1954, S. I. No. 1146. The 1954 Constitution was amended by S. I. Nos. 1955/432; 1956/836; 1957/1363, 1530; 1958/429, 1257, 1522, 1958; 1959/368, 1049, 1772, 1981; 1960/203. All those amendments and the 1954 constitution as thereby amended are printed in Legal Notice 52 of 1960 *Supplement to Official Gazette*, Vol. XLVII, No. 20 (April 14, 1960), Part D.

Report by the Nigeria Constitutional Conference Held in London, May and June 1957 (H.M.S.O., London, 1957), Cmnd. 207.

Report by the Ad-Hoc Meeting of the Nigeria Constitutional Conference Held in Lagos in February 1958 (Federal Government Printer, Lagos, 1958).

Report by the Resumed Nigeria Constitutional Conference Held in London, September and October 1958 (H.M.S.O., London, 1958), Cmnd. 569.

Nigeria Constitutional Discussions Held in London, May 1960 (H.M.S.O., London, 1960), Cmnd. 1063.

The Nigeria (Constitution) Order-in-Council, 1960, S. I. No. 1652 (As Schedules has Federal and Regional Independence Constitutions).

Proposals for the Constitution of the Federal Republic of Nigeria, Sess.

Paper No. 3, 1963. Proposals for the Republican Constitution stemming from an all-party conference held in Lagos.

The Constitution of the Federal Republic of Nigeria. The Republic Constitution, which came into effect on October 1, 1963.

Extremely influential with respect to the decisions not to create new states before independence, inclusion of fundamental rights provisions in the Constitution, and distribution of power with respect to the police between Federal Government and regions was

Nigeria: Report of the Commission Appointed to Enquire into the Fears of Minorities and the Means of Allaying Them (H.M.S.O., London, 1958), Cmnd. 505. Well written; useful maps in pocket showing geographical distribution of adherents of religions and members of major tribes. Comments by Philip Mason, a member of the Commission, are made in *West Africa,* Nos. 22 and 29, 1958, pp. 1115, 1135.) With respect to the fundamental rights provisions, it should be pointed out that *The Convention for the Protection of Fundamental Rights and Fundamental Freedoms of the Member States of the Council of Europe* is the model for many of Nigeria's constitutional guarantees of fundamental rights.

As influential as the Minorities Commission Report was *Nigeria: Report of the Fiscal Commission* (H.M.S.O., London, 1958), Cmnd. 481. Almost all of the Fiscal Commission's proposals with respect to the division of tax jurisdiction between the Federal Goverment and the regions and with respect to the distribution of revenue from the Federal Government to the regions were agreed to and now appear in the Constitution.

A brief critique of the Fiscal Commission's report is in William R. Cotter, "Taxation and Federalism in Nigeria," *British Tax Review,* March-April 1964, p. 97. Much of the article deals with the constitutionality of the Federal Government's Income Tax Management Act of 1961, a portion of which the author persuasively concludes exceeds the Federal Goverment's limited powers with respect to personal income tax. For a general review of African tax policy, including several comments on Nigeria, *see* John F. Due, *Taxation and Economic Development in Tropical Africa* (M.I.T. Press, Cambridge, 1963).

Early documents concerning the fiscal arrangements under Nigerian constitutions are:

Statement of Administrative Government and Financial Procedure under the New Constitution (Government Printer, Lagos, 1946).

Report of the Commission on (Nigeria) Revenue Allocation, J. R. Hicks and Sydney Phillipson, Commissioners (Government Printer, Lagos, 1951).

Report of Fiscal Commissioner on Financial Effects of Proposed New Constitutional Arrangements, Louis Chick, Commissioner (Government Printer, Lagos, 1953).

Some issues arising under the Nigerian Constitution of 1954 as amended through August 1960 were discussed by leading lawyers, law professors, and jurists from Nigeria, the United Kingdom, the United States, and Canada in Lagos in August 1960 at a conference sponsored by the Ford Foundation. Papers read and some comments made at the conference were published in *Constitutional Problems of Federalism in Nigeria,* edited by Lionel Brett (Times Press, Lagos, 1961). Though the section references vary from the corresponding sections in the Independence and Republican Constitutions, and some sections have been changed substantively, the essays contain as much material on the Nigerian Constitution as may be found elsewhere.

The conference and the Constitution are discussed in Taylor Cole, "The Independence Constitution of Nigeria," *The South Atlantic Quarterly,* Vol. LX (Winter 1961), p. 1, which is somewhat revised as Chapter 4 in *The Nigerian Political Scene, op. cit.*

Some articles concentrating on the fundamental rights provisions are

De Smith, S. A., "Fundamental Rights in the New Commonwealth," *International and Comparative Law Quarterly,* Vol. X (1961), pp. 83, 215.

Elias, T. O., "The New Constitution of Nigeria and the Protection of Human Rights and Fundamental Freedoms," *Journal of the International Commission of Jurists,* Vol. II (1959–1960), p. 30. One of the conclusions of Dr. Elias, who later became Nigeria's Attorney-General, is that the enforcement provisions would be "inadequate" in the absence of a widespread system of legal aid.

Grove, David L., "The 'Sentinels' of Liberty? The Nigerian Judiciary and Fundamental Rights," *Journal of African Law,* Vol. VII (1963), p. 152. Discusses the early cases arising under the fundamental rights provisions with emphasis upon (1) the judges' view of their relationship to the legislature (deference: causing the author to query whether it is consistent with the historical purpose of the fundamental rights provisions to curb abuses by regional majorities for the courts to turn about and defer to legislative majorities that restrict individual freedom) and the use of foreign cases (generally have relied upon irrelevant decisions leading to the author's conclusion that what was sought "was not some insight into the problems at hand, but support for a position that had already been adopted").

Kaplan, Philip J., "Fundamental Rights in the Federation of Nigeria," *Syracuse Law Review,* Vol. XIII (1962), p. 434.

"Nigeria — Some Recent Decisions on the Constitution," *International and Comparative Law Quarterly,* Vol. XI (1962), p. 919. Discusses the cases arising out of the Western Region emergency. The writer comments on the disadvantages under which judges brought up in the tradition of the single absolutely sovereign legislature suffer when they must be the arbiters of a federal system in which the legislature's powers are limited.

Insights into federalism and the possibilities for developments and problems under Nigeria's federal constitution can be obtained from, among many other works:

Basu, Durga D. *Commentaries on the Indian Constitution* (S. C. Sakar & Sons, Calcutta, 1955, third ed.). Compares constitutional provisions and cases interpreting them, covering almost all the federal constitutions there have been. Given a warning that some of the cases cited were no longer controlling even at the date of publication, this book is a helpful guide.

Beloff, Max, "The 'Federal Solution' in its Application to Europe, Asia and Africa," *Political Studies,* June 1953, p. 114.

Birch, A. H., *Federalism, Finance and Social Legislation in Canada, Australia and the United States* (Clarendon Press, Oxford, 1955). Includes at end a chapter on the new federations.

Bowie, Robert R. and Carl J. Friedrich, *Studies in Federalism* (Little, Brown and Company, Boston, 1954).

Hicks, U. K., *et al., Federalism and Economic Growth in Underdeveloped Countries* (Oxford University Press, New York, 1961).

Livingston, William S., *Federalism and Constitutional Change* (Oxford, Clarendon Press, 1956).

Macmahon, Arthur W., ed., *Federalism, Mature and Emergent* (Doubleday & Company, Inc., Garden City, N. Y., 1955). A series of essays which together is probably the most comprehensive examination of federalism in any single book.

Rothchild, Donald, *Toward Unity in Africa: A Study of Federalism in British Africa* (Public Affairs Press, Washington, D. C., 1960).

Index

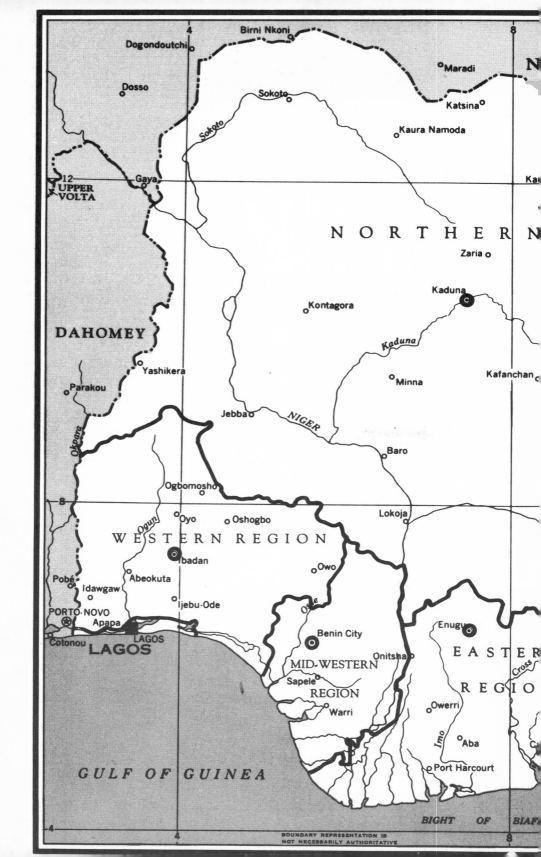